ONE WEEK LOAN

Treasury Securities and Derivatives

Frank J. Fabozzi, CFA
Adjunct Professor of Finance
School of Management
Yale University

Published by Frank J. Fabozzi Associates

**To my wife Donna
and my son Francesco Alfonso**

Cover design by Scott C. Riether

© 1998 By Frank J. Fabozzi Associates
New Hope, Pennsylvania

This publication is designed to provide accurate and authoritative information in regard to the subject matter covered. It is sold with the understanding that the publisher is not engaged in rendering legal, accounting, or other professional services.

ISBN: 1-883249-23-6

Printed in the United States of America

Table of Contents

Acknowledgments

I would like to thank the following individuals who provided me with assistance in various aspects of this project.

Paul Zhao (TIAA-CREF) and William McLellan (Consultant) provided me with valuable comments on the entire manuscript.

Dragomir Krgin (Merrill Lynch) and Jan Mayl (TIPS) reviewed and commented on the material in Chapters 1, 2, and 3 on standard industry calculations Dragomir shared with me his notes on these calculations and furnished me with several examples to illustrate the calculations

Frank Keane (Federal Reserve Bank of New York) provided me with helpful comments on Chapters 1 and 9; Michael Fleming (Federal Reserve Bank of New York) provided me with helpful comments on Chapter 1 and furnished me with a forthcoming paper that I found extremely useful in preparing Chapter 1.

Ram Willner (PIMCO) provided suggestions for improving the discussion on yield curve risk (Chapter 7). Richard Shea (BlackRock Financial Management) reviewed the chapter on taxes (Chapter 10) and provided several suggestions for revising the discussion. Douglas Johnston (Lehman Brothers) provided me with comments on trading strategies with Treasury securities (Chapter 11).

I am grateful to the following individuals for providing me with data used in this book: Ronald Ryan (Ryan Labs), Ruben Rodriquez (BARRA/Global Advanced Technology), Philip Galdi (Merrill Lynch), Jack Malvey (Lehman Brothers), Tom Macirowski (Goldman Sachs), and Marcus Huie (Goldman Sachs).

The background artwork for the cover of this book was provided by Ned Downing of Early American Capital Markets of Wellesley, Massachusetts. A clearer version of the artwork is shown on page v. The artwork is a reprint of American Revolutionary War Debt to French King Louis XVI signed by Benjamin Franklin.

Frank J. Fabozzi

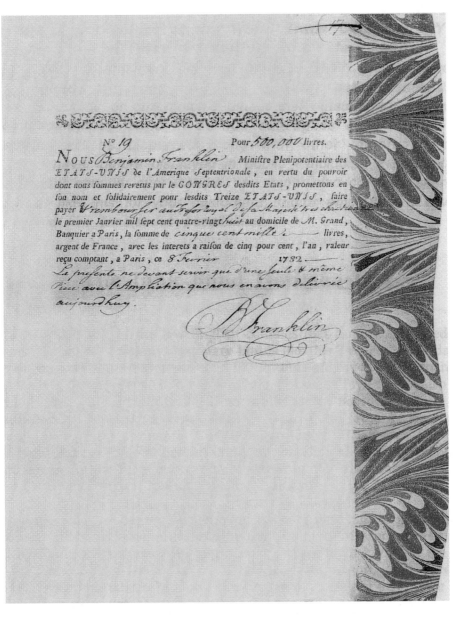

No 19   Pour 500,000 livres.

NOUS *Benjamin Franklin* Ministre Plénipotentiaire des
ÉTATS-UNIS de l'Amérique Septentrionale, en vertu du pouvoir
dont nous sommes revêtus par le CONGRÈS desdits Etats, promettons en
son nom et solidairement pour lesdits Treize ÉTATS-UNIS, faire
payer *& rembourser authorisé de sa Majesté tres chrétienne*
le premier Janvier mil sept cent quatre-vingt *huit* au domicile de M. Grand,
Banquier à Paris, la somme de *cinque cent mille* livres,
argent de France, avec les interets à raison de cinq pour cent, l'an, valeur
reçu comptant, à Paris, ce *8 Février* 1782.
*La présente ne devant servir que d'une seule & même
Pièce avec l'Ampliation que nous en avons delivrée
aujourdhuy.*

B. Franklin

Financing Freedom
Benjamin Franklin signed American Revolutionary War Debt to
French King Louis XVI

Chapter 1

U.S. TREASURY SECURITIES

Treasury securities are issued by the United States Department of the Treasury and are backed by the full faith and credit of the United States government. Market participants view Treasury securities as having no credit risk. Consequently, interest rates on Treasury securities are the benchmark interest rates throughout the U.S. economy as well as in international capital markets.

Two factors account for the prominent role of U.S. Treasury securities: volume (in terms of dollars outstanding) and liquidity. The Department of the Treasury is the largest single issuer of debt in the world. As of early 1997, the amount of marketable Treasury securities outstanding was $3.4 trillion, represented by less than 260 issues. The U.S. corporate bond market by contrast is about $1.4 trillion with over 10,000 issues; the U.S. municipal bond market is about $1.3 trillion, with more than 70,000 separate issuers and millions of individual issues.

The large volume of total debt and the large size of any single issue have contributed to making the Treasury market the most active and hence the most liquid market in the world. The dealer spread between bid and ask prices is considerably narrower than in other sectors of the bond market, and most issues can be purchased easily. Many issues in the corporate and municipal markets are illiquid by contrast, and cannot be traded readily.

In this chapter, we will discuss Treasury securities and the primary and secondary markets for these securities. At the end of this chapter we discuss the risks associated with investing in Treasury securities.

GENERAL FEATURES OF TREASURY SECURITIES

The *par value* of a Treasury security is the amount that the Treasury agrees to repay the security holder by the maturity date. This amount is also referred to as the *principal*, *face value*, or *maturity value*.

The *term to maturity* of a security is the number of years over which the Treasury has promised to meet the conditions of the obligation. The *maturity* of a security refers to the date that the debt will cease to exist, at which time the Treasury will redeem the security by paying the par value. The practice in the bond market is to refer to the "term to maturity" of a security as simply its "maturity" or "term." This is the convention that we shall follow in this book.

As explained later, certain Treasury securities pay interest periodically. The *coupon rate* is the interest rate that the Treasury agrees to pay each year. The annual amount of the interest payment is called the *coupon*. The coupon is determined by multiplying the coupon rate by the par value of the bond. For example, a Treasury

1

security with an 8% coupon rate and a par value of $10,000 will pay annual interest of $800. Treasury securities that have a coupon pay interest semiannually.

Interest income from Treasury securities is subject to federal income taxes but is exempt from state and local income taxes. The federal income tax treatment is explained in Chapter 10.

TYPES OF TREASURY SECURITIES

There are two types of Treasury securities: discount and coupon securities. Treasury coupon securities come in two forms: fixed-rate and variable-rate securities. As explained below, the reference rate for variable-rate securities is the Consumer Price Index.

Treasury Bills

Discount Treasuries are issued at a discount to par value, have no coupon rate, and mature at par value. The current practice of the Treasury is to issue all securities with maturities of one year or less as discount securities. These securities are called *bills*. As discussed in the next section, Treasury bills are issued on a regular basis with initial maturities of 91 days, 182 days, and 364 days. Because of holidays, these days may be either lower or higher by 1 day. In addition, *cash management bills* of varying maturities less than 364 days are occasionally issued on a discount basis. Of the $3.4 trillion of marketable Treasury securities outstanding, approximately $760 billion are Treasury bills.

Treasury Notes and Bonds

All securities with initial maturities of two years or more are issued as coupon securities. Coupon securities are issued at approximately par, have a coupon rate, and mature at par value. Treasury coupon securities issued with original maturities between 2 and 10 years are called *notes*. Treasury coupon securities with original maturities greater than 10 years are called *bonds*. Treasury notes and bonds are referred to as *Treasury coupon securities*.

Treasury coupon securities are currently issued on a regular basis with initial maturities of 2 years, 3 years, 5 years, 10 years, and 30 years. The Treasury also issues Series EE and Series HH bonds. Neither of these bonds are marketable. Therefore, we exclude these Treasury debt obligations from discussions in this book. The Treasury issues other nonmarketable securities to state and local governments that acquire them to reinvest proceeds for advanced refundings of the debt that they issued. These nonmarketable securities that are sold to state and local governments are known as SLUGS.

When describing a Treasury coupon security, the coupon rate is indicated along with the maturity date. For example, the expression "7¼s of 8/15/2004" means an issue with a 7¼% coupon rate maturing on 8/15/2004. On quote sheets, an "*n*" is used to denote a Treasury note. No notation typically follows an issue to identify it as a bond.

The right of the issuer to retire an issue prior to the stated maturity date is referred to as a *call option*. If an issuer exercises this right, the issuer is said to "call the bond." The price which the issuer must pay to retire the issue is referred to as the *call price*. An issuer generally wants the right to retire a bond issue prior to the stated maturity date because it recognizes that at some time in the future the general level of interest rates may fall sufficiently below the issue's coupon rate so that redeeming the issue and replacing it with another issue with a lower coupon rate would be economically beneficial. This right is a disadvantage to the bondholder since proceeds received must be reinvested at a lower interest rate.

None of the currently issued Treasury coupon securities are callable. The 30-year bonds issued through November 1984 were callable but since then have been noncallable. Outstanding callable Treasury bonds are callable five years prior to their maturity date and identified by two dates: when the bond is first callable and the maturity date. The call price is par value. Exhibit 1 lists the callable Treasury bonds outstanding and their coupon rate.

Treasury Inflation Protection Securities

On January 29, 1997, the U.S. Department of the Treasury issued for the first time Treasury securities that adjust for inflation. These securities are popularly referred to as *Treasury inflation protection securities* or TIPS. The first issue was a 10-year note. Subsequently, the Treasury issued a 5-year note in July 1997 and announced that it planned to issue a 10-year note and a 30-year bond in 1998.

Exhibit 1: Callable Treasury Bonds Outstanding

Coupon rate (%)	First Callable	Maturity
7⅝	2/2002	2/2007
7⅞	11/2002	11/2007
8⅜	8/2003	8/2008
8¾	11/2003	11/2008
9⅛	5/2004	5/2009
10⅜	11/2004	11/2009
11¾	2/2005	2/2010
10	5/2005	5/2010
12¾	11/2005	11/2010
13⅞	5/2006	5/2011
14	11/2006	11/2011
10⅜	11/2007	11/2012
12	8/2008	8/2013
13¼	5/2009	5/2014
12½	8/2009	8/2014
11¾	11/2009	11/2014

TIPS work as follows. The coupon rate on an issue is set at a fixed rate. That rate is determined via the auction process described later in the chapter. The coupon rate is called the *real rate* since it is the rate that the investor earns above the inflation rate. For the first TIPS which were auctioned on January 29, 1997 (the 10-year note), the real rate was 3⅜%. The real rate was 3⅝% for the 5-year note auctioned on July 1997.

Inflation-Adjusted Principal

The adjustment for inflation is as follows. The principal that the Treasury Department will base both the dollar amount of the coupon payment and the maturity value will be adjusted semiannually. This is called the *inflation-adjusted principal*. For example, suppose that the coupon rate for a TIPS is 3.5% and the annual inflation rate is 3%. Suppose further that an investor purchases $100,000 of par value (principal) of this issue and that the semiannual inflation rate is 1.5%. Multiplying 1.5% by the initial principal of $100,000 gives the inflation-adjusted principal of $101,500. The dollar amount of the coupon payment for the period is found by multiplying the inflation-adjusted principal times the semiannual coupon rate. In our example, it is $1,776.25 which is found by multiplying $101,500 (the inflation-adjusted principal) by 1.75% (the semiannual coupon rate). Suppose that in the subsequent semiannual period, the inflation rate is 2%. Then the inflation-adjusted principal is found by multiplying the prior inflation-adjusted principal of $101,500 by the semiannual inflation rate of 1%. The new inflation-adjusted principal would then be $102,515. The dollar amount of the coupon payment would be the semiannual coupon rate of 1.75% multiplied by the new inflation-adjusted principal of $102,515, or $1,794.01.

As can be seen, part of the adjustment for inflation comes in the coupon payment since it is based on the inflation-adjusted principal. The majority of the compensation for inflation comes in the form of the adjustment to the principal which is paid at the maturity date. However, the U.S. government has decided to tax the adjustment each year. This feature reduces the attractiveness of TIPS as investments in accounts of tax-paying entities.

Because of the possibility of disinflation (i.e., price declines), the inflation-adjusted principal at maturity may turn out to be less than the initial par value. The Treasury has structured TIPS so that they are redeemed at the greater of the inflation-adjusted principal and the initial par value.

The Reference Inflation Index

Now let's look at the inflation index that the government has decided to use for the inflation adjustment. The index is the non-seasonally adjusted U.S. City Average All Items Consumer Price Index for All Urban Consumers (CPI-U). The CPI is published by the U.S. government and measures the average change in the prices paid by urban consumers for a fixed basket of more than 360 categories of goods and services. The product groups (or categories) covered are housing, food and beverage, apparel and upkeep, medical care, entertainment, transportation, and "other goods and services." There are two versions of the CPI — the Urban Wage Earners and Clerical Workers Price Index (CPI-W) and the All Urban Consumers Price Index (CPI-U). The latter is a broader index and is the one selected by the Treasury to adjust the principal for inflation and is referred to as the *reference CPI*. If the CPI-U is discontinued or altered by law, the U.S. Department of the Treasury will determine an alternative reference inflation index to use.

An inflation-adjusted principal must be calculated for a settlement date. The inflation-adjusted principal will be defined in terms of an *index ratio* which is the ratio of the reference CPI for the settlement date to the reference CPI for the issue date. The reference CPI will be calculated with a 3-month lag. For example, the reference CPI for May 1 will be the CPI-U reported in February. The U.S. Department of the Treasury will publish a daily index ratio for an issue each month.

THE TREASURY AUCTION PROCESS

The Public Debt Act of 1942 grants the Department of the Treasury considerable discretion in deciding on the terms for a marketable security. An issue may be sold on an interest-bearing or discount basis and may be sold on a competitive basis or other basis, at whatever prices the Secretary of the Treasury may establish. However, Congress imposes a restriction on the total amount of bonds outstanding. Although Congress has granted an exemption to this restriction, there have been times when the failure of Congress to extend the exemption has resulted in the delay or cancellation of a Treasury bond offering.

Treasury securities are all issued on an auction basis. Until 1991, in the auction primary dealers and large commercial banks that were not primary dealers would submit bids for their own account and for their customers. Others who wished to participate in the auction process could only submit competitive bids for their own account, not their customers. Consequently, a broker-dealer in government securities that was not a primary dealer could not submit a competitive bid on behalf of its customers. Moreover, unlike primary dealers, non-primary dealers had to make large cash deposits or provide guarantees to assure that they could fulfill their obligation to purchase the securities for which they bid.

In the early 1990s, the Treasury announced that it would allow qualified broker-dealers to bid for their customers at Treasury auctions. If a qualified broker-dealer establishes a payment link with the Federal Reserve System, no deposit or guaranty would be required. Moreover, the auction is no longer handled by the submission of hand-delivered sealed bids to the Federal Reserve. The new auction process is a computerized auction system which can be electronically accessed by qualified broker-dealers.

Auction Cycles

The Treasury believes its borrowing costs will be less if it provides buyers of Treasury securities stable expectations regarding new issues of its debt, so it has regularized its auction cycles. However, there have been occasional changes in its auction cycles. For example, in the past, 20-year bonds have been issued. (The last issue was the 9⅜% of 2/15/06 (noncallable) issued on January 15, 1986.) The 20-year bond was part of a "mini-refunding" wherein the 20-year bond and 4- and 7-year notes were announced together and auctioned sequentially. Today, none of these securities are issued. Previous to the 20-year bond auction cycle, 15-year bonds were issued. (The last 15-year bond was the 11½% of 11/15/95 (noncallable) which was issued on October 14, 1980 and then replaced by 20-year bonds, the first of which was the 11¾% of 2/15/01 issued on January 12, 1981.)

The most dramatic change in the Treasury auction cycle occurred in December 1990, when the Treasury discontinued the quarterly auction of the 4-year note and began a monthly auction of the 5-year note, which had previously been auctioned quarterly as a 5-year, 2-month note. (The 4-year note had been auctioned once a quarter along with the 2-year note. The last 4-year note was the 7⅝% of 12/94 auctioned on December 19, 1990.) The monthly 5-year note settles on the last day of each month and matures five years from the date of issuance (on the last day of the month) and is announced during the third week of each month, on the same cycle as the 2-year note. The 5-year note is therefore no longer a 5-year, 2-month note, but a 5-year note. In 1996, the Treasury changed the auction cycle for the 10-year note from quarterly to six times per annum; in 1997, the Treasury announced it would return to a quarterly auction cycle for the 10-year note.

The current auction cycles are as follows. There are weekly 3-month and 6-month bill auctions; "year-bill" auctions are every fourth week. The 3-month and 6-month bills are auctioned on a Monday. The year-bill is auctioned on a Thursday. If the scheduled auction date is a non-business day, the Treasury typically moves the auction to the next business day.

For coupon securities, there are monthly 2-year note and 5-year note auctions and quarterly auctions for the 3-year note, 10-year note, and 30-year bond (the "refunding" auction). The three current auction cycles for coupon securities are summarized below:

2-year and 5-year	Monthly (issued on the last day of each month)
3-year , 10-year, and 30-year	Quarterly (issued on the 15th of February, May, August, and November)[1]
TIPS	Quarterly (January, April, July, and October)

On the announcement day, the Treasury announces the amount of each issue to be auctioned. It also announces the auction date, settlement date, and maturities to be issued. Due to the regularization of the auction cycles, however,

---

[1] If the scheduled issue date falls on a Saturday, Sunday, or holiday, the securities are issued on the next business day.

these aspects of the auction are usually correctly anticipated. Occasionally an out-standing issue is "re-opened" (that is, the amount of an outstanding note is increased) at an auction instead of a new issue auctioned. In recent years, the Department of the Treasury has re-opened the 10-year note several times.

The typical issue size for Treasury notes is as follows:[2]

2-year issue	$17 billion
3-year issue	$15 billion
5-year issue	$11 billion
10-year issue	$12 billion
10-year reopened	$23 billion

Determination of the Results of an Auction

The auction for Treasury securities is conducted on a competitive bid basis. Competitive bids must be submitted on a yield basis. Non-competitive tenders may also be submitted for up to a $1 million face amount for bills and $5 million face amount for notes and bonds. Such tenders are based only on quantity, not yield.

The auction results are determined by first deducting the total non-competitive tenders and non-public purchases (such as purchases by the Federal Reserve itself) from the total securities being auctioned. The remainder is the amount to be awarded to the competitive bidders. For example, in April 1996 there was an auction for the 2-year Treasury note. The amount auctioned by the Treasury was $19.946 billion. The non-competitive bids totalled $1.169 billion. This meant that there was $18.777 billion to be distributed to competitive bidders. For this auction, there were bids for $47.604 billion

The bids are then arranged from the lowest yield bid to the highest yield bid. This is equivalent to arranging the bids from the highest price to the lowest price. Starting from the lowest yield bid, all competitive bids are accepted until the amount to be distributed to the competitive bidders is completely allocated. The highest yield accepted by the Treasury is referred to as the "stop yield," and bidders at that yield are awarded a percentage of their total tender offer. For the 2-year Treasury auction in April 1996, the stop yield was 5.939%. Bidders higher in yield than the stop yield were not distributed any of the new issue.

At what yield is a winning bidder awarded the auctioned security? At the time of this writing, there are two types of auctions held to determine the yield winning bidders will pay for the auctioned security: multiple-price auctions and single-price auctions. *Single-price auctions* are held for the 2-year and 5-year notes and the TIPS. In a single-price auction, all bidders are awarded securities at the highest yield of accepted competitive tenders (i.e., the stop yield). For example, in the 2-year auction of April 1996, the stop yield was 5.939%.

---

[2] Frank Keane, "Repo Rate Patterns for New Treasury Notes," *Current Issues in Economics and Finance,* September 1996, Table 2.

All other Treasury securities are issued using a *multiple-price auction.* Here the lowest-yield (i.e., highest price) bidders are awarded securities at their bid price. Successively higher-yielding bidders are awarded securities at their bid price until the total amount offered (less non-competitive tenders) is awarded. The price paid by non-competitive bidders is the average price of the competitive bids. For example, the auction result for an actual 364-day Treasury bill offering was as follows:

Total issue	=	$9.00 billion
Less non-competitive bids	=	0.64 billion
Less Federal Reserve	=	2.80 billion
Left for competitive bidders	=	$5.56 billion

Total competitive bids might have been received as follows:

Amount (in Billions)	Bid
$0.20	7.55% (lowest yield/highest price)
0.26	7.56
0.33	7.57
0.57	7.58 (average yield/average price)
0.79	7.59
0.96	7.60
1.25	7.61
1.52	7.62 (stop yield/lowest price)

The Treasury allocated bills to competitive bidders from the low-yield bid to the high-yield bid until $5.56 billion was distributed. Those who bid 7.55% to 7.61% were awarded the entire amount for which they bid. The total that was awarded to these bidders was $4.36 billion, leaving $1.2 billion to be awarded, less than the $1.52 billion bid at 7.62%. Each of the bidders at 7.62% was awarded 79% ($1.2/$1.52) of the amount they bid. For example, if a financial institution bid for $100 million at 7.62%, it would be awarded $79 million. The results of the auction would show 7.55% low, 7.58% average, and 7.62% the stop yield, with 79% awarded at the stop. Bidders higher in yield than 7.62% were shut out.

The difference between the average yield of all the bids accepted by the Treasury and the stop yield is called the "tail." Market participants use the tail as a measure of the success of the auction. The larger the tail, the less successful the auction. This is because the average price at which accepted bidders realized securities was considerably lower than the highest price paid. The 364-day Treasury bill auction had a tail of 4 basis points — the stop yield of 7.62% less the average yield of 7.58%.

The bid-to-cover ratio is the ratio of of the amount of bids submitted relative to the auction size. For the 10-year note, the average bid-to-cover ratio for the auctions from November 1988 to November 1996 was 2.47. The ratio ranged from a high of 3.15 (August 1993) to a low of 1.59 (August 1990). For the 30-

year, the average ratio for the same period was 2.23 with a high of 2.78 (August 1994) and a low of 1.48 (May 1991).[3]

THE SECONDARY MARKET

The secondary market for Treasury securities is an over-the-counter market where a group of U.S. government securities dealers offer continuous bid and ask prices on outstanding Treasuries. There is virtual 24-hour trading of Treasury securities. The three primary trading locations are New York, London, and Tokyo. Trading begins at 8:30 a.m. Tokyo time (7:30 p.m. New York time) and continues to about 4:00 p.m. Tokyo time (3:00 a.m. New York time).[4] Trading then goes on to London where trading begins at 8:00 a.m. London time and then on to New York at 12:30 p.m. London time (7:30 a.m. New York time). In New York trading begins at 7:30 a.m. and continues until 5:30 p.m.[5]

The secondary market is the most liquid financial market in the world. Daily average trading volume for all Treasury securities by primary dealers for the week ending March 19, 1997 was $206.914 billion, with the distribution among Treasury securities as follows:[6]

Treasury bills	$45.170 billion
Coupon securities	
due in 5 years or less	108.231 billion
due in more than 5 years	53.512 billion

In the interdealer market, positions are bought and sold in seconds. The trade size in the interdealer market begins at $5 million for bills and $1 million for coupon securities.

The most recently auctioned Treasury issue for a maturity is referred to as the *on-the-run issue* or *current coupon issue*. Issues auctioned prior to the current coupon issues typically are referred to as *off-the-run issues*. They are not as liquid as an on-the-run issue for a given maturity; that is, the bid-ask spread is larger for off-the-run issues relative to an on-the-run issue.

All Treasury bills and all Treasury coupon securities issued since January 1, 1983 are available only in book-entry registered form at the Federal Reserve System. (Treasury coupon instruments issued prior to January 1, 1983 are also available in bearer form.)

---

[3] As reported in Figure 2 of Lehman Brothers, *Relative Value Report*, Fixed Income Research, November 11, 1996, p. GOV-1.

[4] These are the trading hours when New York is on daylight savings time. The main difference when New York is on standard time is that Tokyo starts an hour earlier relative to New York (6:30 p.m. New York time).

[5] Michael J. Fleming, "The Round-the-Clock Market for U.S. Treasury Securities," *Economic Policy Review*, Federal Reaerve Bank of New York (July 1997), pp. 9-32.

[6] This figure represents immediate transactions of purchases and sales in the market as reported to the Federal Reserve Bank of New York. Immediate transactions are those scheduled for delivery in five days or less.

The normal settlement period for Treasury securities is the business day after the transaction day ("next day" settlement). By prior agreement, transactions may be made for settlement on the same day as the transaction day ("same day" or "spot" settlement), or for settlement on the fifth business day after the transaction day ("corporate" settlement).

Since virtually all Treasury securities are registered instruments with the Federal Reserve System, settlement occurs via members of the Federal Reserve System clearing organization, commercial banks, investment banks, or other brokers (dealers). Settlement occurs via the "Fed wire" on a *delivery versus payment* (DVP) *basis*. Settlement between the Fed and dealers and between dealers must occur by 2:00 p.m. on the settlement day; settlement from customers to dealers must occur by 2:15 p.m. (although some customers receive "dealer time" — that is, may settle with dealers until 2:30 p.m.).

When-Issued Market

Treasury securities are traded prior to the time they are issued by the Treasury. This component of the Treasury secondary market is called the *when-issued market*, or *wi market*. When-issued trading for both bills and coupon securities extends from the day the auction is announced until the issue day. All deliveries on when-issued trades occur on the issue day of the security traded.

Treasury Dealers and Interdealer Brokers

Any firm can deal in government securities, but in implementing its open market operations, the Federal Reserve will deal directly only with dealers that it designates as primary or recognized dealers. Basically, the Federal Reserve wants to be sure that firms requesting status as primary dealers have adequate capital relative to positions assumed in Treasury securities and do a reasonable amount of volume in Treasury securities. Exhibit 2 lists the primary government dealers as of May 1, 1997. Primary dealers include diversified and specialized securities firms, money center banks, and foreign-owned financial entities.

Treasury dealers trade with the investing public and with other dealer firms. When they trade with each other, it is through intermediaries known as *interdealer brokers*. Dealers leave firm bids and offers with interdealer brokers who display the highest bid and lowest offer in a computer network tied to each trading desk and displayed on a monitor. The dealer responding to a bid or offer by "hitting" or "taking" pays a commission to the interdealer broker. The size and prices of these transactions are visible to all dealers at once. The fees charged are negotiable and vary depending on transaction volume. Typically the fee is as follows: for a 3-month bill, ¼ of a hundredth of a point ($12.50 per $1 million); for a 6-month bill, ½ of a hundredth of a point ($25 per $1 million); for a 1-year bill, ¼ of a hundredth of a point ($25 per $1 million); and, for coupon securities, ⅛ of a 32nd of a point ($39.06 per $1 million).[7]

---

[7] These typical fees were reported in Marcia Stigum, *The Money Market* (Homewood, IL: Dow Jones-Irwin, 1990). In a study by Fleming ("The Round-the-Clock Market for U.S. Treasury Securities") these fees were found to be similar in 1996.

Exhibit 2: Primary Government Securities Dealers

BA Securities, Inc.	Aubrey G. Lanston & Co., Inc.
BZW Securities Inc.	Lehman Brothers Inc.
Bear, Stearns & Co., Inc.	Merrill Lynch Government Securities Inc.
BT Securities Corporation	J.P. Morgan Securities, Inc.
Chase Securities, Inc.	Morgan Stanley & Co. Incorporated
CIBC Wood Gundy Securities Corp.	NationsBanc Capital Markets, Inc.
Citicorp Securities, Inc.	Nesbitt Burns Securities Inc.
Credit Suisse First Boston Corporation	The Nikko Securities Co. International, Inc.
Daiwa Securities America Inc.	Nomura Securities International, Inc.
Dean Witter Reynolds Inc.	Paine Webber Incorporated
Deutsche Morgan Grenfell/C.J. Lawrence Inc.	Paribus Corporation
Dillon, Read & Co. Inc.	Prudential Securities Incorporated
Donaldson, Lufkin & Jenrette Securities Corporation	Salomon Brothers Inc.
Eastbridge Capital Inc.	Sanwa Securities (USA) Co., L.P.
First Chicago Capital Markets, Inc.	Smith Barney Inc.
Fuji Securities Inc.	SBC Warburg Inc.
Goldman, Sachs & Co.	UBS Securities LLC
Greenwich Capital Markets, Inc.	Yamaichi International (America), Inc.
HSBC Securities, Inc.	Zions First National Bank

Source: Market Reports Division, Federal Reserve Bank of New York, May 1, 1997.

Six interdealer brokers handle the bulk of daily trading volume. They include Cantor, Fitzgerald Securities Inc.; Garban Ltd.; Liberty Brokerage Inc.; RMJ Securities Corp.; Hilliard Farber & Co. Inc. (Treasury bills only); and, Tullett and Tokyo Securities Inc. These six firms service the primary government dealers and a dozen or so other large government dealers aspiring to be primary dealers.

Dealers use interdealer brokers because of the speed and efficiency with which trades can be accomplished. With the exception of Cantor, Fitzgerald Securities, interdealer brokers do not trade for their own account, and they keep the names of the dealers involved in trades confidential. The quotes provided on the government dealer screens represent prices in the "inside" or "interdealer" market. Historically, primary dealers have resisted attempts to allow the general public to have access to them. However, as a result of government pressure, GovPX Inc. was formed to provide greater public disclosure. GovPX is a joint venture of five of the six interdealer brokers and the primary dealers in which information on best bids and offers, size, and trade price are distributed via Bloomberg, Reuters, and Knight-Ridder. In addition, some dealers have developed an electronic trading system which allows trading between them and investors via Bloomberg. One example is Deutsche Morgan Grenfell's AutoBond System.

A recent study by Michael Fleming of the Federal Reserve Bank of New York examined data provided by GovPX to investigate intraday trading volume and bid-ask spreads for the three major trading locations — New York, London, and Tokyo.[8] The study covered the period April 4, 1994 to August 19, 1994. Fleming reported that 94% of trading occurs in New York, while trading in London and Tokyo is 4% and 2%, respectively. Based on daily volume data from GovPX, he finds that 64% of interdealer trading is in on-the-run issues, 24% is in off-the-run securities, and 12% is in when-issued securities.

Exhibit 3 shows Treasury interdealer trading volume by half hour as reported by Fleming. The pattern is as follows: trading starts in Tokyo at 7:30 p.m. New York time with relatively low trading volume. Volume picks up when London opens at 3:00 a.m. New York time and then remains fairly steady through London trading hours. Trading volume increases in the first half hour of trading after the 7:30 a.m. New York open, jumps higher in the second half hour, and then increases again to its daily peak between 8:30 a.m. and 9:00 a.m. A partial explanation for this peak in trading is the release of important government announcements at 8:30 a.m. and the opening up of Treasury futures trading on the Chicago Board of Trade at 8:20 a.m.[9] From 10:30 a.m. to 1:30 p.m. volume generally declines but rises again to an afternoon peak between 2:30 p.m. and 3:00 p.m. This peak coincides with the closing of futures trading at 3:00 p.m. Volume then declines through 5:30 p.m.

Exhibit 3: U.S. Treasury Securities Interdealer Trading Volume by Half Hour
(April 4, 1994 to August 19, 1994)

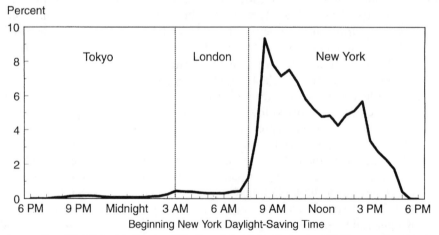

Source: Chart 2 in Michael J. Fleming, "The Round-the-Clock Market for U.S. Treasury Securities," *Economic Policy Review*, Federal Reserve Bank of New York (July 1997).

[8] Fleming, "The Round-the-Clock Market for U.S. Treasury Securities."
[9] Michael J. Fleming and Eli M. Remolona, "Price Formation and Liquidity in the U.S. Treasury Market: Evidence from Interday Patterns Around Announcements," working paper, Federal Reserve Bank of New York, March 1997.

Exhibit 4: U.S. Treasury Securities Interdealer Transactions Volume for On-the-Run Issues by Maturity (April 4, 1994 to August 19, 1994)

On-the-Run Issue	Mean Volume as a Percent of Total Volume*
3-month bill	7.4
6-month bill	6.4
cash management bill	1.0
1-year bill	10.1
2-year note	21.3
3-year note	7.7
5-year note	26.0
10-year note	17.4
30-year bond	2.7
Total	100.00

* Total volume for the on-the-run issues.

Source: Taken from Chart 1 in Michael J. Fleming, "The Round-the-Clock Market for U.S. Treasury Securities," *Economic Policy Review*, Federal Reserve Bank of New York (July 1997).

Trading volume in the interdealer market for the on-the-run issues is reported in Exhibit 4. Notice that about 43% of the trading volume takes place for the 5-year and 10-year notes. It has been suggested that the high volume of trading for these intermediate term notes is due to hedging activity.[10] Interdealer trading volume of on-the-run issues in London and Tokyo is different. While trading volume in Treasury bills is about 25% in New York (see Exhibit 4), Fleming found that it is less than 1% in London and Tokyo.

Information on dealer spreads for the three trading locations for the on-the-run coupon issues are reported in Exhibit 5. The dealer spread is defined as the difference between the highest price a potential buyer is willing to pay (the bid price) and lowest price that a potential seller is willing to sell (the ask price). The bid-ask spreads were calculated each day at half hour intervals and then averaged. (The spreads ignore fees paid on interdealer trades.) As Exhibit 5 indicates, spread increases with maturity — the minor exception being the 3-year and 5-year notes due to the large volume of transactions in the 5-year note that reduces the spread. Based on statistical tests, the spread for all the notes are less in New York than in London and Tokyo. While the average bid-ask spread is larger in New York than in London and Tokyo for the 30-year bond, the difference was not found to be statistically significant. The spread for the 3-year note is not significantly different between New York and London.

---

[10] This has been suggested by Madigan and Stehm. Specifically, it is driven by the hedging of dealer swap transactions. (See: Brian Madigan and Jeff Stehm, "An Overview of the Secondary Market for U.S. Treasury Securities in London and Tokyo," Board of Governors of the Federal Reserve System, *Finance and Economics Discussion Series* 94-17, July 1994.)

Exhibit 5: Average Bid-Ask Spreads for Interdealer Trades for On-the-Run Coupon Issues (April 4, 1994 to August 19, 1994)

On-the-Run Issue	Values in hundredths of a point			
	All Markets	Tokyo	London	New York
2-year note	0.83	1.37	1.12	0.78
3-year note	1.68	2.47	1.79	1.65
5-year note	1.53	2.48	2.04	1.47
10-year note	2.50	3.83	3.73	2.39
30-year bond	6.30	5.93	6.27	6.36

Source: Adapted from Table 4 in Michael J. Fleming, "The Round-the-Clock Market for U.S. Treasury Securities," *Economic Policy Review*, Federal Reserve Bank of New York (July 1997).

Price Quotes

The convention for quoting bids and offers is different for bills and coupon securities. Bids and offers on bills are quoted on a *bank discount basis*, not on a price basis. We will discuss this yield measure in Chapter 3.

Treasury coupon securities trade on a dollar price basis in price units of $1/32$ of 1% of par value. Par is taken to be $100. For example, a quote of 92-14 refers to a price of 92 and $14/32$. The number after the hyphen represents the number of 32nds. Thus the quoted price is 92.4375% of par value. If par value is $100,000, the quoted price is $92,437.50. On the basis of $100,000 par value, a change in price of 1% equates to $1,000, and $1/32$ equates to $31.25. A plus sign following the number of 32nds means that a 64th is added to the price. For example, 92-14+ refers to a price of 92 and $29/64$ or 92.453125% of par value. Prices can be refined to intervals even finer than 64ths (to 128ths and maybe even 256ths). For example, with a quoted price of 92.142, the 2 at the end refers to the number of eighths of 32nds. The price is thus 92 and $57/128$ or 92.4453125.

Sometimes a quote is shown with a decimal rather than a hyphen. The convention in the Treasury coupon market is the same as that with a hyphen. That is, a quote of 92.14 means 92 and $14/32$. In the illustrations throughout this book, we will *not* use this convention. Consequently, when a decimal is used in a price quote it represents a percentage of par value. So, 92.14 would mean 92.14% of par value.

When-issued securities are traded on a yield basis, not a price basis. The price will not be determined until settlement when the Treasury determines the coupon rate based on the auction.

Accrued Interest

The U.S. Treasury does not disburse coupon interest payments every day. Instead, coupon interest is paid every six months. If an investor buys a Treasury coupon security between coupon payments and holds it until the next coupon payment, then the entire coupon interest earned for the period will be paid to the buyer of the security. The seller of the security gives up the coupon interest from the time of the last coupon payment to the time until the security is sold. The amount of interest over this period that will be received by the buyer even though it was earned by the seller is called *accrued interest.*

In the United States and in many countries, the buyer must pay the seller the accrued interest. The amount that the buyer pays the seller is the agreed upon price for the security plus accrued interest. This amount is called the *full price* (*dirty price*). The agreed upon security price without accrued interest is called the *price* (*clean price*).

A security in which the buyer must pay the seller accrued interest is said to be trading *cum coupon.* If the buyer forgoes the next coupon payment, the security is said to be trading *ex coupon.* In the United States, Treasury coupon securities are always traded *cum coupon.*

Calculating Accrued Interest

When calculating accrued interest, three pieces of information are needed: (1) the number of days in the accrued interest period, (2) the number of days in the coupon period, and (3) the dollar amount of the coupon payment. The number of days in the accrued interest period represents the number of days over which the investor has earned interest. Given these values, the accrued interest (AI) assuming semiannual payments is calculated as follows:

$$\text{AI} = \frac{\text{Annual dollar coupon}}{2} \times \frac{\text{Days in AI period}}{\text{Days in coupon period}}$$

For example, suppose that (1) there are 50 days in the accrued interest period, (2) there are 183 days in a coupon period, and (3) the annual dollar coupon per $100 of par value is $8. Then the accrued interest is:

$$\text{AI} = \frac{\$8}{2} \times \frac{50}{183} = \$1.0929$$

Day Count Conventions

The calculation of the number days in the accrued interest period and the number of days in the coupon period begins with the determination of three key dates: trade date, settlement date, and date of previous coupon payment. The *trade date* is the date on which the transaction is executed. The *settlement date* is the date a transaction is completed. For Treasury securities, settlement is the next business day after the trade date. Interest accrues on a Treasury coupon security from and including the date of the previous coupon payment up to but *excluding* the settlement date.

The number of days in the accrued interest period and the number of days in the coupon period may not be simply the actual number of calendar days between two dates. The reason is that there is a market convention for each type of security that specifies how to determine the number of days between two dates. These conventions are called *day count conventions.* There are different day count conventions for Treasury securities than for government agency securities, municipal bonds, and corporate bonds.

For Treasury coupon securities, the day count convention used is to determine the actual number of days between two dates. This is referred to as the "actual/actual" day count convention. For example, consider a Treasury coupon security whose previous coupon payment was May 15. The next coupon payment would be on November 15. Suppose this Treasury security is purchased with a settlement date of September 10. First, the number of days of accrued interest is calculated. The actual number of days between May 15 (the previous coupon date) and September 10 (the settlement date) is 118 days, as shown below:

May 15 to May 31	17 days[11]
June	30 days
July	31 days
August	31 days
September 1 to September 10	9 days[12]
	118 days

The number of days in the coupon period is the actual number of days between May 15 and November 15, which is 184 days. The number of days between the settlement date (September 10) and the next coupon date (November 15) is therefore 66 days (184 days − 118 days).

Coupon Rolls

An important element of both the primary and secondary Treasury markets is the coupon roll. This is a transaction in which a dealer buys from a customer an outstanding on-the-run issue of a given maturity and sells to that same customer the new issue that will be auctioned. The issue to be auctioned is traded in the when-issued market and will not be delivered until after the auction. The transaction is called a "roll" because the customer is rolling the proceeds from the sale of the outstanding issue into the issue that will be auctioned.

In Chapter 11 we will explain this trade (as well as a reverse roll) and how the value of a roll is determined. For now, we only note why rolls are important in the primary and secondary Treasury markets. First, a dealer will do a roll for customers who want to trade into the new issue prior to the auction. This provides greater liquidity for the outstanding issue and facilitates the distribution of the new issue in the primary market. Second, by selling the new issue, a dealer will be positioning itself for bidding on that issue at auction. Thus, the dealer will bid more aggressively at the auction for that issue.

---

[11] Notice that May 15 is counted for purposes of determining the number of days in the accrued interest period.

[12] Notice that the settlement date (September 10) is not included for purposes of determining the number of days in the accrued interest period.

Exhibit 6: Coupon Stripping: Creating Zero-Coupon Treasury Securities

Security

| Par: $100 million |
| Coupon: 10%, semiannual |
| Maturity: 10 years |

Cash flows

| Coupon: $5 million Receipt in: 6 months | Coupon: $5 million Receipt in: 1 year | Coupon: $5 million Receipt in: 1.5 years | .... | Coupon: $5 million Receipt in: 10 years | Principal: $100 million Receipt in: 10 years |

Zero-coupon Treasury securities created

| Maturity value: $5 million Maturity: 6 months | Maturity value: $5 million Maturity: 1 year | Maturity value: $5 million Maturity: 1.5 years | .... | Maturity value: $5 million Maturity: 10 years | Maturity value: $100 million Maturity: 10 years |

STRIPPED TREASURY SECURITIES

The Treasury does not issue zero-coupon notes or bonds. However, because of the demand for zero-coupon instruments with no credit risk and a maturity greater than one year, the private sector has created such securities.

Trademark Products

In August 1982, Merrill Lynch and Salomon Brothers created synthetic zero-coupon Treasury receipts. Merrill Lynch marketed its Treasury receipts as "Treasury Income Growth Receipts" (TIGRs), and Salomon Brothers marketed its as "Certificates of Accrual on Treasury Securities" (CATS). The procedure was to purchase a Treasury coupon security and deposit it in a bank custody account. The firms then issued receipts representing an ownership interest in each coupon payment on the underlying Treasury security in the account and a receipt for ownership of the underlying Treasury security's maturity value. This process of separating each coupon payment, as well as the principal (also called the "corpus"), and selling securities backed by them is referred to as "coupon stripping." Although the receipts created from the coupon stripping process are not issued by the U.S. Treasury, the underlying security deposited in the bank custody account is a debt obligation of the U.S. Treasury, so the cash flows from the underlying security are certain.

To illustrate the process, suppose $100 million of a Treasury note with a 10-year maturity and a coupon rate of 10% is purchased to create zero-coupon Treasury receipts (see Exhibit 6). The cash flows from this Treasury note are 20 semiannual payments of $5 million each ($100 million times 10% divided by 2) and the repayment of principal (corpus) of $100 million 10 years from now. This Treasury note is deposited in a bank custody account. Receipts are then issued, each with a different single payment claim on the bank custody account. As there are 21 different payments to be made by the Treasury, a receipt representing a single payment claim on each payment is issued, which is effectively a zero-coupon instrument. The amount of the maturity value for a receipt on a particular payment, whether coupon or principal, depends on the amount of the payment to be made by the Treasury on the underlying Treasury note. In our example, 20 coupon receipts each have a maturity value of $5 million, and one receipt, the principal, has a maturity value of $100 million. The maturity dates for the receipts coincide with the corresponding payment dates by the Treasury.

Other investment banking firms followed suit by creating their own receipts. For example, Lehman Brothers offered "Lehman Investment Opportunities Notes" (LIONs); E.F. Hutton offered "Treasury Bond Receipts" (TBRs); and Dean Witter Reynolds offered "Easy Growth Treasury Receipts" (ETRs). There were also GATORs, COUGARs, and — moving out of the feline family — DOGS (Dibs on Government Securities). They all are referred to as *trademark zero-coupon Treasury receipts* because they are associated with particular firms. They are also called "animal products" for obvious reasons. Receipts of one firm were rarely traded by competing dealers, so the secondary market was not liquid for any one trademark. Moreover, the investor was exposed to the risk — as small as it may be — that the custodian bank may go bankrupt.

The motivation for coupon stripping lies in the arbitrage available to government dealers when they can purchase a Treasury coupon security for a price that is less than the aggregate amount at which they expect they can sell all the stripped securities. The theoretical reasons why this can occur are discussed in Chapter 2.

Treasury Receipts

To broaden the market and improve liquidity of these receipts, a group of primary dealers in the government market agreed to issue generic receipts that would not be directly associated with any of the participating dealers. These generic receipts are referred to as "Treasury Receipts" (TRs). Rather than representing a share of the trust as the trademarks do, TRs represent ownership of a Treasury security. A common problem with both trademark and generic receipts was that settlement required physical delivery, which is often cumbersome and inefficient.

STRIPS

In February 1985, the Treasury announced its *Separate Trading of Registered Interest and Principal Securities* (STRIPS) program to facilitate the stripping of designated Treasury securities. Specifically, all new Treasury bonds and all new Treasury notes with maturities of 10 years and longer are eligible. The inflation-protection securities may be stripped. The zero-coupon Treasury securities created under the STRIPS program are direct obligations of the U.S. government. Moreover, the securities clear through the Federal Reserve's book-entry system. Creation of the STRIPS program ended the origination of trademarks and Treasury Receipts.

There may be confusion when a market participant refers to a "stripped Treasury." Today, a stripped Treasury typically means a STRIPS product. However, since there are trademark products and TRs still traded in the market, an investor should clarify what product is the subject of the discussion. In the Chapters that follow, we will refer to stripped Treasury securities as simply "strips."

On dealer quote sheets and vendor screens STRIPS are identified by whether the cash flow is created from the coupon (denoted "ci"), principal from a Treasury bond (denoted "bp"), or principal from a Treasury note (denoted "np"). The reason why a distinction is made between the STRIPS created from the coupon and the principal has to do with the tax treatment by non-U.S. entities as discussed below.

Tax Treatment

A disadvantage of a taxable entity investing in stripped Treasury securities is that accrued interest is taxed each year even though interest is not paid. Thus, these instruments are negative cash flow instruments until the maturity date. They have negative cash flow since tax payments on interest earned but not received in cash must be made. A further discussion of the tax treatment of stripped Treasury securities is provided in Chapter 10.

One reason for distinguishing between STRIPS created from the principal and interest is that some foreign buyers have a preference for the STRIPS created from the principal. This preference is due to the tax treatment of the interest in their home country. Some country tax laws treat the interest as a capital gain which receives a preferential tax treatment (i.e., lower tax rate) compared to ordinary interest income if the stripped security was created from the principal.

RISKS ASSOCIATED WITH INVESTING IN TREASURY SECURITIES

While Treasury securities are viewed as free of credit or default risk, they expose investors to varying degrees of other types of risk. The two major risks are interest rate risk and inflation (or purchasing power) risk. For callable issues, there is call risk. There are additional risks that are discussed in later chapters. Some of the risks discussed in later chapters pertain to the risks associated with fixed income portfolio strategies.

Interest Rate Risk

The price of a Treasury security will change in the opposite direction from a change in market interest rates. That is, when interest rates rise, a Treasury security's price will fall; when interest rates fall, a Treasury security's price will rise. For example, consider a hypothetical 6% 20-year Treasury bond. If the yield investors require to buy this bond is 6%, the price of this bond would be $100. However, if the required yield increased to 6.5%, the price of this bond would decline to $94.4479. Thus, for a 50 basis point increase in yield, the bond's price declines by 5.55%. If, instead, the yield declines from 6% to 5.5%, the bond's price will rise by 6.02% to $106.0195.

Since the price of a Treasury security fluctuates with market interest rates, the risk that an investor faces is that the price of a Treasury security held in a portfolio will decline if market interest rates rise. This risk is referred to as *interest rate risk* and is by far the major risk faced by investors in Treasury securities. In Chapter 3, we will see the importance of this risk.

Because interest rate risk is a major concern to investors, it is critical that an investor be able to quantify this risk. As we will see in later chapters, interest rate risk has two dimensions. The first is the exposure of an individual Treasury security to the level of interest rates. We call this *level risk*. In Chapter 6, we explain how to quantify this risk. The second dimension of this risk relates to how a portfolio consisting of Treasury securities with different maturities may change in value when the interest rate for all maturities does not change by the same amount. We call this *yield curve risk* and in Chapter 7 we will see how this risk is measured.

Inflation or Purchasing Power Risk

Inflation risk or *purchasing power risk* arises because of the variation in the value of cash flows from a security due to inflation, as measured in terms of purchasing power. For example, if an investor purchases a Treasury security with a coupon rate of 7%, but the rate of inflation is 8%, the purchasing power of the cash flow has declined. For all but Treasury inflation-protection securities (TIPS), an investor is exposed to inflation risk because the interest rate the Treasury promises to make is fixed for the life of the issue.

Call Risk

As explained earlier, while the Treasury no longer issues callable bonds, there are Treasury bonds outstanding that are callable. From the investor's perspective, there are three disadvantages to owning a callable Treasury bond. First, the cash flow pattern of a callable bond is not known with certainty. Second, because the Treasury will likely call those issues if interest rates at the first call date or thereafter are below the coupon rate, the investor is exposed to reinvestment risk. This is the risk that the investor will have to reinvest the proceeds when the bond is called at relatively lower interest rates. Finally, the capital appreciation potential of a callable Treasury bond will be reduced, because the bond's price will not rise as much as that of a noncallable Treasury bond when rates decline. Because of these disadvantages faced by the investor, a callable Treasury bond is said to expose the investor to *call risk*.

KEY POINTS

1. *Treasury securities are backed by the full faith and credit of the U.S. government and viewed by market participants as having no credit risk.*

2. *The par value (principal, face value, redemption value, or maturity value) is the amount that the U.S. Treasury agrees to repay the security holder by the maturity date.*

3. *The Treasury issues two types of Treasury securities: discount securities and coupon securities (fixed rate and variable rate).*

4. *Treasury discount securities are called bills and have a maturity of one year or less.*

5. *A Treasury note is a coupon-bearing security which when issued has an original maturity between two and 10 years; a Treasury bond is a coupon-bearing security which when issued has an original maturity greater than 10 years.*

6. *In 1997, the Treasury began issuing inflation-protection securities whose principal and coupon payments are indexed to the Consumer Price Index.*

7. *Treasury coupon securities are currently issued on a regular basis with initial maturities of 2 years, 3 years, 5 years, 10 years, and 30 years.*

8. *While there are outstanding Treasury bonds that are callable, the Treasury no longer issues callable bonds.*

9. *Treasury securities are all issued on a competitive bid auction basis with an allowance for non-competitive bids of $1 million or less for bills and $5 million or less for notes and bonds.*

10. *Single-price auctions are held for the 2-year and 5-year notes and the inflation protection bonds; all other Treasury securities are auctioned on a multiple-price basis.*

11. *In a single-price auction, all winning bidders are awarded securities at the highest yield of accepted competitive tenders (i.e., the stop yield).*

12. *In a multiple-price auction, the lowest-yield (i.e., highest price) bidders are awarded securities at their bid price while successively higher-yielding bidders are awarded securities at their bid price until the total amount offered (less non-competitive tenders) is awarded.*

13. *The tail of an auction is the difference between the average yield of all the bids accepted by the Treasury and the stop yield and is a measure of the success of the auction.*

14. *The over-the-counter market for Treasury securities is the most liquid financial market in the world.*

15. *The most recently auctioned Treasury issue for a maturity is referred to as the on-the-run issue or current coupon issue; off-the-run issues are issues auctioned prior to the current coupon issues and are not as liquid as an on-the-run issue for a given maturity.*

16. *Treasury securities are traded prior to the time they are issued by the Treasury in the when-issued market, where trading is carried on from the day the auction is announced until the issue day (between one and two weeks).*

17. *The normal settlement period for Treasury securities is the business day after the transaction day ("next day" settlement).*

18. *Bond prices are quoted as a percentage of par value, with par value equal to 100, and in increments of 32nds of a point and 64ths of a point; the prices can be refined to intervals even finer than 64ths (to 128ths and maybe even 256ths).*

19. *The interest rate that the Treasury agrees to pay each year is called the coupon rate; the coupon is the annual amount of the interest payment and is found by multiplying the par value by the coupon rate.*

20. *The full price (or dirty price) of a Treasury security is the agreed upon price plus accrued interest; the price (or clean price) is the agreed upon price without accrued interest.*

21. *Interest accrues on a Treasury coupon security from and including the date of the previous coupon up to but excluding the settlement date.*

22. *The day count convention used for Treasury coupon securities is the actual number of days since the last coupon payment and the actual number of days in the coupon period (actual/actual).*

23. *A coupon roll is a transaction in which a dealer purchases from a customer an outstanding on-the-run issue of a given maturity and then sells to that same customer the new issue that will be subsequently auctioned.*

24. *Zero-coupon Treasury instruments are created by stripping the coupon payments and principal payment of a Treasury coupon security.*

25. *While there are three types of stripped Treasury securities outstanding— trademark products, Treasury Receipts, and STRIPS — only STRIPS are issued today.*

26. *A disadvantage of a taxable entity investing in stripped Treasury securities is that accrued interest is taxed each year even though interest is not paid; a similar disadvantage exists for TIPS, because the amount of inflation adjustment is taxed currently but paid at maturity.*

27. *While Treasury securities are viewed as being free of credit risk, they still expose an investor to other risks.*

28. *Interest rate risk is the risk that the price of a Treasury security will decline because interest rates rise.*

29. *Interest rate risk has two dimensions — level risk and yield curve risk.*

30. *Inflation risk is the risk that the purchasing power of the cash flows will decline because of inflation.*

31. *Callable Treasury bonds expose investors to call risk which consists of the uncertainty of the cash flows after the first call date, reinvestment risk, and limited price appreciation potential.*

Chapter 2

VALUATION OF TREASURY SECURITIES

In this chapter, we look at how to price or value a Treasury security. In the next chapter we will see how to calculate the yield offered on a Treasury security.

GENERAL PRINCIPLES OF VALUATION

The value of a Treasury security is equal to the present value of its cash flows. Valuation involves the following three steps:

> *Step 1:* Determine the cash flows.
> *Step 2:* Determine the appropriate interest rate or interest rates that should be used to discount the cash flows.
> *Step 3:* Calculate the present value of the cash flows found in step 1 by the interest rate or interest rates determined in step 2.

Cash Flows

Cash flow is simply the cash that is expected to be received at some time from an investment. It does not make any difference whether the cash flow is interest income or repayment of principal. The *cash flows* of a security are the collection of each period's cash flow. With the exception of callable Treasury bonds and inflation protection securities, the cash flows for a Treasury security are simple to project. The cash flows for a Treasury coupon security are the coupon interest payments every six months up to the maturity date and the maturity value at the maturity date. For a Treasury bill and a strip, there is only one cash flow — the maturity value at the maturity date.

For a callable Treasury security, the cash flows up to the first call date are known. They are simply the coupon payments. However, from the first call date to the maturity date, the cash flows are uncertain. The investor does know that the maturity value will be received, but does not know when since the Treasury can pay off the bond prior to the maturity date. Nor does the investor know how many coupon payments there will be after the first call date and up to the maturity date.

A key factor determining whether the U.S. Department of the Treasury will exercise its option to call a callable Treasury bond issue is the level of interest rates in the future relative to the callable issue's coupon rate. Specifically, for a callable Treasury bond, if the prevailing market rate at which the Department of the Treasury can issue a comparable-maturity Treasury note (since callable issues will have no more than five years remaining to maturity), there is an economic incentive to call the issue. What this means is that to properly estimate the cash flows of a callable Treasury bond it is necessary to incorporate into the valuation analysis future interest rate changes and how such changes would affect the incentive for the Department of the Treasury to call an issue. This is accomplished by introducing a parameter in the valuation process that reflects the expected volatility of interest rates. Throughout the remainder of this chapter, our focus will be on noncallable Treasury securities. We discuss the valuation of callable Treasury bonds in Chapter 14.

Determining the Appropriate Rate or Rates

Once the cash flows of a Treasury security are determined, the next step is to determine the appropriate interest rate that should be used to discount the cash flows. One approach is to discount every cash flow by the yield on a comparable-maturity on-the-run Treasury security. Alternatively, it can be argued that each cash flow is unique and therefore it may be more appropriate to value each cash flow using an interest rate specific to that cash flow. In the traditional approach to valuation discussed later in this chapter, we will see that a single interest rate is used. In the contemporary valuation approach, multiple interest rates are used.

Discounting the Cash Flows

Given the cash flows and the appropriate interest rate or interest rates that should be used to discount the cash flows, the final step in valuing a Treasury security is determining the value of the cash flows.

The value of a single cash flow to be received in the future is equal to the amount of money that must be invested today to generate that future value. The resulting value is called the *present value* of a cash flow. (It is also called the *discounted value*.) The present value of a cash flow will depend on when a cash flow will be received (i.e., the timing of a cash flow) and the interest rate used to calculate the present value. The interest rate used is called the *discount rate*.

The present value of a cash flow to be received t years from now if a discount rate i can be earned on any sum invested today is:

$$\text{Present value} = \frac{\text{Cash flow}}{(1+i)^t}$$

To illustrate the present value formula, consider a 4-year Treasury security that has a coupon rate of 10% and has a maturity value of $100. For simplicity, let's assume for now that the security pays interest annually and the same discount rate of 8% should be used to calculate the present value of each cash flow. Then the cash flows for this security are:

Year	Cash Flow
1	$10
2	10
3	10
4	110

The present value of each cash flow is

Year 1: Present value$_1$ = $\dfrac{\$10}{(1.08)^1}$ = $9.2593

Year 2: Present value$_2$ = $\dfrac{\$10}{(1.08)^2}$ = $8.5734

Year 3: Present value$_3$ = $\dfrac{\$10}{(1.08)^3}$ = $7.9383

Year 4: Present value$_4$ = $\dfrac{\$110}{(1.08)^4}$ = $80.8533

The value of this Treasury security is then the sum of the present values of the four cash flows. That is, the present value is $106.6243 ($9.2593 + $8.5734 + $7.9383 + $80.8533).

Present Value Properties
An important property about the present value can be seen from the above illustration. For the first three years, the cash flow is the same ($10) and the discount rate is the same (8%). The present value is lower the further into the future the cash flow will be received. *This is an important property of the present value: for a given discount rate, the further into the future a cash flow is received, the lower its present value.*

Suppose that instead of a discount rate of 8%, a 12% discount rate is used for each cash flow. Then, the present value of each cash flow is:

Year 1: Present value$_1$ = $\dfrac{\$10}{(1.12)^1}$ = $8.9286

Year 2: Present value$_2$ = $\dfrac{\$10}{(1.12)^2}$ = $7.9719

Year 3: Present value$_3$ = $\dfrac{\$10}{(1.12)^3}$ = $7.1178

Year 4: Present value$_4$ = $\dfrac{\$110}{(1.12)^4}$ = $69.9070

The value of this Treasury security is then $93.9253 ($8.9286 + $7.9719 + $7.1178 + $69.9070). The security's value is lower if a 12% discount rate is used compared to an 8% discount rate ($93.9253 versus $106.6243). This is a general property of present value. The higher the discount rate, the lower the present value. Since the value of a Treasury security is the present value of the cash flows, this property carries over to the value of a Treasury security: *the higher the discount rate, the lower a Treasury security's value*. The reverse is also true: *the lower the discount rate, the higher a Treasury security's value*.

Exhibit 1: Price/Discount Rate Relationship for a Noncallable Treasury Security

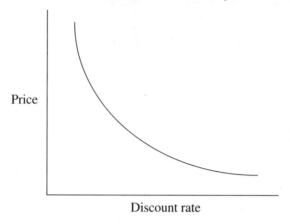

Exhibit 1 shows for a noncallable Treasury security this inverse relationship between a security's value and the discount rate. The shape of the curve in Exhibit 1 is referred to as *convex*.

Relationship between Coupon Rate, Discount Rate, and Price Relative to Maturity Value

Another important property is worth noting. The coupon rate on our hypothetical Treasury security is 10%. When an 8% discount rate is used, the security's value ($106.6243) is greater than the maturity value ($100). A security whose price is greater than its maturity value is said to be trading at a *premium to maturity value* or *premium to par value*. In general, when the discount rate is less than the coupon rate the security will trade at a premium to its maturity value. When a discount rate of 12% is used, the security's value is less than its maturity value ($93.9253). In such cases, the security is said to be trading at a *discount to maturity value* or *discount to par value*. In general, when the discount rate is greater than the coupon rate the security will trade at a discount to its maturity value. A security's value will be equal to its maturity value when the discount rate is equal to the coupon rate. So, if a 10% discount rate is used to calculate the present value of the cash flows, it would be found that the security's value is $100.

Valuation Using Multiple Discount Rates

If instead of the same discount rate for each year, let's suppose that the appropriate discount rates are as follows: year 1, 6.8%; year 2, 7.2%; year 3, 7.6%; and year 4, 8%. Then the present value of each cash flow is:

$$\text{Year 1: Present value}_1 = \frac{\$10}{(1.068)^1} = \$9.3633$$

$$\textit{Year 2: Present value}_2 = \frac{\$10}{(1.072)^2} = \$8.7018$$

$$\textit{Year 3: Present value}_3 = \frac{\$10}{(1.076)^3} = \$8.0272$$

$$\textit{Year 4: Present value}_4 = \frac{\$110}{(1.08)^4} = \$80.8533$$

The present value of this Treasury security assuming the various discount rates is $106.9456.

Valuing Semiannual Cash Flows

In our illustrations, we assumed that the coupon payments are paid once per year. For Treasury coupon securities the payments are semiannual. This does not introduce any complexities into the calculation. The procedure is to simply adjust the coupon payments by dividing the annual coupon payment by 2 and adjust the discount rate by dividing the annual discount rate by 2. The time period t in the present value formula is treated in terms of 6-month periods rather than years.

For example, consider once again the 4-year 10% coupon Treasury security with a maturity value of $100. The cash flow for the first 3.5 years is equal to $5 ($10/2). The last cash flow is $105. If an annual discount rate of 8% is used, the semiannual discount rate is 4%. The present value of each cash flow is then:

$$\textit{Period 1: Present value}_1 = \frac{\$5}{(1.04)^1} = \$4.8077$$

$$\textit{Period 2: Present value}_2 = \frac{\$5}{(1.04)^2} = \$4.6228$$

$$\textit{Period 3: Present value}_3 = \frac{\$5}{(1.04)^3} = \$4.4449$$

$$\textit{Period 4: Present value}_4 = \frac{\$5}{(1.04)^4} = \$4.2740$$

$$\textit{Period 5: Present value}_5 = \frac{\$5}{(1.04)^5} = \$4.1096$$

$$\textit{Period 6: Present value}_6 = \frac{\$5}{(1.04)^6} = \$3.9516$$

$$\textit{Period 7: Present value}_7 = \frac{\$5}{(1.04)^7} = \$3.7996$$

$$\textit{Period 8: Present value}_8 = \frac{\$105}{(1.04)^8} = \$76.7225$$

This Treasury security's value is equal to $106.7327.

Valuing a Treasury Strip

For a Treasury strip there is only one cash flow — the maturity value. The value of a strip that matures N years from now where N is greater than six months is

$$\text{Value of a Treasury strip} = \frac{\text{Maturity value}}{(1 + i/2)^{2N}}$$

For example, a 5-year strip (10-period strip) with a maturity value of $100 discounted at an 8% interest rate (4% semiannual interest rate) is $67.5564, as shown below:

$$\frac{\$100}{(1.04)^{10}} = \$67.5564$$

If the time to maturity is six months or less for a Treasury strip, the value is computed as follows:

$$\text{Value of a Treasury strip} = \frac{\text{Maturity value}}{1 + (i/2) \times g}$$

where

$$g = \frac{\text{number of days from settlement to maturity}}{\text{Number of days in a 6-month period ending at the maturity date}}$$

For example, assume the following:

Maturity date: 11/15/97
Settlement date: 8/19/97
Discount rate: 6%

The number of days from settlement to maturity is 88. The number of days in a 6-month period ending at the maturity date is 184. Therefore, g is 88/184. The value of this Treasury strip is then

$$\frac{\$100}{1 + 0.03 \times (88/184)} = \$98.585512$$

Valuing Treasury Coupon Securities between Coupon Payments

For Treasury coupon securities, a complication arises when the next coupon payment is not six months from now. This happens when a settlement date is between coupon payments. The amount that the buyer pays the seller in such cases is the present value of the cash flows at the settlement date. This is the bond's full price (or dirty price). In Chapter 1, we explained how accrued interest is calculated. Here we will show how the present value formula is modified when a Treasury coupon security is purchased between coupon payments.

First it is necessary to determine the following ratio:

$$w = \frac{\text{Days between settlement date and next coupon payment}}{\text{Days in current coupon period}}$$

As explained in Chapter 1, the number of days between two dates depends on day count conventions used in the Treasury market. Day count conventions are also used to calculate the number of days in the numerator and denominator of the ratio w.

Given w there are then two ways in which the next cash flow can be discounted for a fractional period from the next coupon payment date to the settlement date. The first method uses a discount rate based on compounded interest and the second method uses a discount rate based on simple interest. The two methods are explained below.

Cash Flow Discounted Based on Compounded Interest The present value of the next coupon payment to be received w periods from now when discounted at a compounded interest rate is:

$$\text{Present value of next coupon payment} = \frac{\text{Next coupon payment}}{(1 + i/2)^w}$$

where i is the discount rate.

For any subsequent cash flow, the present value of the cash flow to be received $t + w$ periods from notes assuming the next coupon payment is w periods from now is as follows based on compounding of the discount rate i:

$$\text{Present value}_t = \frac{\text{Cash flow}}{(1 + i/2)^{t+w}}$$

This method for calculating the present value when a security is purchased between coupon payments is called the *Street method* or the *Securities Industry Association (SIA) method*.

To illustrate the procedure, we will use the hypothetical 4-year 10% Treasury security with interest payable semiannually. Assume that this security is purchased between coupon payments and that there are (1) 78 days between the settlement date and the next coupon payment date and (2) 182 days in the current coupon period. Then w is 0.4286. The present value of each cash flow assuming that each is discounted at 8% is

$$\textit{Period 1}: \text{Present value}_0 = \frac{\$5}{(1.04)^{0.4286}} = \$4.9167$$

$$\textit{Period 2}: \text{Present value}_1 = \frac{\$5}{(1.04)^{1.4286}} = \$4.7275$$

$$\textit{Period 3}: \text{Present value}_2 = \frac{\$5}{(1.04)^{2.4286}} = \$4.5457$$

$$\textit{Period 4}: \text{Present value}_3 = \frac{\$5}{(1.04)^{3.4286}} = \$4.3709$$

$$\textit{Period 5}: \text{Present value}_4 = \frac{\$5}{(1.04)^{4.4286}} = \$4.2028$$

$$\textit{Period 6:} \text{ Present value}_5 = \frac{\$5}{(1.04)^{5.4286}} = \$4.0411$$

$$\textit{Period 7:} \text{ Present value}_6 = \frac{\$5}{(1.04)^{6.4286}} = \$3.8857$$

$$\textit{Period 8:} \text{ Present value}_7 = \frac{\$105}{(1.04)^{7.4286}} = \$78.4613$$

The full price is the sum of the present value of the cash flows, which is $109.1517. From the full price must be subtracted the accrued interest to get the (clean) price.

Cash Flow Discounted Based on Simple Interest When simple interest is used, the present value of the next coupon payment to be received w periods from now is computed as follows:

$$\text{Present value of next coupon payment} = \frac{\text{Next coupon period}}{[1 + (w)i/2]}$$

For any subsequent cash flow, the present value to be received t periods from the next coupon payment assuming the next coupon payment is w periods from now based on simple interest and a discount rate of i is:

$$\text{Present value}_t = \frac{\text{Cash flow}}{[1 + (w)i/2](1 + i/2)^t}$$

This method for computing the present value is called the *Treasury method* or the *Fed method*.

Using our hypothetical 4-year 10% Treasury security, the present value of each cash flow is computed below assuming a discount rate of 8%:

$$\textit{Period 1:} \text{ Present value}_0 = \frac{\$5}{1 + (0.4286)(0.04)} = 4.9157$$

$$\textit{Period 2:} \text{ Present value}_1 = \frac{\$5}{[1 + (0.4286)(0.04)](1.04)^1} = 4.7267$$

$$\textit{Period 3:} \text{ Present value}_2 = \frac{\$5}{[1 + (0.4286)(0.04)](1.04)^2} = 4.5449$$

$$\textit{Period 4:} \text{ Present value}_3 = \frac{\$5}{[1 + (0.4286)(0.04)](1.04)^3} = 4.3701$$

$$\textit{Period 5:} \text{ Present value}_4 = \frac{\$5}{[1 + (0.4286)(0.04)](1.04)^4} = 4.2020$$

$$\textit{Period 6:} \text{ Present value}_5 = \frac{\$5}{[1 + (0.4286)(0.04)](1.04)^5} = 4.0404$$

$$Period\ 7\text{: Present value}_6 = \frac{\$5}{[1 + (0.4286)(0.04)](1.04)^6} = 3.8850$$

$$Period\ 8\text{: Present value}_7 = \frac{\$105}{[1 + (0.4286)(0.04)](1.04)^7} = 78.4464$$

The full price is the sum of the present value of the cash flows, which is $109.1311, a value which is less than when computing the cash flows assuming compounding.

THE TRADITIONAL VALUATION APPROACH

The traditional approach to the valuation of a Treasury security has been to discount every cash flow by the same interest rate (or discount rate). For example, consider the three hypothetical 10-year Treasury securities shown in Exhibit 2: a 12% coupon Treasury, an 8% coupon Treasury, and a Treasury strip. The cash flows for each security are shown in the exhibit. The traditional approach to valuation is to use the same discount rate to calculate the present value of all three securities and use the same discount rate for the cash flow for each period. For the three hypothetical securities, suppose that the yield for the 10-year on-the-run Treasury is 10%. Then, the practice is to discount each cash flow using a discount rate of 10%.

Exhibit 2: Cash Flows for Three 10-Year Hypothetical Treasury Securities Per $100 of Par Value
Each period is six months

Period	Coupon Rate 12%	Coupon Rate 8%	Strip (Zero Coupon)
1	$6	$4	$0
2	6	4	0
3	6	4	0
4	6	4	0
5	6	4	0
6	6	4	0
7	6	4	0
8	6	4	0
9	6	4	0
10	6	4	0
11	6	4	0
12	6	4	0
13	6	4	0
14	6	4	0
15	6	4	0
16	6	4	0
17	6	4	0
18	6	4	0
19	6	4	0
20	106	104	100

THE CONTEMPORARY VALUATION APPROACH

The fundamental flaw of the traditional approach is that it views each Treasury security of a given maturity as the same package of cash flows. For example, consider a 10-year Treasury security with an 8% coupon rate. The cash flows per $100 of par value would be 19 payments of $4 every six months and $104 twenty 6-month periods from now. The traditional practice would discount every cash flow using the same interest rate.

The proper way to view the 10-year 8% coupon security is as a package of zero-coupon instruments. Each cash flow should be considered a zero-coupon instrument whose maturity value is the amount of the cash flow and whose maturity date is the date that the cash flow is to be received. Thus, the 10-year 8% coupon security should be viewed as 20 zero-coupon instruments. The reason this is the proper way to value a Treasury security is that it does not allow a market participant to realize an arbitrage profit by taking apart or "stripping" a security and selling off the stripped securities at a higher aggregate value than it would cost to purchase the Treasury security in the market.

By viewing any financial asset as a package of zero-coupon instruments, a consistent valuation framework can be developed. For example, under the traditional approach to the valuation of Treasury securities, a 10-year zero-coupon instrument would be viewed as the same security as a 10-year 8% coupon security. Viewing a Treasury as a package of zero-coupon instruments means that these two securities would be viewed as different packages of zero-coupon instruments and valued accordingly.

The difference between the traditional valuation approach and the contemporary approach is depicted in Exhibit 3 which shows how the three Treasury securities whose cash flows are depicted in Exhibit 2 should be valued. With the traditional approach, the discount rate for all three securities is the yield on the on-the-run 10-year Treasury. With the contemporary approach the discount rate for a cash flow is the theoretical rate that the U.S. Treasury would have to pay if it issued a zero-coupon instrument with a maturity date equal to the maturity date of the cash flow.

Therefore, to implement the contemporary approach it is necessary to determine the theoretical rate that the Department of the Treasury would have to pay to issue a zero-coupon instrument for each maturity. Another name used for the zero-coupon Treasury rate is the *Treasury spot rate*. In Chapter 5 we will explain how the Treasury spot rate can be calculated.

Valuation Using Treasury Spot Rates

To illustrate how Treasury spot rates are used to value a Treasury security, we will use the hypothetical Treasury spot rates shown in the fourth column of Exhibit 4 to value an 8% 10-year Treasury security. The present value of each period's cash flow is shown in the last column. The sum of the present values is the theoretical value for the Treasury security. For the 8% 10-year Treasury it is $115.2619.

Exhibit 3: Comparison of Traditional Approach and Contemporary Approach in Valuing a Treasury Security
Each period is six months

Period	Discount Rate		Cash Flows For*		
	Traditional Approach	Contemporary Approach	12%	8%	0%
1	10-year Treasury rate	1-period Treasury spot rate	$6	$4	$0
2	10-year Treasury rate	2-period Treasury spot rate	6	4	0
3	10-year Treasury rate	3-period Treasury spot rate	6	4	0
4	10-year Treasury rate	4-period Treasury spot rate	6	4	0
5	10-year Treasury rate	5-period Treasury spot rate	6	4	0
6	10-year Treasury rate	6-period Treasury spot rate	6	4	0
7	10-year Treasury rate	7-period Treasury spot rate	6	4	0
8	10-year Treasury rate	8-period Treasury spot rate	6	4	0
9	10-year Treasury rate	9-period Treasury spot rate	6	4	0
10	10-year Treasury rate	10-period Treasury spot rate	6	4	0
11	10-year Treasury rate	11-period Treasury spot rate	6	4	0
12	10-year Treasury rate	12-period Treasury spot rate	6	4	0
13	10-year Treasury rate	13-period Treasury spot rate	6	4	0
14	10-year Treasury rate	14-period Treasury spot rate	6	4	0
15	10-year Treasury rate	15-period Treasury spot rate	6	4	0
16	10-year Treasury rate	16-period Treasury spot rate	6	4	0
17	10-year Treasury rate	17-period Treasury spot rate	6	4	0
18	10-year Treasury rate	18-period Treasury spot rate	6	4	0
19	10-year Treasury rate	19-period Treasury spot rate	6	4	0
20	10-year Treasury rate	20-period Treasury spot rate	106	104	100

* Per $100 of par value.

Exhibit 4: Determination of the Theoretical Value of an 8% 10-Year Treasury

Period	Years	Cash Flow ($)	Spot rate (%)	Present Value ($)
1	0.5	4	3.0000	3.9409
2	1.0	4	3.3000	3.8712
3	1.5	4	3.5053	3.7968
4	2.0	4	3.9164	3.7014
5	2.5	4	4.4376	3.5843
6	3.0	4	4.7520	3.4743
7	3.5	4	4.9622	3.3694
8	4.0	4	5.0650	3.2747
9	4.5	4	5.1701	3.1791
10	5.0	4	5.2772	3.0828
11	5.5	4	5.3864	2.9861
12	6.0	4	5.4976	2.8889
13	6.5	4	5.6108	2.7916
14	7.0	4	5.6643	2.7055
15	7.5	4	5.7193	2.6205
16	8.0	4	5.7755	2.5365
17	8.5	4	5.8331	2.4536
18	9.0	4	5.9584	2.3581
19	9.5	4	6.0863	2.2631
20	10.0	104	6.2169	56.3828
			Total	$115.2619

KEY POINTS

1. Valuing a Treasury security is the process of determining the security's fair value.

2. The valuation process involves three steps: (1) determining the expected cash flows, (2) determining the appropriate interest rate or interest rates that should be used to discount the cash flows, and (3) calculating the present value of the cash flows.

3. A Treasury security's value is the present value of the cash flows.

4. A cash flow is the cash that is expected to be received at some time.

5. The cash flows of a security are the collection of each period's cash flow.

6. With the exception of callable Treasury bonds and inflation-protection securities, the cash flows for all Treasury securities can easily be determined.

7. For Treasury coupon securities, the cash flows are the semiannual coupon payments and the maturity value.

8. For a Treasury strip and bill, there is only one cash flow — the maturity value.

9. The difficulty in determining cash flows for a callable Treasury bond arises because the U.S. Department of the Treasury can alter the cash flows by calling the issue.

10. For a given discount rate, the present value of a single cash flow to be received in the future is the amount of money that must be invested today that will generate that future value.

11. The present value of a cash flow will depend on when a cash flow will be received (i.e., the timing of a cash flow) and the discount rate (i.e., interest rate) used to calculate the present value

12. The present value is lower the further into the future the cash flow will be received.

13. The higher the discount rate, the lower a cash flow's present value and therefore since the value of a security is the present value of the cash flows, the higher the discount rate, the lower a security's value.

14. In general, when the discount rate is less than the coupon rate the security will trade at a premium to its maturity value and when the discount rate is higher than the coupon rate the security will trade at a discount to its maturity value.

15. For securities purchased between coupon payment dates, the next coupon payment can be discounted assuming compounded interest (the Street method) or simple interest (the Treasury method).

16. The traditional valuation methodology is to discount every cash flow of a Treasury security by the same interest rate (or discount rate), thereby incorrectly viewing each security of equal maturity as the same package of cash flows.

17. The contemporary approach values a Treasury security as a package of cash flows, with each cash flow viewed as a zero-coupon instrument and each cash flow discounted at its own unique discount rate.

18. The unique interest rate that should be used to discount each cash flow is the theoretical rate that the Treasury would pay if it issued a zero-coupon instrument.

19. The theoretical Treasury zero-coupon rates are called spot rates.

Chapter 3

YIELD AND RETURN CALCULATIONS

In the previous chapter, we saw how to calculate the price or value of a Treasury coupon security. In this chapter, we look at how to calculate the yield on a Treasury coupon security and bill. Yield measures are based on certain assumptions which limit their use in comparing the relative value of Treasury securities. To understand these limitations, we begin this chapter with an explanation of the sources of return from investing in a Treasury security. At the end of the chapter, we explain how to calculate the potential return from investing in a Treasury security.

SOURCES OF RETURN

When an investor purchases a Treasury security, he or she can expect to receive a dollar return from one or more of the following sources:

1. the coupon interest payments made by the Treasury
2. any capital gain (or capital loss – a negative dollar return) when the security matures, is sold, or is called (in the case of a callable Treasury bond)
3. income from reinvestment of the coupon payments received

Any yield measure that purports to measure the potential return from a Treasury security should consider all three sources of return listed above.

It is important to note that the classification of the sources of return in our discussion in this chapter is different from the treatment under the U.S. tax code. For example, as explained in Chapter 10, for Treasury strips, the tax code treats the difference between the par value and the purchase price as interest income. More specifically, the discount from par value is called an *original interest discount*. In our discussion in this chapter, it would be classified as a capital gain. As a second example, the tax code has rules for the treatment of what it defines as a bond purchased below par value because of changes in market interest rates. The difference between the par value and market price is called a *market discount* and is treated as interest income under the tax code. In our discussion we would define the difference as a capital gain.

Coupon Interest Payments

The most obvious source of return is the periodic coupon interest payments. For strips, the return from this source is zero, despite the fact that the investor is effectively receiving interest by purchasing a security below its par value and realizing interest at the maturity date when the investor receives the par value.

39

Capital Gain or Loss

The proceeds received when a Treasury security matures, is called (in the case of a callable Treasury bond), or is sold may be greater than the purchase price, in which case a *capital gain* results. For a Treasury security held to maturity, there will be a capital gain if it is purchased below par value. A security purchased below par value is said to be purchased at a *discount*. For example, a security purchased for $94.17 with a par value of $100 will generate a capital gain of $5.83 ($100 − $94.17) if held to maturity. For a callable Treasury bond, a capital gain will result if the price at which the bond is called is greater than the purchase price. The call price for a callable Treasury bond is par value. If a Treasury security is sold prior to its maturity (or before it is called, in the case of a callable Treasury bond), a capital gain will result if the proceeds exceed the purchase price. So, if a Treasury security purchased for $94.17 is sold prior to the maturity date for $103, the capital gain would be $8.83 ($103 − $94.17).

A *capital loss* is generated when the proceeds received when a Treasury security matures, is called, or is sold are less then the purchase price. For a Treasury security held to maturity, there will be a capital loss if it is purchased for more than its par value. A security purchased for more than its par value is said to be purchased at a *premium*. For example, a Treasury coupon security purchased for $102.5 with a par value of $100 will generate a capital loss of $2.5 ($102.5 − $100) if held to maturity. For a callable Treasury bond, a capital loss results if its purchase price exceeds par value.

Note that for a Treasury bill or strip, the purchase price will be less than the par value. Therefore, if the issue is held to maturity, only a capital gain (as defined here) will be realized.

Reinvestment Income

A Treasury coupon security makes periodic payments of interest that can be reinvested until the security is removed from the portfolio. The interest earned from reinvesting the interim coupon payments until the security is removed from the portfolio is called *reinvestment income*.

YIELD MEASURES FOR TREASURY COUPON SECURITIES

There are several yield measures cited for Treasury coupon securities. These yield measures are expressed as a percent return rather than a dollar return. Below we explain how each measure is calculated and its limitations. There are additional yield measures for Treasury coupon securities with a remaining maturity of less than one year. We discuss these measures in a later section.

Current Yield

The current yield relates the annual dollar coupon interest to the market price. The formula for the current yield is:

$$\text{Current yield} = \frac{\text{Annual dollar coupon interest}}{\text{Price}}$$

For example, the current yield for a 7% 8-year Treasury security whose price is $94.17 is 7.43% as shown below:

Annual dollar coupon interest = $0.07 \times \$100 = \$7$

Price = $94.17

$$\text{Current yield} = \frac{\$7}{\$94.17} = 0.0743 \text{ or } 7.43\%$$

The current yield will be greater than the coupon rate when the bond sells at a discount; the reverse is true for a bond selling at a premium. For a bond selling at par value, the current yield will be equal to the coupon rate.

The drawback of the current yield is that it considers only the coupon interest and no other source that will impact an investor's return. No consideration is given to the capital gain that the investor will realize when a Treasury security is purchased at a discount and held to maturity; nor is there any recognition of the capital loss that the investor will realize if a Treasury security purchased at a premium is held to maturity.

Yield to Maturity

The most popular measure of yield is the yield to maturity. The *yield to maturity* is the interest rate that will make the present value of the cash flows from a Treasury security equal to its market price plus accrued interest.

Calculation of the yield to maturity of a Treasury security is the reverse process of calculating the price of a security. As explained in the previous chapter, to find the price of a security we determine the cash flows and the appropriate discount rate(s), then we calculate the present value of the cash flows to obtain the price. To find the yield to maturity, we first determine the cash flows. Then we search by trial and error for the interest rate that will make the present value of the cash flows equal to the market price plus accrued interest. In the illustrations presented in this chapter, we assume that the next coupon payment will be six months from now so that there is no accrued interest.

To illustrate, consider a 7% 8-year Treasury coupon security selling for $94.17. The cash flows for this security are (1) 16 payments every six months of $3.50 and (2) a payment 16 6-month periods from now of $100. The present value using various discount (interest) rates is:

Interest rate	3.5%	3.6%	3.7%	3.8%	3.9%	4.0%
Present value	100.00	98.80	97.62	96.45	95.30	94.17

When a 4.0% interest rate is used, the present value of the cash flows is equal to $94.17, which is the assumed price of the security. Hence, 4.0% is the *semiannual yield to maturity*.

The market convention adopted is to double the semiannual yield and call that the yield to maturity. Thus, the yield to maturity for the above security is 8% (2 times 4.0%). The yield to maturity computed using this convention — doubling the semiannual yield — is called a *bond-equivalent yield*.

Yield quotes can be based on the *Street method* or the *Treasury method*. As explained in Chapter 2, the difference between the two yield measures is the procedure used to discount the first coupon payment when it is not exactly six months away. This occurs for two reasons. First, for certain securities, the first coupon payment may be less than six months away. This situation is referred to as an "odd" or "irregular" first coupon payment. When the first coupon payment is less than six months from the date of issuance, the Treasury security is said to have a *short first coupon*.[1] The second circumstance when the first coupon payment may be received in less than six months is when a security is purchased between coupon dates.

The Treasury method (also called the "Fed" method) assumes simple interest over the period from the settlement date to the next coupon payment. The Street method (also called the Securities Industry Association or "SIA" method) assumes compound interest over the period from the settlement date to the next coupon payment. From a practical point of view, once a security is issued and traded in the secondary market, investors and traders use the Street method.

Relationship among Price and Coupon Rate, Current Yield, and Yield to Maturity

The following relationships among the price of a Treasury security, coupon rate, current yield, and yield to maturity hold:

Security selling at	Relationship		
par	coupon rate =	current yield =	yield to maturity
discount	coupon rate <	current yield <	yield to maturity
premium	coupon rate >	current yield >	yield to maturity

Limitations of Yield-to-Maturity Measure

The yield to maturity considers not only the coupon income but any capital gain or loss that the investor will realize by holding a Treasury security to maturity. The yield to maturity also considers the timing of the cash flows. It does consider reinvestment income; however, it assumes that the coupon payments can be reinvested at an interest rate equal to the yield to maturity. So, if the yield to maturity for a Treasury coupon security is 8%, for example, to earn that yield the coupon payments must be reinvested at an interest rate equal to 8%. The following illustration clearly demonstrates this.

---

[1] The Treasury issues a security with a short first coupon when the auction date is the fifteenth or the end of the month, but that day falls on a weekend or holiday. In such cases, the Treasury issues the security on the next business day, but pays the first coupon on the fifteenth or at the end of the month six months later. Thus, the first coupon payment is less than six months away.

Suppose an investor has $94.17 and places the funds in a certificate of deposit that pays 4% every six months for 8 years or 8% per year (on a bond-equivalent basis, i.e., doubling the semiannual rate). At the end of 8 years, the $94.17 investment will grow to $176.38. Instead, suppose an investor buys a 7% 8-year Treasury security selling for $94.17. The yield to maturity for this bond is 8%. The investor would expect that at the end of 8 years, the total dollars from the investment will be $176.38.

Let's look at what the investor will receive. There will be 16 semiannual interest payments of $3.50 which will total $56. When this security matures, the investor will receive $100. Thus, the total dollars that the investor will receive is $156 by holding this security to maturity. But this is less than the $176.38 necessary to produce a yield of 8% on a bond-equivalent basis. The interest shortfall is $20.38 ($176.38 minus $156). How is this deficiency supposed to be made up? If the investor reinvests the coupon payments at a semiannual interest rate of 4% (or 8% annual rate on a bond-equivalent basis), then the interest earned on the reinvested coupon payments will be $20.38. Consequently, of the $82.21 total dollar return ($176.38 minus $94.17) necessary to produce a yield of 8%, about 25% ($20.38 divided by $82.21) must be generated by reinvesting the coupon payments.

Clearly, the investor will only realize the yield to maturity that is stated at the time of purchase only if (1) the coupon payments can be reinvested at the yield to maturity and (2) the security is held to maturity. With respect to the first assumption, the risk that an investor faces is that future interest rates will be less than the yield to maturity at the time the bond is purchased. This risk is referred to as *reinvestment risk*. If the security is not held to maturity, it may have to be sold for less than its purchase price, resulting in a return that is less than the yield to maturity. The risk that a bond will have to be sold at a loss is referred to as *interest rate risk*. We discussed this risk in Chapter 1. In Chapter 7 we will explain how this risk is measured.

A Closer Look at Reinvestment Risk There are two characteristics of a Treasury coupon security that determine the degree of reinvestment risk. First, for a given yield to maturity and a given coupon rate, the longer the maturity the more the bond's total dollar return is dependent on reinvestment income to realize the yield to maturity at the time of purchase. That is, the greater the reinvestment risk. The implication is that the yield-to-maturity measure for long-term Treasury coupon securities tells little about the potential return that an investor may realize if it is held to maturity. For long-term Treasury coupon securities, in high interest rate environments the reinvestment income component may be as high as 80% of the security's potential total dollar return.

The second characteristic that determines the degree of reinvestment risk is the coupon rate. For a given maturity and a given yield to maturity, the higher the coupon rate, the more dependent the security's total dollar return will be on the reinvestment of the coupon payments in order to produce the yield to maturity at the time of purchase. This means that holding maturity and yield to maturity constant, Treasury coupon securities selling at a premium will be more dependent on reinvestment income than Treasury coupon securities selling at par value. In contrast, Treasury coupon securities selling at a discount will be less dependent on reinvestment income than Treasury coupon securities selling at par value. For strips, none of the security's total dollar return is dependent on reinvestment income. So, a strip has no reinvestment risk if held to maturity.

The dependence of the total dollar return on reinvestment income for hypothetical Treasury securities with different coupon rates and maturities is shown in Exhibit 1. The securities are assumed to be selling to yield 8%.

Yield to Call

For a callable Treasury bond, the practice has been to calculate a yield to call as well as a yield to maturity. The procedure for calculating the yield to call is the same as for any yield calculation: determine the interest rate that will make the present value of the expected cash flows equal to the price plus accrued interest. In the case of yield to call, the expected cash flows are the coupon payments to the first call date and the call price of $100. When the yield to call is calculated based on the first call date, it is called the *yield to first call*. Similarly, a yield to any call date can be calculated for a callable Treasury bond.

Limitations of Yield to Call

Let's take a closer look at the yield to call as a measure of the potential return of a callable Treasury security. The yield to call does consider all three sources of potential return from owning a security. However, as in the case of the yield to maturity, it assumes that all cash flows can be reinvested at the calculated yield to call until the assumed call date. As we just demonstrated, this assumption may be inappropriate. Moreover, the yield to call assumes that (1) the investor will hold the issue to the assumed call date and (2) the Department of the Treasury will call the issue on that date.

Exhibit 1: Percentage of Total Dollar Return from Reinvestment Income

	Years to maturity				
	2	3	5	8	15
7% coupon selling to yield 8%					
Price	98.19	97.38	95.94	94.17	91.35
% of total	5.2%	8.6%	15.2%	24.8%	44.5%
8% coupon selling to yield 8%					
Price	100.00	100.00	100.00	100.00	100.00
% of total	5.8%	9.5%	16.7%	26.7%	46.5%
12% coupon selling to yield 8%					
Price	107.26	110.48	116.22	123.30	134.58
% of total	8.1%	12.9%	21.6%	32.5%	51.8%

Yield to Worst

For a callable Treasury bond, a yield can be calculated for every possible call date. In addition, a yield to maturity can be calculated. The lowest of all these possible yields is called the *yield to worst*. The yield to worst measure holds little meaning as a measure of potential return.

YIELD MEASURE FOR STRIPS

Treasury strips do not make coupon payments. They are zero-coupon instruments. Nor is there accrued interest between coupon periods. However, the yield to maturity for a strip is calculated in the same manner as the yield to maturity for a Treasury coupon security. In the case of a strip, it is the interest rate that makes the present value of the maturity value equal to the price. To make yield calculations for strips comparable to that for Treasury coupon securities, the maturity is specified in terms of semiannual periods. That is, a strip that matures in 10 years is treated as maturing in 20 6-month periods.

Since there are no coupon payments to reinvest, the yield to maturity is the yield or return that an investor will realize by holding a strip to maturity. While there is no reinvestment risk, there is still interest rate risk if an investor must sell a strip prior to the maturity date. In fact, as explained in Chapter 6, for two securities with the same maturity, the lower the coupon rate, the greater the price volatility or interest rate risk. Thus, strips have greater interest rate risk than same-maturity Treasury coupon securities. Moreover, the longer the maturity of a security, the greater its interest rate risk. Consequently, long-term strips have substantial interest rate risk. Therefore, while a strip has no reinvestment risk, it has considerable interest rate risk, particularly long-term strips.

TREASURY BILL YIELD MEASURES

As discount securities, Treasury bills do not pay coupon interest. Instead, Treasury bills are issued at a discount from their maturity value; the return to the investor is the difference between the maturity value and the purchase price. Treasury bills discount rate (explained below) is based on an actual/360-day basis.

Yield on a Discount Basis

The convention in the Treasury bill market is to calculate a bill's *yield on a discount basis*. This yield is determined by two variables:

1. the settlement price per $1 of maturity value (denoted by p)
2. the number of days to maturity which is calculated as the number of days between the settlement date and the maturity date (denoted by N_{SM})

The yield on a discount basis (denoted by d) is calculated as follows:

$$d = (1-p)\left(\frac{N_{SM}}{360}\right)$$

We will use two actual Treasury bills to illustrate the calculation of the yield on a discount basis assuming a settlement date in both cases of 8/6/97. The first bill has a maturity date of 1/8/98 and a price of 0.977697222. For this bill, the number of days from the settlement date to the maturity date, N_{SM}, is 155. Therefore, the yield on a discount basis is

$$d = (1-0.97769722)\left(\frac{360}{155}\right) = 5.18\%$$

For our second bill, the maturity date is 7/23/98 and the price is 0.9490075. Assuming a settlement date of 8/16/97, the number of days from the settlement date to the maturity date is 351. The yield on a discount basis for this bill is

$$d = (1-0.9490075)\left(\frac{360}{351}\right) = 5.23\%$$

Given the yield on a discount basis, the price of a bill (per $1 of maturity value) is computed as follows:

$$p = 1 - d(N_{SM}/360)$$

For the 155-day bill selling for a yield on a discount basis of 5.18%, the price per $1 of maturity value is

$$p = 1 - 0.0518\,(155/360) = 0.977697222$$

For the 351-day bill selling for a yield on a discount basis of 5.23%, the price per $1 of maturity value is

$$p = 1 - 0.0523\,(351/360) = 0.9490075$$

The quoted yield on a discount basis is not a meaningful measure of the return from holding a Treasury bill for two reasons. First, the measure is based on a maturity value investment rather than on the actual dollar amount invested. Second, the yield is annualized according to a 360-day year rather than a 365-day year, making it difficult to compare yields on Treasury bills with Treasury notes and bonds which pay interest based on the actual number of days in a year. The use of 360 days for a year is a convention for money market instruments. Despite its shortcomings as a measure of return, this is the method dealers have adopted to quote Treasury bills.

Other Yield Measures for Treasury Bills[2]

Because of the limitations of the yield on a discount basis, dealer quote sheets and reporting services calculate other yield measures that are more useful to compare Treasury bills to Treasury coupon securities. Two yield measures have been reported: *Treasury yield* and *bond-equivalent yield*. A *simple yield* based on a 360-day basis is sometimes reported. Another measure sometimes reported is the *CD-equivalent yield*. This measure is used to compare a Treasury bill yield to the yield on a certificate of deposit.

For all of these measures, the calculation depends on the number of days from the settlement date to the maturity date. Specifically, there are calculations for bills with 182 days or less from the settlement date to the maturity date and calculations for bills with more than 182 days from the settlement date to the maturity date. The reason for the different treatment is as follows. Treasury coupon securities pay interest semiannually. Bills do not pay interest until maturity. Bills with a maturity of less than or equal to 182 days offer the same compounding opportunity as coupon securities in their last coupon period. Bills with a maturity of more than 182 days entail the opportunity cost of foregoing reinvestment of any coupon interest payments relative to Treasury coupon securities.

Bills with 182 Days or Less from Settlement to Maturity

When there are 182 days or less from the settlement date to the maturity date, the computation of the four yield measures is explained below. In each illustration, the 155-day bill will be used assuming a settlement date of 8/16/97 and a yield on a discount basis of 5.18%.

Treasury Yield The Treasury yield uses the actual number of days in a year rather than 360 days, and relates the return to the settlement price rather than the maturity value. Given the yield on a discount basis (d), the formula for the Treasury yield is

$$y = \frac{N_A \, d}{360 - (N_{SM} \, d)}$$

where N_{AY} is the actual number of days in a year. This value is 365 days except if the Treasury bill's issue date is after February 28 of one year and before March 1 of the next year which is a leap year. In such cases, N_{AY} is 366.[3]

For our 155-day bill, the Treasury yield is 5.37% as shown below

$$y = \frac{365(0.0518)}{360 - (155)(0.0518)} = 0.0537 = 5.37\%$$

---

[2] I am grateful to Dragomir Krgin of Merrill Lynch for providing me with the formulae and illustrations presented below.

[3] Another yield measure that is sometimes quoted is the Compucorp (TM) yield. The difference between this measure and the Treasury yield is that 365 is always used in the formula.

Bond-Equivalent Yield The bond-equivalent yield is calculated as follows:

$$y = \left(\frac{1}{p} - 1\right)\frac{2}{F}$$

where

$$F = \frac{\text{Actual number of days from settlement date to maturity date}}{\text{Actual number of days in a 6-month period ending with maturity date}}$$

When calculating the 6-month period ending with the maturity date, the beginning of the period is the same day in a month 6 months before the maturity date or the end of the month (if the maturity date is the end of the month) 6 months before the maturity date. This is illustrated below:

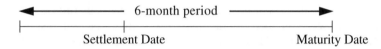

Using the 155-day bill, F is found as follows.

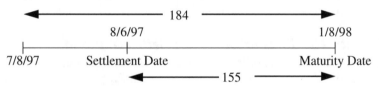

Therefore,

$$F = \frac{155}{184}$$

The Treasury yield is then

$$y = \left(\frac{1}{0.97769722} - 1\right)\left(\frac{2}{155/184}\right) = 5.42\%$$

Simple Interest Yield The simple interest yield relates the return to the settlement price rather than the maturity value; however, the calculation is based on a 360-day basis. The formula for the simple interest yield given the yield on a discount basis is

$$y = \frac{360 \ d}{360 - (N_{SM} \ d)}$$

For the 155-day bill, the simple interest yield is 5.30%, as shown below:

$$y = \frac{360(0.0518)}{360 - (155 \times 0.0518)} = 5.30\%$$

CD-Equivalent Yield The CD-equivalent yield, sometimes called the *money market equivalent yield* or the *medium term CD yield*, makes the quoted yield on a Treasury bill more comparable to the yield quoted on other money market instruments that pay interest on a 360-day basis. It does this by taking into consideration the price of the bill rather than its maturity value. The formula given the yield on a discount basis is

$$y = \frac{360 \ d}{360 - (N_{SM} \ d)}$$

Note that this is the same formula as the simple interest yield. Thus, for bills with a maturity of 182 days or less from the settlement date to the maturity date, the CD-equivalent yield and the simple interest yield are equal.

Bills with More Than 182 Days from Settlement to Maturity

For Treasury bills with more than 182 days from the settlement date to the maturity date, the computations are more complex. The formula for each yield measure is given below. We also show how to calculate p given the quoted yield measure. The 351-day bill will be used in our illustrations.

Treasury Yield To compute the Treasury yield, the period from the settlement date to the maturity is divided into two periods as shown below:

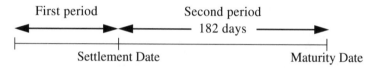

For the first period, simple interest is assumed. For the second period, compound interest is assumed (as with the Street convention discussed earlier). The formula for the Treasury yield is[4]

$$y = \frac{\dfrac{-2N_{SM}}{N_{AY}} + 2\sqrt{\left(\dfrac{N_{SM}}{N_{AY}}\right)^2 - \left(\dfrac{2N_{SM}}{N_{AY}} - 1\right)\left(1 - \dfrac{1}{p}\right)}}{\left(\dfrac{2N_{SM}}{N_{AY}}\right) - 1}$$

For the 351-day bill in our example, the number of days in the year is 365 (i.e., $N_{AY} = 365$). Since p is 0.9490075, the Treasury yield is

$$y = \frac{\dfrac{-2(351)}{365} + 2\sqrt{\left(\dfrac{351}{365}\right)^2 - \left(\dfrac{2(351)}{365} - 1\right)\left(1 - \dfrac{1}{0.9490075}\right)}}{\dfrac{2(351)}{365} - 1} = 5.15\%$$

Given a quote for a Treasury bill based on the Treasury yield formula above, the price per \$1 of maturity value is found as follows:

---

[4] The Compucorp (TM) yield uses the same formula except that 365 is always used for NAY.

$$p = \frac{1}{\left(1 + \frac{y}{2}\right)\left(1 + \frac{y}{2}\left(\frac{2N_{SM}}{N_{AY}} - 1\right)\right)}$$

Bond-Equivalent Yield The bond-equivalent yield is:

$$y = 2\left(\frac{1}{p^{1/(1+F)}} - 1\right)$$

where F was defined earlier.

For the 351-day bill, F is determined as follows:

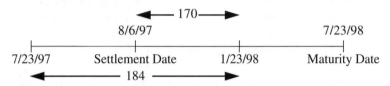

Therefore,

$$F = \frac{170}{184}$$

and the bond-equivalent yield is

$$y = 2\left(\frac{1}{0.9490075^{1/(1 + 170/184)}} - 1\right) = 5.52\%$$

Given a quote on a bond-equivalent yield for a Treasury bill, then the price per $1 of maturity value is computed as follows:

$$p = \frac{1}{\left(1 + \frac{y}{2}\right)^{1 + F}}$$

Simple Interest Yield The computation of the simple interest yield is:

$$y = \left(\frac{1}{p} - 1\right)\left(\frac{360}{N_{SM}}\right)$$

The simple interest yield for the 351-day bill is

$$y = \left(\frac{1}{0.9490075} - 1\right)\left(\frac{360}{351}\right) = 5.51\%$$

Given the simple interest yield, the price per $1 of maturity value is found by

$$p = \cfrac{1}{1 + y\left(\cfrac{N_{SM}}{360}\right)}$$

CD-Equivalent Yield To compute the CD-equivalent yield, the days between the time period must be divided as follows:

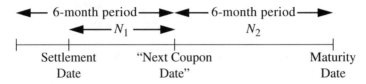

While there is no "next coupon date," for purposes of the calculation, this date is the same day in a month, 6 months before the maturity date or the end of the month (if the maturity date is at the end of the month), 6 months before the maturity date. Then, N_1 is the actual number of days from the settlement date to the "next coupon date," and N_2 is the actual number of days from the "next coupon date" to the maturity date.

The CD-equivalent yield is then calculated as follows:

$$y = \cfrac{360 - (N_1 + N_2) + \sqrt{(N_1 + N_2)^2 - 4N_1 N_2\left(1 - \cfrac{1}{p}\right)}}{2N_1 N_2}$$

For the 351-day bill, N_1 and N_2 are determined as follows:

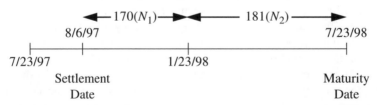

The CD-equivalent yield is then

$$y = \cfrac{360\left[-(170+181)+\sqrt{(170+181)^2 - 4(170)(181)\left(1 - \cfrac{1}{0.9490075}\right)}\,\right]}{2(170)(181)} = 5.44\%$$

The price per $1 of maturity value given a quote on a CD-equivalent yield is

$$p = \cfrac{1}{\left[1 + y\left(\cfrac{N_1}{360}\right)\right]\left[1 + y\left(\cfrac{N_2}{360}\right)\right]}$$

YIELD FOR COUPON TREASURY SECURITIES IN THEIR LAST COUPON PERIOD

There is a special treatment for the yield calculation of Treasury coupon securities in their last coupon period. The convention is to calculate the simple interest rate using the following formula:

$$\text{Yield} = \left(\frac{M - C/2}{\text{Price} + AI} - 1\right) \times \frac{2 \times \text{No. of days in the coupon period}}{\text{No. of days from settlement to maturity}}$$

where M is the maturity value, C is the annual dollar coupon payment, and AI is accrued interest.

The numerator of the first ratio is the semiannual dollar coupon interest minus the accrued interest paid. Thus, it is the dollar return. The denominator of the first ratio is the amount of the investment (i.e, the dirty price). Thus, the first ratio is the return. The second ratio annualizes the return.

A limitation of this measure is that doubling of the number of days in the coupon period never adds up to the number of days in a year, 365. Rather than use an arbitrary convention to assess the potential dollar return, a better method for assessing the relative return of Treasury bills and Treasury coupon securities in their last coupon period is to use the measure described in the next section.

TOTAL RETURN

As we have emphasized, yield measures provide only an estimate of the potential return from investing in a Treasury security if an issue is held to maturity and coupon payments can be reinvested at the calculated yield. If yield measures offer little insight into the potential return, what measure can be used? The proper measure is one that considers the three sources of potential dollar return over the investor's investment horizon. (We discussed these three sources at the outset of this chapter.) It is the return (interest rate) that will make the proceeds (i.e., price plus accrued interest) invested in the Treasury security or portfolio grow to the projected total dollar return at the end of the investment horizon. This interest rate is referred to as the *total return*.

The total return requires that the investor specify (1) an investment horizon, (2) a reinvestment rate, and (3) a selling price for the Treasury security at the end of the investment horizon (which depends on the assumed yield to maturity for the issue at the end of the investment horizon). More formally, the steps for computing a total return over some investment horizon are as follows:

> *Step 1:* Compute the total coupon payments plus the reinvestment income based on an assumed reinvestment rate. The reinvestment rate is one-half

the annual interest rate that the investor assumes can be earned when rein-vesting the coupon interest payments.[5]

Step 2: Determine the projected sale price at the end of the investment hori-zon. We refer to this as the *horizon price.* The horizon price will depend on the projected yield for the security at the end of the investment horizon. We refer to the yield at the end of the investment horizon as the *horizon yield.*

Step 3: Add the values computed in Steps 1 and 2. The sum is the *total future dollars* that will be received from the investment given the assumed rein-vestment rate and projected horizon yield.

Step 4: To obtain the semiannual total return, use the following formula:

$$\left(\frac{\text{Total future dollars}}{\text{Dirty price of bond}} \right)^{1/\text{Length of horizon}} - 1$$

where the dirty price is the price plus accrued interest.

Step 5: Double the interest rate found in Step 4. The resulting interest rate is the total return expressed on a bond-equivalent basis. Instead, the total return can be expressed on an *effective rate basis* by using the following formula:

$$\text{Effective rate} = (1 + \text{Semiannual total return})^2 - 1$$

A graphical depiction of the total return calculation is presented in Exhibit 2.

The decision as to whether to calculate the total return on a bond-equiva-lent basis or an effective rate basis depends on the situation. If the total return is being compared to a benchmark index that is calculated on a bond-equivalent basis, then the total return should be calculated in that way. However, if the investment proceeds are being used to satisfy a liability that is calculated on an effective rate basis, then the total return should be calculated in that way.

Exhibit 2: Graphical Depiction of Total Return Calculation

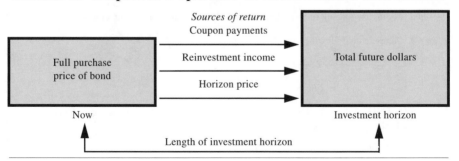

[5] An investor can choose multiple reinvestment rates for cash flows from the security over the investment horizon.

To illustrate the computation of the total return, suppose that an investor with a 3-year investment horizon is considering purchasing a 20-year 8% coupon Treasury bond for $82.84. The next coupon payment is six months from now. The yield to maturity for this issue is 10%. The investor expects that he can reinvest the coupon payments at an annual interest rate of 6% and that at the end of the investment horizon the 17-year Treasury issue will be selling to offer a yield to maturity of 8.5% (i.e., the horizon yield is 8.5%). The total return for this Treasury issue is computed in Exhibit 3.

Comparing Treasury Bills and Coupon Securities in their Last Coupon Period

The total return can be used to assess the outcome from investing in a Treasury bill (which is based on a 360-day year) and a Treasury coupon security in its last coupon period (which is based on a 365-day year). The total number of dollars over a specified investment horizon can be calculated per dollar invested for the two alternatives and then compared.

Exhibit 3: Illustration of Calculation of Total Return

Assumptions:

> Bond: 8% 20-year Treasury bond selling for $82.84 (yield to maturity is 10%)
> Reinvestment rate: 6%
> Investment horizon: 3 years
> Horizon yield: 8.5%

Calculation:

Step 1: Compute the total coupon payments plus the reinvestment income assuming an annual reinvestment rate of 6%, or 3% every six months. The coupon payments are $4 per $100 of par value every 6 months for 3 years or 6 periods (the length of the investment horizon). The total coupon interest plus reinvestment income is $25.874.

Step 2: The projected sale price at the end of 3 years (i.e., the horizon price) assuming that the required yield to maturity for 17-year bonds (i.e., horizon yield) is 8.5% is $95.55.

Step 3: Adding the amount in Steps 1 and 2 gives the total future dollars of $121.424.

Step 4: Compute the following:

$$\left(\frac{\$121.424}{\$82.84}\right)^{\frac{1}{6}} - 1 = (1.46577)^{0.16667} - 1$$

$$= 1.0658 - 1 = 0.0658 \text{ or } 6.58\%$$

Step 5: Doubling 6.58% gives a total return of 13.16% on a bond-equivalent basis. On an effective rate basis, the horizon return is

$$(1.0658)^2 - 1 = 1.1359 - 1 = 0.1359 = 13.59\%$$

Moreover, in comparing funding costs to investment return, an investor must be concerned with different day count conventions for different borrowing vehicles (such as repurchase agreements). Converting to dollars the investment proceeds and the financing costs allows the correct assessment of a strategy.

Portfolio Total Return

To calculate a portfolio's total return, it is first necessary to calculate the total dollars at the end of the investment horizon for each Treasury issue in the portfolio. Then the total dollars are summed. It is this aggregate dollar amount that is used in the total return formula. The denominator is the total dollars invested in all the securities.

Scenario Analysis

Total return enables a portfolio manager to analyze the performance of an individual Treasury issue or a Treasury portfolio based on different interest rate scenarios for horizon yields and reinvestment rates. This type of analysis, referred to as *scenario analysis*, allows a portfolio manager to see how sensitive the performance of a Treasury issue or Treasury portfolio is to each assumption. A portfolio manager should be more comfortable looking at the total return profile using different interest rate assumptions than blindly relying upon the implicit assumptions incorporated into conventional yield measures. We'll illustrate scenario analysis in later chapters.

KEY POINTS

1. *The sources of return from holding a Treasury security to maturity are the coupon interest payments, any capital gain or loss, and reinvestment income.*

2. *Reinvestment income is the interest income generated by reinvesting coupon interest payments from the time of receipt to the security's maturity.*

3. *For a Treasury coupon security, the current yield relates the annual dollar coupon interest to the market price.*

4. *The current yield measure fails to recognize any capital gain or loss and reinvestment income.*

5. *The yield to maturity is the interest rate that will make the present value of the cash flows equal to the market price plus accrued interest.*

6. *The market convention to annualize a semiannual yield is to double it and the resulting annual yield is referred to as a bond-equivalent yield.*

7. *The yield to maturity quoted for Treasury coupon securities is calculated using either the Street method or the Treasury method — the difference between the two yield measures being the procedure used to discount the first coupon payment when it is not exactly six months away.*

8. *The yield to maturity takes into account all three sources of return but assumes that the coupon payments can be reinvested at an interest rate equal to the calculated yield to maturity.*

9. *The yield to maturity will only be realized only if the interim coupon payments can be reinvested at the calculated yield to maturity and the security is held to maturity.*

10. *The risk an investor faces that future reinvestment rates will be less than the yield to maturity at the time a security is purchased is called reinvestment risk.*

11. *Interest rate risk is the risk that if a security is not held to maturity, an investor may have to sell it for less than the purchase price.*

12. *The longer the maturity and the higher the coupon rate, the more a Treasury security's return is dependent on reinvestment income to realize the yield to maturity at the time of purchase.*

13. *For a callable Treasury bond, the yield to call is the interest rate that will make the present value of the expected cash flows to the assumed call date equal to the price plus accrued interest.*

14. *The yield to call does consider all three sources of potential return but assumes that all coupon payments can be reinvested at the calculated yield to call until the assumed call date, the investor will hold the bond to the assumed call date, and the Department of the Treasury will call the issue on the assumed call date.*

15. *The yield to worst is the lowest yield from among all possible yield to calls and the yield to maturity.*

16. *The convention in the Treasury bill market is to calculate a bill's yield on a discount basis.*

17. *The quoted yield on a discount basis is not a meaningful measure of the return from holding a bill because the measure is based on a maturity value investment and the yield is annualized according to a 360-day rather than 365-day year.*

18. *To make Treasury bill yields more comparable to yields quoted on Treasury coupon securities, a "Treasury yield" and a "bond-equivalent yield" are computed by dealer firms and reporting services.*

19. *A simple interest yield is computed assuming a 360-day basis.*

20. *A CD-equivalent yield is computed to compare Treasury bill yields with other money market instruments that pay interest on a 360-day basis.*

21. *The formula for computing the yield for a Treasury bill depends on whether there are 182 days or less from the settlement date to the maturity date or more than 182 days.*

22. *There is a special treatment for the yield calculation of Treasury coupon securities in their last coupon period.*

23. *For a Treasury security in its last coupon period the convention is to calculate a simple interest rate.*

24. *The proper measure for assessing the potential return from investing in a Treasury security is the total return.*

25. *Calculation of the total return to an investment horizon that is less than the maturity date requires specification of the reinvestment rate and the horizon yield.*

26. *The horizon yield is needed to obtain the horizon price of the Treasury security at the end of the investment horizon.*

27. *Scenario analysis involves calculating the total return under different assumptions regarding the reinvestment rate and horizon yield.*

Chapter 4

THE TERM STRUCTURE OF INTEREST RATES

The yields offered on Treasury securities represent the base interest rate or minimum interest rate that investors demand if they purchased a non-Treasury security. For this reason market participants continuously monitor the yields on Treasury securities, particularly the yields on the on-the-run issues. In this chapter we will discuss the historical relationship that has been observed between the yields offered on-the-run Treasury securities and maturity. The relationship between the yield on Treasury securities and maturity is called the *term structure of interest rates*. Economic theories about the term structure of interest rates are presented in the next chapter where we also explain two important pieces of information that are derived from the term structure — spot rates and forward rates.

In this chapter we also present empirical evidence showing how changes in the term structure of interest rates have affected the historical returns on Treasury portfolios. Once we understand the factors that affect Treasury portfolio returns, we can develop measures for assessing the impact of changes in the term structure of interest rates on a Treasury portfolio. These measures are explained and illustrated in Chapters 6 and 7.

THE YIELD CURVE

Treasuries of different maturities trade at different yield levels. As we just noted, this is called the term structure of interest rates. Exhibit 1 shows the yield for the on-the-run issues for three days: 10/24/94, 12/28/89, and 3/3/89. In Exhibit 2, this relationship is drawn for the three days whose yields are reported in Exhibit 1. The graphical depiction of this relationship is called the *yield curve*.

Exhibit 1: Yields On-the-Run Treasury Issues for Three Days

Maturity	Yields on		
(years)	10/24/94	12/28/89	3/3/89
2	6.81%	7.96%	9.48%
3	7.12	7.88	9.39
4	not issued	7.91	9.43
5	7.51	7.86	9.38
7	not issued	7.95	9.34
10	7.84	7.91	9.31
30	8.04	7.96	9.13

Source: Ryan Labs, Inc.

Exhibit 2: Treasury Yield Curve Shape on Three Days

Yields on 10/24/94 — Normal

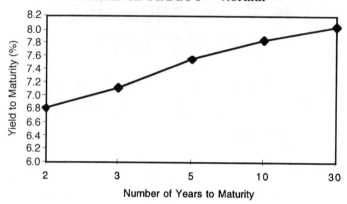

Number of Years to Maturity

Yields on 12/28/89 — Flat

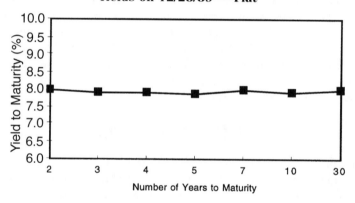

Number of Years to Maturity

Yields on 3/3/89 — Inverted

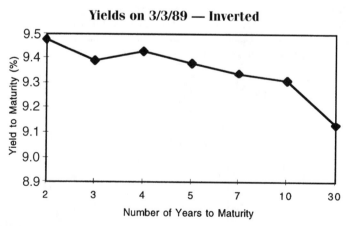

Number of Years to Maturity

Exhibit 3: Average Daily Slope of the Treasury Yield Curve (30-Year Yield minus 2-Year Yield) by Month from January 1989 to August 1997

Year	Jan	Feb	Mar	Apr	May	June	July	Aug	Sept	Oct	Nov	Dec
In basis points												
1997	88	72	68	68	72	72	58					
1996	110	103	90	86	73	77	76	81	83	91	77	77
1995	36	52	68	79	79	86	94	90	75	67	78	73
1994	217	203	194	175	147	149	146	134	134	123	97	29
1993	298	302	296	313	277	266	259	235	217	208	208	210
1992	263	267	231	264	271	283	327	323	347	348	303	288
1991	115	119	120	127	149	157	156	173	178	202	238	268
1990	17	15	−7	3	10	9	34	82	96	99	94	92
1989	−25	−37	−51	−43	−21	−15	25	−3	−13	2	11	8

Slope is defined as the average daily spread between the 30-year and 2-year Treasury yields for the month.
Source: Ryan Labs, Inc.

Historically, three shapes have been observed for the yield curve. Exhibit 2 shows these three shapes for the yields reported in Exhibit 1. The most common relationship is a yield curve in which the longer the maturity, the higher the yield. That is, investors are rewarded for holding longer maturity Treasuries in the form of a higher potential yield. This shape is referred to as a *normal* or *positively sloped yield curve*. The yield curve on 10/24/94 was an example. A *flat yield curve* is one in which the yield for all maturities is approximately equal. The yield curve on 12/28/89 was an example. There have been times when the relationship between maturities and yields were such that the longer the maturity the lower the yield. Such a downward sloping yield curve is referred to as an *inverted* or a *negatively sloped yield curve*. On 3/3/89 the yield curve exhibited this characteristic.

Slope of the Yield Curve

Market participants talk about the difference between long-term Treasury yields and short-term Treasury yields. The spread between these yields for two maturities is referred to as the *steepness* or *slope of the yield curve*. There is no industry-wide accepted definition of the maturity used for the long-end and the maturity for the short-end of the yield curve. Some market participants define the slope of the yield curve as the difference between the 30-year yield and the 3-month yield — that is, the difference between the longest and shortest Treasury securities issued. Other market participants define the slope of the yield curve as the difference between the 30-year yield and the 2-year yield.

Exhibit 3 reports for the period January 1989 to July 1997 the average monthly slope of the Treasury yield curve as defined by the average daily spread for the month between the 30-year yield and 2-year yield. Note that the yield curve was the steepest in September and October 1992, about 348 basis points. For the period reported, the yield curve was inverted for most of 1989, with the largest inversion occurring in March 1989. Exhibit 4 reports the steepness of the yield curve at the long end for the same period. The long end is defined as the spread between the 30-year bond yield and 10-year note yield. Note the flatter slope of the long end of the yield curve.

Yield Curve Shifts

A shift in the yield curve refers to the relative change in the yield for each Treasury maturity. A *parallel shift in the yield curve* refers to a shift in which the change in the yield for all maturities is the same. A *nonparallel shift in the yield curve* means that the yield for all maturities does not change by the same number of basis points.

Historically, two types of nonparallel yield curve shifts have been observed: a twist in the slope of the yield curve and a change in the humpedness or curvature of the yield curve. All of these shifts are graphically portrayed in Exhibit 5. A *twist in the slope of the yield curve* refers to a flattening or steepening of the yield curve. A *flattening of the yield curve* means that the slope of the yield curve (i.e., the spread between the yield on a long-term and short-term Treasury) has decreased; a steepening of the yield curve means that the slope of the yield curve has increased. This is depicted in the second panel of Exhibit 5.

The other type of nonparallel shift, a change in the humpedness of the yield curve, is referred to as a *butterfly shift*. A *positive butterfly shift* means that the yield curve becomes less humped. A *negative butterfly shift* means that the yield curve become more humped. This is depicted in the third panel of Exhibit 5.

Exhibit 4: Average Daily Slope of the Treasury Yield Curve (30-Year Yield minus 10-Year Yield) by Month from January 1989 to July 1997

Year	Jan	Feb	Mar	Apr	May	June	July	Aug	Sept	Oct	Nov	Dec
					In basis points							
1997	29	25	19	25	25	29	29					
1996	44	35	34	24	14	18	18	18	22	29	32	23
1995	7	15	25	30	32	41	45	38	36	34	33	35
1994	58	51	43	31	23	30	29	27	26	20	14	6
1993	76	87	90	90	83	90	84	65	64	62	50	55
1992	56	52	43	50	49	58	76	81	93	95	74	68
1991	18	18	18	17	20	19	18	24	30	41	51	61
1990	5	3	−2	−3	−3	−4	3	11	14	14	14	6
1989	−17	−17	−19	−15	−3	−1	6	1	−3	−1	3	−5

Slope is defined as the average daily spread between the 30-year and 10-year Treasury yields for the month.
Source: Ryan Labs, Inc.

Exhibit 5: Types of Yield Curve Shifts

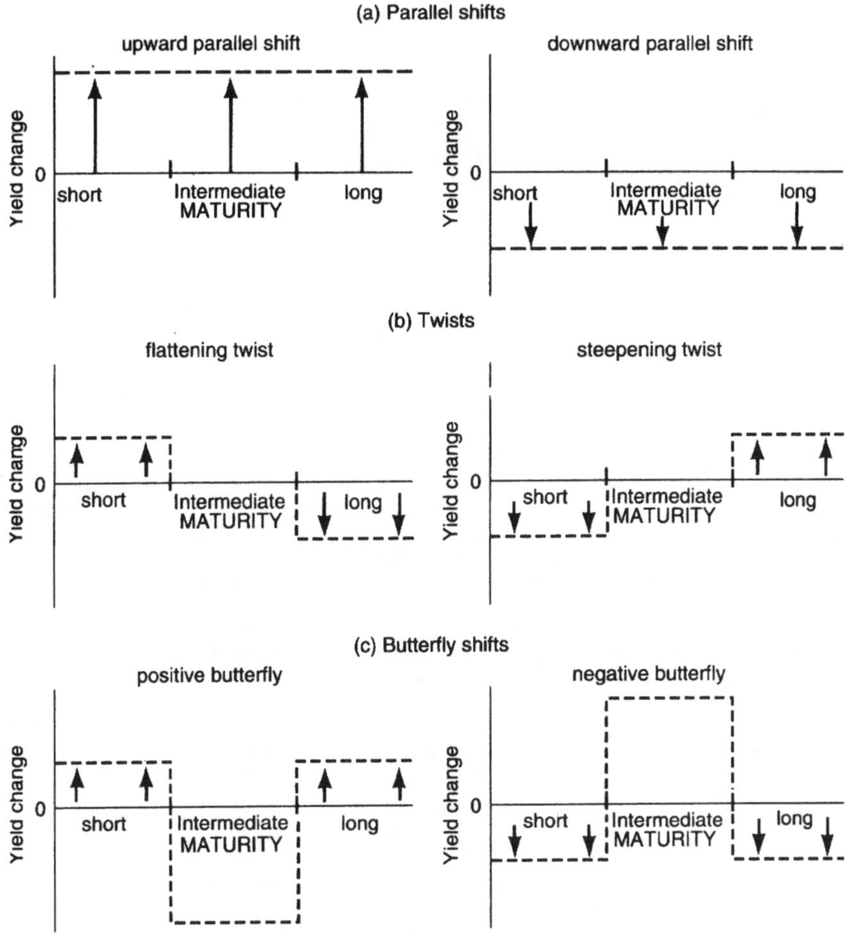
(a) Parallel shifts
upward parallel shift
downward parallel shift
Yield change
0
short
Intermediate
MATURITY
long
(b) Twists
flattening twist
steepening twist
(c) Butterfly shifts
positive butterfly
negative butterfly

TREASURY RETURNS RESULTING FROM YIELD CURVE MOVEMENTS

As we discussed in Chapter 3, a yield measure is a promised return if certain assumptions are satisfied. At the end of that chapter, we explained that the total return is a more appropriate measure of the potential return from investing in a Treasury security. The potential return for a short investment horizon depends critically on how interest rates change; that is, it is a function of how the yield curve changes.

Exhibit 6: Factors Explaining Treasury Returns

Factor 1: Changes in the level of interest rates
Factor 2: Changes in the yield curve slope
Factor 3: Changes in the curvature of the yield curve

Zero Coupon Maturity	Variance of Total Returns Explained	Proportion of Total Explained Variance Accounted for by		
		Factor 1	Factor 2	Factor 3
6 months	99.5%	79.5%	17.2%	3.3%
1 year	99.4	89.7	10.1	0.2
2 years	98.2	93.4	2.4	4.2
5 years	98.8	98.2	1.1	0.7
8 years	98.7	95.4	4.6	0.0
10 years	98.8	92.9	6.9	0.2
14 years	98.4	86.2	11.5	2.2
18 years	95.3	80.5	14.3	5.2
Average	98.4	89.5	8.5	2.0

Source: Robert Litterman and José Scheinkman, "Common Factors Affecting Bond Returns," *Journal of Fixed Income* (June 1991), p. 58. This copyrighted material is reprinted from Institutional Investor, Inc., *Journal of Fixed Income*, 488 Madison Avenue, New York, New York 10022.

Empirical studies that have investigated the factors that have affected the historical returns on Treasury portfolios support this. A study by Robert Litterman and José Scheinkman found that three factors explained historical returns.[1] The first factor was changes in the level of rates, the second factor was changes in the slope of the yield curve, and the third factor was changes in the curvature of the yield curve.

Litterman and Scheinkman employed regression analysis to determine the relative contribution of these three factors in explaining the returns on zero-coupon Treasury securities of different maturities. Exhibit 6 summarizes their results. The second column of the exhibit shows the coefficient of determination, popularly referred to as the "R^2," for each zero-coupon maturity. In general, the R^2 measures the percentage of the variance in the dependent variable (i.e., the return on the zero-coupon Treasury security) explained by the independent variables (i.e., the three factors). For example, an R^2 of 0.8 means that 80% of the variation of the return on a zero-coupon Treasury security is explained by the three factors. Therefore, 20% of the variation of the return cannot be explained by these three factors. The R^2 will have a value between 0% and 100%. As can be seen in the second column, the R^2 was very high for all maturities, meaning that the three factors had a very strong predictive or explanatory power.

The last three columns show the relative contribution that each of the three factors had in explaining the return on the zero-coupon Treasury security of

---

[1] Robert Litterman and José Scheinkman, "Common Factors Affecting Bond Returns," *Journal of Fixed Income* (June 1991), pp. 54-61.

a given maturity. For example, let's look at the 18-year zero. The second column indicates that 95% of the variance of the return in the 18-year zero is explained by the three factors. The first factor represents changes in the level of rates, holding all other factors constant (in particular, yield curve slope) and contributes about 81% of the explanatory power. This factor has the greatest explanatory power for all the maturities, averaging about 90%. The implication is that the most important factor that a manager of a Treasury portfolio should control for is exposure to changes in the level of interest rates. For this reason it is important to have a way to measure or quantify this risk. We shall see how this is done in Chapter 6.

The second factor, changes in the yield curve slope, is the second largest contributing factor. For the 18-year zero-coupon Treasury, the relative contribution is about 14.3%. The average relative contribution is 8.5%. Thus, changes in the yield curve slope are, on average, about one tenth as significant as changes in the level of rates. While the relative contribution is only 8.5%, this can still have a significant impact on the return for a Treasury portfolio and a portfolio manager must control for this risk. In Chapter 7, we discuss how this risk can be measured.

The third factor, changes in the curvature of the yield curve, contributes relatively little to explaining historical returns.

Similar results were also found by Frank Jones who analyzed the types of yield curve shifts that occurred between 1979 and 1990.[2] His findings indicate that parallel shifts and twists in the yield curve were responsible for 91.6% of Treasury returns, while 3.4% of the return is attributable to butterfly shifts and the balance, 5%, to unexplained factor shifts. In addition, he found that the three types of yield curve shifts are not independent, with the two most common types of yield curve shifts being (1) a downward shift in the yield curve combined with a steepening of the yield curve and (2) an upward shift in the yield curve combined with a flattening of the yield curve. These two types of combination shifts in the yield curve are depicted in Exhibit 7.

Frank Jones quantified the correlation between the three types of yield curve changes and these results are reported in Exhibit 8. He also estimated the statistical relationships between these changes. He found that a 50 basis point upward shift in the yield curve is consistent with a 12.5 basis point flattening of the yield curve and a 2 basis point more positive butterfly (less humpedness). He finds that these changes are typical for very large yield changes.

YIELD SPREAD BETWEEN
TREASURY COUPON SECURITIES AND STRIPS

There is a yield spread at which strips and Treasury securities trade. The spread varies over time depending on market expectations for future interest rates. Recall

---

[2] Frank J. Jones, "Yield Curve Strategies," *Journal of Fixed Income* (September 1991), pp. 43-51.

that strips eliminate reinvestment risk. Consequently, the yield at the time of purchase on strips is the pre-tax return that will be realized if an issue is held to maturity. Strips trade with a liquidity premium relative to Treasury securities and there is an adverse tax consequence for taxable entities who purchase these instruments. These disadvantages of strips are reflected in the yield spread.

Exhibit 7: Combinations of Yield Curve Shifts

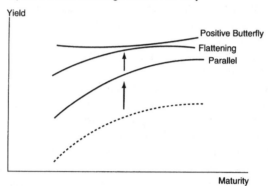

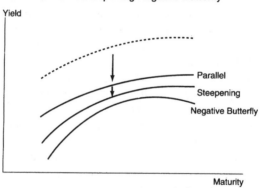

Exhibit 8: Shift, Twist, and Butterfly Correlation Matrix

	Upward shift	Flattening twist	Positive butterfly
Upward shift	1.00	0.41	0.32
Flattening twist	0.41	1.00	0.22
Positive butterfly	0.32	0.22	1.00

Source: Adapted from Frank J. Jones, "Yield Curve Strategies," *Journal of Fixed Income* (September 1991), Table 1. This copyrighted material is reprinted from Institutional Investor, Inc., *Journal of Fixed Income*, 488 Madison Avenue, New York, New York 10022.

Exhibit 9: Yield Spread Between Treasury Strips and Treasury Coupon Securities

	Yield Spread vs. Benchmark Treasury Security (in basis points)							
	8/30/96				12/8/05			
Current	On	Prior 90 days			On	Prior 90 days		
Issues	8/30/96	High	Low	Avg.	12/8/95	High	Low	Avg.
3-mo	4	86	0	18	9	29	−10	7
6-mo	17	34	11	21	5	20	−5	6
1-year	−11	29	−11	12	2	14	−3	5
2-year	−2	12	−2	7	3	11	1	5
3-year	3	13	1	6	4	8	4	6
5-year	1	8	1	4	−1	3	−1	1
10-year	17	28	14	19	16	26	16	21
30-year	30	38	23	30	29	38	25	31

	Yield Spread vs. Closest Duration Coupon Treasury (in basis points)							
	8/30/96				12/08/05			
Current	On	Prior 90 days			On	Prior 90 days		
Issues	8/30/96	High	Low	Avg.	12/08/95	High	Low	Avg.
3-mo	0	87	−12	−4	−2	5	−18	−7
6-mo	−5	1	−13	−5	−2	2	−11	−4
1-year	−24	−1	−24	−10	−6	3	−11	−4
2-year	−1	3	−3	1	−1	3	−5	0
3-year	−4	−2	−6	−4	0	4	−1	1
5-year	−11	−8	−14	−10	−6	−5	−12	−8
10-year	−13	−9	−16	−12	−82	−63	−83	−73

Source: Lehman Brothers, *Relative Value Report*, Fixed Income Research, December 11, 1995 and September 3, 1996 issues, p. T-1.

The upper panel of Exhibit 9 shows the yield spread between strips and Treasury coupon securities of the same maturity on 8/30/96 and 12/8/95. The high, low, and average spread for 90 days prior to these dates is also shown. A more appropriate comparison is the yield spread between strips and Treasury coupon securities with the same duration. As explained in Chapter 6, duration is a measure of a security's price sensitivity to interest rate changes. The lower panel of Exhibit 9 provides the same information as the upper panel using a Treasury coupon security with the closest duration. Note that the Treasury coupon security is typically an off-the-run issue and therefore reflects a liquidity premium relative to an on-the-run issue.

KEY POINTS

1. The relationship between the yield on Treasury securities and maturity is called the term structure of interest rates.

2. The yield curve is the graphical depiction of the term structure of interest rates.

3. Historically, three shapes have been observed for the yield curve: (1) normal or positively sloped (i.e., the longer the maturity, the higher the yield), (2) flat (i.e., the yield for all maturities is approximately equal), and (3) inverted or negatively sloped (i.e., the longer the maturity the lower the yield).

4. The spread between long-term Treasury yields and short-term Treasury yields is referred to as the steepness or slope of the yield curve.

5. Some investors define the slope as the spread between the 30-year yield and the 3-month yield and others as the spread between the 30-year yield and the 2-year yield.

6. A shift in the yield curve refers to the relative change in the yield for each Treasury maturity.

7. A parallel shift in the yield curve refers to a shift in which the change in the yield for all maturities is the same; a nonparallel shift in the yield curve means that the yield for all maturities does not change by the same number of basis points.

8. Historically, the two types of nonparallel yield curve shifts that have been observed are a twist in the slope of the yield curve and a change in the humpedness of the yield curve.

9. A flattening of the yield curve means that the slope of the yield curve has decreased; a steepening of the yield curve means that the slope has increased.

10. A butterfly shift is the other type of nonparallel shift — a change in the humpedness of the yield curve.

11. Historical evidence suggests that the three types of yield curve shifts are not independent with the two most common types of yield curve shifts being (1) a downward shift in the yield curve combined with a steepening of the yield curve and (2) an upward shift in the yield curve combined with a flattening of the yield curve.

12. The spread between yields on Treasury coupon securities and strips depends on expectations regarding future interest rates, the lower liquidity for strips, and the tax disadvantage associated with strips.

Chapter 5

SPOT RATES, FORWARD RATES, AND THEORIES OF THE TERM STRUCTURE OF INTEREST RATES

In Chapter 2, we saw how to value a Treasury security using spot rates. However, we did not demonstrate how the Treasury spot rate curve can be constructed. In this chapter, we will see how this is done using the yields on Treasury securities. We will then see how additional information useful to market participants can be extrapolated from the Treasury yield curve: forward rates. These rates can be viewed as the market's consensus of future interest rates. This view, however, is predicated on a particular theory about the term structure of interest rates. At the end of this chapter, we discuss several theories of the term structure of interest rates.

CONSTRUCTING THE THEORETICAL TREASURY SPOT RATE CURVE

There are two methodologies that have been used to derive the theoretical Treasury spot rate curve: (1) bootstrapping the on-the-run Treasury yield curve and (2) estimation using econometric methods.

Bootstrapping the On-the-Run Treasury Yield Curve

Probably the most common method for constructing the theoretical Treasury spot rate curve is the bootstrapping of the on-the-run Treasury yield curve. We will illustrate the general principles of this methodology first, and then discuss how this is modified in practice. We will use the price, annualized yield to maturity, and maturity for the 20 hypothetical Treasury securities shown in Exhibit 1. Our focus is on the first four columns of the exhibit. Our goal is to explain how the values in the last column of the exhibit are derived. Notice that these values are the spot rates that were used in Chapter 2.

Throughout the analysis and illustrations to come, it is important to remember that the basic principle is that the value of a Treasury coupon security should be equal to the value of the package of zero-coupon Treasury securities that duplicates the coupon bond's cash flows.

Consider the 6-month Treasury bill in Exhibit 1. Since a Treasury bill is a zero-coupon instrument, its annualized yield of 3.00% is equal to the spot rate. Similarly, for the 1-year Treasury, the quoted yield of 3.30% is the 1-year spot rate. Given these two spot rates, we can compute the spot rate for a theoretical 1.5-year zero-coupon Treasury. The price of a 1.5-year Treasury should equal the present value of the three cash flows from the 1.5-year coupon Treasury, where the yield used for discounting is the spot rate corresponding to the cash flow. Since all the coupon bonds are selling at par, the yield to maturity for each bond is the coupon rate. Using $100 as par, the cash flows for the 1.5-year coupon Treasury is:

$$
\begin{array}{lll}
0.5 \text{ year} & 0.035 \times \$100 \times 0.5 = & \$1.75 \\
1.0 \text{ year} & 0.035 \times \$100 \times 0.5 = & \$1.75 \\
1.5 \text{ years} & 0.035 \times \$100 \times 0.5 + \$100 = & \$101.75
\end{array}
$$

The present value of the cash flows is then:

$$
\frac{1.75}{(1+z_1)^1} + \frac{1.75}{(1+z_2)^2} + \frac{101.75}{(1+z_3)^3}
$$

where:

z_1 = one-half the 6-month theoretical spot rate,
z_2 = one-half the 1-year theoretical spot rate, and
z_3 = one-half the 1.5-year theoretical spot rate.

Since the 6-month spot rate and 1-year spot rate are 3.00% and 3.30%, respectively, we know that:

$$z_1 = 0.0150 \text{ and } z_2 = 0.0165$$

Exhibit 1: Maturity and Yield to Maturity for 20 Hypothetical Treasury Securities

Period	Years	Yield to maturity (%)	Price	Spot rate (%)
1	0.5	3.00	—	3.0000
2	1.0	3.30	—	3.3000
3	1.5	3.50	100.00	3.5053
4	2.0	3.90	100.00	3.9164
5	2.5	4.40	100.00	4.4376
6	3.0	4.70	100.00	4.7520
7	3.5	4.90	100.00	4.9622
8	4.0	5.00	100.00	5.0650
9	4.5	5.10	100.00	5.1701
10	5.0	5.20	100.00	5.2772
11	5.5	5.30	100.00	5.3864
12	6.0	5.40	100.00	5.4976
13	6.5	5.50	100.00	5.6108
14	7.0	5.55	100.00	5.6643
15	7.5	5.60	100.00	5.7193
16	8.0	5.65	100.00	5.7755
17	8.5	5.70	100.00	5.8331
18	9.0	5.80	100.00	5.9584
19	9.5	5.90	100.00	6.0863
20	10.0	6.00	100.00	6.2169

We can compute the present value of the 1.5-year coupon Treasury security as:

$$\frac{1.75}{(1+z_1)^1} + \frac{1.75}{(1+z_2)^2} + \frac{101.75}{(1+z_3)^3} = \frac{1.75}{(1.015)^1} + \frac{1.75}{(1.0165)^2} + \frac{101.75}{(1+z_3)^3}$$

Since the price of the 1.5-year coupon Treasury security is par, the following relationship must hold:

$$\frac{1.75}{(1.015)^1} + \frac{1.75}{(1.0165)^2} + \frac{101.75}{(1+z_3)^3} = 100$$

We can solve for the theoretical 1.5-year spot rate as follows:

$$1.7241 + 1.6936 + \frac{101.75}{(1+z_3)^3} = 100$$

$$\frac{101.75}{(1+z_3)^3} = 96.5822$$

$$(1+z_3)^3 = \frac{101.75}{96.5822}$$

$$z_3 = 0.0175265 = 1.7527\%$$

Doubling this yield we obtain the bond-equivalent yield of 3.5053%, which is the theoretical 1.5-year spot rate. That rate is the rate that the market would apply to a 1.5-year zero-coupon Treasury security if, in fact, such a security existed.

Given the theoretical 1.5-year spot rate, we can obtain the theoretical 2-year spot rate. The cash flows for the 2-year coupon Treasury in Exhibit 1 is:

0.5 year	$0.039 \times \$100 \times 0.5$	=	\$1.95
1.0 year	$0.039 \times \$100 \times 0.5$	=	\$1.95
1.5 years	$0.039 \times \$100 \times 0.5$	=	\$1.95
2.0 years	$0.039 \times \$100 \times 0.5 + \$100$	=	\$101.95

The present value of the cash flows is then:

$$\frac{1.95}{(1+z_1)^1} + \frac{1.95}{(1+z_2)^2} + \frac{1.95}{(1+z_3)^3} + \frac{101.95}{(1+z_4)^4}$$

where z_4 = one-half the 2-year theoretical spot rate.

Since the 6-month spot rate, 1-year spot rate, and 1.5-year spot rate are 3.00%, 3.30%, and 3.5053%, respectively, then:

$$z_1 = 0.0150, z_2 = 0.0165, \text{ and } z_3 = 0.017527$$

Therefore, the present value of the 2-year coupon Treasury security is:

$$\frac{1.95}{(1.0150)^1} + \frac{1.95}{(1.0165)^2} + \frac{1.95}{(1.017527)^3} + \frac{101.95}{(1+z_4)^4}$$

Since the price of the 2-year coupon Treasury security is par, the following relationship must hold:

$$\frac{1.95}{(1.0150)^1} + \frac{1.95}{(1.0165)^2} + \frac{1.95}{(1.017527)^3} + \frac{101.95}{(1+z_4)^4} = 100$$

We can solve for the theoretical 2-year spot rate as follows:

$$\frac{101.95}{(1+z_4)^4} = 94.3407$$

$$(1+z_4)^4 = \frac{101.95}{94.3407}$$

$$z_4 = 0.019582 = 1.9582\%$$

Doubling this yield, we obtain the theoretical 2-year spot rate bond-equivalent yield of 3.9164%.

One can follow this approach sequentially to derive the theoretical 2.5-year spot rate from the calculated values of z_1, z_2, z_3, and z_4 (the 6-month-, 1-year-, 1.5-year-, and 2-year rates), and the price and coupon of the bond with a maturity of 2.5 years. Further, one could derive theoretical spot rates for the remaining 15 half-yearly rates.

The spot rates thus obtained are shown in the last column of Exhibit 1. They represent the term structure of Treasury rates for maturities up to ten years at the particular time to which the bond price quotations refer.

In practice, the on-the-run Treasury yield curve is used to construct the theoretical spot rate curve using the bootstrapping method. There are several shortcomings to this methodology. Notice in our illustration we used 20 hypothetical issues that were assumed to be trading at par. In practice, there are only seven on-the-run issues available: 6-month Treasury bill, 1-year Treasury bill, 2-year Treasury note, 3-year Treasury note, 5-year Treasury note, 10-year Treasury note, and 30-year Treasury bond.[1] In addition, the five coupon issues may not be trading at par because market yields may have changed subsequent to the auction of an issue. To cope with this problem the following is done. The yield for each on-the-run coupon issue is used as the coupon rate for the issue and the price for each issue is then par.

Moreover, there is a gap between maturities that must be filled in. A theoretical spot rate curve with semiannual rates for 30-years requires 60 spot rates (1.5 years, 2 years, 2.5 years, 3 years, 3.5 years, 4-years, etc.) There is no 4-year on-the-run issue. The 4-year rate must be extrapolated from the 3-year and 5-year rates.

---

[1] As explained in Chapter 1, at one time there was a 4-year Treasury note, a 7-year Treasury note, and a 20-year Treasury bond.

The 2.5-year rate must be extrapolated from the 2-year and 3-year rates. Typically a simple linear extrapolation method is used. The major problem with the linear extrapolation method comes where large gaps in maturities exist. These are the gaps between the 5-year and 10-year maturities and between the 10-year and 30-year maturities. In practice, to reduce this problem at the long end (i.e., the gap between the 10-year and 30-year maturities), the analysis is supplemented by including the yield on the off-the-run 20-year and 25-year maturity Treasury issues.

Estimation Using Econometric Methods

As we have just explained, there are problems with the bootstrapping method. Another problem is that it fails to use all of the information in the Treasury market by ignoring off-the-run issues. The objective in empirical estimation of the theoretical spot rate curve is to construct a curve such that it (1) fits the data sufficiently well and (2) is a sufficiently smooth function.[2]

   Several econometric models have been proposed to estimate the theoretical spot rate curve.[3] The most commonly used econometric model is the one developed by Oldrich Vasicek and Gifford Fong.[4] The econometric method used is the exponential spline method. The model produces spot rates that are a smooth, continuous function of maturity. Moreover, the model has desirable asymptotic properties for long maturities, and exhibits sufficient flexibility to fit a wide variety of shapes of the yield curve.

   In Exhibit 2, the theoretical spot rate curve generated using the bootstrapping method (using the on-the-run Treasury issues supplemented with the 20-year and 25-year off-the-run issues) and the Merrill Lynch exponential spline model are shown for January 29, 1997. Also shown in the exhibit is the spot rate curve constructed using the Treasury strips, where the strips are created from the coupon, not principal. The exponential spline method provides a better estimate of the actual Treasury strips curve.

WHY TREASURIES MUST BE PRICED BASED ON SPOT RATES

As explained in Chapter 2, the theoretical spot rates are used to value a Treasury security. We illustrated this at the end of Chapter 2 where we used the spot rates shown in Exhibit 1 of this chapter to value an 8% 10-year Treasury security. We

---

[2] For a further discussion of the desirable properties of models for estimating the term structure, see Terence C. Langetieg and Stephen J. Smoot, "An Appraisal of Alternative Spline Methodologies for Estimating the Term Structure of Interest Rates," working paper, University of Southern California, December 1981.

[3] Earlier models include Willard R. Carleton and Ian Cooper, "Estimation and Uses of the Term Structure of Interest Rates," *Journal of Finance* (September 1976), pp. 1067-1083; and, J. Houston McCulloch, "Measuring the Term Structure of Interest Rates," *Journal of Business* (January 1971), pp. 19-31.

[4] Oldrich A. Vasicek and H. Gifford Fong, "Term Structure Modeling Using Exponential Splines," *Journal of Finance* (May 1982), pp. 339-348. For an example of a dealer model, see Arnold Shapiro et al, "Merrill Lynch Exponential Spline Model," Merrill Lynch, Global Fixed Income Research (August 8, 1994).

reproduce the calculations in Exhibit 3. The theoretical value is $115.2619. We can use this security and the spot rates in Exhibit 1 to demonstrate the economic forces that will assure that the actual market price of a Treasury security will not depart significantly from its theoretical value.

Look again at Exhibit 1. From the yield curve, the yield on the 10-year Treasury is 6%. Suppose that the market prices the 8% 10-year issue at a 6% yield. That is, suppose that all the cash flows are discounted at 6%. The security would then be valued at $114.8775.

The question is, could this security trade at $114.8775 in the market? Let's see what would happen if the 8% 10-year Treasury traded at $114.8775. Suppose that a dealer firm buys this issue at $114.8775 and strips it. By stripping it, we mean creating zero-coupon instruments as depicted in Exhibit 3. By stripping this issue, the dealer firm creates 20 zero-coupon instruments guaranteed by the U.S. Treasury.[5]

How much can the 20 zero-coupon instruments be sold for by the dealer firm? Expressed equivalently, at what yield can each of the zero-coupon instruments be sold? The answer is in Exhibit 1. The yield at which each zero-coupon instrument can be sold is the spot rate shown in the last column.

Exhibit 2: Comparison of Spot Rate Curve Generated by Bootstrapping Method and Exponential Spline Method
(As of January 29, 1997)

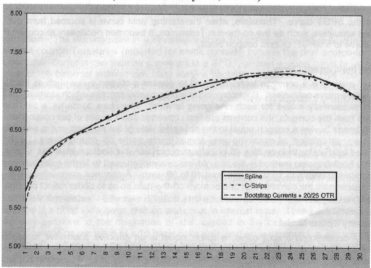

Source: Figure 1 in Philip H. Galdi and Shenglin Lu, "Valuing Embedded Options in Corporate/Government Securities," Merrill Lynch, Global Fixed Income Research (February 27, 1997), p. 4. Reprinted by permission. Copyright 1997 Merrill Lynch, Pierce, Fenner & Smith Incorporated.

---

[5] As shown in Exhibit 3, 21 zero-coupon instruments are created since the last coupon and the maturity value are sold separately. In our illustrations, we do not make any distinction between the last coupon and maturity value.

Exhibit 3: Determination of the Theoretical Value of an 8% 10-Year Treasury

Period	Years	Cash flow ($)	Spot rate (%)	Present value ($)	Present value at 6% ($)
1	0.5	4	3.0000	3.9409	3.8835
2	1.0	4	3.3000	3.8712	3.7704
3	1.5	4	3.5053	3.7968	3.6606
4	2.0	4	3.9164	3.7014	3.5539
5	2.5	4	4.4376	3.5843	3.4504
6	3.0	4	4.7520	3.4743	3.3499
7	3.5	4	4.9622	3.3694	3.2524
8	4.0	4	5.0650	3.2747	3.1576
9	4.5	4	5.1701	3.1791	3.0657
10	5.0	4	5.2772	3.0828	2.9764
11	5.5	4	5.3864	2.9861	2.8897
12	6.0	4	5.4976	2.8889	2.8055
13	6.5	4	5.6108	2.7916	2.7238
14	7.0	4	5.6643	2.7055	2.6445
15	7.5	4	5.7193	2.6205	2.5674
16	8.0	4	5.7755	2.5365	2.4927
17	8.5	4	5.8331	2.4536	2.4201
18	9.0	4	5.9584	2.3581	2.3496
19	9.5	4	6.0863	2.2631	2.2811
20	10.0	104	6.2169	56.3828	57.5823
			Total	$115.2619	114.8775

We can use Exhibit 3 to determine the proceeds that would be received per $100 of par value of the 8% 10-year issue stripped. The next-to-last column shows how much would be received for each coupon sold as a zero-coupon instrument. The total proceeds received from selling the zero-coupon Treasury securities created would be $115.2619 per $100 of par value of the Treasury issue purchased by the dealer. Since the dealer purchased the issue for $114.8775, this would result in an arbitrage profit of $0.3844 per $100 of the 8% 10-year Treasury issue purchased.

To understand why the dealer has the opportunity to realize this arbitrage profit, look at the last column of Exhibit 3 which shows how much the dealer paid for each cash flow by buying the entire package of cash flows (i.e., by buying the issue). For example, consider the $4 coupon payment in four years. By buying the 10-year Treasury bond priced to yield 6%, the dealer effectively pays a price based on 6% (3% semiannual) for that coupon payment, or, equivalently, $3.1576. Under the assumptions of this illustration, however, investors were willing to accept a lower yield to maturity (the 4-year spot rate), 5.065% (2.5325% semiannual), to purchase a zero-coupon Treasury security with four years to maturity. Thus investors were willing to pay $3.2747. On this one coupon payment, the dealer realizes a profit equal to the difference between $3.2747 and $3.1576 (or $0.1171). From all the cash flows, the total profit is $0.3844. In this instance, coupon stripping results in the sum of the parts being greater than the whole.

Suppose that, instead of the observed yield to maturity from Exhibit 1, the yields that investors want are the same as the theoretical spot rates that are shown in the exhibit. As can be seen in Exhibit 3, if we use these spot rates to discount the cash flows, the total proceeds from the sale of the zero-coupon Treasury securities would be equal to $115.2619, making coupon stripping uneconomic since the proceeds from stripping would be the same as the cost of purchasing the issue.

In our illustration of coupon stripping, the price of the Treasury security is less than its theoretical price. Suppose instead that the price of the Treasury coupon security is greater than its theoretical price. In this case, investors can create a portfolio of zero-coupon Treasury securities such that the cash flows of the portfolio replicates the cash flows of the mispriced Treasury coupon security. By doing so, the investor will realize a yield higher than the yield on the Treasury coupon security. For example, suppose that the market price of the 10-year Treasury coupon security we used in our illustration is $116. An investor could buy 20 outstanding zero-coupon stripped Treasury securities with a maturity value identical to the cash flows shown in the third column of Exhibit 3. The cost of purchasing this portfolio of stripped Treasury securities would be $115.2619. Thus, an investor is effectively purchasing a portfolio of stripped Treasury securities that has the same cash flows as an 8% 10-year Treasury coupon security at a cost of $115.2619 instead of $116.

It is the process of coupon stripping and reconstituting that will prevent the market price of Treasury securities from departing significantly from their theoretical value.

FORWARD RATES

Market participants typically have different views about what they expect future interest rates to be. Under a certain theory of the term structure of interest rates described later in this chapter and based on arbitrage arguments, the market's consensus of future interest rates can be extrapolated from the Treasury yield curve. These rates are called *forward rates*.

Examples of forward rates that can be calculated from the Treasury yield curve are the:

- 6-month forward rate six months from now
- 6-month forward rate three years from now
- 1-year forward rate one year from now
- 3-year forward rate two years from now
- 5-year forward rate three years from now

Since the forward rates are extrapolated from the Treasury yield curve, these rates are sometimes referred to as *implicit forward rates*.

To illustrate how forward rates are derived, we begin with the derivation of 6-month forward rates. The 6-month forward rates are sometimes referred to as *short-term forward rates*. The structure of short-term forward rates is called the *forward rate curve*.

Deriving 6-Month Forward Rates

To illustrate the process of extrapolating 6-month forward rates, we will use the yield curve and corresponding spot rate curve from Exhibit 1. Consider an investor who has a 1-year investment horizon and is faced with the following two alternatives:

Alternative 1: Buy a 1-year Treasury bill, or
Alternative 2: Buy a 6-month Treasury bill, and when it matures in six months buy another 6-month Treasury bill.

The investor will be indifferent toward the two alternatives if they produce the same return over the 1-year investment horizon. The investor knows the spot rate on the 6-month Treasury bill and the 1-year Treasury bill. However, he does not know what yield will be available on a 6-month Treasury bill that will be purchased six months from now. That is, he does not know the 6-month forward rate six months from now. Given the spot rates for the 6-month Treasury bill and the 1-year Treasury bill, the forward rate on a 6-month Treasury bill is the rate that equalizes the dollar return between the two alternatives.

To see how that rate can be determined, suppose that an investor purchased a 6-month Treasury bill for X. At the end of six months, the value of this investment would be:

$$X(1 + z_1)$$

where z_1 is one-half the bond-equivalent yield (BEY) of the theoretical 6-month spot rate.

Let f represent one-half the forward rate (expressed as a BEY) on a 6-month Treasury bill available six months from now. If the investor were to renew his investment by purchasing that bill at that time, then the future dollars available at the end of one year from the X investment would be:

$$X(1 + z_1)(1 + f)$$

Now consider an alternative investment in a 1-year Treasury bill. If we let z_2 represent one-half the BEY of the theoretical 1-year spot rate, then the future dollars available at the end of one year from the X investment would be:

$$X(1 + z_2)^2$$

This is depicted in Exhibit 4.

Exhibit 4: Graphical Depiction of the 6-Month Forward Rate Six Months from Now

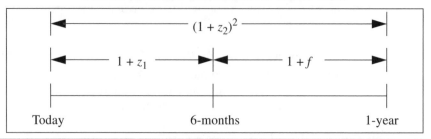

Now, we are prepared to analyze the investor's choices and what this says about forward rates. The investor will be indifferent toward the two alternatives confronting him if he makes the same dollar investment (X) and receives the same future dollars from both alternatives at the end of one year. That is, the investor will be indifferent if:

$$X (1 + z_1) (1 + f) = X (1 + z_2)^2$$

Solving for f, we get:

$$f = \frac{(1 + z_2)^2}{(1 + z_1)} - 1$$

Doubling f gives the BEY for the 6-month forward rate six months from now.

We can illustrate the use of this formula with the theoretical spot rates shown in Exhibit 1. From that exhibit, we know that:

6-month bill spot rate = 0.030, therefore $z_1 = 0.0150$
1-year bill spot rate = 0.033, therefore $z_2 = 0.0165$

Substituting into the formula, we have:

$$f = \frac{(1.0165)^2}{(1.0150)} - 1 = 0.0180 = 1.8\%$$

Therefore, the forward rate on a 6-month Treasury security is 3.6% (1.8% × 2) BEY.

Let's confirm our results. If X is invested in the 6-month Treasury bill at 1.5% and the proceeds then reinvested at the 6-month forward rate of 1.8%, the total proceeds from this alternative would be:

$$X (1.015) (1.018) = 1.03327 X$$

Investment of X in the 1-year Treasury bill at one-half the 1-year rate, 1.0165%, would produce the following proceeds at the end of one year:

$$X (1.0165)^2 = 1.03327 X$$

Both alternatives have the same payoff if the 6-month Treasury bill yield six months from now is 1.8% (3.6% on a BEY). This means that, if an investor is guaranteed a 1.8% yield (3.6% BEY) on a 6-month Treasury bill six months from now, he will be indifferent toward the two alternatives.

The same line of reasoning can be used to obtain the 6-month forward rate beginning at any time period in the future. For example, the following can be determined:

- the 6-month forward rate three years from now
- the 6-month forward rate five years from now

The notation that we use to indicate 6-month forward rates is $_1f_m$ where the subscript 1 indicates a 1-period (6-month) rate and the subscript m indicates the period beginning m periods from now. When m is equal to zero, this means the current rate. Thus, the first 6-month forward rate is simply the current 6-month spot rate. That is,

$$_1f_0 = z_1$$

The general formula for determining a 6-month forward rate is:

$$_1f_m = \frac{(1 + z_{m+1})^{m+1}}{(1 + z_m)^m} - 1$$

For example, suppose that the 6-month forward rate four years (8 6-month periods) from now is sought. In terms of our notation, m is 8 and we seek $_1f_8$. The formula is then:

$$_1f_8 = \frac{(1 + z_9)^9}{(1 + z_8)^8} - 1$$

From Exhibit 1, since the 4-year spot rate is 5.065% and the 4.5-year spot rate is 5.1701%, z_8 is 2.5325% and z_9 is 2.58505%. Then,

$$_1f_8 = \frac{(1.0258505)^9}{(1.025325)^8} - 1 = 3.005\%$$

Doubling this rate gives a 6-month forward rate four years from now of 6.01%

Exhibit 5 shows all of the 6-month forward rates for the Treasury yield curve and corresponding spot rate curve shown in Exhibit 1. The set of these forward rates is the short-term forward rate curve.

Relationship between Spot Rates and Short-Term Forward Rates

Suppose an investor invests X in a 3-year zero-coupon Treasury security. The total proceeds three years (six periods) from now would be:

$$X(1 + z_6)^6$$

Exhibit 5: Six-Month Forward Rates: The Short-Term Forward Rate Curve

Notation	Forward Rate
$_1f_0$	3.00
$_1f_1$	3.60
$_1f_2$	3.92
$_1f_3$	5.15
$_1f_4$	6.54
$_1f_5$	6.33
$_1f_6$	6.23
$_1f_7$	5.79
$_1f_8$	6.01
$_1f_9$	6.24
$_1f_{10}$	6.48
$_1f_{11}$	6.72
$_1f_{12}$	6.97
$_1f_{13}$	6.36
$_1f_{14}$	6.49
$_1f_{15}$	6.62
$_1f_{16}$	6.76
$_1f_{17}$	8.10
$_1f_{18}$	8.40
$_1f_{19}$	8.72

The investor could instead buy a 6-month Treasury bill and reinvest the proceeds every six months for three years. The future dollars or dollar return will depend on the 6-month forward rates. Suppose that the investor can actually reinvest the proceeds maturing every six months at the calculated 6-month forward rates shown in Exhibit 5. At the end of three years, an investment of X would generate the following proceeds:

$$X (1 + z_1) (1 + {}_1f_1) (1 + {}_1f_2) (1 + {}_1f_3) (1 + {}_1f_4) (1 + {}_1f_5)$$

Since the two investments must give the same proceeds at the end of four years, the two previous equations can be equated:

$$X (1 + z_6)^6 = X (1 + z_1) (1 + {}_1f_1) (1 + {}_1f_2) (1 + {}_1f_3) (1 + {}_1f_4) (1 + {}_1f_5)$$

Solving for the 3-year (six-period) spot rate, we have:

$$z_6 = [(1 + z_1) (1 + {}_1f_1) (1 + {}_1f_2) (1 + {}_1f_3) (1 + {}_1f_4) (1 + {}_1f_5)]^{1/6} - 1$$

Exhibit 6: Graphical Depiction of Forward Rates

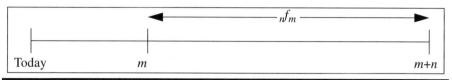

This equation tells us that the 3-year spot rate depends on the current 6-month spot rate and the five 6-month forward rates. In fact, the right-hand side of this equation is a geometric average of the current 6-month spot rate and the five 6-month forward rates.

Let's use the values in Exhibits 1 and 5 to confirm this result. Since the 6-month spot rate in Exhibit 1 is 3%, z_1 is 1.5% and therefore

$$z_6 = [(1.015)(1.018)(1.0196)(1.02575)(1.0327)(1.03165)]^{1/6} - 1$$
$$= 0.023761 = 2.3761\%$$

Doubling this rate gives 4.7522%. This agrees with the spot rate shown in Exhibit 1.

In general, the relationship between a T-period spot rate, the current 6-month spot rate, and the 6-month forward rates is as follows:

$$z_T = [(1 + z_1)(1 + {}_1f_1)(1 + {}_1f_2) \dots (1 + {}_1f_{T-1})]^{1/T} - 1$$

Therefore, discounting at the forward rates will give the same present value as discounting at spot rates.

Forward Rates for Any Period

We can take the analysis of forward rates much further. It is not necessary to limit ourselves to 6-month forward rates. The Treasury yield curve can be used to calculate the forward rate for any time in the future for any investment horizon.

To demonstrate how this is done, we must redefine our earlier notation. Before we defined ${}_1f_m$ as the 1-period (or 6-month) forward rate m periods from now. We will now let ${}_nf_m$ be the forward rate for an investment of n periods beginning m periods from now. This is depicted in Exhibit 6. For example, ${}_4f_6$ is the 4-period forward rate beginning six periods from now.

Now let's see how the spot rates can be used to calculate forward rates for a period greater than six months. We assume in the illustration that there are zero-coupon Treasury securities available. The existence of these securities is not necessary for determination of the forward rates. The assumption just simplifies the presentation.

Suppose that an investor with a 5-year investment horizon is considering the following two alternatives:

Alternative 1: Buy a 5-year (10-period) zero-coupon Treasury security
Alternative 2: Buy a 3-year (6-period) zero-coupon Treasury security, and when it matures in three years buy a 2-year zero-coupon Treasury security

By investing $X in a 5-year zero-coupon security Treasury today, the investor will have the following at the end of five years:

$$X(1 + z_{10})^{10}$$

where z_{10} is one-half the BEY of the theoretical 10-period spot rate.

With the second alternative, the amount available at the end of three years from investing $X in a 3-year zero-coupon Treasury security would be:

$$X(1 + z_6)^6$$

The amount at the end of five years depends on the forward rate for a 2-year investment beginning three years from now. In terms of our formula, it depends on $_4f_6$. The amount at the end of five years would then be:

$$X(1 + z_6)^6 (1 + {_4f_6})^4$$

The investor will be indifferent toward the two alternatives confronting him if he makes the same dollar investment ($X) and receives the same future dollars from both alternatives at the end of five years. That is, the investor will be indifferent if:

$$X(1 + z_{10})^{10} = X(1 + z_6)^6 (1 + {_4f_6})^4$$

Solving for $_4f_6$, we get:

$$_4f_6 = \left[\frac{(1 + z_{10})^{10}}{(1 + z_6)^6}\right]^{1/4} - 1$$

Doubling $_4f_6$ gives the BEY for the 2-year forward rate three years from now.

We can illustrate the use of this formula with the theoretical spot rates shown in Exhibit 5. From that exhibit, we know that the:

5-year spot rate = 5.2772%, therefore $z_{10} = 0.026386$
3-year spot rate = 4.7520%, therefore $z_6 = 0.023760$

Substituting these into the formula, we have:

$$_4f_6 = \left[\frac{(1.026386)^{10}}{(1.023760)^6}\right]^{1/4} - 1 = 0.03034 = 3.034\%$$

Therefore, the 2-year forward rate three years from now is 6.068% (3.034% × 2) BEY.

In general, the formula for any forward rate is:

$$_nf_m = \left[\frac{(1 + z_{m+n})^{m+n}}{(1 + z_m)^m}\right]^{1/n} - 1$$

Forward Rate as a Hedgeable Rate

A natural question about forward rates is how well they do at predicting future interest rates. Studies have demonstrated that forward rates do not do a good job at predicting future interest rates.[6] Then, why the big deal about understanding forward rates? The reason is that forward rates indicate how an investor's expectations must differ from the market consensus in order to make the correct decision.

A forward rate may not be realized. That is irrelevant. The fact is that a forward rate indicates to the investor if his expectation about a rate in the future is less than the corresponding forward rate, then he would be better off investing now to lock in the forward rate. For this reason, as well as others explained later, some market participants prefer not to talk about forward rates as being market consensus rates. Instead they refer to forward rates as being *hedgeable rates*.

THEORIES OF THE TERM STRUCTURE OF INTEREST RATES

In Chapter 4, we presented several shapes that have been observed for the Treasury yield curve. Two major theories have evolved to account for these observed shapes of the yield curve: the *expectations theory* and the *market segmentation theory*.

There are several forms of the expectations theory — the *pure expectations theory*, the *liquidity theory*, and the *preferred habitat theory*. All share a hypothesis about the behavior of short-term forward rates and also assume that the forward rates in current long-term bonds are closely related to the market's expectations about future short-term rates. These three theories differ, however, on whether other factors also affect forward rates, and how. The pure expectations theory postulates that no systematic factors other than expected future short-term rates affect forward rates; the liquidity theory and the preferred habitat theory assert that there are other factors. Accordingly, the last two forms of the expectations theory are sometimes referred to as *biased expectations theories*. The relationship among the various theories is described below and summarized in Exhibit 7.

The Pure Expectations Theory

According to the pure expectations theory, forward rates exclusively represent expected future rates. Thus, the entire term structure at a given time reflects the market's current expectations of the family of future short-term rates. Under this view, a rising term structure must indicate that the market expects short-term rates to rise throughout the relevant future. Similarly, a flat term structure reflects an expectation that future short-term rates will be mostly constant, while a falling term structure must reflect an expectation that future short-term rates will decline.

---

[6] Eugene F. Fama, "Forward Rates as Predictors of Future Spot Rates," *Journal of Financial Economics* Vol. 3, No. 4, 1976, pp. 361-377.

Exhibit 7: Term Structure Theories

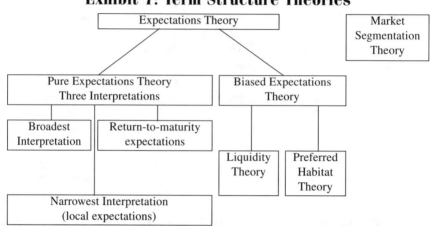

Drawbacks of the Theory

The pure expectations theory suffers from one shortcoming, which, qualitatively, is quite serious. It neglects the risks inherent in investing in bonds. If forward rates were perfect predictors of future interest rates, then the future prices of bonds would be known with certainty. The return over any investment period would be certain and independent of the maturity of the instrument acquired. However, with the uncertainty about future interest rates and, therefore, about future prices of bonds, these instruments become risky investments in the sense that the return over some investment horizon is unknown.

There are two risks that cause uncertainty about the return over some investment horizon. The first is the uncertainty about the price of the bond at the end of the investment horizon. For example, an investor who plans to invest for five years might consider the following three investment alternatives: (1) invest in a 5-year bond and hold it for five years; (2) invest in a 12-year bond and sell it at the end of five years; and, (3) invest in a 30-year bond and sell it at the end of five years. The return that will be realized for the second and third alternatives is not known because the price of each of these bonds at the end of five years is unknown. In the case of the 12-year bond, the price will depend on the yield on 7-year bonds five years from now; and the price of the 30-year bond will depend on the yield on 25-year bonds five years from now. Since forward rates implied in the current term structure for a 7-year bond five years from now and a 25-year bond five years from now are not perfect predictors of the actual future rates, there is uncertainty about the price for both bonds five years from now. Thus, there is price risk; that is, the price of the bond may be lower than currently expected at the end of the investment horizon. As explained in Chapter 6, interest rate risk increases with the length of the bond's maturity.

The second risk involves the uncertainty about the rate at which the proceeds from a bond that matures prior to the end of the investment horizon can be reinvested until the maturity date, that is, reinvestment risk. For example, an investor who plans to invest for five years might consider the following three alternative investments: (1) invest in a 5-year bond and hold it for five years; (2) invest in a 6-month instrument and, when it matures, reinvest the proceeds in 6-month instruments over the entire 5-year investment horizon; and, (3) invest in a 2-year bond and, when it matures, reinvest the proceeds in a 3-year bond. The risk in the second and third alternatives is that the return over the 5-year investment horizon is unknown because rates at which the proceeds can be reinvested until the end of the investment horizon are unknown.

Interpretations of the Theory

There are several interpretations of the pure expectations theory that have been put forth by economists. These interpretations are not exact equivalents nor are they consistent with each other, in large part because they offer different treatments of the two risks associated with realizing a return that we have just explained.[7]

The broadest interpretation of the pure expectations theory suggests that investors expect the return for any investment horizon to be the same, regardless of the maturity strategy selected.[8] For example, consider an investor who has a 6-month investment horizon. According to this theory, it makes no difference if a 5-year, 12-year, or 30-year bond is purchased and held for five years since the investor expects the return from all three bonds to be the same over the 5-year investment horizon. A major criticism of this very broad interpretation of the theory is that, because of price risk associated with investing in bonds with a maturity greater than the investment horizon, the expected returns from these three very different bond investments should differ in significant ways.[9]

A second interpretation, referred to as the *local expectations* form of the pure expectations theory, suggests that the return will be the same over a short-term investment horizon starting today. For example, if an investor has a 1-month investment horizon, buying a 5-year, 10-year or 20-year bond will produce the same 1-month return.

This is illustrated in Exhibit 8 for a 6-month investment horizon for three of the bonds in Exhibit 1 — the 1-year, 5-year, and 10-year issues. For the 6-month issue in Exhibit 1, the total return is the 6-month spot rate of 3%. Panel A of Exhibit 8 shows the cash flows for the 1-year issue six months from now. If the short-term forward rate is realized, the 6-month forward rate is 3.6% as indicated in Exhibit 5. The price of the 1-year issue six months from now when discounted at the 6-month forward rate is shown in Exhibit 8. Adding this price to the coupon and dividing by the initial price of $100 gives a 6-month total return of 1.5% and a 1-year total return of 3%. This is the same total return as the 6-month issue. Panels B and C of Exhibit 8 show the same calculations for the 5-year and 10-year issues assuming that the 6-month forward rates shown in Exhibit 5 are realized 6-months from now. As can be seen, the total return is 3%. Thus, in each case, the total return over a 6-month horizon is the same and it is equal to the current 6-month spot rate.

---

[7] These formulations are summarized by John Cox, Jonathan Ingersoll, Jr., and Stephen Ross, "A Re-examination of Traditional Hypotheses About the Term Structure of Interest Rates," *Journal of Finance* (September 1981), pp. 769-799.

[8] F. Lutz, "The Structure of Interest Rates," *Quarterly Journal of Economics* (1940-41), pp. 36-63.

[9] Cox, Ingersoll and Ross, pp. 774-775.

Exhibit 8: Total Return Over a 6-Month Investment Horizon if 6-Month Forward Rates are Realized

Panel A: Total return on 1-year issue if forward rates are realized			
Period	Cash flows ($)	6-month forward rate (%)	Price at horizon ($)
1	101.650	3.60	99.85265
Price at horizon: 99.85265		Total proceeds: 101.5027	
Coupon: 1.65		Total return: 3.00%	

Panel B: Total return on 5-year issue if forward rates are realized			
Period	Cash flows ($)	6-month forward rate (%)	Present value ($)
1	2.600	3.60	2.55403
2	2.600	3.92	2.50493
3	2.600	5.15	2.44205
4	2.600	6.54	2.36472
5	2.600	6.33	2.29217
6	2.600	6.23	2.22293
7	2.600	5.79	2.16039
8	2.600	6.01	2.09736
9	102.600	6.24	80.26096
		Total:	98.89954
Price at horizon: 98.89954		Total proceeds: 101.4995	
Coupon: 2.60		Total return: 3.00%	

Panel C: Total return on 10-year issue if forward rates are realized			
Period	Cash flows ($)	6-month forward rate (%)	Present value ($)
1	3.000	3.60	2.94695
2	3.000	3.92	2.89030
3	3.000	5.15	2.81775
4	3.000	6.54	2.72853
5	3.000	6.33	2.64482
6	3.000	6.23	2.56492
7	3.000	5.79	2.49275
8	3.000	6.01	2.42003
9	3.000	6.24	2.34681
10	3.000	6.48	2.27316
11	3.000	6.72	2.19927
12	3.000	6.97	2.12520
13	3.000	6.36	2.05970
14	3.000	6.49	1.99497
15	3.000	6.62	1.93105
16	3.000	6.76	1.86791
17	3.000	8.10	1.79521
18	3.000	8.40	1.72285
19	103.000	8.72	56.67989
		Total:	98.50208
Price at horizon: 98.50208		Total proceeds: 101.5021	
Coupon: 3.00		Total return: 3.00%	

It has been demonstrated that the local expectations formulation, which is narrow in scope, is the only interpretation of the pure expectations theory that can be sustained in equilibrium.[10]

The third and final interpretation of the pure expectations theory suggests that the return that an investor will realize by rolling over short-term bonds to some investment horizon will be the same as holding a zero-coupon bond with a maturity that is the same as that investment horizon. (A zero-coupon bond has no reinvestment risk, so that future interest rates over the investment horizon do not affect the return.) This variant is called the *return-to-maturity expectations* interpretation. For example, let's once again assume that an investor has a 5-year investment horizon. By buying a 5-year zero-coupon bond and holding it to maturity, the investor's return is the difference between the maturity value and the price of the bond, divided by the price of the bond. According to the return-to-maturity expectations, the same return will be realized by buying a 6-month instrument and rolling it over for five years. At this time, the validity of this interpretation is subject to considerable doubt.

Biased Expectations Theories

There are two forms of the biased expectations theory: the liquidity theory and the preferred habitat theory.

The Liquidity Theory

We have explained that the drawback of the pure expectations theory is that it does not consider the risks associated with bond investments. We have just shown that there is indeed risk in holding a long-term bond for one period, and that risk increases with the bond's maturity because maturity and price volatility are directly related.

Given this uncertainty, and considering that investors typically do not like uncertainty, some economists and financial analysts have suggested a different theory. This theory states that investors will hold longer-term maturities if they are offered a long-term rate higher than the average of expected future rates by a risk premium that is positively related to the term to maturity.[11] Put differently, the forward rates should reflect both interest rate expectations and a "liquidity" premium (really a risk premium), and the premium should be higher for longer maturities.

According to this theory, which is called the *liquidity theory of the term structure*, forward rates will not be an unbiased estimate of the market's expectations of future interest rates because they embody a liquidity premium. Thus, an upward-sloping yield curve may reflect expectations that future interest rates either (1) will rise, or (2) will be unchanged or even fall, but with a liquidity premium increasing fast enough with maturity so as to produce an upward-sloping yield curve.

---

[10] Cox, Ingersoll, and Ross.

[11] John R. Hicks, *Value and Capital* (London: Oxford University Press, 1946), second ed., pp. 141-145.

The Preferred Habitat Theory

Another theory, known as the *preferred habitat theory*, also adopts the view that the term structure reflects the expectation of the future path of interest rates as well as a risk premium. However, the preferred habitat theory rejects the assertion that the risk premium must rise uniformly with maturity.[12] Proponents of the preferred habitat theory say that the latter conclusion could be accepted if all investors intend to liquidate their investment at the shortest possible date while all borrowers are anxious to borrow long. This assumption can be rejected since institutions have holding periods dictated by the nature of their liabilities.

The preferred habitat theory asserts that if there is an imbalance between the supply and demand for funds within a given maturity range, investors and borrowers will not be reluctant to shift their investing and financing activities out of their preferred maturity sector to take advantage of any imbalance. However, to do so, investors must be induced by a yield premium in order to accept the risks associated with shifting funds out of their preferred sector. Similarly, borrowers can only be induced to raise funds in a maturity sector other than their preferred sector by a sufficient cost savings to compensate for the corresponding funding risk.

Thus, this theory proposes that the shape of the yield curve is determined by both expectations of future interest rates and a risk premium, positive or negative, to induce market participants to shift out of their preferred habitat. Clearly, according to this theory, yield curves sloping up, down, or flat are all possible.

Market Segmentation Theory

The *market segmentation theory* also recognizes that investors have preferred habitats dictated by the nature of their liabilities. This theory also proposes that the major reason for the shape of the yield curve lies in asset/liability management constraints (either regulatory or self-imposed) and/or creditors (borrowers) restricting their lending (financing) to specific maturity sectors.[13] However, the market segmentation theory differs from the preferred habitat theory in that it assumes that neither investors nor borrowers are willing to shift from one maturity sector to another to take advantage of opportunities arising from differences between expectations and forward rates. Thus, for the segmentation theory, the shape of the yield curve is determined by the supply of and demand for securities within each maturity sector.

---

[12] Franco Modigliani and Richard Sutch, "Innovations in Interest Rate Policy," *American Economic Review* (May 1966), pp. 178-197.
[13] This theory was suggested in J.M. Culbertson, "The Term Structure of Interest Rates," *Quarterly Journal of Economics* (November 1957), pp. 489-504.

KEY POINTS

1. There are two methodologies that have been used to derive the theoretical Treasury spot rate curve: (1) bootstrapping the on-the-run Treasury yield curve and (2) using econometric methods for estimation.

2. The bootstrapping method uses on-the-run Treasury issues to generate the spot rate curve using arbitrage arguments.

3. The basic principle underlying the bootstrapping method is that the value of the cash flows from an on-the-run Treasury issue when discounted at the spot rates must be equal to the observed market price.

4. In practice, the bootstrapping method must be modified to allow for on-the-run issues not trading at par and for the gaps in maturities.

5. To mitigate the problem of maturity gaps, in practice, 20-year and 25-year issues are used in the bootstrapping method.

6. An econometric method called exponential splines is used to statistically estimate the spot rate curve using yields on all Treasury issues.

7. The economic force that assures that Treasury securities will be priced in the market based on spot rates is the opportunity for dealers to profit from stripping Treasury securities or for investors to risklessly enhance portfolio returns.

8. Using arbitrage arguments, the market's consensus of future interest rates can be extrapolated from the Treasury yield curve or equivalently, the spot rate curve.

9. These rates are called forward rates or implied forward rates and the set of short-term (6-month) forward rates is the short-term forward rate curve.

10. The spot rate for a given period is related to the forward rates, specifically, the spot rate is a geometric average of the current 6-month spot rate and the subsequent 6-month forward rates.

11. Forward rates should be viewed as hedgeable rates.

12. The two major theories for explaining the observed shapes of the Treasury yield curve are the expectations theory and the market segmentation theory.

13. The three forms of the expectations theory (the pure expectations theory, the liquidity theory, and the preferred habitat theory) assume that the forward rates in current long-term bonds are closely related to the market's expectations about future short-term rates.

14. *The three forms of the expectations theory differ on whether other factors also affect forward rates, and how.*

15. *The pure expectations theory postulates that no systematic factors other than expected future short-term rates affect forward rates.*

16. *Because forward rates are not perfect predictors of future interest rates, the pure expectations theory neglects the risks (interest rate risk and reinvestment risk) associated with investing in Treasury securities.*

17. *The broadest interpretation of the pure expectations theory suggests that investors expect the return for any investment horizon to be the same, regardless of the maturity strategy selected.*

18. *The local expectations form of the pure expectations theory suggests that the return will be the same over a short-term investment horizon starting today and it is this narrow interpretation that economists have demonstrated is the only interpretation that can be sustained in equilibrium.*

19. *The return-to-maturity expectations interpretation of the pure expectations theory suggests that the return that an investor will realize by rolling over short-term Treasury securities to some investment horizon will be the same as holding a zero-coupon Treasury with a maturity that is the same as that investment horizon.*

20. *The liquidity theory and the preferred habitat theory assert that there are other factors that affect forward rates and these two theories are therefore referred to as biased expectations theories.*

21. *The liquidity theory states that investors will hold longer-term maturities only if they are offered a risk premium and therefore forward rates should reflect both interest rate expectations and a liquidity risk premium.*

22. *The preferred habitat theory in addition to adopting the view that forward rates reflect the expectation of the future path of interest rates as well as a risk premium argues that the risk premium need not reflect a liquidity premium but the demand and supply of funds in a given maturity range.*

23. *The market segmentation theory recognizes that investors have preferred maturity sectors dictated by the nature of their liabilities but it goes further than the preferred habitat theory by assuming that neither investors nor borrowers are willing to shift from one maturity sector to another to take advantage of opportunities arising from differences between expectations and forward rates.*

Chapter 6

MEASURING LEVEL RISK

To effectively control a Treasury portfolio's exposure to interest rate risk, it is necessary to quantify the sensitivity of a portfolio to a change in rates. In Chapter 4 we explained the factors that affect a Treasury portfolio's return — changes in the level of rates, changes in the slope of the yield curve, and changes in the curvature of the yield curve. In this chapter and the next we look at how to measure exposure to the first two factors. Our focus in this chapter is on measuring level risk.

PRICE VOLATILITY CHARACTERISTICS OF TREASURY SECURITIES

A fundamental principle of a noncallable Treasury security is that its price changes in the opposite direction from a change in the security's yield. Exhibit 1 illustrates this property for four hypothetical Treasury securities, where the prices are shown assuming a par value of $100.

When the price/yield relationship for any noncallable Treasury security is graphed, it exhibits the shape shown in Exhibit 2. Notice that as the yield rises, the security's price declines. However, this relationship is not linear (that is, it is not a straight line). The shape of the price/yield relationship for any noncallable Treasury security is referred to as *convex*. The price/yield relationship that we have discussed refers to an instantaneous change in yield.

Exhibit 1: Price/Yield Relationship for Four Hypothetical Noncallable Treasury Securities

Yield (%)	Price ($)			
	6%/5 year	6%/20 year	9%/5 year	9%/20 year
4.00	108.9826	127.3555	122.4565	168.3887
5.00	104.3760	112.5514	117.5041	150.2056
5.50	102.1600	106.0195	115.1201	142.1367
5.90	100.4276	101.1651	113.2556	136.1193
5.99	100.0427	100.1157	112.8412	134.8159
6.00	100.0000	100.0000	112.7953	134.6722
6.01	99.9574	99.8845	112.7494	134.5287
6.10	99.5746	98.8535	112.3373	133.2472
6.50	97.8944	94.4479	110.5280	127.7605
7.00	95.8417	89.3225	108.3166	121.3551
8.00	91.8891	80.2072	104.0554	109.8964

Exhibit 2: Price/Yield Relationship for a Noncallable Treasury Security

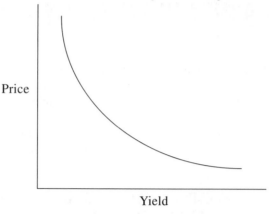

Properties of Noncallable Treasury Securities

Exhibit 3 uses the four hypothetical noncallable Treasury securities in Exhibit 1 to show the percentage change in each security's price for various changes in the yield, assuming that the initial yield for all four securities is 6%. An examination of Exhibit 3 reveals several properties concerning the price volatility of a noncallable Treasury security.

> *Property 1:* Although the prices of all noncallable Treasury securities move in the opposite direction from the change in yield, the percentage price change is not the same for all securities.
>
> *Property 2:* For small changes in yield, the percentage price change for a given security is roughly the same whether the yield increases or decreases.
>
> *Property 3:* For large changes in yield, the percentage price change is not the same for an increase in yield as it is for a decrease in yield.
>
> *Property 4:* For a given large change in basis points, in absolute terms the percentage price increase is greater than the percentage price decrease.

The implication of Property 4 is that if an investor is long a Treasury security, the price appreciation that will be realized if the yield decreases by a large number of basis points is greater than the capital loss that will be realized if the yield rises by the same number of basis points. For an investor who is short a Treasury security, the reverse is true: the potential capital loss is greater than the potential capital gain if the yield changes by a large number of basis points.

An explanation for these four properties of price volatility lies in the convex shape of the price/yield relationship.

Exhibit 3: Instantaneous Percentage Price Change for Four Hypothetical Noncallable Treasury Securities
(Initial yield for all four securities is 6%)

New Yield (%)	Percent Price Change			
	6%/5 year	6%/20 year	9%/5 year	9%/20 year
4.00	8.98	27.36	8.57	25.04
5.00	4.38	12.55	4.17	11.53
5.50	2.16	6.02	2.06	5.54
5.90	0.43	1.17	0.41	1.07
5.99	0.04	0.12	0.04	0.11
6.01	−0.04	−0.12	−0.04	−0.11
6.10	−0.43	−1.15	−0.41	−1.06
6.50	−2.11	−5.55	−2.01	−5.13
7.00	−4.16	−10.68	−3.97	−9.89
8.00	−8.11	−19.79	−7.75	−18.40

Characteristics of a Treasury Security that Affect its Price Volatility

There are two characteristics of a noncallable Treasury security that determine its price volatility: term to maturity and coupon.

Characteristic 1: For a given coupon rate and initial yield, the longer the maturity of a Treasury security the greater the security's price sensitivity to changes in market interest rates.

Characteristic 2: For a given maturity and initial yield, the lower the coupon rate the greater the Treasury security's price sensitivity to changes in market interest rates.

These properties can be verified by examining Exhibit 3.

An implication of the first characteristic is that investors who want to increase a Treasury portfolio's price volatility because they expect interest rates to fall, all other factors being constant, should hold securities with long maturities in the portfolio. To reduce a Treasury portfolio's price volatility in anticipation of a rise in interest rates, securities with short maturities should be held in the portfolio. Another implication is that Treasury bills because of their short maturity have little price volatility.

An implication of the second characteristic is that Treasury strips will have greater price volatility risk than same-maturity Treasury coupon securities. Long-term Treasury strips will have substantial price volatility.

The Effects of Yield to Maturity

As the level of interest rates changes, the degree of price sensitivity of a security to changes in interest rates changes. Specifically, the higher the level of interest rates, the lower the price sensitivity.

To see this, we can compare a 6% 20-year Treasury initially selling at a yield of 6%, and the same Treasury issue initially selling at a yield of 10%. At the 6% yield level, the security's price is initially $100. If the yield level is 10%, the security's price is $65.68. If the yield increases by 100 basis points from the 6% yield level, the security would drop in price by $10.68 (10.68%). After the assumed increase in yield at the 10% level, the same security would trade at a price of $59.88, for a price decline of only $5.80 (or 8.83%). Thus, we see that in a low interest rate environment, a Treasury security is more volatile in both percentage price change and absolute price change, as long as the other bond characteristics are the same.

An implication of this is that, for a given change in interest rates, price sensitivity is lower when the level of interest rates in the market is high, and price sensitivity is higher when the level of interest rates is low.

PRICE VALUE OF A BASIS POINT AS A MEASURE OF INTEREST RATE RISK

One measure of the dollar price sensitivity of a Treasury security to interest rate changes is the *price value of a basis point* (PVBP). This measure, also referred to as the *dollar value of an 01* (DV01), is the change in the price of a Treasury security if the yield changes by 1 basis point.[1] Typically, the price value of a basis point is expressed as the absolute value of the change in price; consequently, the greater the price value of a basis point, the greater the dollar price volatility. As we noted earlier, price changes are almost symmetric for small changes in yield. Thus, it does not make a great deal of difference whether we increase or decrease yields to calculate the price value of a basis point. In practice, an average of the change resulting from both an up and a down movement in yield is used.

We will illustrate the calculation of the price value of a basis point using the 9% 20-year Treasury assuming this security is selling to yield 6%. As can be seen in Exhibit 1:

yield at 6.00% = 134.6722
yield at 5.99% = 134.8159
yield at 6.01% = 134.5287

The PVBP per $100 of par value if the yield decreases by 1 basis point is:

134.8159 − 134.6722 = 0.1437

This value is almost identical to the PVBP if the yield increases by 1 point:

134.6722 − 134.5287 = 0.1435

---

[1] The term dollar value of an 01 appears to be more commonly used for Treasury bills, while the term price value of a basis point is more commonly use for Treasury coupon securities.

Some investors calculate the price value of more than 1 basis point. The principle of calculating the price value of any number of basis points is the same. For example, the price value of 10 basis points is found by computing the difference between the initial price and the price if the yield changed by 10 basis points. Consider once again the 9% 20-year Treasury trading to yield 9%, then:

yield at 6.00% = 134.6722
yield at 5.90% = 136.1193
yield at 6.10% = 133.2472

The price value of 10 basis points per $100 of par value if the yield decreases by 10 basis points is:

136.1193 − 134.6722 = 1.4471

The price value of 10 basis points per $100 of par value if the yield decreases by 10 basis points is:

134.6722 − 133.2472 = 1.4250

The price value of 10 basis is then the average of the two changes:

(1.4471 + 1.4250)/2 = 1.4361

Since the relationship is still nearly symmetric for a 10 basis point change in yield up or down, the price value of 10 basis points is approximately equal to 10 times the price value of 1 basis point. However, for larger changes in yield, there will be a difference if the yield is increased or decreased, and the price change for a large number of basis points can no longer be approximated by multiplying the price value of 1 basis point by the number of basis points. Most investors who derive the price value for large movements in yields (such as 100 basis points), will average the PVBPs for an up move and a down move to get the PVBP of interest.

Exhibit 4 shows graphically what happens to the price value of a basis point at different yield levels. Notice that the price value of a basis point is smaller the higher the initial yield. This agrees with what we pointed out earlier that at low levels of interest rates, the price value of a basis point is greater than at higher levels.

YIELD VALUE OF A 32ND

Another measure of dollar price volatility of a Treasury security is the *yield value of a 32nd*. This measure is found by first calculating the Treasury security's yield if the price is increased by a 32nd. Then the difference between the initial yield and the new yield is the yield value of a 32nd.

Exhibit 4: Graphical Illustration of the Price Value of a Basis Point

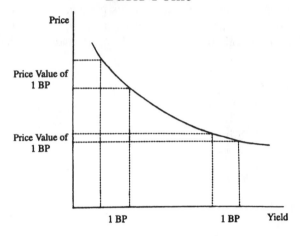

Exhibit 5: Graphical Depiction of Yield Value of a 32nd

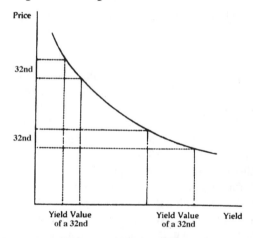

The smaller the yield value of a 32nd price change, the greater the *dollar* price volatility of a Treasury security. This is because it would take more 32nds in price movement to change the yield a specified number of basis points. This is illustrated graphically in Exhibit 5.

Calculation of the yield value of a 32nd for the four hypothetical Treasury securities in Exhibit 1 is shown in Exhibit 6 assuming each security is trading to yield 6%. Notice that the yield value of a 32nd for the two 5-year securities is greater than for the two 20-year securities. This agrees with our earlier statement that the lower the yield value of a 32nd, the greater the dollar price volatility.

Exhibit 6: Calculation of the Yield Value of a 32nd for Four Hypothetical Treasury Securities Trading at 6%

Decreasing the price by a 32nd:

Security	Initial price Minus a 32nd	Yield at new new price	Yield value of a 32nd
6% 5 year	99.968750	6.007328	0.007328
6% 20 year	99.968750	6.002704	0.002704
9% 5 year	112.764054	6.006807	0.006807
9% 20 year	134.640908	6.002177	0.002177

Increasing the price by a 32nd:

Security	Initial price Plus a 32nd	Yield at new new price	Yield value of a 32nd
6% 5 year	100.031250	5.992674	0.007326
6% 20 year	106.031250	5.997297	0.002703
9% 5 year	112.826554	5.993195	0.006805
9% 20 year	134.703408	5.997824	0.002176

Average: Yield Value of a 32nd

6% 5 year	0.007327
6% 20 year	0.002704
9% 5 year	0.006806
9% 20 year	0.002176

DURATION AS A MEASURE OF INTEREST RATE RISK

The most obvious way to measure a Treasury security's price sensitivity as a percentage of its current price to changes in interest rates is to change rates by a small number of basis points and calculate how its price will change. To do this, we introduce the following notation. Let

Δy = change in the yield of the security (in decimal)
V_0 = initial value of the security
V_- = value of the security if the yield is decreased by Δy
V_+ = value of the security if the yield is increased by Δy

We are interested in the percentage change in the price of a security when interest rates change. The percentage change in price per basis point change is found by dividing the percentage price change by the number of basis points (Δy times 100). That is:

$$\frac{V_- - V_0}{V_0(\Delta y)100}$$

Similarly, the percentage change in price per basis point change for an increase in yield (Δy times 100) is:

$$\frac{V_0 - V_+}{V_0(\Delta y)100}$$

As explained earlier, the percentage price change for an increase and decrease in interest rates may not be the same. Consequently, the average percentage price change per basis point change in yield can be calculated. This is done as follows:

$$\frac{1}{2}\left[\frac{V_- - V_0}{V_0(\Delta y)100} + \frac{V_0 - V_+}{V_0(\Delta y)100}\right]$$

or equivalently,

$$\frac{V_- - V_+}{2V_0(\Delta y)100}$$

The approximate percentage price change for a 100 basis point change in yield is found by multiplying the previous formula by 100. The name popularly used to refer to the approximate percentage price change is *duration*. Thus,

$$\text{Duration} = \frac{V_- - V_+}{2V_0\Delta y} \qquad (1)$$

To illustrate this formula, consider the hypothetical 9% 20-year Treasury trading to yield 6%. The initial price (V_0) is 134.6722. Suppose the yield is changed by 20 basis points. If the yield is decreased to 5.8%, the value of this security (V_-) would be 137.5888. If the yield is increased to 6.2%, the value of this security (V_+) would be 131.8439. Thus,

$$\Delta y = 0.002$$
$$V_0 = 134.6722$$
$$V_- = 137.5888$$
$$V_+ = 131.8439$$

Substituting these values into the duration formula,

$$\text{Duration} = \frac{137.5888 - 131.8439}{2(134.6722)(0.002)} = 10.66$$

Interpreting Duration

The duration of a security can be interpreted as the approximate percentage change in the price for a 100 basis point change in interest rates. Thus a Treasury security with a duration of 4.8 will change by approximately 4.8% for a 100 basis point change in interest rates. For a 50 basis point change, the security's price will change by approximately 2.4%; for a 25 basis point change, 1.2%, etc.

An investor who anticipates a decline in interest rates will extend (i.e., increase) the portfolio's duration. Suppose that the investor increases the current portfolio duration of 4 to 6. This means that for a 100 basis point change in interest rates, the portfolio will change by about 2% more than if the portfolio duration was left unchanged at 4.

Dollar Duration

Duration is related to percentage price change. However, for two Treasury securities with the same duration, the dollar price change will not be the same if the prices are not the same. For example, consider two hypothetical Treasury issues, W and X. Suppose that both issues have a duration of 5, but that W is trading at par while X is trading at 90. A 100 basis point change for both bonds will change the price by approximately 5%. This means a price change of $5 (5% times $100) for W and a price change of $4.5 (5% times $90) for X.

The dollar price volatility of a Treasury security can be measured by multiplying duration by the full dollar price and the number of basis points (in decimal form). That is:

Dollar price change = Duration × Dollar price × Δy

where Δy is the yield change (in decimal).

The dollar price volatility for a 100 basis point change in yield is:

Dollar price change = Duration × Dollar price × 0.01

or equivalently,

Dollar price change = Duration × Dollar price /100

The dollar price change calculated using the above formula is called *dollar duration*. In some contexts, dollar duration refers to the price change for a 100 basis point change in yield. The dollar duration for any number of basis points can be computed by scaling the dollar price change accordingly. For example, for a 50 basis point change in yields, the dollar price change or dollar duration is:

Dollar price change = Duration × Dollar price/200

For a 1 basis point change in yield, the dollar price change will give the same result as the price value of a basis point.

The dollar duration for a 100 basis point change in yield for issues W and X is:

For W: Dollar duration = 5 × $100/100 = $5.0
For X: Dollar duration = 5 × $90/100   = $4.5

Exhibit 7: Price/Yield Relationship for a Noncallable Treasury Bond and a Callable Treasury Bond

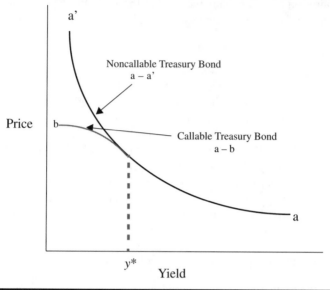

Duration for a Callable Treasury Bond

Thus far our discussion has focused on price volatility for a noncallable Treasury security. The form of duration that we have discussed for these securities is called *modified duration*. This form of duration assumes that when interest rates change, the cash flows of a security do not change. What this means is that in calculating the values of V_- and V_+ in the duration formula, the same cash flows used to calculate V_0 are used. Therefore, the change in the security's price when interest rates change is due solely to discounting at the new yield level.

The assumption that the cash flows will not change when interest rates change makes sense for noncallable Treasury securities. This is because the payments made by the U.S. Department of the Treasury to current holders of its obligations do not change when interest rates change. However, the same cannot be said for callable Treasury bonds. For these securities, a change in yield will alter the *expected* cash flows because the U.S. Department of the Treasury has the option to call the security and thereby alter the cash flows (i.e., stop coupon payments from the call date to the maturity date and repay the principal before the scheduled maturity date).

The price/yield relationship for callable Treasury bonds is shown in Exhibit 7. As yields in the market decline, the concern is that the Treasury will call the issues that it is permitted to call. The exact yield level at which investors begin to view the issue likely to be called may not be known, but we do know that there is some level. In Exhibit 7, at yield levels below $y*$, the price/yield relationship for the callable Treasury bond departs from the price/yield relationship for the noncallable Treasury bond. For example, suppose the market yield is such that a noncallable Treasury bond would be selling for 120. If the same bond is callable at par, investors would not pay 120. If they did and the bond is called, investors would receive 100 for a bond they purchased for 120. Notice that in Exhibit 7 for a range of yields below y^*, there is price compression — that is, there is limited price appreciation as yields decline. The portion of the callable Treasury bond price/yield relationship below y^* is said to be *negatively convex.*

Negative convexity means that the price appreciation will be less than the price depreciation for a large change in yield of a given number of basis points. A noncallable Treasury security is said to exhibit *positive convexity*; that is, the price appreciation will be greater than the price depreciation for a large change in yield. The price changes resulting from Treasury bonds exhibiting positive convexity and negative convexity are summarized below:

Change in interest rates	Absolute value of percentage price change for:	
	Positive convexity	Negative convexity
−100 basis points	X%	less than Y%
+100 basis points	less than X%	Y%

A valuation model for callable Treasury bonds is needed to estimate what the new value will be when interest rates change. When V_- and V_+ are the values produced from these valuation models, the resulting duration takes into account both the discounting at different interest rates and how the expected cash flows can change. When duration is calculated in this manner, it is referred to as *effective duration* or *option-adjusted duration.*

Macaulay Duration

It is worth comparing the modified duration formula presented above to that commonly found in the literature. It is common in the literature to find the following formula for modified duration for a semiannual-pay bond on a coupon anniversary date:

$$\frac{1}{(1 + \text{yield}/2)} \left[\frac{1 \times \text{PVCF}_1 + 2 \times \text{PVCF}_2 + ... + n \times \text{PVCF}_n}{2 \times \text{Price}} \right] \tag{2}$$

where

$\quad n \quad = \quad$ number of periods until maturity (i.e., number of years to maturity times 2)

$\quad$ yield $\quad = \quad$ yield to maturity of the security

$\quad$ PVCF$_t$ $\quad = \quad$ present value of the cash flow in period t discounted at the yield to maturity

The expression in the brackets of the modified duration formula given by equation (2) is a measure formulated in 1938 by Frederick Macaulay.[2] This measure is popularly referred to as *Macaulay duration.* Thus, modified duration is commonly expressed as:

$$\text{Modified duration} = \frac{\text{Macaulay duration}}{(1 + \text{yield}/2)}$$

The general formulation for duration as given by equation (1) provides a short-cut procedure for determining a Treasury security's modified duration. Because it is easier to calculate the modified duration using the short-cut procedure, many vendors of analytical software will use equation (1) rather than equation (2) to reduce computation time. But, once again, it must be emphasized that modified duration may be a flawed measure of a callable Treasury bond's price sensitivity to interest rate changes.

Duration of a Treasury Portfolio

A Treasury portfolio's duration can be obtained by calculating the weighted average of the duration of the Treasury securities in the portfolio. The weight is the proportion of the portfolio that a security comprises. Mathematically, a Treasury portfolio's duration can be calculated as follows:

$$W_1 D_1 + W_2 D_2 + W_3 D_3 + \dots + W_K D_K$$

where

W_i = market value of security i/market value of the portfolio
D_i = duration of security i
K = number of securities in the portfolio

To illustrate this calculation, consider the following hypothetical portfolio of Treasury securities in which all issues are noncallable:

Security	Par amount owned	Price
10%, 5-year	$4 million	$4,000,000
8%, 15-year	5 million	4,231,375
14%, 30-year	1 million	1,378,586

In this illustration, it is assumed that the next coupon payment for each security is six months from now. The market value for the portfolio is $9,609,961. The market price per $100 value of each security, its yield to maturity, and its duration are given below:

Security	Price	Yield to Maturity (%)	Duration
10%, 5-year	100.0000	10	3.861
8%, 15-year	84.6275	10	8.047
14%, 30-year	137.8590	10	9.168

In this illustration, K is equal to 3 and:

$$W_1 = 4,000,000/9,609,961 = 0.416 \quad D_1 = 3.861$$

---

[2] Frederick Macaulay, *Some Theoretical Problems Suggested by the Movement of Interest Rates, Bond Yields, and Stock Prices in the U.S. Since 1856* (New York: National Bureau of Economic Research, 1938).

$$W_2 = 4{,}231{,}375/9{,}609{,}961 = 0.440 \qquad D_2 = 8.047$$
$$W_3 = 1{,}378{,}586/9{,}609{,}961 = 0.144 \qquad D_3 = 9.168$$

The portfolio's duration is:

$$0.416\ (3.861) + 0.440\ (8.047) + 0.144\ (9.168) = 6.47$$

A portfolio duration of 6.47 means that for a 100 basis change in the yield for all three Treasury securities, the market value of the portfolio will change by approximately 6.47%. But keep in mind, the yield on all three Treasury securities must change by 100 basis points for the duration measure to be useful. This is a critical assumption and its importance cannot be overemphasized. We shall return to this point in the next chapter.

Similarly, the dollar duration of a Treasury portfolio can be obtained by calculating the weighted average of the dollar duration of the Treasury securities in the portfolio.

CONVEXITY MEASURE AS A SECOND ORDER APPROXIMATION OF PRICE CHANGE

Notice that the duration measure indicates that regardless of whether the yield change is up or down, the approximate percentage price change is the same. However, this does not agree with the properties of a Treasury security's price volatility described earlier in this chapter. Specifically, Property 2 states that for small changes in yield, the percentage price change will be the same for an increase or decrease in yield. Property 3 states that for large changes in yield this is not true. This suggests that duration is only a good approximation of the percentage price change for a small change in yield.

To see this, consider once again the 9% 20-year Treasury security selling to yield 6% with a duration of 10.66. If yields increase instantaneously by 10 basis points (from 6% to 6.1%), then using duration the approximate percentage price change would be −1.066% (−10.66% divided by 10, remembering that duration is the percentage price change for a 100 basis point change in yield). Notice from Exhibit 3 that the actual percentage price change is −1.07%. Similarly, if the yield decreases instantaneously by 10 basis points (from 6.00% to 5.90%), then the percentage change in price would be +1.066%. From Exhibit 3, the actual percentage price change would be +1.07%. This example illustrates that for small changes in yield, duration does an excellent job of approximating the percentage price change.

Instead of a small change in yield, let's assume that yields increase by 200 basis points, from 6% to 8%. The approximate percentage price change is −21.32% (−10.66% times 2). As can be seen from Exhibit 3, the actual percentage change in price is only −18.40%. Moreover, if the yield decreases by 200 basis points from 6% to 4%, the approximate percentage price change based on duration would be +21.32%, compared to an actual percentage price change of +25.04%. Thus, the approximation is not as good for a 200 basis point change in yield.

Duration is in fact a first approximation for a small change in yield. The approximation can be improved by using a second approximation. This approximation is referred to as a *security's convexity*. The use of this term in the industry is unfortunate since the term convexity is also used to describe the shape or curvature of the price/yield relationship, as explained earlier in this chapter. The convexity measure of a security can be used to approximate the change in price that is not explained by duration.

Convexity Measure

The convexity measure of a Treasury security can be approximated using the following formula:

$$\text{Convexity measure} = \frac{V_+ + V_- - 2V_0}{2V_0(\Delta y)^2} \tag{3}$$

where the notation is the same as used earlier for duration [equation (1)].

For our hypothetical 9% 20-year Treasury selling to yield 6%, we know that for a 20-basis-point-change in yield

$$
\begin{aligned}
\Delta y &= 0.0020 \\
V_+ &= 131.8439 \\
V_- &= 137.5888 \\
V_0 &= 134.6722
\end{aligned}
$$

Substituting these values into the convexity measure formula, we get

$$\text{Convexity measure} = \frac{137.5888 + 131.8439 - 2(134.6722)}{2(134.6722)(0.002)^2} = 81.96$$

Percentage Price Change Adjustment for Convexity

Given the convexity measure, the approximate percentage price change adjustment due to the security's convexity (i.e., the percentage price change not explained by duration) is:

$$\text{Convexity measure} \times (\Delta y)^2$$

We call this the *convexity adjustment.*

For example, for the 9% 20-year Treasury security, the convexity adjustment to the percentage price change if the yield increases from 6% to 8% is

$$81.96 \times (0.02)^2 = 0.0328 = 3.28\%$$

If the yield decreases from 6% to 4%, the convexity adjustment to the approximate percentage price change would also be 3.28%.

The approximate percentage price change based on duration and the convexity adjustment is found by simply adding the two estimates. So, for example, if yields change from 6% to 8%, the estimated percentage price change would be:

Estimated change approximated by duration = −21.32%
Convexity adjustment = + 3.28%
Total estimated percentage price change = −18.04%

The actual percentage price change is −18.40%.

For a decrease of 200 basis points, from 6% to 4%, the approximate percentage price change would be as follows:

Estimated change approximated by duration = +21.32%
Convexity adjustment = +3.28%
Total estimated percentage price change = +24.60%

The actual percentage price change is +25.04%. Thus, duration combined with the convexity adjustment does a good job of estimating the sensitivity of a security's price change to large changes in yield.

Modified Convexity and Effective Convexity

The prices used in equation (3) to calculate convexity can be obtained by either assuming that when yield changes the expected cash flows do not change or they do change. In the former case, the resulting convexity is referred to as *standard convexity*. Actually, in the industry, convexity is not qualified by the adjective "standard." Thus, in practice the term convexity typically means the cash flows are assumed not to change when yields change. *Effective convexity*, in contrast, assumes that the cash flows do change when yield changes. This is the same distinction made for duration.

As with duration, for callable Treasury bonds the effective duration should be used. For noncallable Treasury securities, either convexity measure will have a positive value.[3] For callable Treasury bonds, the calculated effective convexity can be negative when the calculated standard convexity gives a positive value.

---

[3] Hence, dealer firms such as Goldman Sachs refer to the convexity adjustment as the "convexity gain."

KEY POINTS

1. *The price/yield relationship for a noncallable Treasury security is convex.*

2. *A property of a noncallable Treasury security is that for a small change in yield, the percentage price change is roughly the same whether the yield increases or decreases.*

3. *A property of a noncallable Treasury security is that for a large change in yield, the percentage price change is not the same for an increase in yield as it is for a decrease in yield.*

4. *A property of a noncallable Treasury security is that for a given change in basis points, the percentage price increase is greater than the percentage price decrease.*

5. *The coupon and maturity of a Treasury security affect its price volatility.*

6. *For a given term to maturity and initial yield, the lower the coupon rate the greater the price volatility of a Treasury security.*

7. *For a given coupon rate and initial yield, the longer the term to maturity, the greater the price volatility.*

8. *For a given change in yield, price volatility is less when yield levels in the market are high than when yield levels are low.*

9. *Three measures of the price sensitivity of a Treasury security to changes in interest rates are the price value of a basis point, the yield value of a 32nd, and duration.*

10. *The price value of a basis point (also called the dollar value of an 01) is the change in the price if the yield changes by one basis point.*

11. *The yield value of a 32nd is the change in a Treasury security's yield if the price is changed by a 32nd.*

12. *The smaller the yield value of a 32nd, the greater the dollar price volatility.*

13. *The percentage price change of a security can be estimated by changing the yield by a small number of basis points and observing how the price changes.*

14. *Duration is the approximate percentage change in a security's price for a 100 basis point change in yield.*

15. *The dollar duration of a security measures the dollar price change when interest rates change.*

16. *Given the duration of a Treasury security and its price, the dollar duration can be calculated.*

17. *Callable Treasury bonds exhibit negative convexity which means that the percentage price change for a rise in rates is greater than for a decline in rates by the same number of basis points.*

18. *Modified duration is not as useful a measure of the price sensitivity for callable Treasury bonds.*

19. *Effective duration or option-adjusted duration is the approximate percentage price change of a callable Treasury bond for a 100 basis point change in yield allowing for the expected cash flows to change as a result of the change in yield.*

20. *The estimate of the price sensitivity of a Treasury security to a change in yield based on duration can be improved by using a bond's convexity measure.*

21. *As with duration, the convexity of a callable Treasury bond can be measured assuming that the cash flows do not change when yield changes (standard convexity) or assuming that the cash flows do change when yield changes (effective convexity).*

Chapter 7

MEASURING YIELD CURVE RISK

As explained in Chapter 4, the return on a portfolio of Treasury securities is affected not only by changes in the level of interest rates, but by how the yield curve shifts. The different types of shifts that have been observed are documented in Chapter 4. When using a Treasury portfolio's duration to measure the exposure to interest rate changes, it is assumed that any change in interest rates is the result of a parallel shift in the yield curve. A parallel shift means that the yield for all maturities changes by the same number of basis points.

In this chapter, we will see that duration, as well as convexity, is an inadequate measure of interest rate risk when the yield curve does not change in a parallel manner. As a result, it is necessary to be able to measure the exposure of a Treasury portfolio to shifts in the yield curve. Three approaches for measuring this exposure are described in this chapter — yield curve reshaping duration, key rate duration, and yield curve specific duration.

DURATION, CONVEXITY, AND
NONPARALLEL YIELD CURVE SHIFTS

To illustrate the limitations of duration and convexity, let's first look at how two portfolios consisting of hypothetical Treasury securities with the same portfolio duration will perform if the yield curve does not shift in a parallel fashion. Consider the three hypothetical Treasury securities shown in Exhibit 1. A is the short-term Treasury security, B is the long-term Treasury security, and C is the intermediate-term Treasury security. Each Treasury security is selling at par, and it is assumed the next coupon payment is six months from now. The duration and convexity for each security are calculated in the exhibit. Since all the securities are trading at par value, the duration and convexities are then the dollar duration and dollar convexity per $100 of par value.

Suppose that the following two Treasury portfolios are constructed. The first portfolio consists of only security C, the 10-year issue, and shall be referred to as the "bullet portfolio." The second portfolio consists of 51.86% of security A and 48.14% of security B, and this portfolio shall be referred to as the "barbell portfolio."

The dollar duration of the bullet portfolio is 6.49821. Recall that dollar duration is a measure of the dollar price sensitivity of a security or a portfolio. The dollar duration of the barbell is the weighted average of the dollar duration of the two Treasury securities in the portfolio and is computed below:

$$0.5186 (4.21122) + 0.4814 (9.89681) = 6.49821$$

Exhibit 1: Three Hypothetical Treasury Securities to Illustrate the Limitations of Duration and Convexity

Treasury issue	Coupon rate (%)	Price	Yield to maturity (%)	Maturity (years)
A	6.5	100	6.5	5
B	8.0	100	8.0	20
C	7.5	100	7.5	10

Calculation of duration and convexity:
Change yield up and down by 10 basis points

Treasury issue	Value if rate changes by		Duration	Convexity
	+10 bp	−10 bp		
A	99.5799	100.4222	4.21122	10.67912
B	99.0177	100.9970	9.89681	73.63737
C	99.3083	100.6979	6.49821	31.09724

The dollar duration of the barbell is equal to the dollar duration of the bullet. In fact, the barbell portfolio was designed to produce this result.

Duration is just a first approximation of the change in price resulting from a change in interest rates. The convexity measure provides a second approximation. The dollar convexity measure of the two portfolios is not equal. The dollar convexity measure of the bullet portfolio is 31.09724. The dollar convexity measure of the barbell is a weighted average of the dollar convexity measure of the two Treasury securities in the portfolio. That is,

$$0.5186 (10.67912) + 0.4814 (73.63737) = 40.98658$$

Thus, the bullet has a dollar convexity measure that is less than that of the barbell portfolio. Below is a summary of the dollar duration and dollar convexity of the two portfolios:

Parameter	Treasury Portfolio	
	Bullet	Barbell
Dollar duration	6.49821	6.49821
Dollar convexity	31.09724	40.98658

Which is the better Treasury portfolio in which to invest? The answer depends on the portfolio manager's investment objectives and investment horizon. Let's assume a 6-month investment horizon. The last column of Exhibit 2 shows the difference in the total return over a 6-month investment horizon for the two Treasury portfolios, assuming that the yield curve shifts in a "parallel" fashion.[1]

---

[1] Note that no assumption is needed for the reinvestment rate since the three bonds shown in Exhibit 1 are assumed to be trading right after a coupon payment has been made and therefore there is no accrued interest.

As explained in Chapter 4, by parallel it is meant that the yield for the short-term security (A), the intermediate-term security (C), and the long-term security (B) changes by the same number of basis points, shown in the first column of the exhibit. The total return reported in the second column of Exhibit 2 is:

bullet portfolio's total return − barbell portfolio's total return

Thus a positive value in the last column means that the bullet portfolio outperformed the barbell portfolio while a negative sign means that the barbell portfolio outperformed the bullet portfolio.

Which portfolio is the better investment alternative if the yield curve shifts in a parallel fashion *and* the investment horizon is six months? The answer depends on the amount by which yields change. Notice in the last column that the if yields change by less than 100 basis points, the bullet portfolio will outperform the barbell portfolio. The reverse is true if yields change by more than 100 basis points.

Exhibit 2: Performance of Bullet and Barbell Treasury Portfolios Over a 6-Month Horizon Assuming a Parallel Yield Curve Shift: Scenario Analysis

Yield change	Price plus coupon ($)			Total return (%)		
(in b.p.)	A	B	C	Bullet	Barbell	Difference[*]
−300	115.6407	141.0955	126.7343	53.47	55.79	−2.32
−250	113.4528	133.6753	122.4736	44.95	46.38	−1.43
−200	111.3157	126.8082	118.3960	36.79	37.55	−0.76
−150	109.2281	120.4477	114.4928	28.99	29.26	−0.27
−100	107.1888	114.5512	110.7559	21.51	21.47	0.05
−50	105.1965	109.0804	107.1775	14.35	14.13	0.22
−25	104.2176	106.4935	105.4453	10.89	10.63	0.26
0	103.2500	104.0000	103.7500	7.50	7.22	0.28
25	102.2935	101.5961	102.0907	4.18	3.92	0.27
50	101.3481	99.2780	100.4665	0.93	0.70	0.23
100	99.4896	94.8852	97.3203	−5.36	−5.45	0.09
150	97.6735	90.7949	94.3050	−11.39	−11.28	−0.11
200	95.8987	86.9830	91.4146	−17.17	−16.79	−0.38
250	94.1640	83.4271	88.6433	−22.71	−22.01	−0.70
300	92.4686	80.1070	85.9857	−28.03	−26.96	−1.06

* A positive sign indicates that the bullet portfolio outperformed the barbell portfolio; a negative sign indicates that the barbell portfolio outperformed the bullet portfolio.

Exhibit 3: Performance of Bullet and Barbell Treasury Portfolios Over a 6-Month Horizon Assuming a Flattening of the Yield Curve: Scenario Analysis

Yield change for C (in bp)	Price plus coupon ($)			Total return (%)		
	A	B	C	Bullet	Barbell	Difference[*]
−300	114.3218	145.8342	126.7343	53.47	58.98	−5.51
−250	112.1645	138.0579	122.4736	44.95	49.26	−4.31
−200	110.0573	130.8648	118.3960	36.79	40.15	−3.36
−150	107.9989	124.2057	114.4928	28.99	31.60	−2.62
−100	105.9879	118.0356	110.7559	21.51	23.58	−2.06
−50	104.0232	112.3139	107.1775	14.35	16.03	−1.67
−25	103.0578	109.6094	105.4453	10.89	12.42	−1.53
0	102.1036	107.0033	103.7500	7.50	8.92	−1.42
25	101.1603	104.4914	102.0907	4.18	5.53	−1.35
50	100.2279	102.0699	100.4665	0.93	2.23	−1.30
100	98.3949	97.4829	97.3203	−5.36	−4.09	−1.27
150	96.6037	93.2142	94.3050	−11.39	−10.06	−1.33
200	94.8531	89.2380	91.4146	−17.17	−15.70	−1.47
250	93.1421	85.5311	88.6433	−22.71	−21.04	−1.67
300	91.4697	82.0718	85.9857	−28.03	−26.11	−1.92

Assumptions:
Change in yield of security C results in a change in the yield of security A plus 30 basis points.
Change in yield of security C results in a change in the yield of security B minus 30 basis points.
* A positive sign indicates that the bullet portfolio outperformed the barbell portfolio; a negative sign indicates that the barbell portfolio outperformed the bullet portfolio.

Now let's look at what happens if the yield curve does not shift in a parallel fashion. The last columns of Exhibits 3 and 4 show the relative performance of the two Treasury portfolios for a nonparallel shift of the yield curve. Specifically, in Exhibit 3 it is assumed that if the yield on C (the intermediate-term security) changes by the amount shown in the first column, A (the short-term security) will change by the same amount plus 30 basis points, whereas B (the long-term security) will change by the same amount shown in the first column less 30 basis points. That is, the nonparallel shift assumed is a flattening of the yield curve. For this yield curve shift, the barbell will outperform the bullet for the yield changes assumed in the first column. While not shown in the exhibit, for changes greater than 300 basis points for C, the opposite would be true. In Exhibit 4, the nonparallel shift assumes that for a change in C's yield, the yield on A will change by the same amount less 30 basis points, whereas that on B will change by the same amount plus 30 basis points. That is, it assumes that the yield curve will steepen. In this case, the bullet portfolio would outperform the barbell portfolio for all but a change in yield greater than 250 basis points for C.

Exhibit 4: Performance of Bullet and Barbell Treasury Portfolios Over a 6-Month Horizon Assuming a Steepening of the Yield Curve: Scenario Analysis

Yield change	Price plus coupon ($)			Total return (%)		
for C (in bp)	A	B	C	Bullet	Barbell	Difference*
−300	116.9785	136.5743	126.7343	53.47	52.82	0.65
−250	114.7594	129.4918	122.4736	44.95	43.70	1.24
−200	112.5919	122.9339	118.3960	36.79	35.14	1.65
−150	110.4748	116.8567	114.4928	28.99	27.09	1.89
−100	108.4067	111.2200	110.7559	21.51	19.52	1.99
−50	106.3863	105.9874	107.1775	14.35	12.39	1.97
−25	105.3937	103.5122	105.4453	10.89	8.98	1.91
0	104.4125	101.1257	103.7500	7.50	5.66	1.84
25	103.4426	98.8243	102.0907	4.18	2.44	1.74
50	102.4839	96.6046	100.4665	0.93	−0.69	1.63
100	100.5995	92.3963	97.3203	−5.36	−6.70	1.34
150	98.7582	88.4758	94.3050	−11.39	−12.38	0.99
200	96.9587	84.8200	91.4146	−17.17	−17.77	0.60
250	95.2000	81.4080	88.6433	−22.71	−22.88	0.17
300	93.4812	78.2204	85.9857	−28.03	−27.73	−0.30

Assumptions:
Change in yield of security C results in a change in the yield of security A minus 30 basis points.
Change in yield of security C results in a change in the yield of security B plus 30 basis points.
* A positive sign indicates that the bullet portfolio outperformed the barbell portfolio; a negative sign indicates that the barbell portfolio outperformed the bullet portfolio.

The key point here is that looking at measures such as yield (yield-to-maturity or some type of portfolio yield measure), duration, or convexity tells us little about performance over some investment horizon because performance depends on the magnitude of the change in yields and how the yield curve shifts.

YIELD CURVE RESHAPING DURATIONS

It should be clear from our illustrations that neither the duration nor the convexity of a portfolio or position measures the exposure to yield curve risk. The sensitivity of a portfolio to changes in the shape of the yield curve can be approximated. In this section and the two that follow we describe three approaches to measuring yield curve risk.[2]

---

[2] Some vendors of analytical systems have developed proprietary models for measuring slope changes. See, for example, Wesley Phoa, "Dissecting Yield Curve Risk," in Frank J. Fabozzi (ed), *Managing Fixed Income Portfolios* (New Hope, PA: Frank J. Fabozzi Associates, 1997). The model described is the one developed by Capital Management Sciences.

The first approach looks at the sensitivity of a portfolio to a change in the slope of the yield curve. The first question is to define what is meant by the slope of the yield curve. There are several definitions that have been used to describe the slope of the yield curve. Some market participants define yield curve slope as the difference in the Treasury yield curve at two maturity levels. For instance, the yield curve slope can be defined as the difference between the yield on the 30-year on-the-run Treasury and the 2-year on-the-run Treasury.

The *yield curve reshaping duration* introduced by Klaffky, Ma, and Nozari focuses on three points on the yield curve: 2-year, 10-year and 30-year, and the spread between the 10-year and 2-year issues and the spread between the 30-year and 10-year issues.[3] The former spread is referred to as the short end of the yield curve, and the latter spread the long end of the yield curve. Klaffky, Ma and Nozari refer to the sensitivity of a portfolio to changes in the short end of the yield curve as *short-end duration* (SEDUR) and to changes in the long-end of the yield curve as *long-end duration* (LEDUR). These concepts, however, are applicable to other points on the yield curve.

To calculate the SEDUR of each security in the portfolio, the percentage change in the security's price is calculated for (1) a steepening of the yield curve at the short end by 50 basis points, and (2) a flattening of the yield curve at the short end of the yield curve by 50 basis points. Then the security's SEDUR is computed as follows:

$$\text{SEDUR} = \frac{V_s - V_f}{2V_0 \Delta y}$$

where

V_s = security's price if the short-end of the yield curve steepens by 50 basis points

V_f = security's price if the short-end of the yield curve flattens by 50 basis points

V_0 = security's current market price

To calculate the LEDUR, the same procedure is used for each security in the portfolio: calculate the price for (1) a flattening of the yield curve at the long end by 50 basis points, and (2) a steepening of the yield curve at the long end of the yield curve by 50 basis points. Then the security's LEDUR is computed in the following manner:

$$\text{LEDUR} = \frac{V_f - V_s}{2V_0 \Delta y}$$

The SEDUR and LEDUR are equivalent to the formula for calculating duration given in the previous chapter.

---

[3] Thomas E. Klaffky, Y.Y. Ma, and Ardavan Nozari, "Managing Yield Curve Exposure: Introducing Reshaping Durations," *Journal of Fixed Income* (December 1992), pp. 5-15

Exhibit 5: Bonds and Portfolios Used to Illustrate the Calculation of SEDUR and LEDUR

Security	Coupon rate (%)	Price ($)	Yield to maturity (%)	Maturity (years)
U	6.0	100	6.0	2
V	8.0	100	8.0	30
W	7.0	100	7.0	10

Portfolios

	Percentage of bond in portfolio	
Security	Portfolio 1	Portfolio 2
U	42.5	22.0
V	47.5	22.0
W	10.0	56.0

Dollar Duration and Convexity

	Dollar duration	Dollar convexity
Security U	1.85855	2.22220
Security V	11.31258	107.12569
Security W	7.10631	32.15018
Portfolio 1	6.87718	51.86454
Portfolio 2	6.87718	42.06064

We will use the three securities in Exhibit 5, securities U, V, and W, to demonstrate how to calculate SEDUR and LEDUR. From these three securities two portfolios are constructed as shown in the second panel of the exhibit. Portfolio 1 is concentrated in the 10-year maturity sector, while portfolio 2 is more heavily distributed in the 2-year and 30-year maturity sectors. Both portfolios, however, have the same dollar duration of 6.877182.

The SEDUR for the 2-year issue, U, is found by steepening the yield curve by 50 basis points and flattening it by 50 basis points. These values can be found by decreasing the yield on the 2-year by 50 basis points and increasing it by 50 basis points. The resulting values are V_s = 99.0763 and V_f = 100.9349. Using the formula for SEDUR:

$$\frac{100.9349 - 99.0763}{2(100)(0.005)} = 1.85860$$

The SEDUR for the 30-year issue is zero. Since the analysis proceeds from the shifting of the yield curve holding the 10-year yield constant, the SEDUR for the 10-year issue is zero.

Similarly, for the 2-year issue and the 10-year issue the LEDUR is zero. For the 30-year issue, the LEDUR is found by steepening the yield curve by 50 basis points and flattening it by 50 basis points. This means increasing and decreasing the yield on the 30-year issue by 50 basis points. The resulting values are V_s = 96.5259 and V_f = 103.6348. Using the formula for LEDUR:

$$\frac{103.6348 - 96.5259}{2(100)(0.005)} = 7.10899$$

The portfolio SEDUR and LEDUR are the weighted averages of the corresponding durations for each security in the portfolio. The SEDUR for the two portfolios is calculated as follows:

Portfolio 1: 0.425 (1.85860) + 0.475 (0) + 0.10 (0) = 0.789
Portfolio 2: 0.22 (1.85860) + 0.22 (0) + 0.56 (0) = 0.409

The LEDUR for the two portfolios is calculated as follows:

Portfolio 1: 0.425 (0) + 0.475 (0) + 0.10 (7.10889) = 0.711
Portfolio 2: 0.22 (0) + 0.22 (0) + 0.56 (7.10889) = 3.981

The various duration measures for the two portfolios are summarized below:

	Duration	SEDUR	LEDUR
Portfolio 1	6.88	0.789	0.711
Portfolio 2	6.88	0.409	3.981

These measures indicate that while both portfolios are exposed to the same risk for a small parallel shift in the level of interest rates, for a nonparallel shift, portfolio 1's exposure at the short end of the yield curve is about twice that of portfolio 2's. That is, if the short end of the yield curve shifted by 50 basis points, portfolio 1's value will change by 0.39% while portfolio 2's will change by about 0.20%. Portfolio 2's exposure to a shift in the long end of the yield curve, however, is considerably greater than portfolio 1's. A shift of 50 basis points at the long end will change portfolio 2's value by approximately 2% but portfolio 1's by about 0.36%. As emphasized earlier in the chapter, just focusing on duration would have masked the yield curve exposure.

So far, we have looked at only bonds with maturities at the three points on the yield curve that are used to define the short end and long end. The methodology can be generalized to other maturities as follows:

1. the shift in yields begins with the 10-year Treasury
2. at the short end, the steepening or flattening of the yield curve for any maturity other than two years is proportionate to the 10-year to 2-year spread.
3. at the long end, the steepening or widening for any security with a maturity greater than 10 years is assumed to be proportionate to the change in the 30-year to 10-year spread.

KEY RATE DURATIONS

The second approach to measure yield curve risk is to change the yield for a particular maturity of the yield curve and determine the sensitivity of a security or portfolio to this change holding all other yields constant. The sensitivity of the change in value to a particular change in yield is called *rate duration*. There is a rate duration for every point on the yield curve. Consequently, there is not one rate duration, but a vector of durations representing each maturity on the yield curve. The total change in value if all rates change by the same number of basis points is simply the duration of a security or portfolio to a change in the level of rates. That is, it is the measure of level risk for a parallel shift in the yield curve as discussed in the previous chapter.

This approach was first suggested by Donald Chambers and Willard Carleton in 1988[4] who called it "duration vectors." Robert Reitano suggested a similar approach in a series of papers and called the durations "partial durations."[5] The most popular version of this approach is that developed by Thomas Ho in 1992.[6]

Ho's approach focuses on 11 key maturities of the spot rate curve. The rate durations are called *key rate durations*. The specific maturities on the spot rate curve for which a key rate duration is measured are 3 months, 1 year, 2 years, 3 years, 5 years, 7 years, 10 years, 15 years, 20 years, 25 years, and 30 years. Changes in rates between any two key rates are calculated using a linear approximation.

The impact of any type of yield curve shift can be quantified using key rate durations. A level shift can be quantified by changing all key rates by the same number of basis points and determining based on the corresponding key rate durations the affect on the value of a portfolio. The impact of a steepening of the yield curve can be found by (1) decreasing the key rates at the short end of the yield curve and determining the change in the portfolio value using the corresponding key rate durations, and (2) increasing the key rates at the long end of the yield curve and determining the change in the portfolio value using the corresponding key rate durations.

The key rate durations are superior to the yield curve reshaping durations for assessing yield curve risk. To illustrate the key rate duration methodology, suppose that instead of a set of 11 key rates, there are only three key rates — 2 years, 16 years, and 30 years.[7] The effective duration of a zero-coupon security is the number of years to maturity. Thus, the three key rate durations are 2, 16, and 30. Consider the following two $100 portfolios comprised of 2-year, 16-year, and 30-year issues:

Portfolio	2-year issue	16-year issue	30-year issue
I	$50	$0	$50
II	$0	$100	$0

---

[4] Donald Chambers and Willard Carleton, "A Generalized Approach to Duration," *Research in Finance* 7(1988).

[5] See, for example, Robert R. Reitano, "Non-Parallel Yield Curve Shifts and Durational Leverage," *Journal of Portfolio Management* (Summer 1990), pp. 62-67, and "A Multivariate Approach to Duration Analysis," *ARCH* 2(1989).

[6] Thomas S.Y. Ho, "Key Rate Durations: Measure of Interest Rate Risk," *Journal of Fixed Income* (September 1992), pp. 29-44.

[7] This is the numerical example used by Ho (p. 33).

The key rate durations, denoted $D(i)$, for the three issues and the effective duration are as follows:

Issue	$D(1)$	$D(2)$	$D(3)$	Effective Duration
2-year	2	0	0	2
16-year	0	16	0	16
30-year	0	0	30	30

A portfolio's key rate duration is the weighted average of the security's in the portfolio. The key rate duration and the effective duration for each portfolio are calculated below:

Portfolio I
$D(1) = (50/100) \times 2 + (0/100) \times 0 + (50/100) \times 0 = 1$
$D(2) = (50/100) \times 0 + (0/100) \times 0 + (50/100) \times 0 = 0$
$D(3) = (50/100) \times 0 + (0/100) \times 0 + (50/100) \times 30 = 15$
Effective duration $= (50/100) \times 2 + (0/100) \times 16 + (50/100) \times 30 = 16$

Portfolio II
$D(1) = (0/100) \times 0 + (100/100) \times 0 + (0/100) \times 0 = 0$
$D(2) = (0/100) \times 0 + (100/100) \times 16 + (0/100) \times 0 = 16$
$D(3) = (0/100) \times 0 + (100/100) \times 0 + (0/100) \times 0 = 0$
Effective duration $= (0/100) \times 2 + (100/100) \times 16 + (0/100) \times 30 = 16$

Thus, the key rate durations differ for the two portfolios. However, the effective duration for each portfolio is the same. Despite the same effective duration, the performance of the two portfolios will not be the same for a nonparallel shift in the spot rates. Consider the following three scenarios:

Scenario 1: All spot rates shift down 10 basis points.
Scenario 2: The 2-year key rate shifts up 10 basis points and the 30-year rate shifts down 10 basis points.
Scenario 3: The 2-year key rate shifts down 10 basis points and the 30-year rate shifts up 10 basis points.

The return for the two portfolios for each of these scenarios is as follows:

Portfolio	Scenario 1	Scenario 2	Scenario 3
I	1.6	1.4	−1.4
II	1.6	0	0

Thus, only for the parallel yield curve shift (scenario 1) do the two portfolios have identical performance based on their effective durations.

Let's look at three actual Treasury portfolios to make the concept of key rate duration more concrete. Exhibit 6 shows three Treasury portfolios as of April 23, 1997. The first portfolio has 12 Treasury securities with approximately equal dollar amounts in each maturity. This portfolio is a ladder portfolio. The second portfolio is a barbell portfolio and the third a bullet portfolio. The effective duration for each Treasury portfolio is 4.7. Exhibit 6 shows the key rate durations for each security and the key rate durations for each portfolio. The key rate duration profile for each portfolio is graphed in Exhibit 7.

LEVEL, SLOPE, AND CURVATURE DURATION

Ram Willner has suggested another approach to yield curve risk measures.[8] The approach involves representing the yield curve by a mathematical function that is described in terms of level, slope, curvature, and location of the yield curve hump (i.e., the maximum point of curvature).[9] Given the estimated yield curve, exposure to changes in the parameters — level, slope, and curvature — can be calculated.

Mathematical Representation of the Yield Curve

The mathematical representation of the yield curve used by Willner is:[10]

$$Y = L + (S + C)\frac{(1 - e^{-M/H})}{M/H} - C(e^{-M/H})$$

where

Y = yield to maturity
H = constant associated with curve hump positioning
M = maturity of security (in years)
e = 2.71828

and L, S, and C are the parameters that must be estimated.

The properties of this yield curve function are as follows. First, as maturity increases, holding all other factors constant, the yield to maturity approaches L. The implication is that the estimated parameter L represents the long-run rate and therefore provides the level of the yield curve.

Second, as maturity decreases, the yield approaches $L + S$. Therefore, $L + S$ represents the short rate. It then follows that the spread between the long rate and short rate is $-S$ and for some constant long maturity, M, the slope of the yield curve is $-S/M$.

Third, for either very short-term maturities or very long-term maturities, the parameter C does not appear. It does appear for intermediate maturities. Therefore, the parameter C is represents the curvature of the yield curve over intermediate maturities.

---

[8] Ram Willner, "A New Tool for Portfolio Managers: Level, Slope, and Curvature Durations," *Journal of Fixed Income* (June 1996), pp. 48-59.

[9] In Chapter 11 a definition of curvature is provided based on three points on the yield curve.

[10] This mathematical representation was developed by Nelson and Siegel and is the solution to differential equations describing rational interest rate behavior. See, C. Nelson and A. Siegel, "Parsimonious Modeling of Yield Curves," *Journal of Business* 60 (1987).

Exhibit 6: Key Rate and Effective Durations for Three Treasury Portfolios (April 23, 1997): Ladder, Barbell, and Bullet

LADDER PORTFOLIO

Bond	Code	Cusip	Coupon	Maturity	Description	Size	3Mo	1yr	2yr	3yr	5yr	7yr	10yr	15yr	20yr	25Yr	30yr	Eff Dur
1	TB	912810EW	6.000	2/15/26	TB 2/26 6.000	4,057,595	0.02	0.06	0.12	0.26	0.47	0.73	1.33	1.69	1.57	1.45	4.60	12.31
2	TN	912827X4	6.375	3/31/01	TN 3/01 6.375	11,679,547	0.01	0.06	0.11	1.79	1.45	0.00	0.00	0.00	0.00	0.00	0.00	3.42
3	TB	912810ET	7.625	2/15/25	TB 2/25 7.625	11,124,914	0.01	0.06	0.12	0.27	0.49	0.76	1.38	1.76	1.62	2.32	2.81	11.63
4	TC	912810BR	8.500	5/15/99	TC 599 8.500	2,987,478	0.06	0.00	0.00	0.00	0.00	0.00	0.00	0.00	0.00	0.00	0.00	0.06
5	TB	912810BG	8.750	8/15/20	TB 8/20 8.750	5,348,333	0.02	0.06	0.12	0.28	0.50	0.78	1.42	1.81	2.80	2.74	0.00	10.56
6	TB	912810DS	10.625	8/15/15	TB 8/15 10.625	1,944,533	0.02	0.07	0.15	0.30	0.53	0.83	1.50	3.01	2.77	0.00	0.00	9.16
7	TC	912810CM	11.750	2/15/10	TC 2/10 11.750	7,323,250	0.02	0.08	0.15	0.36	0.62	3.10	1.03	0.01	0.01	0.00	0.00	5.36
8	TN	912810DL	12.500	8/15/14	TN 8/14 12.500	1,212,780	0.02	0.07	0.14	0.33	0.59	0.91	3.19	1.86	0.00	0.00	0.00	7.13
9	TN	91282QAQ	0.000	5/15/99	TN 599 0.000	37,154,780	0.00	0.66	0.86	0.00	0.00	0.00	0.00	0.00	0.00	0.00	0.00	1.52
10	TN	91282QAT	0.000	5/15/99	TN 5/99 0.000	10,840,357	0.00	1.54	0.00	0.70	0.00	0.00	0.00	0.00	0.00	0.00	0.00	2.24
11	TN	91282QBA	0.000	5/15/99	TN 5/99 0.000	8,472,702	0.00	0.00	0.00	1.84	2.09	0.00	0.00	0.00	0.00	0.00	0.00	3.93
Total Portfolio							0.01	0.25	0.49	0.50	0.49	0.50	0.50	0.50	0.50	0.50	0.50	4.75

BARBELL PORTFOLIO

Bond	Code	Cusip	Coupon	Maturity	Description	Size	3Mo	1yr	2yr	3yr	5yr	7yr	10yr	15yr	20yr	25Yr	30yr	Eff Dur
1	TN	9128272P	6.625	3/31/02	TN 3/02 6.625	86,528,320	0.02	0.06	0.12	0.34	3.60	0.00	0.00	0.00	0.00	0.00	0.00	4.14
2	TC	912810BR	8.500	5/15/99	TC 599 8.500	59,853,088	0.07	0.00	0.00	0.00	0.00	0.00	0.00	0.00	0.00	0.00	0.00	0.07
3	TB	912810DY	8.750	5/15/17	TB 5/17 8.750	63,761,372	0.01	0.06	0.12	0.28	0.50	0.78	1.41	1.80	4.69	0.06	0.00	9.73
Total Portfolio							0.03	0.04	0.08	0.22	1.49	0.25	0.46	0.59	1.53	0.02	0.00	4.71

BULLET PORTFOLIO

Bond	Code	Cusip	Coupon	Maturity	Description	Size	3Mo	1yr	2yr	3yr	5yr	7yr	10yr	15yr	20yr	25Yr	30yr	Eff Dur
1	TN	9128272H	5.875	2/15/00	TN 2/00 5.875	2,388,518	0.01	0.05	0.52	1.94	0.00	0.00	0.00	0.00	0.00	0.00	0.00	2.53
2	TN	912827V4	6.125	9/30/00	TN 9/00 6.125	3,949,212	0.01	0.05	0.11	2.26	0.61	0.00	0.00	0.00	0.00	0.00	0.00	3.04
3	TN	912827J	6.250	2/15/07	TN 2/07 6.250	26,670,642	0.02	0.06	0.11	0.25	0.45	1.00	5.20	0.00	0.00	0.00	0.00	7.08
4	TB	912810BQ	6.250	8/15/23	TB 8/23 6.250	7,015,242	0.01	0.06	0.12	0.27	0.48	0.74	1.34	1.71	1.58	3.99	1.51	11.82
5	TN	9128272J	7.125	9/30/99	TN 9/99 7.125	1,146,557	0.02	0.06	1.23	0.90	0.00	0.00	0.00	0.00	0.00	0.00	0.00	2.20
6	TB	912810BM	7.250	8/15/22	TB 8/22 7.250	1,059,479	0.02	0.06	0.12	0.27	0.49	0.76	1.37	1.75	1.62	4.51	0.32	11.30
7	TB	912810DX	7.500	11/15/16	TB 11/16 7.500	2,360,381	0.02	0.06	0.12	0.27	0.48	0.75	1.36	2.12	4.74	0.00	0.00	9.93
8	TC	912810BR	8.500	5/15/99	TC 599 8.500	33,761,656	0.06	0.00	0.00	0.00	0.00	0.00	0.00	0.00	0.00	0.00	0.00	0.06
9	TB	22655P9	8.750	11/15/08	TB 11/08 8.750	18,540,286	0.01	0.06	0.13	0.29	0.51	0.80	3.98	1.45	0.00	0.00	0.00	7.24
Total Portfolio							0.03	0.04	0.10	0.30	0.30	0.51	2.34	0.50	0.24	0.30	0.10	4.75

Source: Global Advanced Technology

Exhibit 7: Key Rate Duration Profile for Three Treasury Portfolios (April 23, 1997): Ladder, Barbell, and Bullet
(a) Ladder Portfolio

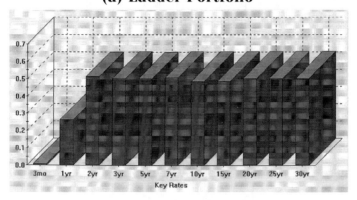

(b) Barbell Portfolio

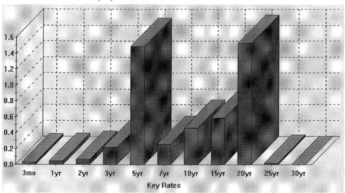

(c) Bullet Portfolio

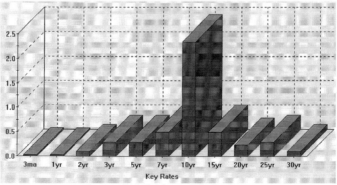

Source: Global Advanced Technology

To summarize:

- *L* represents the level of rates
- −*S* represents the spread between the long-term and short-term rates
- −*S/M* represents the slope of the yield curve
- *C* represents the curvature of the yield curve

KEY POINTS

1. *When using a portfolio's duration and convexity to measure the exposure to interest rates, it is assumed that the yield curve shifts in a parallel fashion.*

2. *For a nonparallel shift in the yield curve, duration and convexity do not provide adequate information about the risk exposure.*

3. *Exposure of a portfolio to a shift in the yield curve is called yield curve risk.*

4. *One method to measure yield curve risk is to calculate a portfolio's yield curve reshaping duration.*

5. *Yield curve reshaping duration decomposes the yield curve into a short end and a long end.*

6. *The sensitivity of a portfolio to changes in the short end of the yield curve is called short-end duration (SEDUR) and to changes in the long end of the yield curve is called long-end duration (LEDUR).*

7. *An alternative approach to measure yield curve risk is to change the yield for a particular maturity of the yield curve and determine the sensitivity of a security or portfolio to this change holding all other yields constant.*

8. *Key rate duration is the sensitivity of the change in a portfolio's value to a particular key rate.*

9. *The most popular version of key rate duration uses 11 key maturities of the spot rate curve (3 months, 1, 2, 3, 5, 7, 10, 15, 20, 25, and 30 years).*

10. *A third approach to measuring a portfolio's yield curve risk is by estimating the yield curve by a mathematical function that describes the yield curve in terms of level, slope, curvature, and location of the yield curve hump (i.e., the maximum point of curvature).*

11. *From the mathematical function, the exposure to a change in level, slope, curvature, and location of the hump can be determined, thereby summarizing the total price change in bond price.*

Chapter 8

MEASURING HISTORICAL YIELD VOLATILITY AND FORECASTING YIELD VOLATILITY

Investors are concerned with the volatility of Treasury yields. In this chapter we will look at historical volatility of Treasury yields and how to measure historical volatility. At the end of the chapter we will explain how to forecast yield volatility.

HISTORICAL VOLATILITY

A study by Ryan Labs, Inc. documented the history of interest rate volatility for the on-the-run Treasury issues since the inception of the auction for each maturity series through December 31, 1995. Exhibit 1 shows this history in terms of the basis point change in yield for the rolling 12-month periods for the 2-year and 30-year maturity series. Reported in the exhibit is the percentage of times that the number of basis points in the interval was observed. The auction of the 2-year maturity series began in August 1974 and there were 257 observations; for the 30-year maturity series which began in May 1973, there were 260 observations.

Exhibit 2 provides summary statistics regarding the historical basis point movements. Note that while the average basis point change of −7 and −3 basis points for the 2-year and 30-year, respectively, was small, this masks the volatility because of the averaging of significant upward and downward movements of yields. What is apparent from all the summary statistics reported is that interest rate volatility is greater for the 2-year yield than the 30-year yield. That is, interest rate volatility is greater at the short end of the yield curve. While not reported in the exhibit, this relationship holds for the 3-year, 5-year, and 10-year Treasury maturity series — that is, the longer the maturity, the lower the interest rate volatility. The maximum basis point change occurred consistently at high yield levels.

Exhibit 3 reports the history of interest rate volatility in terms of the percentage change in yield for the same period for the 2-year and 30-year issues. Exhibit 4 provides summary statistics. Again, the average change has little meaning and it can be seen that the longer maturity series exhibited less interest rate volatility than the shorter maturity series. The magnitude of the percentage change depends on the level of yields. It was found that the maximum percentage positive yield change occurred at low yield levels while the maximum percentage negative yield change occurred at high yield levels.

125

Exhibit 1: The History of 2-Year and 30-Year Treasury Interest Rate Volatility in Terms of Basis Point Changes
(Rolling 12-Month Periods from Inception of Auction to December 31, 1995)

Basis point change in yield	Percentage of time observed for	
	2-Year (257 obs)	30-Year (260 obs)
−550 to −500	0.8%	0.0%
−500 to −450	2.3	0.0
−450 to −400	1.2	0.8
−400 to −350	1.2	0.4
−350 to −300	1.6	3.5
−300 to −250	1.2	2.7
−250 to −200	7.0	2.7
−200 to −150	6.6	3.8
−150 to −100	9.3	5.8
−100 to −50	10.9	11.5
−50 to 0	12.1	17.7
0 to 50	7.0	13.5
50 to 100	8.2	18.1
100 to 150	8.6	7.3
150 to 200	8.9	4.6
200 to 250	5.8	3.5
250 to 300	3.1	1.9
300 to 350	1.2	2.3
350 to 400	0.0	0.0
400 to 450	0.4	0.0
450 to 500	1.2	0.0
500 to 650	1.6	0.0

Source: Ryan Labs, Inc.

Exhibit 2: Summary Statistics for The History of 2-Year and 30-Year Treasury Interest Rate Volatility in Terms of Basis Point Changes
(Rolling 12-Month Periods from Inception of Auction to December 31, 1995)

	2-Year	30-Year
Average change (bp)	−7.21	−2.82
One standard deviation (bp)	−209 to 194	−149 to 144
Two standard deviations (bp)	−411 to 396	−296 to 290
Maximum positive change (bp)	611	350
(beginning date - ending date)	7/80 - 7/81	9/80 - 9/81
(beginning yield - ending yield)	9.69% - 15.8%	11.69% - 15.18%
Maximum negative change (bp)	−546	−415
(beginning date - ending date)	9/81 - 9/82	3/85 - 3/86
(beginning yield - ending yield)	16.72% - 11.27%	11.63% - 7.48%

Source: Ryan Labs, Inc.

Exhibit 3: The History of 2-Year and 30-Year Treasury Interest Rate Volatility in Terms of Percentage Yield Changes
(Rolling 12-Month Periods from Inception of Auction to December 31, 1995)

Percentage change in yield	Percentage of time observed for	
	2-Year (257 obs)	30-Year (260 obs)
−40 to −35	1.17%	0.38%
−35 to −30	5.84	1.92
−30 to −25	7.78	1.15
−25 to −20	5.84	5.77
−20 to −15	7.00	5.00
−15 to −10	9.73	10.38
−10 to −5	7.39	9.23
−5 to 0	9.34	15.00
0 to 5	5.06	12.31
5 to 10	7.39	12.31
10 to 15	6.61	11.92
15 to 20	5.84	4.62
20 to 25	3.11	4.23
25 to 30	4.67	3.46
30 to 35	4.67	1.92
35 to 40	1.95	0.38
40 to 45	0.78	0.00
45 to 50	1.17	0.00
50 to 55	1.17	0.00
55 to 60	0.78	0.00
60 to 65	0.78	0.00
65 to 70	0.00	0.00
70 to 75	0.78	0.00
75 to 80	0.78	0.00
80 to 85	0.39	0.00

Source: Ryan Labs, Inc.

Exhibit 4: Summary of the History of 2-Year and 30-Year Treasury Interest Rate Volatility in Terms of Percentage Yield Changes
(Rolling 12-Month Periods from Inception of Auction to December 31, 1995)

	2-Year	30-Year
Average change (%)	1.72	0.70
One standard deviation (%)	−23 to 26	−14 to 15
Two standard deviations (%)	−47 to 51	−29 to 30
Maximum positive change (%)	81	37
(beginning date - ending date)	12/93 - 12/94	3/80 - 3/81
(beginning yield - ending yield)	4.25% - 7.69%	9.02% - 12.32%
Maximum negative change (%)	−37	−36
(beginning date - ending date)	9/91 - 9/92	3/85 - 3/86
(beginning yield - ending yield)	6.03% - 3.82%	11.63% - 7.48%

Source: Ryan Labs, Inc.

MEASURING HISTORICAL YIELD VOLATILITY

Market participants seek a measure of yield volatility. The measure used is the standard deviation or variance. In this section, we explain these statistical measures. In the next section we look at how to forecast Treasury yield volatility. We begin with some fundamental concepts from the theory of probability and statistics.

Probability Distributions and their Properties

A *random variable* is a variable for which a probability can be assigned to each possible value that can be taken by the variable. A *probability distribution* or *probability function* describes all the values that the random variable can take on and the probability associated with each.

Summary Measures of a Probability Distribution

Various measures are used to summarize the probability distribution of a random variable. The two most often used measures are the expected value and the variance (or standard deviation).

The *expected value* of a probability distribution is the weighted average of the distribution. The weights in this case are the probabilities associated with the random variable X. The expected value of a random variable is denoted by $E(X)$ and is computed as follows:

$$E(X) = P_1 X_1 + P_2 X_2 + ... + P_n X_n$$

where P_i is the probability associated with the outcome X_i.

One is interested not only in the expected value of a probability distribution but also in the dispersion of the random variable around the expected value. A measure of dispersion of the probability distribution is the *variance* of the distribution. The variance of a random variable X, denoted by $\text{var}(X)$, is computed using the following formula:

$$\text{var}(X) = [X_1 - E(X)]^2 P_1 + [X_2 - E(X)]^2 P_2 + ... + [X_n - E(X)]^2 P_n$$

Notice that the variance is simply a weighted average of the deviations of each possible outcome from the expected value, where the weight is the probability of an outcome occurring. The greater the variance, the greater the distribution of the possible outcomes for the random variable. The reason that the deviations from the expected value are squared is to avoid outcomes above and below the expected value from canceling each other out.

The problem with using the variance as a measure of dispersion is that it is in terms of squared units of the random variable. Consequently, the square root of the variance, called the *standard deviation*, is used as a better measure of the degree of dispersion. Mathematically this can be expressed as follows:

Exhibit 5: Normal Distribution

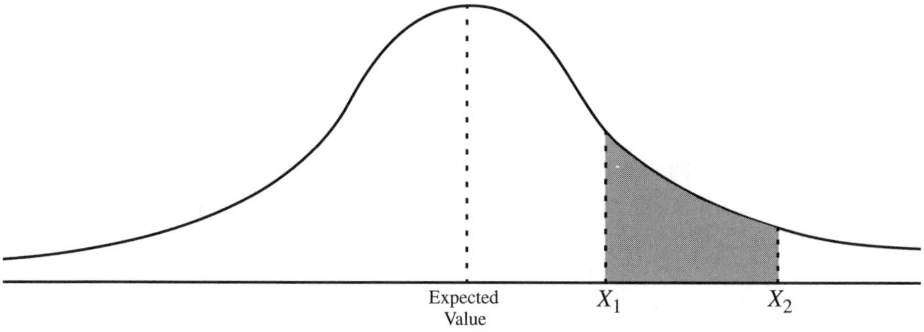

Probability of realizing a value between X_1 and X_2 is shaded area.

$$\text{std}(X) = \sqrt{\text{var}(X)}$$

where std(X) denotes the standard deviation of the random variable X.

Normal Distribution

A probability distribution can be classified according to the values that a random variable can realize. When the value of the random variable can only take on specific values, then the probability distribution is referred to as a *discrete probability distribution*. If, instead, the random variable can take on any possible value within the range of outcomes, then the probability distribution is said to a *continuous probability distribution*.

When a random variable is either the price, yield, or return on a financial asset, the distribution can be assumed to be a continuous probability distribution. This means that it is possible to obtain, for example, a yield of 7.92367% or 8.15432% and any value in between. In practice, we know that financial assets are not quoted in such a way.

In many applications involving probability distributions, it is assumed that the underlying probability distribution is a *normal distribution*. An example of a normal distribution is shown in Exhibit 5. A normal distribution is an example of a continuous probability distribution.

The area under the normal distribution or normal curve between any two points on the horizontal axis is the probability of obtaining a value between those two values. For example, the probability of realizing a value for the random variable X that is between X_1 and X_2 in Exhibit 5 is shown by the shaded area. The entire area under the normal curve is equal to 1 which means the sum of the probabilities is 1.

The normal distribution has the following properties:

Property 1. The point in the middle of the normal curve is the expected value for the distribution.

Property 2. The distribution is symmetric around the expected value. That is, half of the distribution is to the left of the expected value and the other half is to the right. Thus, the probability of obtaining a value less than the expected value is 50%. The probability of obtaining a value greater than the expected value is also 50%.

Property 3. The probability that the actual outcome will be within a range of one standard deviation above the expected value and one standard deviation below the expected value is 68.3%.

Property 4. The probability that the actual outcome will be within a range of two standard deviations above the expected value and two standard deviations below the expected value is 95.5%.

Property 5. The probability that the actual outcome will be within a range of three standard deviations above the expected value and three standard deviations below the expected value is 99.7%.

Calculating Standard Deviation from Historical Data

Above we provided the formula for calculating the standard deviation and variance of a random variable given a discrete probability distribution. The variance of a random variable using historical data is calculated using the following formula:

$$\text{Variance} = \sum_{t=1}^{T} \frac{(X_t - \bar{X})^2}{T-1} \tag{1}$$

and then

$$\text{Standard deviation} = \sqrt{\text{Variance}}$$

where

X_t = observation t on variable X
$\bar{X}$ = the sample mean for variable X
T = the number of observations in the sample

Our focus is on yield volatility. More specifically, we are interested in the percentage change in daily yields. So, X_t will denote the percentage change in yield from day t and the prior day, $t-1$. If we let y_t denote the yield on day t and y_{t-1} denote the yield on day $t-1$, then X_t which is the natural logarithm of percentage change in yield between two days, can be expressed as:

$$X_t = 100[\text{Ln}(y_t/y_{t-1})]$$

For example, on 10/18/95 the Treasury 30-year zero rate was 6.555% and on 10/19/95 it was 6.593%. Therefore, the natural logarithm of X for 10/19/95 is:

$$X = 100[\text{Ln}(6.593/6.555)] = 0.57804$$

To illustrate how to calculate a daily standard deviation from historical data, consider the data in Exhibit 6 which show the yield on Treasury 30-year zeros from 10/8/95 to 11/12/95 in the third column. From the 26 observations, 25 days of percentage yield changes are calculated in the fourth column. The fifth column shows the square of the deviations of the observations from the mean. The bottom of Exhibit 6 shows the calculation of the daily mean for the 25 observations, the variance, and the standard deviation. The daily standard deviation is 0.6360493%.

The daily standard deviation will vary depending on the 25 days selected. For example, the daily yields from 8/20/95 to 9/24/95 were used to generate 25 daily percentage yield changes. The computed daily standard deviation was 0.8452714%.

Exhibit 6: Calculation of Daily Standard Deviation Based on 25 Daily Observations for 30-Year Treasury Zeros (October 9, 1995 to November 12, 1995)

t	Date	y_t	$X_t = 100[Ln(y_t/y_{t-1})]$	$(X_t - \overline{X})^2$
0	08-Oct-95	6.694		
1	09-Oct-95	6.699	0.06720	0.02599
2	10-Oct-95	6.710	0.16407	0.06660
3	11-Oct-95	6.675	−0.52297	0.18401
4	12-Oct-95	6.555	−1.81411	2.95875
5	15-Oct-95	6.583	0.42625	0.27066
6	16-Oct-95	6.569	−0.21290	0.01413
7	17-Oct-95	6.583	0.21290	0.09419
8	18-Oct-95	6.555	−0.42625	0.11038
9	19-Oct-95	6.593	0.57804	0.45164
10	22-Oct-95	6.620	0.40869	0.25270
11	23-Oct-95	6.568	−0.78860	0.48246
12	24-Oct-95	6.575	0.10652	0.04021
13	25-Oct-95	6.646	1.07406	1.36438
14	26-Oct-95	6.607	−0.58855	0.24457
15	29-Oct-95	6.612	0.07565	0.02878
16	30-Oct-95	6.575	−0.56116	0.21823
17	31-Oct-95	6.552	−0.35042	0.06575
18	01-Nov-95	6.515	−0.56631	0.22307
19	02-Nov-95	6.533	0.27590	0.13684
20	05-Nov-95	6.543	0.15295	0.06099
21	06-Nov-95	6.559	0.24424	0.11441
22	07-Nov-95	6.500	−0.90360	0.65543
23	08-Nov-95	6.546	0.70520	0.63873
24	09-Nov-95	6.589	0.65474	0.56063
25	12-Nov-95	6.539	−0.76173	0.44586
		Total	−2.35025	9.7094094

Sample mean = $\overline{X} = \dfrac{-2.35025}{25} = -0.09401\%$

Variance = $\dfrac{9.7094094}{25 - 1} = 0.4045587$

Std = $\sqrt{0.4045587} = 0.6360493\%$

Exhibit 7: Comparison of Daily and Annual Volatility for a Different Number of Observations (Ending Date November 12, 1995) for Various Treasury Zeros

Number of observations	Daily standard deviation (%)	Annualized standard deviation (%)		
		250 days	260 days	365 days
Treasury 30-Year Zero				
683	0.4901505	7.75	7.90	9.36
60	0.6282858	9.93	10.13	12.00
25	0.6360493	10.06	10.26	12.15
10	0.6242041	9.87	10.06	11.93
Treasury 10-Year Zero				
683	0.7497844	11.86	12.09	14.32
60	0.7408469	11.71	11.95	14.15
25	0.7091771	11.21	11.44	13.55
10	0.7458877	11.79	12.03	14.25
Treasury 5-Year Zero				
683	1.0413025	16.46	16.79	19.89
60	0.8267317	13.07	13.33	15.79
25	0.7224093	11.42	11.65	13.80
10	0.8345784	13.20	13.46	15.94

Determining the Number of Observations

In our illustration, we used 25 observations for the daily percentage change in yield. The appropriate number depends on the situation at hand. For example, traders concerned with overnight positions might use the 10 most recent days (i.e., two weeks). A bond portfolio manager who is concerned with longer term volatility might use 25 days (about one month).

The selection of the number of observations can have a significant effect on the calculated daily standard deviation. This can be seen in Exhibit 7 which shows the daily standard deviation for the Treasury 30-year zero, Treasury 10-year zero, and Treasury 5-year zero for 60 days, 25 days, 10 days, and 683 days ending 11/12/95.

Annualizing the Standard Deviation

The daily standard deviation can be annualized by multiplying it by the square root of the number of days in a year.[1] That is,

$$\text{Daily standard deviation} \times \sqrt{\text{Number of days in a year}}$$

---

[1] For any probability distribution, it is important to assess whether the value of a random variable in one period is affected by the value that the random variable took on in a prior period. Casting this in terms of yield changes, it is important to know whether the yield today is affected by the yield in a prior period. The term *serial correlation* is used to describe the correlation between the yield in different periods. Annualizing the daily yield by multiplying the daily standard deviation by the square root of the number of days in a year assumes that serial correlation is not significant.

Exhibit 8: Comparison of Daily Standard Deviation Calculated for Two 25-Day Periods

Dates		Daily standard deviation(%)	Annualized standard deviation(%)		
From	To		250 days	260 days	365 days
Treasury 30-Year Zero					
10/8/95	11/12/95	0.6360493	10.06	10.26	12.15
8/20/95	9/24/95	0.8452714	13.36	13.63	16.15
Treasury 10-Year Zero					
10/8/95	11/12/95	0.7091771	11.21	11.44	13.55
8/20/95	9/24/95	0.9044855	14.30	14.58	17.28
Treasury 5-Year Zero					
10/8/95	11/12/95	0.7224093	11.42	11.65	13.80
8/20/95	9/24/95	0.8145416	12.88	13.13	15.56

Market practice varies with respect to the number of days in the year that should be used in the annualizing formula above. Typically, either 250 days, 260 days, or 365 days are used.

Thus, in calculating an annual standard deviation, the investor must decide on:

1. the number of daily observations to use
2. the number of days in the year to use to annualize the daily standard deviation.

Exhibit 7 shows the difference in the annual standard deviation for the daily standard deviation based on the different number of observations and using 250 days, 260 days, and 365 days to annualize. Exhibit 8 compares the 25-day annual standard deviation for two different time periods for the 30-year zero, 10-year zero, and 5-year zero.

Interpreting the Standard Deviation

What does it mean if the annual standard deviation for the 30-year zero is 12%. It means that if the prevailing yield is 8%, then the annual standard deviation is 96 basis points (12% times 8%).

Assuming that the yield volatility is approximately normally distributed, we can use the normal probability to construct an interval or range for what the future yield will be. For example, we know that there is a 68.3% probability that the yield will be between one standard deviation below and above the expected value. The expected value is the prevailing yield. If the annual standard deviation is 96 basis points and prevailing yield is 8%, then there is a 68.3% probability that the yield next year will be between 7.04% (8% minus 96 basis points) and 8.96% (8% plus 96 basis points). For three standard deviations below and above the prevailing yield, there is a 99.7% probability that the yield next year will be in this interval. Using the numbers above, three standard deviations is 288 basis points (3 times 96 basis points). The interval is then 5.22% (8% minus 288 basis points) and 10.88% (8% plus 288 basis points).

The interval or range constructed is called a *confidence interval*. Our first interval of 7.04%-8.96% is a 68.3% confidence interval. Our second interval of 5.22%-10.88% is a 99.7% confidence interval. A confidence interval with any probability can be constructed using a normal probability distribution table.

HISTORICAL VERSUS IMPLIED VOLATILITY

Market participants estimate yield volatility in one of two ways. The first way is by estimating historical yield volatility. This is the method that we have thus far described in this chapter. The resulting volatility is called *historical volatility*. The second way is to estimate yield volatility based on the observed prices of interest rate options. Yield volatility calculated using this approach is called *implied volatility*.

The implied volatility is based on some option pricing model. We discuss option pricing models in Chapter 14. One of the inputs to any option pricing model in which the underlying is a Treasury security or Treasury futures contract is expected yield volatility. If the observed price of an option is assumed to be the fair price and the option pricing model is assumed to be the model that would generate that fair price, then the implied yield volatility is the yield volatility that when used as an input into the option pricing model would produce the observed option price.

There are several problems with using implied volatility. First, it is assumed the option pricing model is correct. Second, option pricing models typically assume that volatility is constant over the life of the option. Therefore, interpreting an implied volatility becomes difficult.

FORECASTING YIELD VOLATILITY

As can be seen, the yield volatility as measured by the standard deviation can vary based on the time period selected and the number of observations. Now we turn to the issue of forecasting yield volatility. There are several methods. Before describing these methods, let's address the question of what mean should be used in the calculation of the forecasted standard deviation.

Suppose at the end of 10/24/95 a trader is interested in a forecast for volatility using the 10 most recent days of trading and updating that forecast at the end of each trading day. What mean value should be used?

The trader can calculate a 10-day moving average of the daily percentage yield change. Exhibit 6 shows the daily percentage change in yield for the Treasury 30-year zero from 10/9/95 to 11/12/95. To calculate a moving average of the daily percentage yield change on 10/24/95, the trader would use the 10 trading days from 10/11/95 to 10/24/95. At the end of 10/25/95, the trader will calculate the 10-day average by using the percentage yield change on 10/25/95 and would exclude the percentage yield change on 10/11/95. That is, the trader will use the 10 trading days from 10/12/95 to 10/25/95.

Exhibit 9 shows the 10-day moving average calculated from 10/24/95 to 11/12/95. Notice the considerable variation over this period. The 10-day moving average ranges from −0.20324% to 0.07902%. For the period from 4/15/93 to 11/12/95, the 10-day moving average ranged from −0.61705% to 0.60298%.

Rather than using a moving average, it is more appropriate to use an expectation of the average. It has been argued that it would be more appropriate to use a mean value of zero.[2] In that case, the variance as given by equation (1) simplifies to:

$$\text{Variance} = \sum_{t=1}^{T} \frac{X_t^2}{T-1} \qquad (2)$$

Now let's look at the various methods for forecasting daily volatility.

Exhibit 9: 10-Day Moving Daily Average for Treasury 30-Year Zero

10-Trading Days Ending	Daily Average (%)
24-Oct-95	−0.20324
25-Oct-95	−0.04354
26-Oct-95	0.07902
29-Oct-95	0.04396
30-Oct-95	0.00913
31-Oct-95	−0.04720
01-Nov-95	−0.06121
02-Nov-95	−0.09142
05-Nov-95	−0.11700
06-Nov-95	−0.01371
07-Nov-95	−0.11472
08-Nov-95	−0.15161
09-Nov-95	−0.02728
12-Nov-95	−0.11102

[2] Jacques Longerstacey and Peter Zangari, *Five Questions about RiskMetrics*[TM], JP Morgan Research Publication 1995.

Exhibit 10: Moving Daily Standard Deviation Based on 10-Days of Observations

10-Trading Days Ending	Daily Standard Deviation (%)
24-Oct-95	0.75667
25-Oct-95	0.81874
26-Oct-95	0.58579
29-Oct-95	0.56886
30-Oct-95	0.59461
31-Oct-95	0.60180
01-Nov-95	0.61450
02-Nov-95	0.59072
05-Nov-95	0.57705
06-Nov-95	0.52011
07-Nov-95	0.59998
08-Nov-95	0.53577
09-Nov-95	0.54424
12-Nov-95	0.60003

Equally-Weighted Average Method

The daily standard deviation given by equation (2) assigns an equal weight to all observations.[3] So, if a trader is calculating volatility based on the most recent 10 days of trading, each day is given a weight of 10%.

For example, suppose that a trader is interested in the daily volatility of the Treasury 30-year zero yield and decides to use the 10 most recent trading days. Exhibit 10 reports the 10-day volatility for various days using the data in Exhibit 6 and the formula for the variance given by equation (2). For the period 4/15/93 to 11/12/95, the 10-day volatility ranged from 0.16370% to 1.33006%.

Weighted Average Method

There is reason to suspect that market participants give greater weight to recent movements in yield or price when determining volatility. To give greater importance to more recent information, observations further in the past should be given less weight. This can be done by revising the variance as given by equation (2) as follows:

$$\text{Variance} = \sum_{t=1}^{T} \frac{W_t X_t^2}{T-1} \tag{3}$$

[3] In April 1995, the Basel Committee on Banking Supervision at the Bank for International Settlements proposed that volatility (as measured by the standard deviation) be calculated based on an equal weighting of daily historical observations using one year of observations. Moreover, the committee proposed that volatility estimates should be updated at least quarterly.

where W_t is the weight assigned to observation t such that the sum of the weights is equal to 1 (i.e., $\sum W_t = 1$) and the further the observation from today, the lower the weight.

The weights should be assigned so that the forecasted volatility reacts faster to a recent major market movement and declines gradually as we move away from any major market movement. One approach is to use an *exponential moving average.*[4] The formula for the weight W_t in an exponential moving average is:

$$W_t = (1 - \beta)\beta^t$$

where ß is a value between 0 and 1. The observations are arrayed so that the closest observation is $t = 1$, the second closest is $t = 2$, etc.

For example, if ß is 0.90, then the weight for the closest observation ($t = 1$) is:

$$W_1 = (1 - 0.90) (0.90)^1 = 0.09$$

For $t = 5$ and ß equal to 0.90, the weight is:

$$W_5 = (1 - 0.90) (0.90)^5 = 0.05905.$$

Exhibit 11 shows the weights that would be assigned to 76 observations for different values for ß. Notice that the smaller the value of ß, the lower the relative weight assigned to further observations. For example, for ß equal to 0.80, the weight assigned to the first observation is 16%. For the 16th observation, a weight of only 0.6% is assigned. In contrast, for ß equal to 0.95, the corresponding values for the first and 16th observations are 4.8% and 2.2%, respectively.

The parameter ß is measuring how quickly the information contained in past observations is "decaying" and hence is referred to as the "decay factor." The smaller the ß, the faster the decay. What decay factor to use depends on how fast the mean value for the random variable X changes over time. A random variable whose mean value changes slowly over time will have a decay factor close to 1. A discussion of how the decay factor should be selected is beyond the scope of this book.[5]

ARCH Method and Variants

A times series characteristic of financial assets suggests that a period of high volatility is followed by a period of high volatility. Furthermore, a period of relative stability in returns appears to be followed by a period that can be characterized in the same way. This suggests that volatility today may depend upon recent prior volatility. This can be modeled and used to forecast volatility.

---

[4] This approach is suggested by JP Morgan *RiskMetrics*[TM].
[5] A technical description is provided in *RiskMetrics*[TM]*—Technical Document*, pp. 77-79.

Exhibit 11: Weights for Exponential Weighted Moving Average for Various Values of ß

Observation	Assumed value for ß				
	0.99	0.95	0.90	0.85	0.80
1	0.00990	0.04750	0.09000	0.12750	0.16000
2	0.00980	0.04513	0.08100	0.10838	0.12800
3	0.00970	0.04287	0.07290	0.09212	0.10240
4	0.00961	0.04073	0.06561	0.07830	0.08192
5	0.00951	0.03869	0.05905	0.06656	0.06554
6	0.00941	0.03675	0.05314	0.05657	0.05243
7	0.00932	0.03492	0.04783	0.04809	0.04194
8	0.00923	0.03317	0.04305	0.04087	0.03355
9	0.00914	0.03151	0.03874	0.03474	0.02684
10	0.00904	0.02994	0.03487	0.02953	0.02147
11	0.00895	0.02844	0.03138	0.02510	0.01718
12	0.00886	0.02702	0.02824	0.02134	0.01374
13	0.00878	0.02567	0.02542	0.01814	0.01100
14	0.00869	0.02438	0.02288	0.01542	0.00880
15	0.00860	0.02316	0.02059	0.01310	0.00704
16	0.00851	0.02201	0.01853	0.01114	0.00563
17	0.00843	0.02091	0.01668	0.00947	0.00450
18	0.00835	0.01986	0.01501	0.00805	0.00360
19	0.00826	0.01887	0.01351	0.00684	0.00288
20	0.00818	0.01792	0.01216	0.00581	0.00231
21	0.00810	0.01703	0.01094	0.00494	0.00184
22	0.00802	0.01618	0.00985	0.00420	0.00148
23	0.00794	0.01537	0.00886	0.00357	0.00118
24	0.00786	0.01460	0.00798	0.00303	0.00094
...					
38	0.00683	0.00712	0.00182	0.00031	0.00004
39	0.00676	0.00676	0.00164	0.00027	0.00003
40	0.00669	0.00643	0.00148	0.00023	0.00003
41	0.00662	0.00610	0.00133	0.00019	0.00002
42	0.00656	0.00580	0.00120	0.00016	0.00002
43	0.00649	0.00551	0.00108	0.00014	0.00001
44	0.00643	0.00523	0.00097	0.00012	0.00001
...					
70	0.00495	0.00138	0.00006	0.00000	0.00000
71	0.00490	0.00131	0.00006	0.00000	0.00000
72	0.00485	0.00124	0.00005	0.00000	0.00000
73	0.00480	0.00118	0.00005	0.00000	0.00000
74	0.00475	0.00112	0.00004	0.00000	0.00000
75	0.00471	0.00107	0.00004	0.00000	0.00000
76	0.00466	0.00101	0.00003	0.00000	0.00000

The statistical model used to estimate this time series property of volatility is called an *auto*regressive *c*onditional *h*eteroscedasticity or ARCH model.[6] The term "conditional" means that the value of the variance depends on or is conditional on the value of the random variable. The term heteroscedasticity means that the variance is not equal for all values of the random variable.

The simplest ARCH model is

$$\sigma_t^2 = a + b(X_{t-1} - \overline{X})^2 \tag{4}$$

where

$$\sigma_t^2 \quad = \text{ variance on day } t$$
$$X_{t-1} - \overline{X} \quad = \text{ deviation from the mean on day } t-1$$

and a and b are parameters.

The parameters a and b must be estimated statistically. The statistical technique of regression analysis is used to estimate the parameters.

Equation (4) states that the estimate of the variance on day t depends on how much the observation on day $t-1$ deviates from the mean. Thus, the variance on day t is "conditional" on the deviation from day $t-1$. The reason for squaring the deviation is that it is the magnitude, not the direction of the deviation, that is important for forecasting volatility.[7] By using the deviation on day $t-1$, recent information (as measured by the deviation) is being considered when forecasting volatility.

The ARCH model can be generalized in two ways. First, information for days prior to $t-1$ can be included into the model by using the squared deviations for several prior days. For example, suppose that four prior days are used. Then equation (4) can be generalized to:

$$\sigma_t^2 = a + b_1(X_{t-1} - \overline{X})^2 + b_2(X_{t-2} - \overline{X})^2$$
$$+ b_3(X_{t-3} - \overline{X})^2 + b_4(X_{t-4} - \overline{X})^2 \tag{5}$$

where a, b_1, b_2, b_3, and b_4 are parameters to be estimated statistically.

A second way to generalize the ARCH model is to include not only squared deviations from prior days as a random variable that the variance is conditional on but also the estimated variance for prior days. For example, the following equation generalizes equation (4) for the case where the variance at time t is conditional on the deviation squared at time $t-1$ and the variance at time $t-1$:

$$\sigma_t^2 = a + b(X_{t-1} - \overline{X})^2 + c\sigma_{t-1}^2 \tag{6}$$

where a, b, and c are parameters to be estimated statistically.

---

[6] See Robert F. Engle, "Autoregressive Conditional Heteroskedasticity with Estimates of Variance of U.K. Inflation," *Econometrica* 50 (1982), pp. 987-1008.

[7] The variance for the unconditional variance (i.e., a variance that does not depend on the prior day's deviation) is $\sigma_t^2 = a/(1-b)$.

Suppose that the variance at time t is assumed to be conditional on four prior periods of squared deviations and three prior variances, then equation (4) can be generalized as follows:

$$\sigma_t^2 = a + b_1(X_{t-1} - \overline{X})^2 + b_2(X_{t-2} - \overline{X})^2 + b_3(X_{t-3} - \overline{X})^2$$

$$+ b_4(X_{t-4} - \overline{X})^2 + c_1\sigma_{t-1}^2 + c_2\sigma_{t-2}^2 + c_3\sigma_{t-3}^2 \qquad (7)$$

where the parameters to be estimated are a, the b_i's (i=1,2,3,4), and c_j's (j=1,2,3).

Equations (5), (6), and (7) are referred to as *generalized* ARCH or GARCH models. GARCH models are conventionally denoted as follows: GARCH(i,j) where i indicates the number of prior squared deviations included in the model and j the number of prior variances in the model. Equations (5), (6), and (7) would be denoted GARCH(4,0), GARCH(1,1), and GARCH(4,3), respectively.

There have been further extensions of ARCH models but these extensions are beyond the scope of this chapter.[8]

---

[8] For an excellent overview of these extensions as well as the GARCH models, see Robert F. Engle, "Statistical Models for Financial Volatility," *Financial Analysts Journal* (January-February 1993), pp. 72-78.

KEY POINTS

1. Interest rate volatility is greater at the short end of the yield curve than at the long end.

2. The magnitude of the percentage change in yield depends on the level of yields.

3. Historically, the maximum percentage positive yield change has occurred at low yield levels while the maximum percentage negative yield change has occurred at high yield levels.

4. A random variable is a variable for which a probability can be assigned to each possible value that can be taken by the variable.

5. A probability distribution describes all the values that the random variable can take on and the probability associated with each.

6. The expected value of a probability distribution is the weighted average of the probability distribution.

7. Variance is a measure of the dispersion of the random variable around its expected value.

8. The standard deviation is the square root of the variance and is a commonly used measure of volatility.

9. The greater the standard deviation, the greater the variability of the random variable around the expected value.

10. A normal distribution is a symmetric probability distribution and the area under the normal distribution or normal curve between any two points on the horizontal axis is the probability of obtaining a value between those two values.

11. Yield volatility can be estimated from daily yield observations.

12. The observation used in the calculation of the standard deviation is the natural logarithm of the percentage change in yield between two days.

13. The selection of the number of observations and the time period can have a significant effect on the calculated daily standard deviation.

14. A daily standard deviation is annualized by multiplying it by the square root of the number of days in a year.

15. Typically, either 250 days, 260 days, or 365 days are used to annualize the daily standard deviation.

16. *A confidence interval gives a range for possible values of a random variable and a probability associated with that range.*

17. *Implied volatility can also be used to estimate yield volatility based on some option pricing model.*

18. *In forecasting volatility, it is more appropriate to use an expectation of zero for the mean value.*

19. *The simplest method for forecasting volatility is weighting all observations equally.*

20. *A forecasted volatility can be obtained by assigning greater weight to more recent observations.*

21. *Generalized autoregressive conditional heteroscedasticity (GARCH) models can be used to capture the times series characteristic of yield volatility in which a period of high volatility is followed by a period of high volatility and a period of relative stability appears to be followed by a period that can be characterized in the same way.*

Chapter 9

REPURCHASE AGREEMENTS

There are strategies in which an investor borrows funds to purchase Treasury securities. The expectation of the investor is that the return earned by investing in the Treasury securities purchased with the borrowed funds will exceed the borrowing cost. There are several sources of funds available to an investor to borrow funds. When securities are to be purchased with the borrowed funds, the most common practice is to use the securities as collateral for the loan. In such instances, the transaction is referred to as a *collateralized loan*. In this chapter, we will look at one type of collateralized loan called a repurchase agreement. There are basically two parties in this transaction: the borrower of the funds and the lender of the funds. For the lender of the funds, a repurchase agreement represents an investment. For the borrower of funds, a repurchase agreement can be used to create leverage. We begin this chapter with a discussion of the advantages and disadvantages of leverage.

THE PRINCIPLE OF LEVERAGING

The investment principle of borrowing funds in the hope of earning a return in excess of the cost of funds is called *leveraging*. The attractive feature of leveraging is that it magnifies the return that will be realized from investment in a security for a given change in the price of that security. That's the good news. The bad news is that leveraging also magnifies any loss.

To illustrate this, consider an investor who wants to purchase a 30-year U.S. Treasury bond in anticipation of a decline in interest rates six months from now. Suppose that the investor has $1 million to invest. The $1 million is referred to as the investor's *equity*. Assuming that the coupon rate for the 30-year Treasury bond is 8% with the next coupon payment six months from now and the bond can be purchased at par value, then the investor can purchase $1 million of par value of an 8% coupon 30-year Treasury bond with the equity available.

Exhibit 1 shows the return that will be realized assuming various yields six months from now at which the 8% coupon 30-year Treasury bond will trade. The dollar return consists of the coupon payment six months from now and the change in the value of the 30-year Treasury bond. At the end of six months, the 30-year Treasury bond is a 29.5-year Treasury bond. The percent return is found by dividing the dollar return by the $1 million equity investment and then annualizing by simply multiplying by 2. Notice that the range for the annualized percent return based on the assumed yields six months from now ranges from −29.8% to +63.0%.

Exhibit 1: Annual Return from a $1 Million Investment in a 30-Year 8% Coupon Treasury Bond Held for Six Months

Assumed yield six months from now (%)	Price per $100 par value ($)	Price per $1 million par value ($)	Semiannual coupon payment ($)	Dollar return ($)	Annualized percent return* (%)
10.00	81.12	811,200	40,000	−148,800	−29.8
9.50	85.23	852,300	40,000	−107,700	−21.5
9.00	89.72	897,200	40,000	−62,800	−12.6
8.50	94.62	946,200	40,000	−13,800	−2.8
8.00	100.00	1,000,000	40,000	40,000	8.0
7.50	105.91	1,059,100	40,000	99,100	19.8
7.00	112.41	1,124,100	40,000	164,100	32.8
6.50	119.58	1,195,800	40,000	235,800	47.2
6.00	127.51	1,275,100	40,000	315,100	63.0

* Annualized by doubling semiannual return.

In our illustration, the investor did not borrow any funds. Hence, the strategy is referred to as an "unleveraged strategy." Now let's suppose that the investor can borrow $1 million to purchase an additional $1 million of par value of the 30-year 8% coupon Treasury bond. Assume further that the loan agreement specifies that: (1) the maturity of the loan is six months, (2) the annual interest rate is 9%, and (3) $2 million par value of the 30-year 8% coupon Treasury bond is used as collateral. Therefore, the loan is a collateralized loan. The collateral for this loan is the $2 million par value of the 30-year 8% Treasury bond purchased by the investor. The $2 million invested comes from the $1 million of equity and $1 million of borrowed funds. In this strategy, the investor is using leverage. Since the investor has the use of $2 million in proceeds and has equity of $1 million, this amount of leverage is said to be "2-to-1 leverage."

Exhibit 2 shows the annual percent return for this leveraged strategy assuming the same yields at the end of six months as in Exhibit 1. The return is measured relative to the $1 million equity investment made by the investor, not the $2 million. The dollar return on the $1 million of equity invested adjusts for the cost of the borrowing.

By using borrowed funds, the range for the annualized percent return is wider (−68.5% to +117.0%) than in the case where no funds are borrowed (−29.8% to 63.0%). This example clearly shows how leveraging is a two-edged sword — it can magnify returns both up and down. Notice that if the market yield does not change at the end of six months for the 30-year Treasury bond, then the unleveraged strategy would have generated an 8% annual return. In contrast, the 2-to-1 leveraging strategy would produce only a 7% annual return. The reason for this is that while the value of the 30-year Treasury bond did not change, it cost the investor $45,000 to borrow $1 million for six months but only earned coupon interest of $40,000 on the $1 million.

Exhibit 2: Annual Return from a $2 Million Investment in a 30-Year 8% Coupon Treasury Bond Held for Six Months Using $1 Million of Borrowed Funds

Assumed yield six months from now (%)	Price per $100 par value ($)	Price per $2 million par value ($)	Semiannual coupon payment ($)	Dollar return* ($)	Annualized percent return** (%)
10.00	81.12	1,622,400	80,000	−342,600	−68.5
9.50	85.23	1,704,600	80,000	−260,400	−52.1
9.00	89.72	1,794,400	80,000	−170,600	−34.1
8.50	94.62	1,892,400	80,000	−72,600	−14.5
8.00	100.00	2,000,000	80,000	35,000	7.0
7.50	105.91	2,118,200	80,000	153,200	30.6
7.00	112.41	2,248,200	80,000	283,200	56.6
6.50	119.58	2,391,600	80,000	426,600	85.3
6.00	127.51	2,550,200	80,000	585,200	117.0

* After deducting interest expense of $45,000 ($1 million × 9%/2).
** Annualized by doubling semiannual return.

Suppose that instead of borrowing $1 million, the investor can find a lender who is willing to lend for six months $11 million at an annual interest rate of 9%. The investor can now purchase $12 million of 30-year 8% coupon Treasury bonds —$1 million of equity and $11 million of borrowed funds. The lender requires that the entire $12 million of Treasury bonds be used as collateral for this loan. Since there is $12 million invested and $1 million of equity, this strategy is said to have "12-to-1 leverage."

Exhibit 3 shows the annual return assuming the same yields for the 30-year Treasury six months from now as in Exhibits 1 and 2. Notice the considerably wider range for the annual return for the 12-to-1 leverage strategy compared to the 2-to-1 leverage strategy and the unleveraged strategy. In the case where the yield remains at 8%, the 12-to-1 strategy results in an annual return of −3%.

Exhibit 4 shows the range for different degrees of leverage. The greater the leverage, the wider the range of potential outcomes, and therefore the greater the risk.

Let's look at this from the lender's perspective. The lender is exposed to the risk that the borrower will default. The lender seeks to protect against this risk by requiring that the borrower use the security purchased as collateral for the loan. Should the borrower default, the lender can sell the collateral and use the proceeds invested to pay off the borrower's debt obligation. In a collateralized loan, the risk is that the security's value will be less than the amount borrowed. In a collateralized loan, the lender can protect against this by requiring the frequent marking to market of the collateral. If the collateral's value falls below some level, the lending agreement can specify that additional collateral must be put up by the borrower in the form of cash or additional securities.

Exhibit 3: Annual Return from a $12 Million Investment in a 30-Year 8% Coupon Treasury Bond Held for Six Months Using $11 Million of Borrowed Funds

Assumed yield six months from now (%)	Price per $100 par value ($)	Price per $11 million par value ($)	Semiannual coupon payment ($)	Dollar return ($)*	Annualized percent return (%)**
10.00	81.12	9,734,400	480,000	−2,228,600	−456.1
9.50	85.23	10,227,600	480,000	−1,787,400	−357.5
9.00	89.72	10,766,400	480,000	−1,248,600	−249.7
8.50	94.62	11,354,400	480,000	−660,600	−132.1
8.00	100.00	12,000,000	480,000	−15,000	−3.0
7.50	105.91	12,709,200	480,000	694,200	138.8
7.00	112.41	13,489,200	480,000	1,474,200	294.8
6.50	119.58	14,349,600	480,000	2,334,600	466.9
6.00	127.51	15,301,200	480,000	3,286,200	657.2

* After deducting interest expense of $495,000 ($11 million × 9%/2).
** Annualized by doubling semiannual return.

Exhibit 4: Annual Return For Various Degrees of Leverage

Assumed yield six months from now (%)	Annual return for $1 million of equity and debt of $X million					
	$0	$1	$2	$4	$5	$11
10.00	−29.8%	−68.5%	−107.3%	−146.0%	−223.6%	−456.1%
9.50	−21.5	−52.1	−82.6	−113.2	174.2	−357.5
9.00	−12.6	−34.1	−55.7	−77.2	120.4	−249.7
8.50	−2.8	−14.5	−26.3	−38.0	61.6	−132.1
8.00	8.0	7.0	6.0	5.0	3.0	−3.0
7.50	19.8	30.6	41.5	52.3	73.9	138.8
7.00	32.8	56.6	80.5	104.3	151.9	294.8
6.50	47.2	85.3	123.5	161.6	238.0	466.9
6.00	63.0	117.0	171.1	225.1	333.1	657.2

TERMS OF A REPURCHASE AGREEMENT

A *repurchase agreement* is the sale of a security with a commitment by the seller to buy the same security back from the purchaser at a specified price at a designated future date. The price at which the seller must subsequently repurchase the security for is called the *repurchase price* and the date that the security must be repurchased is called the *repurchase date*. Basically, a repurchase agreement is a collateralized loan, where the collateral is the security sold and subsequently repurchased. The agreement is best explained with an illustration.

Suppose a government securities dealer has purchased $10 million of a particular Treasury security. Where does the dealer obtain the funds to finance that position? Of course, the dealer can finance the position with its own funds or by borrowing from a bank. Typically, however, the dealer uses the repurchase agreement or "repo" market to obtain financing. In the repo market the dealer can use the $10 million of the Treasury security as collateral for a loan. The term of the loan and the interest rate that the dealer agrees to pay are specified. The interest rate is called the *repo rate*. When the term of the loan is one day, it is called an *overnight repo;* a loan for more than one day is called a *term repo*. The transaction is referred to as a repurchase agreement because it calls for the sale of the security and its repurchase at a future date. Both the sale price and the purchase price are specified in the agreement. The difference between the purchase (repurchase) price and the sale price is the dollar interest cost of the loan.

Back to the dealer who needs to finance $10 million of a Treasury security that it purchased and plans to hold overnight. Suppose that a customer of the dealer has excess funds of $10 million. (The customer might be a municipality with tax receipts that it has just collected, and no immediate need to disburse the funds.) The dealer would agree to deliver ("sell") $10 million of the Treasury security to the customer for an amount determined by the repo rate and buy ("repurchase") the same Treasury security from the customer for $10 million the next day. Suppose that the overnight repo rate is 6.5%. Then, as will be explained below, the dealer would agree to deliver the Treasury securities for $9,998,194 and repurchase the same securities for $10 million the next day. The $1,806 difference between the "sale" price of $9,998,194 and the repurchase price of $10 million is the dollar interest on the financing.

The following formula is used to calculate the dollar interest on a repo transaction:

Dollar interest = (Dollar principal) × (Repo rate) × Repo term/360

Notice that the interest is computed on a 360-day basis. In our example, at a repo rate of 6.5% and a repo term of one day (overnight), the dollar interest is $1,806 as shown below:

$10,000,000 × 0.065 × 1/360 = $1,806

The advantage to the dealer of using the repo market for borrowing on a short-term basis is that the rate is lower than the cost of bank financing. (The reason for this is explained below.) From the customer's perspective, the repo market offers an attractive yield on a short-term secured transaction that is highly liquid.

While the example illustrates financing a dealer's long position in the repo market, dealers can also use the market to cover a short position. For example, suppose a government dealer sold $10 million of Treasury securities two weeks ago and must now cover the position — that is, deliver the securities. The dealer can do a *reverse repo* (agree to buy the securities and sell them back). Of course, the dealer eventually would have to buy the Treasury security in the market in order to cover its short position. In this case, the dealer is actually making a collateralized loan to its customer. The customer is then using the funds obtained from the collateralized loan to create leverage.

There is a good deal of Wall Street jargon describing repo transactions.[1] To understand it, remember that one party is lending money and accepting a security as collateral for the loan; the other party is borrowing money and providing collateral to borrow the money. When someone lends securities in order to receive cash (i.e., borrow money), that party is said to be "reversing out" securities. A party that lends money with the security as collateral is said to be "reversing in" securities. The expressions "to repo securities" and "to do repo" are also used. The former means that someone is going to finance securities using the security as collateral; the latter means that the party is going to invest in a repo. Finally, the expressions "selling collateral" and "buying collateral" are used to describe a party financing a security with a repo on the one hand, and lending on the basis of collateral, on the other.

Rather than using industry jargon, investment guidelines should be clear as to what a manager is permitted to do. For example, a client may have no objections to its money manager using a repo as a short-term investment — that is, the money manager may lend funds on a short-term basis. The investment guidelines will set forth how the loan arrangement should be structured to protect against credit risk. We'll discuss this below. However, if a client does not want a money manager to use the repo agreement as a vehicle for borrowing funds (thereby, creating leverage), it should state so.

Most participants in the United States use the Public Securities Association (PSA) Master Repurchase Agreement. Paragraphs 1 ("Applicability"), 2 ("Definitions"), 4 ("Margin Maintenance"), 8 ("Segregation of Purchased Securities"), 11 ("Events of Default"), and 19 ("Intent") of this agreement are reproduced in the appendix to this chapter.[2]

---

[1] The jargon relating to repo transactions gets even more confusing when we look at the use of this vehicle by the Federal Reserve. The Federal Reserve influences short-term interest rates through its open market operations — that is, by the outright purchase or sale of government securities. This is not the common practice followed by the Fed, however. It uses the repo market instead to implement monetary policy by purchasing or selling collateral. By buying collateral (i.e., lending funds), the Fed injects money into the financial markets, thereby exerting downward pressure on short-term interest rates. When the Fed buys collateral for its own account, this is called a *system repo*. The Fed also buys collateral on behalf of foreign central banks in repo transactions that are referred to as *customer repos*. It is primarily through system repos that the Fed attempts to influence short-term rates. By selling securities for its own account, the Fed drains money from the financial markets, thereby exerting upward pressure on short-term interest rates. This transaction is called a *matched sale*. Note the language that is used to describe the transactions of the Fed in the repo market. When the Fed lends funds based on collateral, we call it a system or customer repo, not a reverse repo. Borrowing funds using collateral is called a matched sale, not a repo. The terminology can be confusing, which is why we use the expressions "buying collateral" and "selling collateral" to describe what parties in the market are doing.

[2] In Europe, the PSA/ISMA Global Master Repurchase Agreement has become widely accepted. For more information, see the PSA's website, www.PSA.com.

In the agreement, Paragraph 1 refers to one party as the "Seller" and the other party as the "Buyer." The Seller is the party delivering the security or equivalently borrowing funds. The "Buyer" is the party lending funds. The agreement covers all repurchase transactions where a party is the lender of funds and the other party is the borrower of funds.

CREDIT RISKS

Despite the fact that there may be high-quality collateral underlying a repo transaction, both parties to the transaction are exposed to credit risk. Why does credit risk occur in a repo transaction? Consider our initial example where the dealer uses $10 million of government securities as collateral to borrow. If the dealer cannot repurchase the government securities, the customer may keep the collateral; if interest rates on government securities increase subsequent to the repo transaction, however, the market value of the government securities will decline, and the customer will own securities with a market value less than the amount it lent to the dealer. If the market value of the security rises instead, the dealer will be concerned with the return of the collateral, which then has a market value higher than the loan.

Repos should be carefully structured to reduce credit risk exposure. The amount lent should be less than the market value of the security used as collateral, thereby providing the lender with some cushion should the market value of the security decline. The amount by which the market value of the security used as collateral exceeds the value of the loan is called *repo margin* or simply margin. Margin is also referred to as the "haircut." Repo margin is generally between 1% and 3%. For borrowers of lower credit worthiness and/or when less liquid or more price sensitive securities are used as collateral, the repo margin can be 10% or more.

Another practice to limit credit risk is to mark the collateral to market on a regular basis. (Marking a position to market means recording the value of a position at its market value.) When market value changes by a certain percentage, the repo position is adjusted accordingly. The decline in market value below a specified amount will result in a *margin deficit*. Paragraph 4(a) of The PSA Master Repurchase Agreement (reproduced in the appendix) gives the "Seller" (the dealer in our example) the option to cure the margin deficit by either providing additional cash to the "Buyer" or by transferring "additional Securities reasonably acceptable to Buyer." Suppose instead that the market value rises above the amount required for margin. This results in a *margin excess*. In such instances, Paragraph 4(b) grants the "Buyer" the option to give the "Seller" cash equal to the amount of the margin excess or to transfer purchased securities to the "Seller."

Since the PSA Master Repurchase Agreement covers all transactions where a party is on one side of the transaction, the discussion of margin maintenance in Paragraph 4 is in terms of "the aggregate Market Value of all Purchased

Securities in which a particular party hereto is acting as Buyer" and "the aggregate Buyer's Margin Account for all such Transactions." Thus, maintenance margin is not looked at from an individual transaction or security perspective. However, Paragraph 4(e) permits the "Buyer" and "Seller" to agree to override this provision so as to apply the margin maintenance requirement to a single transaction.

The price to be used to mark positions to market is defined in Paragraph 2(h) — definition of "Market Value." The price is one "obtained from a generally recognized source agreed to by the parties or the most recent closing bid quotation from such a source." For complex securities that do not trade frequently, there is difficulty in obtaining a price at which to mark a position to market.

One concern in structuring a repo is delivery of the collateral to the lender. The most obvious procedure is for the borrower to deliver the collateral to the lender or to the cash lender's clearing agent. In such instances, the collateral is said to be "delivered out." At the end of the repo term, the lender returns the collateral to the borrower in exchange for the principal and interest payment. This procedure may be too expensive though, particularly for short-term repos, because of costs associated with delivering the collateral. The cost of delivery would be factored into the transaction through a lower repo rate. The risk of the lender not taking possession of the collateral is that the borrower may sell the security or use the same security as collateral for a repo with another party.

As an alternative to delivering out the collateral, the lender may agree to allow the borrower to hold the security in a segregated customer account. Of course, the lender still faces the risk that the borrower may use the collateral fraudulently by offering it as collateral for another repo transaction. If the borrower of the cash does not deliver out the collateral, but instead holds it, then the transaction is called a *hold-in-custody repo* (HIC repo). Despite the credit risk associated with a HIC repo, it is used in some transactions when the collateral is difficult to deliver (such as in whole loans) or the transaction amount is small and the lender of funds is comfortable with the reputation of the borrower of the cash.

Another method is for the borrower to deliver the collateral to the lender's custodial account at the borrower's clearing bank. The custodian then has possession of the collateral that it holds on behalf of the lender. This practice reduces the cost of delivery because it is merely a transfer within the borrower's clearing bank. If, for example, a dealer enters into an overnight repo with Customer A, the next day the collateral is transferred back to the dealer. The dealer can then enter into a repo with Customer B for, say, five days without having to redeliver the collateral. The clearing bank simply establishes a custodian account for Customer B and holds the collateral in that account. This specialized type of repo arrangement is called a *tri-party repo*.[3] Tri-party repos account for about half of all repo arrangements.

---

[3] The third-party agent may also be an international clearing house such as Euroclear.

The responsibilities of the third party are as follows. First, it is responsible for marking the collateral to market and reporting these values each day to the two parties. Second, if the borrower of funds wishes to substitute collateral, the third-party agent verifies that the collateral satisfies the requirements set forth in the agreement.

There are also *four-party repos*. The difference between a tri-party repo and a four-party repo is that there is a sub-custodian that is the custodian for the lender. This arrangement does not provide any additional protection to the lender. Rather, in the rare circumstances that it is used, it is because of legal requirements. For example, the investment guidelines might specify that in a repo the custodian must be a bank in a particular city. If the borrower of fund's custodian in a tri-party repo is not located in that city, a sub-custodian in the specified city must be used.

Paragraph 8 ("Segregation of Purchased Securities") of the PSA Master Repurchase Agreement deals with the possession of the collateral. There are special disclosure provisions when the "Seller" retains custody of the collateral.

Paragraph 11 ("Events of Default") sets forth the events that will trigger a default of one of the parties and the options available to the nondefaulting party. In the case of a bankruptcy by the borrower, the bankruptcy code in the United States affords the lender of funds in a qualified repo transaction a special status. It does so by exempting certain types of repos from the stay provisions of the bankruptcy law. This means that the lender of funds can immediately liquidate the collateral to obtain cash.[4] Paragraph 19 ("Intent") of the PSA Master Repurchase Agreement is included for this purpose.

PARTICIPANTS IN THE MARKET

Because it is used by Treasury dealers to finance positions and cover short positions, the repo market has evolved into one of the largest sectors of the money market. Financial and nonfinancial firms participate in the market as both sellers and buyers, depending on the circumstances they face. Thrifts and commercial banks are typically net sellers of collateral (i.e., net borrowers of funds); money market funds, bank trust departments, municipalities, and corporations are typically net buyers of collateral (i.e., providers of funds).

While a dealer firm uses the repo market as the primary means for financing its inventory of Treasury securities and covering short Treasury positions, it will also use the repo market to run a "matched book" where it takes on repos and

---

[4] The bankruptcy provisions differ for financial and nonfinancial institutions. If the defaulting party is a broker/dealer, the Securities Investors Protection Act (SIPA) governs. In the case of a bankruptcy, the Securities Investors Protection Corporation (SIPC) becomes the trustee. The SPIC then has the power to set aside transfers from the defaulting broker/dealer's assets to the nondefaulting party. Thus, there is not the same protection afforded under the bankruptcy code to a nondefaulting party when the defaulting party is a broker/dealer. When the defaulting party is a federally insured financial institution, the FDIC Act governs. With respect to repos, the provisions are similar to those in the bankruptcy code.

reverse repos with the same maturity. The firm does so to capture the spread at which it enters into the repo agreement (i.e., arrangement to borrow funds) and reverse repo agreement (i.e., arrangement to lend funds). For example, suppose that a dealer enters into a term repo of ten days with a money market fund and a reverse repo rate with a thrift for ten days, for which the collateral is identical. This means that the dealer is borrowing funds from the money market fund and lending money to the thrift. If the repo rate on the repo is 7.5% and the repo rate on the reverse repo is 7.55%, the dealer is borrowing at 7.5% and lending at 7.55%, locking in a spread of 0.05% (five basis points).

Another participant is the repo broker. To understand the role of the repo broker, suppose that a dealer has shorted $50 million of a security. It will then survey its regular customers to determine if it can borrow, via a reverse repo, the security it shorted. Suppose that it cannot find a customer willing to do a repo transaction (repo from the customer's point of view, reverse repo from the dealer's). At that point, the dealer will use the services of a repo broker.

DETERMINANTS OF THE REPO RATE

There is not one repo rate. The rate varies from transaction to transaction depending on a variety of factors: quality of collateral, term of the repo, delivery requirement, availability of collateral, and the prevailing federal funds rate.

The higher the credit quality and liquidity of the collateral, the lower the repo rate. The effect of the term of the repo on the rate depends on the shape of the yield curve. As noted earlier, if delivery of the collateral to the lender is required, the repo rate will be lower. If the collateral can be deposited with the bank of the borrower, a higher repo rate is paid.

The more difficult it is to obtain the collateral, the lower the repo rate. To understand why this is so, remember that the borrower (or equivalently the seller of the collateral) has a security that lenders of cash want, for whatever reason. Such collateral is referred to as *hot* or *special collateral*. (Collateral that does not have this characteristic is referred to as *general collateral*.) The party that needs the hot collateral will be willing to lend funds at a lower repo rate in order to obtain the collateral.

While these factors determine the repo rate on a particular transaction, the federal funds rate determines the general level of repo rates. The repo rate generally will be a rate lower than the federal funds rate, because a repo involves collateralized borrowing, while a federal funds transaction is unsecured borrowing.

Transparency in the repo market is increasing. GovPX recently developed a repo index that provides repo rates weighted by volume from on-the-run Treasuries and general collateral. The repo rates are from the interdealer market. In 1995, CS First Boston introduced an interactive system for the electronic pricing and trading of repos. The system, RepoTrade, tracks general collateral and special issue rates. Moreover, it allows on-line execution.

Special Repo Rates

The sector of the repo market that gets the most play is the on-the-run Treasury coupon securities sector. Often, these securities trade on special when there is exceptional demand from the dealer community to borrow them to cover short positions. The on-the-run 5-year and 10-year Treasury notes are sectors of the market most often on special.[5]

Two studies have examined the pattern of special repo rates for on-the-run Treasury securities. Darrell Duffie looked at special repo rates from 1988-1992[6] and Frank Keane of the Federal Reserve Bank of New York investigated the period June 1992-January 1995.[7] Both researchers found a regular pattern in the repo rates as the Treasury auction cycle progresses. Here we summarize the findings of the Keane study because it covers a more recent period.

As noted earlier, the repo rate for special or "hot" collateral is less than that for general collateral. The spread between the general overnight repo rate and the special overnight repo rate is a measure of the degree of "specialness." Keane investigated this specialness spread over the Treasury auction cycle for new Treasury notes (2-, 3-, 5-, and 10-year notes). The motivation for focusing on the on-the-run notes is that the bulk of trading and hedging occur with these issues.

For a note with a given maturity, an auction cycle for the purposes of the study was defined as the number of business days from the date of issuance of a note to the date of issuance of a new note with the same maturity. Exhibits 5 and 6 show the average specialness spread for each day of the auction cycles for the notes issued monthly (2-year and 5-year notes) and the notes issued quarterly (3-year and 10-year notes), respectively.

The results reported in these two exhibits suggest that for all newly issued notes the average specialness spread increases up to the announcement days for the next issue to be auctioned (the shaded area in the exhibits). Then the average specialness decreases. The reason for this pattern is that the proportion of the issue available to the repo market declines over the cycle as more of the issue is tied up in investment portfolios. Hence, with reduced supply, the average specialness spread increases. Once the next issue to be auctioned is announced, trading in that issue increases because of the expected greater supply, causing the average specialness spread to decline for the current issue.

Keane also looked at the costs associated with using the repo market to cover a short position when the security is on special. Recall that a dealer using the repo market to acquire collateral earns the repo rate. An issue on special has a lower repo rate than the repo rate for general collateral. Consequently, the specialness spread is effectively a cost associated with covering a short position. That is, because the dealer earns a below market rate for providing financing, this is a cost of covering the short position.

---

[5] Bloomberg Financial Markets provides information on issues on special. [Type NI RP<Go>]

[6] Darrell Duffie, "Special Repo Rates," *Journal of Finance* (June 1996), pp. 493-526.

[7] Frank Keane, "Repo Rate Patterns for New Treasury Notes," *Current Issues in Economics and Finance* published by the Federal Reserve Bank of New York (September 1996).

Exhibit 5: Average Spread Between General and Special Repo Rates for 2-Year and 5-Year On-the-Run Treasury Notes Over Auction Cycle: June 12, 1992-January 25, 1995

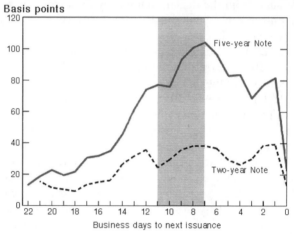

Note: The spread is called the "specialness spread." The spread is calculated using overnight rates for the period. The monthly auction cycle extends from one issue date to the next. The shaded area indicates announcement days for the next issue.

Source: Frank Keane, "Repo Rate Patterns for New Treasury Notes," *Current Issues in Economics and Finance* published by the Federal Reserve Bank of New York (September 1996), Chart 1, p. 3.

Exhibit 6: Average Spread Between General and Special Repo Rates for 3-Year and 10-Year On-the-Run Treasury Notes Over Auction Cycle: June 12, 1992-January 25, 1995

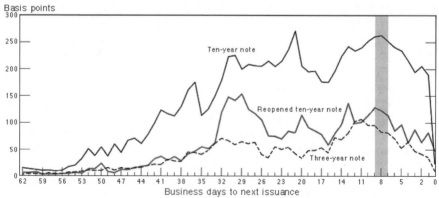

Note: The spread is called the "specialness spread." The spread is calculated using overnight rates for the period. The quarterly auction cycle extends from one issue date to the next. The shaded area indicates announcement days for the next issue.

Source: Frank Keane, "Repo Rate Patterns for New Treasury Notes," *Current Issues in Economics and Finance* published by the Federal Reserve Bank of New York (September 1996), Chart 2, p. 3.

Exhibit 7: Potential Specialness Costs for New Treasury Notes, Adjusted to Typical Holding Periods (Basis Points)

Average Specialness	Holding Periods			
Spread	Overnight	7 Days	30 Days	90 Days
25	0.1	0.5	2.1	6.3
50	0.1	1.0	4.2	12.5
100	0.3	1.9	8.3	25.0
200	0.6	3.9	16.7	50.0
400	1.1	7.8	33.3	100.0

Note: Keane converted annual repo spreads to an overnight holding period by dividing the specialness spread by 360. For longer terms, Keane used the repo market convention of multiplying rather compounding to convert the annual specialness spread. The marginal cost of repo specialness is the adjusted amounts multiplied by the dollar value of the repo loan.

Source: Frank Keane, "Repo Rate Patterns for New Treasury Notes," *Current Issues in Economics and Finance* published by the Federal Reserve Bank of New York (September 1996), Table 1, p. 4.

Keane converted the specialness spread into a "specialness cost" for typical holding periods. This is shown in Exhibit 7. For example, a 200 basis point annualized specialness spread translates into a 50 basis point cost for a 90 days repo period. A spread of 400 basis points only adds 1 basis point to a cost of covering an overnight short position.

Exhibit 8 reports for each note the observed specialness spread and the cumulative average specialness cost over the auction cycle and the cost per month. The costs are even less than that reported in Exhibit 7. This is because the costs are sometimes offset by the fact the on-the-run issue trades at a slight premium due to the demand for the issue. A dealer who uses the repo market for covering a short position can capture the premium by shorting the on-the-run note early in the auction cycle when it is trading at a premium and buying it in the market after the next issue to be auctioned is announced and the demand for the issue has declined.

The specialness cost is a cost of using the repo market to hedge a position. To place this cost in the proper perspective, it can be compared to the cost of not hedging a position. This is measured by the potential price volatility that a dealer is exposed to by not hedging. Exhibit 8 shows the average daily and weekly price exposure for each new issue in the second quarter of 1994. The time period used is one in which there was significant price volatility. As can be seen, the daily and weekly price exposures far exceed the average monthly specialness cost.

HOT (SPECIAL) COLLATERAL AND ARBITRAGE

Earlier in this chapter, we explained how an investor can use collateralized borrowing to create a leveraged Treasury position and we explained the risk associated with such a position. In certain circumstances a borrower of funds via a repo transaction can generate an *arbitrage opportunity*. This occurs when it is possible to borrow funds at a lower rate than the rate that can be earned by reinvesting those funds.

Exhibit 8: Observed Specialness Spread, Specialness Costs, and Unhedged Price Risk Exposure for New Treasury Notes (Basis Points)

Issue	Average Specialness Spread	Specialness Cost		Price Exposure*	
		Cumulative Over Cycle	Per Month	Daily	Weekly
2-year	27	2	2	28	69
3-year	41	10	3	42	99
5-year	58	5	5	72	154
10-year	143	35	12	117	241
10-year, reopened	62	15	5	117	241

* Based on data from the second quarter 1994 and assumes confidence intervals of two standard deviations.
Source: Adapted from Tables 2 and 3 of Frank Keane, "Repo Rate Patterns for New Treasury Notes," *Current Issues in Economics and Finance* published by the Federal Reserve Bank of New York (September 1996).

Such opportunities arise when a portfolio includes securities that are hot or special and the manager can reinvest at a rate higher than the repo rate. For example, suppose that a manager has hot collateral in a portfolio, Bond X, that lenders of funds are willing to take as collateral for two weeks charging a repo rate of 3%. Suppose further that the manager can invest the funds in a 2-week Treasury bill (the maturity date being the same as the term of the repo) and earn 4%. Assuming that the repo is properly structured so that there is no credit risk, then the manager has locked in a spread of 1% for two weeks. This is a pure arbitrage. The manager faces no risk. Of course, the manager is exposed to the risk that Bond X would decline in value, but this risk would exist as long as the manager intended to hold that security in the portfolio anyway.

APPENDIX:
SELECTED PARAGRAPHS FROM THE PUBLIC SECURITIES
ASSOCIATION MASTER REPURCHASE AGREEMENT

1. **Applicability**

From time to time the parties hereto may enter into transactions in which one party ("Seller") agrees to transfer to the other ("Buyer") securities or financial instruments ("Securities") against the transfer of funds by Buyer, with a simultaneous agreement by Buyer to transfer to Seller such Securities at a date certain or on demand, against the transfer of funds by Seller. Each such transaction shall be referred to herein as a "Transaction" and shall be governed by this Agreement, including any supplemental terms or conditions contained in Annex I hereto, unless otherwise agreed in writing.

2. **Definitions**

(a) "Act of Insolvency", with respect to any party, (i) the commencement by such party as debtor of any case or proceeding under any bankruptcy, insolvency, reorganization, liquidation, dissolution or similar law, or such party seeking the appointment of a receiver, trustee, custodian or similar official for such party or any substantial part of its property, or (ii) the commencement of any such case or proceeding against such party, or another seeking such an appointment, or the filing against a party of an application for a protective decree under the provisions of the Securities Investor Protection Act of 1970, which (A) is consented to or not timely contested by such party, (B) results in the entry of an order for relief, such an appointment, the issuance of such a protective decree or the entry of an order having a similar effect, or (C) is not dismissed within 15 days, (iii) the making by a party of a general assignment for the benefit of creditors, or (iv) the admission in writing by a party of such party's inability to pay such party's debts as they become due;

(b) "Additional Purchased Securities", Securities provided by Seller to Buyer pursuant to Paragraph 4(a) hereof;

(c) "Buyer's Margin Amount", with respect to any Transaction as of any date, the amount obtained by application of a percentage (which may be equal to the percentage that is agreed to as the Seller's Margin Amount under subparagraph (q) of this Paragraph), agreed to by Buyer and Seller prior to entering into the Transaction, to the Repurchase Price for such Transaction as of such date;

(d) "Confirmation", the meaning specified in Paragraph 3(b) hereof;

(e) "Income", with respect to any Security at any time, any principal thereof then payable and all interest, dividends or other distributions thereon;

(f) "Margin Deficit", the meaning specified in Paragraph 4(a) hereof;

(g) "Margin Excess", the meaning specified in Paragraph 4(b) hereof;

(h) "Market Value", with respect to any Securities as of any date, the price for such Securities on such date obtained from a generally recognized source agreed to by the parties or the most recent closing bid quotation from such a source, plus accrued Income to the extent not included therein (other than any Income credited or transferred to, or applied to the obligations of, Seller pursuant to Paragraph 5 hereof) as of such date (unless contrary to market practice for such Securities);

(i) "Price Differential", with respect to any Transaction hereunder as of any date, the aggregate amount obtained by daily application of the Pricing Rate for such Transaction to the Purchase Price for such Transaction on a 360 day per year basis for the actual number of days during the period commencing on (and including) the Purchase Date for such Transaction and ending on (but excluding) the date of determination (reduced by any amount of such Price Differential previously paid by Seller to Buyer with respect to such Transaction);

(j) "Pricing Rate", the per annum percentage rate for determination of the Price Differential;

(k) "Prime Rate", the prime rate of U.S. money center commercial banks as published in *The Wall Street Journal;*

(l)"Purchase Date", the date on which Purchased Securities are transferred by Seller to Buyer;

(m) "Purchase Price", (i) on the Purchase Date, the price at which Purchased Securities are transferred by Seller to Buyer, and (ii) thereafter, such price increased by the amount of any cash transferred by Buyer to Seller pursuant to Paragraph 4(b) hereof and decreased by the amount of any cash transferred by Seller to Buyer pursuant to Paragraph 4(a) hereof or applied to reduce Seller's obligations under clause (ii) of Paragraph 5 hereof;

(n) "Purchased Securities", the Securities transferred by Seller to Buyer in a Transaction hereunder, and any Securities substituted therefor in accordance with Paragraph 9 hereof. The term "Purchased Securities" with respect to any Transaction at any time also shall include Additional Purchased Securities delivered pursuant to Paragraph 4(a) and shall exclude Securities returned pursuant to Paragraph 4(b);

(o) "Repurchase Date", the date on which Seller is to repurchase the Purchased Securities from Buyer, including any date determined by application of the provisions of Paragraphs 3(c) or 11 hereof;

(p) "Repurchase Price", the price at which Purchased Securities are to be transferred from Buyer to Seller upon termination of a Transaction, which will be determined in each case (including Transactions terminable upon demand) as the sum of the Purchase Price and the Price Differential as of the date of such determination, increased by any amount determined by the application of the provisions of Paragraph 11 hereof;

(q) "Seller's Margin Amount", with respect to any Transaction as of any date, the amount obtained by application of a percentage (which may be equal to the percentage that is agreed to as the Buyer's Margin Amount under subparagraph (c) of this Paragraph), agreed to by Buyer and Seller prior to entering into the Transaction, to the Repurchase Price for such Transaction as of such date.

4. Margin Maintenance

(a) If at any time the aggregate Market Value of all Purchased Securities subject to all Transactions in which a particular party hereto is acting as Buyer is less than the aggregate Buyer's Margin Amount for all such Transactions (a "Margin Deficit"), then Buyer may by notice to Seller require Seller in such Transactions, at Seller's option, to transfer to Buyer cash or additional Securities reasonably acceptable to Buyer ("Additional Purchased Securities"), so that the cash and aggregate Market Value of the Purchased Securities, including any such Additional Purchased Securities, will thereupon equal or exceed such aggregate Buyer's Margin Amount (decreased by the amount of any Margin Deficit as of such date arising from any Transactions in which such Buyer is acting as Seller).

(b) If at any time the aggregate Market Value of all Purchased Securities subject to all Transactions in which a particular party hereto is acting as Seller exceeds the aggregate Seller's Margin Amount for all such Transactions, at such time (a "Margin Excess"), then Seller may by notice to Buyer require Buyer in such Transactions, at Buyer's option, to transfer cash or Purchased Securities to Seller, so that the aggregate Market Value of the Purchased Securities, after deduction of any such cash or any Purchased Securities so transferred, will thereupon not exceed such aggregate Seller's Margin Amount (increased by the amount of any Margin Excess as of such date arising from any Transactions in which such Seller is acting as Buyer).

(c) Any cash transferred pursuant to this Paragraph shall be attributed to such Transactions as shall be agreed upon by Buyer and Seller.

(d) Seller and Buyer may agree, with respect to any or all Transactions hereunder, that the respective rights of Buyer or Seller (or both) under subparagraphs (a) and (b) of this Paragraph may be exercised only where a Margin Deficit or Margin Excess exceeds a specified dollar amount or a specified percentage of the Repurchase Prices for such Transactions (which amount or percentage shall be agreed to by Buyer and Seller prior to entering into any such Transactions).

(e) Seller and Buyer may agree, with respect to any or all Transactions hereunder, that the respective rights of Buyer and Seller under subparagraphs (a) and (b) of this Paragraph to require the elimination of a Margin Deficit or a Margin Excess, as the case may be, may be exercised whenever such a Margin Deficit or Margin Excess exists with respect to any single Transaction hereunder (calculated without regard to any other Transaction outstanding under this Agreement).

8. Segregation of Purchased Securities

To the extent required by applicable law, all Purchased Securities in the possession of Seller shall be segregated from other securities in its possession and shall be identified as subject to this Agreement. Segregation may be accomplished by appropriate identification on the books and records of the holder, including a financial intermediary or a clearing corporation. Title to all Purchased Securities shall pass to Buyer and, unless otherwise agreed by Buyer and Seller, nothing in this Agreement shall preclude Buyer from engaging in repurchase transactions with the Purchased Securities or otherwise pledging or hypothecating the Purchased Securities, but no such transactions shall relieve Buyer of its obligations to transfer Purchased Securities to Seller pursuant to Paragraphs 3, 4 or 11 hereof, or of Buyer's obligation to credit or pay Income to, or apply Income to the obligations of, Seller pursuant to Paragraph 5 hereof.

11. Events of Default

In the event that (i) Seller fails to repurchase or Buyer fails to transfer Purchased Securities upon the applicable Repurchase Date, (ii) Seller or Buyer fails, after one business day's notice, to comply with Paragraph 4 hereof, (iii) Buyer fails to comply with Paragraph 5 hereof, (iv) an Act of Insolvency occurs with respect to Seller or Buyer, (v) any representation made by Seller or Buyer shall have been incorrect or untrue in any material respect when made or repeated or deemed to have been made or repeated, or (vi) Seller or Buyer shall admit to the other its inability to, or its intention not to, perform any of its obligations hereunder (each an "Event of Default"):

(a) At the option of the nondefaulting party, exercised by written notice to the defaulting party (which option shall be deemed to have been exercised, even if no notice is given, immediately upon the occurrence of an Act of Insolvency), the Repurchase Date for each Transaction hereunder shall be deemed immediately to occur.

(b) In all Transactions in which the defaulting party is acting as Seller, if the nondefaulting party exercises or is deemed to have exercised the option referred to in subparagraph (a) of this Paragraph, (i) the defaulting party's obligations hereunder to repurchase all Purchased Securities in such Transactions shall thereupon become immediately due and payable, (ii) to the extent permitted by applicable law, the Repurchase Price with respect to each such Transaction shall be increased by the aggregate amount obtained by daily application of (x) the greater of the Pricing Rate for such Transaction or the Prime Rate to (y) the Repurchase Price for such Transaction as of the Repurchase Date as determined pursuant to subparagraph (a) of this Paragraph (decreased as of any day by (A) any amounts retained by the nondefaulting party with respect to such Repurchase Price pursuant to clause (iii) of this subparagraph, (B) any proceeds from the sale of Purchased Securities pursuant to subparagraph (d)(i) of this Paragraph, and (C) any amounts credited to the account of the defaulting party pursuant to subparagraph (e) of this Paragraph) on a 360 day per year basis for the actual number of days during the period from and including the date of the Event of Default giving rise to such option to but excluding the date of payment of the Repurchase Price as so increased, (iii) all Income paid after such exercise or deemed exercise shall be retained by the nondefaulting party and applied to the aggregate unpaid Repurchase Prices owed by the defaulting party, and (iv) the defaulting party shall immediately deliver to the nondefaulting party any Purchased Securities subject to such Transactions then in the defaulting party's possession.

(c) In all Transactions in which the defaulting party is acting as Buyer, upon tender by the nondefaulting party of payment of the aggregate Repurchase Prices for all such Transactions, the defaulting party's right title and interest in all Purchased Securities subject to such Transactions shall be deemed transferred to the nondefaulting party, and the defaulting party shall deliver all such Purchased Securities to the nondefaulting party.

(d) After one business day's notice to the defaulting party (which notice need not be given if an Act of Insolvency shall have occurred, and which may be the notice given under subparagraph (a) of this Paragraph or the notice referred to in clause (ii) of the first sentence of this Paragraph), the nondefaulting party may:

(i) as to Transactions in which the defaulting party is acting as Seller, (A) immediately sell, in a recognized market at such price or prices as the nondefaulting party may reasonably deem satisfactory, any or all Purchased Securities subject to such Transactions and apply the proceeds thereof to the aggregate unpaid Repurchase Prices and any other amounts owing by the defaulting party hereunder

or (B) in its sole discretion elect, in lieu of selling all or a portion of such Purchased Securities, to give the defaulting party credit for such Purchased Securities in an amount equal to the price therefor on such date, obtained from a generally recognized source or the most recent closing bid quotation from such a source, against the aggregate unpaid Repurchase Prices and any other amounts owing by the defaulting party hereunder; and

(ii) as to Transactions in which the defaulting party is acting as Buyer, (A) purchase securities ("Replacement Securities") of the same class and amount as any Purchased Securities that are not delivered by the defaulting party to the nondefaulting party as required hereunder or (B) in its sole discretion elect, in lieu of purchasing Replacement Securities, to be deemed to have purchased Replacement Securities at the price therefor on such date, obtained from a generally recognized source or the most recent closing bid quotation from such a source.

(e) As to Transactions in which the defaulting party is acting as Buyer, the defaulting party shall be liable to the nondefaulting party (i) with respect to Purchased Securities (other than Additional Purchased Securities), for any excess of the price paid (or deemed paid) by the nondefaulting party for Replacement Securities therefor over the Repurchase Price for such Purchased Securities and (ii) with respect to Additional Purchased Securities, for the price paid (or deemed paid) by the nondefaulting party for the Replacement Securities therefor. In addition, the defaulting party shall be liable to the nondefaulting party for interest on such remaining liability with respect to each such purchase (or deemed purchase) of Replacement Securities from the date of such purchase (or deemed purchase) until paid in full by Buyer. Such interest shall be at a rate equal to the greater of the Pricing Rate for such Transaction or the Prime Rate.

(f) For purposes of this Paragraph 11, the Repurchase Price for each Transaction hereunder in respect of which the defaulting party is acting as Buyer shall not increase above the amount of such Repurchase Price for such Transaction determined as of the date of the exercise or deemed exercise by the nondefaulting party of its option under subparagraph (a) of this Paragraph.

(g) The defaulting party shall be liable to the nondefaulting party for the amount of all reasonable legal or other expenses incurred by the nondefaulting party in connection with or as a consequence of an Event of Default, together with interest thereon at a rate equal to the greater of the Pricing Rate for the relevant Transaction or the Prime Rate.

(h) The nondefaulting party shall have, in addition to its rights hereunder, any rights otherwise available to it under any other agreement or applicable law.

19. Intent

(a) The parties recognize that each Transaction is a "repurchase agreement" as that term is defined in Section 101 of Title 11 of the United States Code, as amended (except insofar as the type of Securities subject to such Transaction or the term of such Transaction would render such definition inapplicable), and a "securities contract" as that term is defined in Section 741 of Title 11 of the United States Code, as amended.

(b) It is understood that either party's right to liquidate Securities delivered to it in connection with Transactions hereunder or to exercise any other remedies pursuant to Paragraph 11 hereof, is a contractual right to liquidate such Transaction as described in Sections 555 and 559 of Title 11 of the United States Code, as amended.

KEY POINTS

1. *Treasury securities can be used as collateral to borrow funds via a repurchase agreement.*

2. *Leveraging is the investment principle of borrowing funds in the hope of earning a return in excess of the cost of funds.*

3. *Leveraging magnifies the potential gain that will be realized from investing in a Treasury security for a given change in the price of that security but also magnifies the potential loss.*

4. *A repurchase agreement is the sale of a Treasury security with a commitment by the seller to buy the security back from the purchaser at the repurchase price at the repurchase date.*

5. *The difference between the repurchase price and the sale price is the dollar interest cost of the loan.*

6. *Interest in a repurchase agreement is computed on a 360-day basis.*

7. *In a repurchase agreement, the lender of funds is borrowing securities and is making a short-term investment.*

8. *There is a good deal of Wall Street jargon describing repo transactions but basically one party is buying collateral (and making a short-term investment) and the other party is selling collateral (and obtaining financing).*

9. *Rather than using industry jargon, investment guidelines should be clear as to what a manager is permitted to do with respect to repo transactions.*

10. *In a repurchase agreement the lender is exposed to the risk that the borrower will default.*

11. *To reduce credit risk there is over collateralization of the loan (i.e., there is a repo margin) and the collateral is marked to market on a regular basis.*

12. *When the market value of the collateral declines by a certain percentage, a repo agreement can specify either a margin call or repricing of the repo.*

13. *One concern in structuring a repo is delivery of the collateral to the lender.*

14. *When the borrower must deliver the collateral to the lender or to the cash lender's clearing agent, the collateral is said to be "delivered out" and at the repurchase date the lender returns the collateral to the borrower in exchange for the principal and interest payment.*

15. *If the lender agrees to allow the borrower to hold the security in a segregated customer account, then the transaction is called a hold-in-custody repo and exposes the lender to greater credit risk than delivering out the securities.*

16. *A tri-party repo is an alternative to delivering out the collateral which requires that the borrower deliver the collateral to the lender's custodial account at the borrower's clearing bank.*

17. *In certain circumstances a four-party repo is used to satisfy legal requirements, with the fourth party being a sub-custodian for the lender.*

18. *In the case of a bankruptcy by the borrower, in general the bankruptcy code in the United States affords the lender of funds in a qualified repo transaction the right to immediately liquidate the collateral to obtain cash.*

19. *In structuring a repo agreement, most participants in the United States use the Public Securities Association Master Repurchase Agreement.*

20. *The repo rate for a particular transaction will depend on the quality of the collateral, term of the repo, delivery requirement, availability of collateral, and the prevailing federal funds rate.*

21. *Collateral that is highly sought after by dealers is called hot or special collateral and can be used as a cheap source of repo financing.*

22. *For new Treasury notes, there is a consistent pattern in special repo rates.*

23. *The spread between the general overnight repo rate and the special overnight repo rate is a measure of the degree of specialness of a Treasury note.*

24. *Empirical evidence suggests that for all newly issued Treasury notes the average specialness spread increases up to the announcement day for the next issue to be auctioned and then decreases.*

25. *The specialness spread is effectively a dealer's cost for covering a short position since a dealer earns a below market rate for providing financing in order to acquire a note.*

26. *The specialness cost associated with using the repo market when measured against an unhedged price exposure indicates that the repo market is an effective means for covering a short position.*

Chapter 10

TAX TREATMENT

In this chapter, we look at the key provisions in the federal tax law that pertain to the tax treatment of interest income and the gain or loss resulting from transactions in Treasury securities by individuals.

INCOME DEFINED

Investors often use the term "income" in a very casual way. The Internal Revenue Code (IRC), however, provides a more precise definition of income. The IRC distinguishes between gross income, adjusted gross income, taxable income, and alternative minimum taxable income.

Gross income is all income that is subject to income tax. For example, interest income is subject to taxation. However there is statutory exemption for interest from certain types of debt obligations. For such obligations, interest income is not included in gross income.

For individuals, *adjusted gross income* is gross income minus certain business and other deductions. For example, an important deduction from gross income to arrive at adjusted gross income is the deduction for certain contributions to qualified tax-deferred retirement plans.

Taxable income is the amount upon which the tax liability is determined. For an individual, it is found by subtracting the personal exemption allowance and itemized deductions (other than those deductible in arriving at adjusted gross income) from adjusted gross income.

Alternative minimum taxable income (AMTI) is a taxpayer's taxable income with certain adjustments for specified tax preferences designed to cause AMTI to approximate economic income. For individuals a taxpayer's tax liability is the greater of (1) the tax computed at regular tax rates on taxable income and (2) the tax computed at a lower rate on AMTI. This parallel tax system, the alternative minimum tax, is designed to prevent taxpayers from avoiding significant tax liability as a result of taking advantage of exclusions from gross income, deductions, and tax credits otherwise allowed under the IRC.

TAX BASIS AND DETERMINATION OF CAPITAL GAIN OR LOSS

The IRC provides for a special tax treatment on the sale or exchange of a capital asset. Treasury securities qualify as capital assets in the hands of a qualified owner.

Tax Basis

In order to understand the tax treatment of a Treasury security, the tax basis of a capital asset must first be defined. In most instances, the original tax basis of a Treasury security is the taxpayer's total cost on the date of acquisition. The *adjusted basis* is the original tax basis increased by capital additions and decreased by capital recoveries (i.e, return of principal). That is,

adjusted basis = original tax basis + capital additions – capital recoveries

Capital Gain or Loss

The proceeds received from the sale of a Treasury security are compared to the adjusted basis to determine if the transaction produced a capital gain or capital loss. If the proceeds exceed the adjusted basis, the taxpayer realizes a capital gain; a capital loss is realized when the adjusted basis exceeds the proceeds received by the taxpayer.

The rules are summarized below:

Situation	Result
Proceeds > adjusted basis	Capital gain
Proceeds < adjusted basis	Capital loss
Proceeds = adjusted basis	No capital gain or loss

How capital gains and losses are treated for tax purposes is described later in this chapter.

INTEREST INCOME

Interest received by a taxpayer is included in gross income, unless a specific statutory exemption indicates otherwise. A portion of the income realized from holding a Treasury security may be in the form of capital appreciation rather than interest income. The tax treatment of the income component that represents capital appreciation differs depending on when the Treasury security was issued.

As explained later, the IRC provides for different tax treatment for certain capital gains and losses on the one hand and ordinary income and losses on the other. For Treasury securities issued after July 18, 1984, part of the capital appreciation will be treated as ordinary income. Under the current tax law, capital gains are taxed at a lower tax rate than ordinary income. Taxpayers get less favorable treatment for capital losses than ordinary losses. Thus, the tax treatment of income from holding a Treasury security may have a major impact on the after-tax return realized by an investor.

Because of the potential importance of distinguishing between income in the form of a capital gain (or loss) and interest income, the investor must be familiar with certain rules set forth in the IRC. These rules are summarized below.

Accrued Interest

Interest on Treasury coupon securities is paid semiannually. Accrued interest is the interest earned by the seller from holding a security until the disposal date. Suppose that the accrued interest for a Treasury security with a par value of $100,000 is $4,000 and the next coupon payment is $6,000. Let us look at the tax position of the seller and the buyer, assuming that our hypothetical security is selling for $90,000 in the market and that the seller's adjusted basis for this Treasury security is $87,000.

The buyer must pay the seller $94,000, $90,000 for the market price plus $4,000 of accrued interest. The seller must treat the accrued interest of $4,000 as interest income. The $90,000 is compared to the seller's adjusted basis of $87,000 to determine whether the seller has realized a capital gain or capital loss. Obviously, the seller has realized capital appreciation of $3,000. When the buyer receives the coupon interest payment of $6,000 only $2,000 is included in gross income as interest income. The basis of the security for the buyer is $90,000, not $94,000.

Bond Purchased at a Discount

A security purchased at a price less than its redemption value at maturity is said to be bought at a discount. The tax treatment of the discount depends upon whether the discount represents original-issue discount or market discount.

Original-Issue Discount Bonds

When bonds are issued, the original-issue price may be less than the maturity value. Such bonds are said to be issued at an *original-issue discount* (OID). The amount of the original-issue discount is the difference between the maturity value and the original-issue price. The tax law requires that a portion of the original-issue discount must be accrued and included in gross income. There is a corresponding increase in the adjusted basis of the bond. Consequently, original-issue discount obligations are less attractive in taxable portfolios than in nontaxable portfolios.

There are exceptions to this rule. First, the rule does not apply to noninterest bearing obligations with a maturity of no more than one year. Therefore, the OID rule does not apply to Treasury bills. When bills are held by investors who report for tax purposes on a cash rather than an accrual basis, the discount is not recognized until the issue matures. Another rule is that the original-issue discount must exceed a certain dollar amount. That is, just because there is an original-issue discount does not automatically mean that the discount must be accrued and reported in gross income. Generally, when Treasury coupon securities are issued, the Treasury sets the price close enough to par so that any discount is not large enough to require application of the OID rule.

Although the OID rule does not apply to Treasury bills and Treasury coupon securities, they do apply to Treasury strips. In the case of strips, original-issue discount is measured by the difference between the maturity value and the purchase price of the holder, not the adjusted-issue price. The effect of this rule is that it is not possible to have a market discount (discussed below) or premium because a Treasury strip is considered issued on the date any investor purchases it.

The amount of the original-issue discount amortized is based on the *constant-yield method* (also called the *effective method* or *scientific method*) and included in gross income based on the number of days in the tax year that the Treasury strip is held. With this method the amount of the original-issue discount to be included in gross income in the first year is found by multiplying the purchase price by the yield to maturity. The interest calculated is the amount of the original-issue discount amortized for the year. That amount is then added to the adjusted basis. In the second year, the interest is found by multiplying the adjusted basis by the yield to maurity. With the constant-yield method, the accrual is lower in the earlier years, increasing over the life of the strip on a compounding basis.

Treasury Coupon Securities Purchased at a Market Discount

When a Treasury coupon security is purchased at a market discount, the tax treatment depends on when the bond was issued. For securities issued after July 18, 1984, any capital appreciation must be separated into a portion that is attributable to interest income (as represented by the amortization of the market discount with which it is purchased) and a portion that is attributable to capital gain. The portion representing interest income is taxed as ordinary income when the security is sold. This is called *accrued market discount*.

The taxpayer can elect to include accrued market discount in gross income. The motivation for doing so is that if interest expenses were incurred to finance the purchase of the security, the interest expenses would be deferred if the accrued market discount is deferred.

Accrued market discount must be determined using the straight-line method unless the taxpayer elects the constant-yield method. (With the straight line method annual interest income is calculated by dividing the accrued market discount by the number of years to maturity.) The amount of accrued market discount that is included in gross income as interest is limited to the amount of the security's capital appreciation. For Treasury securities issued on or prior to July 18, 1984, any capital appreciation is treated as a capital gain.

There are two implications of these rules. First, from a tax perspective, Treasury coupon securities issued before July 18, 1984 and selling at a discount will be more attractive than securities issued after that date and selling at a discount. This will be reflected in the market price of those issues.[1] Consequently, investors that are in low marginal tax rates will find that they may be overpaying for bonds issued before July 18, 1984. The second implication is that it is not in the best interest of the investor to select the straight-line method to compute the accrued market discount because that method will cause the capital gain portion of any gain on sale to be lower (and the interest portion higher) than if the constant-yield method is elected.

---

[1] For an extensive statistical analysis of the implications of the differential tax treatment, see Ehud I. Ronn and Yongjai Shin, "Tax Effects in U.S. Government Bond Markets," Chapter 13 in Frank J. Fabozzi (ed.), *Advances in Fixed Income Valuation Modeling and Risk Management* (New Hope, PA: Frank J. Fabozzi Associates, 1997), pp. 233-250.

The rules for the treatment of market discount for Treasury coupon securities are summarized below:

1. For Treasury coupon securities issued on or prior to July 18, 1984 any capital appreciation is treated as a capital gain.
2. For Treasury coupon securities issued after July 18, 1984:
   a. Accrued market discount is taxed as ordinary income and is taxed when the security is sold or paid off or currently if the taxpayer elects so.
   b. Accrued market discount can be determined using either the straight-line method or the constant-yield method.

Treasury Coupon Securities Purchased at a Premium

When a Treasury coupon security is purchased at a price greater than its maturity value, the issue is said to be purchased at a *premium*. For a Treasury coupon security issued after September 27, 1985, the taxpayer may elect to amortize the premium over the remaining life of the security under a compound interest method similar to the method of accruing original-issue discount. The premium on a Treasury security issued prior to September 28, 1985 may, however, be amortized on a straight-line basis. An election to amortize bond premiums applies to *all* bonds (Treasury and taxable non-Treasury issues) held when the election is made and to *all* bonds acquired thereafter. The amount amortized reduces the amount of the interest income that will be included as taxable gross income. In turn, the basis is reduced by the amount of the amortization.

CAPITAL GAINS TAX TREATMENT

The tax treatment of a capital gain or loss on the sale of a Treasury security depends on whether the gain or loss is classified as "long term" or "short term." In turn, characterization of long term and short term depends on how long the Treasury security was held. Prior to the change in the tax law, long term was defined as more than one year; otherwise, any gain or loss was classified as short term. In 1997, the tax law was changed. The rules for classification as long term and the applicable maximum tax rate on any capital gain became more complicated. Below we summarize the current rules.

In general, for assets sold on or after July 29, 1997, the holding period for classification as a long-term capital gain or loss is more than 18 months. There is a favorable tax treatment for long-term capital gains for individuals. The current maximum tax rate on ordinary income is 39.6%. For long-term capital gains held for more than 18 months, the maximum tax rate is 20% for individuals who are in the 28% or higher tax bracket. For individuals in the lowest tax bracket, the maximum tax rate is 10% for long-term capital gains held for more than 18 months.

For the acquisition of assets after December 31, 2000, there is another provision. Specifically, for assets held for longer than five years, the maximum tax rate on any capital gains will be 18% for individuals in the highest tax bracket and 8% for individuals in the lowest tax bracket.

While the classification of a capital gain or capital loss as either long term or short term applies on a security-by-security basis, the tax rate is not applied on a security-by-security basis. The aggregate of all long-term capital gains and losses are combined to produce either a net long-term capital gain or net long-term capital loss. The same is done for all short-term capital gains and losses to obtain either a net short-term capital gain or net short-term capital loss. Then an overall net capital gain or net capital loss is determined by combining these amounts. One of the following will occur:

> overall net short-term capital gain
> overall net long-term capital gain
> overall net short-term capital loss
> overall net long-term capital loss

The special tax rates apply to an overall net long-term capital gain.

KEY POINTS

1. The tax code distinguishes between gross income, adjusted gross income, taxable income, and alternative minimum taxable income.

2. The adjusted basis of a capital asset is its original basis increased by capital additions and decreased by capital recoveries.

3. The proceeds received from the sale of a Treasury security are compared to the adjusted basis to determine if the transaction produced a capital gain or capital loss.

4. The tax treatment of the income component from holding a Treasury security that represents capital appreciation differs depending on when the security was issued.

5. For Treasury securities issued after July 18, 1984, part of the capital appreciation will be treated as ordinary income and taxed at the ordinary income tax rate.

6. Under the current tax law, capital gains are taxed at a lower tax rate than ordinary income; taxpayers get less favorable treatment for capital losses than ordinary losses.

7. The tax treatment of Treasury securities acquired at a discount depends upon whether the discount represents original-issue discount or market discount.

8. For a strip, the difference between the maturity value and the purchase price is the original-issue discount.

9. Each year a portion of the original-issue discount must be amortized, with the accrued interest added to gross income and added to the original basis.

10. For Treasury coupon securities issued after July 18, 1984 that are purchased at a market discount, any capital appreciation must be separated into a portion that is attributable to interest income and a portion that is attributable to capital gain.

11. The portion representing interest income, called accrued market discount, is taxed as ordinary income only when the bond is sold or matures.

12. Accrued market discount can be determined using either the straight-line method or the constant-yield method.

13. A taxpayer can elect to have the accrued market interest included in gross income and will elect to do so if there are interest expenses to finance the position that would otherwise have to be deferred.

14. *The treatment of accrued market discount for Treasury coupon securities issued on or prior to July 18, 1984 is that any capital appreciation is treated as a capital gain.*

15. *An implication of Treasury coupon securities issued before July 18, 1984 and selling at a discount is that they will be more attractive than Treasury coupon securities issued after that date and selling at a discount.*

16. *For a Treasury coupon security issued after September 27, 1985 that is purchased at a premium, the taxpayer may elect to amortize the premium over the remaining life of the security using the constant yield method, while for a security issued prior to September 28, 1985 a straight-line basis may be used.*

17. *Capital gains and losses are classified as either long term or short term depending on the length of time the capital asset is held.*

18. *The tax law provides for a preferential tax treatment of long-term capital gains.*

19. *A capital gain is classified as long term if it is held for more than 18 months.*

20. *Capital gains treatment is not done on a security-by-security basis but applies to any overall net capital gain.*

Chapter 11

CASH MARKET TRADING STRATEGIES

Now that we are familiar with the mechanics of the Treasury cash market and the repo market, we will look at several trading strategies. There are trades that are undertaken to position the investor for an anticipated change in interest rates. Such trades are referred to as *rate anticipation trades*. They simply involve trades to alter the duration of a portfolio — increasing it if rates are expected to rise and decreasing it if rates are expected to fall. Rate anticipation trades are *market directional trades*. In this chapter we will describe three types of trades — yield curve trades, relative value trades, and roll trades. The primary motivation of such trades is not driven by expectations about the direction or the *level* of the market.

YIELD CURVE TRADES

Yield curve trades are driven by expectations of changes in the shape of the yield curve. Changes in the yield curve can be defined in terms of changes in the level, slope, and curvature. We described these characteristics in previous chapters. Yield curve trades deal primarily with changes in the slope and curvature. However, changes in the shape of the yield curve are related to changes in the level of rates.

     The slope of the yield curve between two maturity sectors is measured as the spread between the two yields. There are various definitions of the curvature of the yield curve. One measure that is used is based on the yield for three maturities: a short maturity, intermediate maturity, and long maturity. The curvature is measured relative to these three maturities by the difference between the yield on the intermediate maturity (i.e., the bullet) and the dollar duration yield of a combination of the short and long maturities (i.e., the barbell).[1]

     Below we describe three types of yield curve trades: (1) pure slope trade, (2) duration and cash neutral trade, and (3) duration neutral trade with equal dollar duration in each wing.[2]

Pure Slope Trade

In a *pure slope trade*, there are three instruments. There are two Treasury coupon issues (with one issue having a longer maturity than the other) and a cash equiva-

---

[1] See Antti Ilmanen, *Weighting Yield Curve Slope and Curvature Trades*, Salomon Brothers, Economic and Market Analysis, November 20, 1996, p.1.

[2] For empirical evidence on the performance of yield curve strategies, see Steven V. Mann and Pradipkumar Ramanlal, "The Relative Performance of Yield Curve Strategies," *Journal of Portfolio Management* (Summer 1997), pp. 64-71.

lent such as an overnight repo. Depending on whether the expectation is for a flattening or steepening of the yield curve in the relevant sector, the following trade is implemented:

Expectation of a yield curve flattening:

Sell the shorter maturity coupon issue
Buy both the longer maturity coupon issue and the cash equivalent

Expectation of yield curve steepening;

Buy the shorter maturity coupon issue
Sell both the longer maturity coupon issue and the cash equivalent

In the case of the yield curve flattening trade, the proceeds from the short sale of the short maturity coupon issue are used to acquire the positions in the long maturity coupon issue and the cash equivalent. The entire amount from the short sale is allocated to the long maturity coupon issue and the cash equivalent.

The amount of the position taken in the longer maturity coupon issue and the cash equivalent depends on the dollar duration of the longer maturity coupon issue and the shorter maturity coupon issue. The positions are created so that the dollar duration of the center is equal to the dollar duration of the wings. Thus, this strategy is neutral with respect to a small parallel shift in the yield curve and hence is referred to as a *duration-neutral trade*. However, the positions are exposed to large shifts because of the different convexity of the two positions. However, this exposure is small. Consequently, this trade is a pure play on expected changes in the slope of the yield curve in the longer maturity coupon and shorter maturity coupon issues involved in the trade.

To illustrate the general principles of a pure slope trade, we will use the hypothetical Treasury securities shown in Exhibit 1. For convenience, we have assumed each security is priced at par and the next coupon payment is six months from now. For the cash equivalent, we will assume an investment in an overnight repo. The assumption is that the overnight repo rate will be unchanged over the period of the trade We examine this trade over a 2-week period.

Exhibit 1: Two Hypothetical Treasury Notes Used to Illustrate a Pure Slope Trade

Security	Coupon rate	Price	Yield	Duration	Convexity
5-year note	6.4%	$100	6.4%	4.221897	10.7120
10-year note	6.6	100	6.6	7.236540	33.0245

Assumed overnight repo rate: 4.93%

In this illustration we will assume that the trader expects a flattening of the yield curve over the next two weeks in the 5-year/10-year sector. The trader will therefore sell the shorter maturity coupon issue (the 5-year note in our illustration), and buy the 10-year note and keep the balance in cash earning the overnight repo rate. The trade must be constructed so as to be duration neutral for a parallel shift in the yield curve.

Let's assume that the trader sells $10 million par of the 5-year note. The $10 million to be purchased of the 10-year and invested in the cash equivalent is determined so as to keep the dollar duration of the two positions the same. Since the 5-year note is trading at par, its dollar duration per $100 of par value is 4.221897 (see Exhibit 1). The dollar duration for the 10-year note/cash equivalent combination is found as follows:

$$\text{Dollar duration combined position} = \frac{\text{Market value of 10-year note}}{\$10 \text{ million}}$$
$$\times \text{Dollar duration of 10-year note per \$100 par}$$
$$+ \frac{\text{Market value of cash equivalent}}{\$10 \text{ million}} \times \text{Dollar duration of cash equivalent}$$

Since the dollar duration of the cash equivalent is zero and the dollar duration of the 10-year note is 7.236540, then the market value of the two instruments to be purchased is determined by setting the previous equation equal to the dollar duration of the 5-year note (4.221897). That is,

$$4.221897 = \frac{\text{Market value of 10-year note}}{\$10 \text{ million}} \times 7.236540$$

Solving the above equation, the market value of the 10-year note to be purchased is $5.83414 million. Since the 10-year note is trading at par, the par amount purchased is $5.83414 million. The balance is the amount invested in cash, $4.16586 million.

Thus, the trade is as follows for an anticipated flattening of the yield curve in the 5-year/10-year sector:

Sell $10 million par/market value of the 5-year note
Buy $5.83414 million par/market value of the 10-year note
Invest $4.16586 million in a cash equivalent

Exhibit 2 shows the profit and loss statement for various outcomes two weeks after the trade is executed. The results for the following five scenarios are shown:

Scenario 1: A flattening of the yield curve assuming that the 10-year rate declines 7 basis points to 6.53% while the 5-year rate stays at 6.4%

Scenario 2: A flattening of the yield curve assuming that the 5-year rate increases 7 basis points to 6.47% while the 10-year rate stays at 6.6%

Scenario 3: No change in yields

Exhibit 2: Profit and Loss Analysis of a Pure Slope Trade
Trade:

> Sell $10 million par/market value of the 5-year note
> Buy $5.83414 million par/market value of the 10-year note
> Invest $4.16586 million in a cash equivalent

In all scenarios, the interest from the cash equivalent assuming a repo rate of 4.93% for the two weeks is (the repo rate is based on 360 days):

> $4.16586 million $\times$ 0.0493 $\times$ (14/360) = $7,986.88

Scenario 1: A flattening of the yield curve assuming that the 10-year rate declines 7 basis points to 6.53% while the 5-year rate stays at 6.4%

Security	Yield	Two weeks later Price	Accrued interest
5-year	6.40%	99.996419	0.247514
10-year	6.53	100.503011	0.255249

	Market value	Accrued interest	Total
Position sold:			
5-year	$9,999,641.90	$24,751.40	$10,024,393.30
Position purchased:			
10-year	$5,863,446.16	$14,891.48	$5,878,337.65
Cash	4,165,860.00	7,986.88	4,173,846.88
Total	$10,029,306.16	$22,878.36	$10,052,184.53
Profit from the trade			$27,791.23

Scenario 2: A flattening of the yield curve assuming that the 5-year rate increases 7 basis points to 6.47% while the 10-year rate stays at 6.6%

Security	Yield	Two weeks later Price	Accrued interest
5-year	6.47%	99.703313	0.247514
10-year	6.60	99.996194	0.255249

	Market value	Accrued interest	Total
Position sold:			
5-year	$9,970,331.30	$24,751.40	$9,995,082.70
Position purchased:			
10-year	$5,833,877.95	$14,891.48	$5,848,769.44
Cash	4,165,860.00	7,986.88	4,173,846.88
Total	$9,999,737.95	$22,878.36	$10,022,616.32
Profit from the trade			$27,533.62

Exhibit 2 (Continued)

Scenario 3: No change in yields

Security	Yield	Two weeks later Price	Accrued interest
		Two weeks later	
5-year	6.40%	99.996419	0.247514
10-year	6.60	99.996194	0.255249

	Market value	Accrued interest	Total
Position sold:			
5-year	$9,999,641.90	$24,751.40	$10,024,393.30
Position purchased:			
10-year	$5,833,877.95	$14,891.48	$5,848,769.44
Cash	4,165,860.00	7,986.88	4,173,846.88
Total	$9,999,737.95	$22,878.36	$10,022,616.32
Loss from the trade			$1,776.98

Scenario 4: A steepening of the yield curve assuming that the 10-year rate increases 7 basis points to 6.67% while the 5-year rate stays at 6.4%

		Two weeks later	
Security	Yield	Price	Accrued interest
5-year	6.40%	99.996419	0.247514
10-year	6.67	99.492595	0.255249

	Market value	Accrued interest	Total
Position sold:			
5-year	$9,999,641.90	$24,751.40	$10,024,393.30
Position purchased:			
10-year	$5,804,497.48	$14,891.48	$5,819,388.97
Cash	4,165,860.00	7,986.88	4,173,846.88
Total	$9,970,357.48	$22,878.36	$9,993,235.85
Loss from the trade			$31,157.45

Scenario 5: A steepening of the yield curve assuming that the 5-year rate decreases 7 basis points to 6.33% while the 10-year rate stays at 6.6%

		Two weeks later	
Security	Yield	Price	Accrued interest
5-year	6.33%	100.290562	0.247514
10-year	6.60	99.996194	0.255249

	Market value	Accrued interest	Total
Position sold:			
5-year	$10,029,056.20	$24,751.40	$10,053,807.60
Position purchased:			
10-year	$5,833,877.95	$14,891.48	$5,848,769.44
Cash	4,165,860.00	7,986.88	4,173,846.88
Total	$9,999,737.95	$22,878.36	$10,022,616.32
Loss from the trade			$31,191.28

Scenario 4: A steepening of the yield curve assuming that the 10-year rate increases 7 basis points to 6.67% while the 5-year rate stays at 6.4%

Scenario 5: A steepening of the yield curve assuming that the 5-year rate decreases 7 basis points to 6.33% while the 10-year rate stays at 6.6%

Note that in the two scenarios in which the yield curve flattens by 7 basis points, there is a profit; for the scenarios in which the yield curve steepens, there is a loss. In the scenario where rates do not change, there is a loss. This is due to the fact that the accrued interest for the 5-year note exceeds the accrued interest for the 10-year note and the interest on the cash equivalent.

For a large parallel change in yields, the trade is not protected against a change in the level of rates. The reason is that the convexity of the 10-year note/cash leg of the trade is better than that of the 5-year note.

A factor that would impact the profit and loss analysis is if the 10-year note is on special. The yield/price of the 10-year note will reflect this. However, the specialness may not be fully reflected in the price. In such instances, the profit in each scenario can be increased (and the loss reduced) by using the 10-year note to obtain cheap financing and use the proceeds to invest at the general repo rate. That is, it can be used to obtain cheap financing.

Duration and Cash Neutral Trade

Another trade that seeks to capitalize on expectations about changes in the slope of the yield curve involves three Treasury securities. Unlike a pure slope trade which involves a position in a cash equivalent, in this trade no position is taken in a cash equivalent. Trades of this nature are called *butterfly trades.*

There are three Treasury securities in this butterfly trade. We shall refer to these securities in this trade as follows:

short maturity issue: the issue with the shortest maturity from among the three issues

long maturity issue: the issue with the longest maturity from among the three issue

intermediate maturity issue: the issue between the shortest maturity issue and longest maturity issue

The body or center of the butterfly in the duration and cash neutral trade is the intermediate maturity coupon issue. The wings of the butterfly in this trade are the long maturity coupon issue and the short maturity coupon issue.

As with the pure slope trade, the risk exposure to small parallel shifts in the level of rates is neutralized by creating a position so that the dollar duration of the center of the butterfly is equal to the dollar duration of the wings. This butterfly trade is called a *duration and cash neutral trade.* Since there is no cash in this trade, the investor is fully invested in the bond market.

The goal of the trade is to capitalize on the expected flattening or steepening of the slope of the intermediate maturity/long maturity sector of the yield curve. We will refer to this as the *slope of the long end of the yield curve*. However, the trade is also affected by how the intermediate maturity/short maturity sector performs relative to the long end of the yield curve. We will refer to the slope of the intermediate maturity and short maturity sector as the *short end of the yield curve*.

Depending on whether the expectation is for a flattening or steepening of the yield curve in the relevant sector, the following trade is implemented:

Expectation of a yield curve flattening:

Sell the intermediate maturity issue
Buy both the long maturity and short maturity issues

Expectation of yield curve steepening:

Buy the intermediate maturity issue
Sell both the long maturity and short maturity issues

To illustrate this trade, we will use three hypothetical Treasury coupon issues — a 2-year note (short maturity issue), 5-year note (intermediate maturity issue), and 10-year note (long maturity issue). Information about these notes is given in Exhibit 3.

We will assume that the trader expects a flattening of the long end of the yield curve (i.e., the slope of the 5-year and 10-year sector). The trader will therefore sell the intermediate maturity issue (the 5-year note in our illustration) and buy the 2-year note (the short maturity issue) and the 10-year note (the long maturity issue). The trade must be constructed so as to be duration neutral for a small parallel shift in the yield curve.

Let's assume that the trader sells $10 million par of the 5-year note. The $10 million used to be purchased the 2-year note and the 10-year note is determined so as to keep the dollar duration of the position the same as the 5-year note. Since the 5-year note is trading at par, its dollar duration per $100 of par value is 4.221897 (see Exhibit 3). The dollar duration for the 2-year note/10-year note combination is found as follows:

$$\text{Dollar duration of 2-year note/10-year note} = \frac{\text{Market value of 2-year note}}{\$10 \text{ million}}$$

$$\times \text{Dollar duration of 2-year note per \$100 par}$$

$$+ \frac{\text{Market value of 10-year note}}{\$10 \text{ million}}$$

$$\times \text{Dollar duration of 10-year note per \$100 par}$$

Exhibit 3: Three Hypothetical Treasury Notes Used to Illustrate a Duration and Cash Neutral Trade

Security	Coupon rate	Price	Yield	Duration	Convexity
2-year note	6.0%	$100	6.0%	1.858500	2.2240
5-year note	6.4	100	6.4	4.221897	10.7120
10-year note	6.6	100	6.6	7.236540	33.0245

Since the dollar duration of the 2-year note and 10-year is 1.8585 and 7.236540, respectively, then the market value of the two securities to be purchased is determined by setting the previous equation equal to the dollar duration of the 5-year note (4.221897). That is,

$$4.2211897 = \frac{\text{Market value of 2-year note}}{\$10 \text{ million}} \times 1.8585$$
$$+ \frac{\text{Market value of 10-year note}}{\$10 \text{ million}} \times 7.236540$$

Since there is a constraint that the proceeds from the short sale of the 5-year note of $10 million must be invested in the 2-year and 10-year notes, the following relationship holds:

$10 million = Market value of 2-year note + Market value of 10-year note

Equivalently,

Market value of 2-year = $10 million – Market value of 10-year note

Substituting into the equation for duration above, we have

$$4.2211897 = \frac{\$10 \text{ million} - \text{Market value of 10-year note}}{\$10 \text{ million}} \times 1.8585$$
$$+ \frac{\text{Market value of 10-year note}}{\$10 \text{ million}} \times 7.236540$$

Solving the above equation, the market value of the 10-year note to be purchased is $4.3932 million. Since the 10-year note is trading at par, the par amount purchased is $4.3932 million. The balance is the amount invested in the 2-year note, $5.6068 million.

Thus, the trade is as follows for an anticipated flattening of the yield curve in the 5-year/10-year sector:

Sell $10 million par/market value of the 5-year note
Buy $5.6068 million par/market value of the 2-year note
Buy $4.3932 million par/market value of the 10-year note

A profit and loss analysis has been computed for this trade for several scenarios. The results of the analysis are reported in Exhibit 4. The following five scenarios are analyzed:

Exhibit 4: Profit and Loss Analysis of a Duration and Cash Neutral Trade

Trade:

Sell $10 million par/market value of the 5-year note
Buy $5.6068 million par/market value of the 2-year note
Buy $4.3932 million par/market value of the 10-year note

Scenario 1: A flattening of the yield curve resulting from a decline in the 10-year yield by 10 basis points while the 2-year and 5-year yields are unchanged.

Security	Yield	Two weeks later Price	Accrued interest
2-year note	6.00%	99.996849	0.232044
5-year note	6.40	99.996419	0.247514
10-year note	6.50	100.721208	0.255249

	Market value	Accrued interest	Total
Position sold:			
5-year note	$9,999,641.90	$24,751.40	$10,024,393.30
Position purchased:			
2-year note	$5,606,623.33	$13,010.24	$5,619,633.57
10-year note	4,424,884.11	11,213.60	4,436,097.71
Total	$10,031,507.44	$24,223.84	$10,055,731.28
Profit on trade			$31,337.98

Scenario 2: A steepening of the yield curve resulting from a rise in the 10-year yield by 10 basis points while the 2-year and 5-year yields are unchanged.

Security	Yield	Two weeks late Price	Accrued interest
2-year note	6.00%	99.996849	0.232044
5-year note	6.40	99.996419	0.247514
10-year note	6.70	99.277746	0.255249

	Market value	Accrued interest	Total
Position sold:			
5-year note	$9,999,641.90	$24,751.40	$10,024,393.30
Position purchased:			
2-year note	$5,606,623.33	$13,010.24	$5,619,633.57
10-year note	4,361,469.94	11,213.60	4,372,683.54
Total	$9,968,093.27	$24,223.84	$9,992,317.11
Loss on trade			$32,076.19

Exhibit 4 (Continued)

Scenario 3: No change in the yield curve with all yields unchanged.

Security	Yield	Two weeks later		
		Price	Accrued interest	
2-year note	6.00%	99.996849	0.232044	
5-year note	6.40	99.996419	0.247514	
10-year note	6.60	99.996194	0.255249	

	Market value	Accrued interest	Total
Position sold:			
5-year note	$9,999,641.90	$24,751.40	$10,024,393.30
Position purchased:			
2-year note	$5,606,623.33	$13,010.24	$5,619,633.57
10-year note	4,393,032.79	11,213.60	4,404,246.39
Total	$9,999,656.12	$24,223.84	$10,023,879.97
Loss on trade			$513.33

Scenario 4: A flattening of the yield curve resulting from a rise in the 2-year yield by 5 basis points, a fall in the 10-year by 5 basis points while the 5-year is unchanged

Security	Yield	Two weeks later		
		Price	Accrued interest	
2-year note	6.05%	99.905644	0.232044	
5-year note	6.40	99.996419	0.247514	
10-year note	6.55	100.357877	0.255249	

	Market value	Accrued interest	Total
Position sold:			
5-year note	$9,999,641.90	$24,751.40	$10,024,393.30
Position purchased:			
2-year note	$5,601,509.65	$13,010.24	$5,614,519.89
10-year note	4,408,922.25	11,213.60	4,420,135.85
Total	$10,010,431.90	$24,223.84	$10,034,655.74
Profit on trade			$10,262.44

Scenario 5: A steepening of the yield curve resulting from a fall in the 2-year yield by 5 basis points, a rise in the 10-year by 5 basis points while the 5-year is unchanged

Security	Yield	Two weeks later		
		Price	Accrued interest	
2-year note	5.95%	100.088161	0.232044	
5-year note	6.40	99.996419	0.247514	
10-year note	6.65	99.636154	0.255249	

	Market value	Accrued interest	Total
Position sold:			
5-year note	$9,999,641.90	$24,751.40	$10,024,393.30
Position purchased:			
2-year note	$5,611,743.01	$13,010.24	$5,624,753.25
10-year note	4,377,215.52	11,213.60	4,388,429.12
Total	$9,988,958.53	$24,223.84	$10,013,182.37
Loss on trade			$11,210.93

Scenario 1: A flattening of the yield curve resulting from a decline in the 10-year yield by 10 basis points while the 2-year and 5-year yields are unchanged.

Scenario 2: A steepening of the yield curve resulting from a rise in the 10-year yield by 10 basis points while the 2-year and 5-year yields are unchanged

Scenario 3: No change in the yield curve with all yields unchanged.

Scenario 4: A flattening of the yield curve resulting from a rise in the 2-year yield by 5 basis points, a fall in the 10-year by 5 basis points while the 5-year is unchanged

Scenario 5: A steepening of the yield curve resulting from a fall in the 2-year yield by 5 basis points, a rise in the 10-year by 5 basis points while the 5-year is unchanged

For the two scenarios where the slope of the long end of the yield changes, the slope of the short end remains unchanged. The results for these two scenarios is as expected. The trade produces a profit if there is a flattening of the yield curve at the long end but a loss if there is a steepening of the yield curve at the long end. If the slope of the yield curve does not change at the long end or short end, there is a small loss because of the greater interest paid on the 5-year note relative to interest earned for the 2-year note/10-year note combination.

The last two scenarios show what happens if both the slope of the long end and short end change by 5 basis points. Scenario 4 shows that if both ends flatten in this instance, then there is profit produced by this trade. A steepening of both the long end and short end will produce a loss in this instance (scenario 5).

Obviously, the outcome of this trade will depend on the relative movements of the yield for the 2-year, 5-year, and 10-year notes. Thus, it depends to some extent on how the curvature of the yield curve changes. Historical analysis of these relative movements will guide the trader in developing appropriate scenarios to assess the potential outcomes of the trade before it is executed in order to assess the risk exposure. Consequently, the duration and cash neutral trade is not a pure curve slope trade but has an element of a curvature trade.[3]

Duration Neutral Trade with Equal Dollar Duration in Each Wing

The duration and cash neutral trade has a different dollar duration in each wing. An alternative weighting of a duration neutral trade is to place an equal dollar duration in each wing. Such a trade requires not only the three securities in a duration and cash neutral trade, but also a cash equivalent. This type of trade is a combination of a slope trade and a curvature trade.[4]

---

[3] Ilmanen, *Weighting Yield Curve Slope and Curvature Trades*, p. 2.
[4] Ilmanen, *Weighting Yield Curve Slope and Curvature Trades*, p. 2.

For an anticipated flattening of the yield curve, the trade would involve:

Sell the intermediate maturity issue
Borrow funds
Buy the short maturity and long maturity issues

The trade is constructed so that the purchase of the issues in the wings has the same dollar duration and the total dollar duration of the wings is equal to the dollar duration of the center (i.e., intermediate maturity issue). The need to borrow funds comes about because the funds required to purchase the issues in each wing so as to satisfy the duration constraint may exceed the proceeds received from the sale of the intermediate maturity issue.

For an anticipated steepening of the yield curve, the trade would involve:

Buy the intermediate maturity issue
Invest in a cash equivalent
Sell the short maturity and long maturity issues

Once again, the trade is constructed so that the purchase of each issue constituting the wings has the same dollar duration and the total dollar duration of the wings is equal to the dollar duration of the center. The investment in the cash equivalent may result because the funds invested in the intermediate maturity issue may be less than the proceeds received from the short sale of the short and long maturity issues.

To illustrate how to determine the amount to buy or sell of each security, we will use the three notes in Exhibit 3 and use the reverse repo as a financing vehicle if funds must be borrowed. Suppose that $10 million of the 5-year note is shorted. The dollar duration of the short position per $100 of par value is 4.221897. Therefore, the dollar duration of each wing must be equal to one half the dollar duration of the 5-year note, or 2.110949. Setting the dollar duration of the lower wing (i.e., the dollar duration of the 2-year note) equal to 2.110949, we have:

$$2.110949 \times \$10 \text{ million} = 1.858500 \times \text{Market value of 2-year note}$$

or

Market value of 2-year note = $11.3583 million

For the 10-year note, the procedure is the same:

$$2.110949 \times \$10 \text{ million} = 7.236540 \times \text{Market value of 10-year note}$$

or

Market value of 10-year note = $2.9171 million

To purchase $11.3583 million of the 2-year note and $0.2917 of the 10-year note will cost more than the 5-year note sold short. The difference between $14.2754 million cost of purchasing the notes in the wings and the proceeds from the sale of $10 million of the 5-year note, $4.2754 million must be financed in the repo market.

RELATIVE VALUE TRADES

A *relative value trade* is based on the expectation that one Treasury issue's yield is rich or cheap and subsequently the market will bring the yield back to its fair yield level. There are several issues in constructing a relative value trade.

First, it is necessary to have a benchmark to determine whether an issue is trading rich or cheap. Typically, this begins with a valuation model. The model must incorporate any unique features about this security. These features would include whether or not an issue is on special or if it is the cheapest-to-deliver. Moreover, as explained in Chapter 10, there is a different tax treatment for issues with a market discount depending on when they were issued.

Statistical models are used to determine the extent to which the yield or price of a Treasury issue differs from the model-derived theoretical value. For example, the degree of mispricing may be measured in statistical terms by the number of standard deviations that the market value is above or below the model derived value. The greater the number of standard deviations that the market value differs from the model-derived value, the greater the likelihood, based on the model, that the issue is mispriced.

A model can be simply based on historical relationships regarding the average spread of a Treasury off-the-run issue relative to an on-the-run issue. The key is that the success of the trade will depend on how good the valuation model is.

Once an issue is identified as mispriced, the next step is to take the appropriate position. Of course, if the issue is cheap it should be purchased. If the issue is expensive, it should be sold or shorted (if permissible). However, buying or selling without any offsetting position exposes the trader to the issue's interest rate risk. This risk may be unacceptable. Consequently, a relative value trade may involve an opposite position in another issue with the same dollar duration. The procedure for matching dollar durations is the same as in the pure slope curve described earlier in the chapter.

Lehman Brothers' Curve Spread Trading Strategy

To illustrate a relative value trade, we will use a trade recommended by Lehman Brothers. On June 9, 1997, the government strategists at Lehman Brothers, Douglas Johnston and Stuart Sparks, recommended a trade of the old 10-year issue at the time (the 6.25s of 2/15/07) versus more seasoned issues in that maturity sector (such as the 7s of 7/15/06).[5] Here we describe the analysis behind that recom-

---

[5] Lehman Brothers, *Relative Value*, Fixed Income Research, June 9, 1997, pp. GOV-2-GOV-4.

mended relative value trade. In particular, the trade shows the reliance on models and the need to backtest trade strategies.

A Treasury issue that trades special in the repo market will sell at a premium (i.e., higher price/lower yield) relative to an appropriate cash market Treasury benchmark issue that trades as general collateral. How rich the issue will trade depends on two factors: (1) the level of the special repo rate compared to the level of general collateral and (2) the shape of the term structure of the special repo rates compared to the shape of the term structure of the general collateral rates.

The valuation model used by the Lehman Brothers' strategists to determine the fair value of the security is a proprietary model, the Lehman Brothers Fitted Treasury Curve. The model gives the rates that should be used to discount the cash flows of a Treasury issue to determine that issue's fair value. Based on the computed fair value and the cash flows, a yield can be derived. Lehman Brothers defines the issue's "spread" as the difference between the model-derived yield and the market yield (as traditionally calculated). This spread is called the *curve spread*.[6]

The fitted Treasury curve is constructed from issues that are trading as general collateral. Consequently, the curve is a benchmark for off-the-run issues. The curve spread then calculated measures the spread relative to general collateral without the need for adjusting for coupon and maturity.

In the early life of an on-the-run issue, the curve spread will be large. This is a reflection of the financing advantage of the issue. However, over time the curve spread for the issue approaches zero as the financing advantage is eliminated. That is, its market value will approach the fair value as indicated by the fitted Treasury curve. The strategists at Lehman Brothers noted that it takes about one year for this to occur in the 10-year sector. Thus, an old on-the-run 10-year issue that is less than one year seasoned will likely have a positive curve spread.

The question is whether or not the calculated curve spread for an issue reflects its fair value as measured by the fitted Treasury curve. Lehman Brothers developed a model to estimate the expected financing advantage of an issue which is compared to the capital loss that is to be expected when the issue's curve spread becomes zero (i.e., the issue becomes fairly priced). Specifically, an estimated *financing implied curve spread* was constructed by dividing the expected financing advantage over an issue's remaining term by the horizon price value of 1 basis point. The trading rule was then based on the following for an issue that was a candidate for this trade:

- an issue is rich if the financing implied curve spread is sufficiently narrow compared to the actual curve spread
- an issue is cheap if the financing implied curve spread is sufficiently wide compared to the actual curve spread

---

[6] This spread is similar to a zero-volatility spread.

Exhibit 5: Profit and Loss Statistics for Curve Spread Trading Strategy for the On-the-Run 10-Year Issue

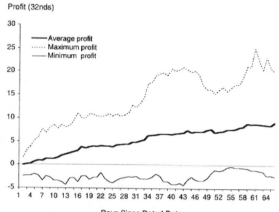

Profit (32nds)

Days Since Dated Date

* Trading strategy tested over the last 18 auction cycles.
Source: Figure 4 of Lehman Brothers, *Relative Value*, Fixed Income Research, June 9, 1997, pp. GOV-3.

The strategists performed a backtest of this strategy over the 18 auction cycles for the 10-year issue prior to the May 1997 auction. Lehman Brothers uses a 0.5 basis point threshold for triggering the buy or sell trade. The average profit and loss results of the strategy if the trade was put on for a 3-month time period are shown in Exhibit 5. The average profit was 8 ticks ($250,000 for a $100 million notional position). The maximum gain was 20 ticks and the maximum loss was 3 ticks. Transaction costs were not considered.

The results are based on an average of the prior 18 auction cycles. The two Lehman Brothers strategists applied their trading strategy to the old 10-year issue at the time — the 6.25s of 2/15/07 — from 2/17/97 to 6/5/97. Exhibit 6 shows the financing implied curve and the actual curve for the period and Exhibit 7 shows the strategy's profit. The profit on the strategy was 8 ticks.

At the outset of our discussion we stated that the strategists at Lehman Brothers suggested trading out of the 6.25s of 2/15/07 to a more seasoned security in that maturity sector. The recommendation was based on the trading strategy just described. Using their model, the analysts found that the 6.25s of 2/15/07 was above fair value based on the following. The overnight repo rate was 4.75% which meant a 67 basis point financing advantage. From the model, the estimated financing implied curve spread was −6.3 basis points. The actual curve spread at the same time was −7.3 basis points. As noted earlier, the buy/sell signal is based on 0.5 basis points. Since the financing implied curve spread of −6.3 basis points is narrower than the actual curve spread of −7.3 basis points, the model signals a sale of the 6.25s of 2/15/07. The model also indicates when a buy recommendation would be signaled. In this case, the overnight financing advantage would have had to increase by about 50 basis points.

Exhibit 6: Financing Implied Curve and Actual Curve Spread for the 6.25s of 2/15/2007: 2/17/97-6/5/97

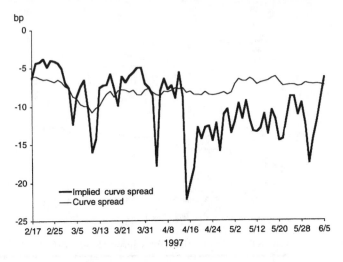

Source: Figure 5 of Lehman Brothers, *Relative Value*, Fixed Income Research, June 9, 1997, pp. GOV-4.

Exhibit 7: Profit and Loss for Curve Spread Trading Strategy for the 6.25s of 2/15/2007: 2/17/97-6/5/97

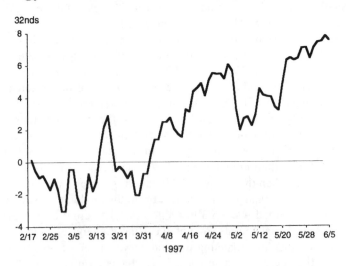

Source: Figure 6 of Lehman Brothers, *Relative Value*, Fixed Income Research, June 9, 1997, pp. GOV-4.

ROLL AND REVERSE ROLL TRADES

In Chapter 1 we provided a brief description of a roll trade. In this trade an investor sells an outstanding issue and buys the issue to be auctioned. In a *reverse roll*, the investor buys the outstanding issue and sells the issue to be auctioned.

Regular settlement for the sale of the outstanding issue is the next business day. For coupon issues, quotes are in terms of price. The issue to be auctioned cannot be delivered until after the auction. That is, there is a forward settlement of the purchase for the issue to be auctioned. When-issued securities are quoted in terms of yield rather than price. Once the auction results are determined, the price of the when-issued security is calculated based on the coupon set by the Treasury.

Dealers provide quotes on roll trades. The quote is expressed as the spread between the yield on the outstanding issue and the yield on the issue to be auctioned. These quotes are available from the various on-line services.

Factors Affecting the Spread on the Roll

Whether an investor should buy the roll or sell the roll (i.e., a reverse roll) requires an analysis of several factors. Below we describe these factors. They include:[7]

1. Financing value
2. Curve value
3. Bad days value
4. Repo value
5. Liquidity value

Financing Value

To illustrate the significance of financing value in deciding whether to buy or sell the roll, we begin with a simple case. The simple case involves a reopened issue. The reason why this is a simple case is that the issues bought and sold are identical.

Let's use a hypothetical 10-year 7% coupon issue that was auctioned on 5/15 of some year. The maturity date for this issue is 5/15 ten year later. Suppose that the Treasury announces on 8/1 that this issue will be reopened and auctioned with settlement on 8/15. That is, the Treasury will auction a 7% coupon issue with a maturity date of 5/15 10 years later. The objective of the exercise is to determine at what yield the investor would breakeven if she did the roll trade on 8/1.

First we must determine how much money the dealer must pay the investor for the issue sold to the dealer on 8/1. Suppose that on 8/1 the outstanding issue is trading at 100.75 (bid price) for a yield of 6.8893%. If the issue is sold, settlement is on 8/2. The number of days from the last coupon payment to 8/2

---

[7] The terminology used here for the factors are those used by Douglas Johnston and Stuart Sparks of Lehman Brothers and discussed in their reports that appear in the weekly Lehman Brothers publication, *Relative Value*.

(i.e., the number of days of accrued interest) is 79. The proceeds that will be received by selling this issue (i.e, the full price) is the price of 100.75 plus accrued interest of 1.5027. Thus, the proceeds received will be 102.2527.

The full price is important since this is the amount the dealer must finance to acquire the proceeds from the investor who is putting on the roll trade. This amount must be financed from 8/2 to the settlement date of the new issue on 8/15. That is, the dealer must finance this position in the repo market for 13 days. Suppose that the repo rate is 5%. Then the dealer's financing cost is:

$$102.2527\ (0.05)\ (13/360) = 0.1846$$

The total proceeds paid to the investor to purchase the issue on 8/2 (102.2527) plus the financing cost to carry the issue to 8/15 (0.1846) is 102.4373. This amount represents what the dealer must recover from selling the newly auctioned issue at settlement on 8/15.

When the new issue settles on 8/15 the proceeds that the dealer will receive from the investor consists of the agreed upon sale price (the forward price) plus the accrued interest. Let's look first at the accrued interest. The accrued interest from the issue date of 5/15 to the settlement date of the new issue (8/15) is 1.7500. Since the dealer must recover 102.4373 on 8/15 to breakeven and will receive 1.7500 in accrued interest, the price that the dealer must receive for the sale of the new issue is 100.6873 (102.4373 − 1.7500). To obtain this price, the dealer must offer to sell the new issue to the investor at a yield so that the price is 100.6873. The yield is 6.8978%.

Consequently, due to financing the dealer breaks even if he buys the outstanding issue for 100.75 (bid price) and sells the new issue for 100.6873 (offer price). Equivalently, the dealer breaks even if buys the outstanding issue for 6.8893% (bid yield) and sells the new issue for 6.8978%. The difference between the offer yield for the new issue and the bid yield for the outstanding issue is 0.85 basis points. Equivalently, this spread on the roll is the spread that will make the investor indifferent between holding the outstanding issue or rolling into the new issue.[8]

We can see how the financing cost affects the spread on the roll. Exhibit 8 shows the spread for five repo rates — 4.0%, 4.5%, 5.0%, 5.5%, and 6.0%. The lower the repo rate the higher the spread on the roll. Exhibit 8 also shows the effect on the spread on the roll based on the proximity to the settlement date for the new issue. The closer the roll trade is to the date when the new issue will be auctioned, the smaller the spread on the roll.

---

[8] It should be noted that the convention for calculating the price and yield in the when-issued market is different from that used in the secondary market. In the when-issued market the Treasury method is used. In the secondary market the Street method is used. Despite the difference in the conventions, the spread on the roll uses the respective convention in each market. However, the difference in the spread on the roll if adjusted to keep the conventions used the same is typically not material.

Exhibit 8: Dealer Price and Yield Needed to Breakeven on Roll Trade and Dealer Quote

Trade date information:			
Trade date	8/2	8/6	8/10
No. of days	13	9	5
Price	100.7500	100.7500	100.7500
Accrued interest	1.5027	1.5788	1.6549
Bid yield	6.8893	6.8891	6.8890
New issue settlement date information:			
Accrued interest	1.7500	1.7500	1.7500
Price ($) needed to breakeven on roll			
Repo rate			
4.0	100.6504	100.6811	100.7118
4.5	100.6689	100.6939	100.7189
5.0	100.6873	100.7067	100.7260
5.5	100.7058	100.7195	100.7331
6.0	100.7242	100.7323	100.7402
Yield (%) to breakeven on roll			
Repo rate			
4.0	6.9030	6.8987	6.8943
4.5	6.9000	6.8969	6.8933
5.0	6.8978	6.8950	6.8923
5.5	6.8952	6.8932	6.8913
6.0	6.8926	6.8914	6.8903
Spread for roll due to financing (in basis points)			
Repo rate(%)			
4.00	1.37	0.96	0.53
4.50	1.07	0.78	0.43
5.00	0.85	0.59	0.33
5.50	0.59	0.41	0.23
6.00	0.33	0.23	0.13

In our illustration the roll on the spread was positive. However, the spread can be negative.

Curve Value

The scenario just presented is simple in that it is assumes that the issue to be auctioned and the outstanding issue are the same. The same principles apply when the issues are not the same (i.e, when the roll does not involve the reopening of an outstanding issue). However, the analysis must take into account that the duration of the outstanding issue if owned on the settlement date of the new issue will not be the same as the duration of the new issue.

An analysis of the roll trade must estimate what the duration (and convexity) will be on the new issue. A pricing model is needed to estimate what the affect of the difference in interest rate risk measures will be. In a positive yield curve environment, a duration extension would result in a positive value for the curve value.

Bad Days Value

In the analysis of the cash flows in determining the effect of financing on the spread on the roll, next day settlement is assumed. However, if the settlement day is a holiday, this must be taken into consideration. The number of days that settlement is postponed due to holidays (for either the outstanding issue or newly auctioned issue) is referred to as *bad days*. Also, the cash flows that occur on a non-business day need to be adjusted since the Street yield convention does not make the adjustment.

Repo Value

In the analysis of the roll, no recognition is given to the fact that in the future the new issue most likely will have a financing advantage over the outstanding issue. The investor would be willing to give up yield by rolling from the outstanding issue to the new issue in order to benefit from favorable future financing via reverse repos. The *repo value* is an estimate of that financing advantage.

The estimate of the repo value depends on how long the new issue is expected to be held in order to take advantage of the favorable financing and the amount of the financing advantage. For example, in their analysis of the 10-year roll for the 8/15/07 new issue, Douglas Johnston and Stuart Sparks estimated the potential repo value by looking at the on-the-run 10-year note and the old on-the-run 10-year note (i.e., the previous on-the-run 10-year note) for five previous cycles. The historical financing advantage was calculated and the yield give-up that would have been exchanged for this financing advantage was computed. The amount of the yield give-up is based on the number of days the positions were held from the settlement date of the newly auctioned on-the-run 10-year issue up to 150 days later. The results are shown in Exhibit 9.

Exhibit 9: Historical Financing Advantage Expressed as Yield as a Function of Holding Period for On-the-Run 10-Year Note versus Old On-the-Run 10-Year Note

Days Held	Feb '06-Nov '05	May '06-Feb '06	July '06-May '06	Oct '06-July '06	Feb '07-Oct '06
15	0.66	2.60	0.07	−0.09	0.38
30	−0.08	2.97	0.00	−0.61	0.23
45	−1.33	4.05	−0.01	−0.89	0.34
60	−2.54	4.79	−0.14	−0.96	0.04
75	−3.85	4.87	−0.79	−1.17	−0.80
90	−4.76	6.17	−0.95	−1.83	−1.77
105	−7.06	7.48	−0.96	−2.24	−2.94
120	−7.21	8.81	−1.00	−3.14	−3.52
135	−8.42	8.81	−1.03	−3.68	−3.61
150	−7.68	9.28	−1.05	−4.00	−3.70

Source: Figure 3 in Lehman Brothers, *Relative Value*, Fixed Income Research, July 28, 1997, GOV-2.

Liquidity Value

Typically, the new issue will trade with better liquidity than the outstanding issue. A subjective estimate of the value of this liquidity must be considered in assessing a roll trade. Tighter bid-ask spread and ease of execution all contribute to this estimate. This estimated value, called the *liquidity value*, is the amount the investor is willing to give up in yield by rolling into the new issue.

Buy or Sell the Roll

Given the quoted spread on the roll and the factors that affect the roll, the question is whether the investor should buy or sell the roll. Buying the roll means selling the outstanding issue and buying the new issue. Selling the roll means buying the outstanding issue and selling the new issue.

Buying the roll should be done when the estimated pickup in yield is less than the quoted spread on the roll. Selling the roll should be done when the estimated pickup in yield is greater than the quoted spread on the roll.

Buying the Roll

We can use the 3-year roll around May 4, 1997 to illustrate when buying the roll would be recommended.[9] The new issue was to be auctioned on May 15, 1997. The bid-ask spread for the roll by dealers was 4.0 bp/3.75 bp. The analysts on the government desk at Lehman Brothers estimated the following:

Financing value based on a repo rate of 5%	1.4 bp
Curve value	2.5 bp
Bad days value	0 bp
Liquidity and repo values	−2.0 bp
Estimated net pickup	1.9 bp

The liquidity and repo values were estimated assuming that the new issue would trade, on average, 22 basis points above the outstanding issue in financing.

Since the estimated net pickup is 1.9 basis points but the quoted spread on the roll is greater, the analysts recommended buying the 3-year roll. That is, the investor could get a greater yield pick-up by buying the roll from the dealer.

Selling the Roll

We can use the roll for the 10-year for the 6.25s of 2/15/07 around May 4, 1997 to demonstrate when the sale of a roll is recommended.[10] This trade would involve selling on about May 4, 1997 the new 10-year issue that was to be auctioned on May 15, 1997.

---

[9] This information is taken from Lehman Brothers, *Relative Value*, Fixed Income Research, May 5, 1997, GOV-1 and GOV-2.

[10] This information is taken from Lehman Brothers, *Relative Value*, Fixed Income Research, May 5, 1997, GOV-1 and GOV-2.

On May 4, 1997 the bid-ask spread for the roll trade was 1.5 bp/1.25 bp. Based on a repo rate of 3.5%, the financing was estimated to be worth 1.2 bp. The curve value was estimated to be worth 1 bp because of the duration that would arise from the roll. (The duration extension was estimated to be 0.14 and since the yield curve was positive, this made the curve value positive.) There were no bad days. Therefore, financing value and curve value were worth 2.2 basis points. But since the bid-ask quote was less than 2.2 (+1.5) basis points, this meant that the market was assigning a give up of −0.7 basis points for the repo value plus the liquidity value. From this it can be determined that the May issue must trade 30 basis points more special than the outstanding issue. (At the time, the May issue was expected to be on-the-run for only two months and not expected to finance well.) Based on the analysis by the two strategists at Lehman Brothers, this premium was too high. As a result, the analysts recommended selling the 10-year roll.

KEY POINTS

1. *Yield curve trades seek to capitalize on changes in the slope and/or curvature of the yield curve.*

2. *Yield curve trades include pure slope trades, duration and cash neutral trades, and duration neutral trades with equal dollar duration in each wing.*

3. *A pure slope trade involves a position in two Treasury securities and a cash equivalent; the positions are determined so as to be duration neutral.*

4. *A duration and cash neutral trade involves a position in three Treasury securities and no position in cash.*

5. *A duration and cash neutral trade is not a pure slope trade because there is some exposure to changes in curvature.*

6. *A duration neutral trade with equal dollar duration in each wing is a combination slope trade and curvature trade.*

7. *A duration neutral trade with equal dollar duration in each wing requires a cash position (either financing or lending overnight).*

8. *Historical information about changes in the slope and curvature for the relevant maturity sector is needed to properly structure a duration and cash neutral trade and a duration neutral trade with equal dollar duration in each wing.*

9. *A relative value trade requires a valuation model for assessing any mispricing.*

10. *A relative value trade typically involves a long position in the cheap issue and short position in the expensive issue, with the positions created so as to be duration neutral.*

11. *A roll trade involves a position in the outstanding on-the-run issue and the opposite position in the issue to be auctioned.*

12. *Buying the roll to achieve a yield pick-up involves selling the outstanding issue and buying the new issue; selling the roll to achieve a yield pick up involves buying the outstanding issue and selling the new issue.*

13. *Dealers quote the spread on the roll.*

14. *The factors that affect the value of a roll are the financing value, the curve value, the bad days value, the repo value, and the liquidity value.*

15. *If the roll value (i.e., estimated net yield pick-up based on the factors) is less than the dealer quoted spread on the roll, the investor should buy the roll; if the roll value is greater than the dealer quoted spread on the roll, then the investor should sell the roll.*

Chapter 12

TREASURY FUTURES CONTRACTS

Futures contracts are agreements that require a party to the agreement either to buy or sell something at a designated future date at a predetermined price. That is, one party is agreeing to make delivery and the other is agreeing to take delivery of something. The price at which the parties agree to transact in the case of a futures contract is called the *futures price*. The designated date on which the parties must transact is called the *settlement* or *delivery date*. Futures contracts are standardized agreements as to the delivery date (or month) and quality of the deliverable, and are traded on organized exchanges. Our focus in this chapter is on futures contracts in which the underlying is a Treasury security. We shall refer to these contracts as Treasury futures contracts. In Chapter 14 we explain how Treasury futures are priced and in Chapter 15 we shall see how they can be used to control interest rate risk.

MECHANICS OF FUTURES TRADING

Treasury futures contracts have settlement dates in the months of March, June, September, or December. This means that at a predetermined time in the contract settlement month the contract stops trading, and a price is determined by the exchange for settlement of the contract. The contract with the closest settlement date is called the *nearby futures contract*. The next futures contract is the one that settles just after the nearby contract. The contract farthest away in time from settlement is called the *most distant futures contract*.

A party to a futures contract has two choices as to how to liquidate a position. First, a position can be liquidated prior to the settlement date. For this purpose, the party must take an offsetting position in the same contract. For the buyer of a futures contract, this means selling the same number of identical futures contracts; for the seller of a futures contract, this means buying the same number of identical futures contracts. The alternative is to wait until the settlement date. At that time the party purchasing a Treasury futures contract accepts delivery of the underlying at the futures settlement price; the party that sells a Treasury futures contract liquidates the position by delivering the underlying at the futures settlement price.

Associated with every futures exchange is a clearinghouse, which performs several functions. One of these functions is to guarantee that the two parties to the contract will perform. When an investor takes a position in the futures market, the clearinghouse effectively takes the opposite position and agrees to satisfy the terms set forth in the contract. Because of the clearinghouse, the investor need not worry about the financial strength and integrity of the party taking the opposite side of the contract. After initial execution of an order, the relationship between the two parties ends. The clearinghouse interposes itself as the buyer for every sale and the seller for every purchase. Thus either party is free to liquidate a position without involving the other party in the original contract, and without worry that the other party may default. Besides its guarantee function, the clearinghouse makes it simple for parties to a futures contract to unwind their positions prior to the settlement date.

When a position is first taken in a futures contract, the parties must deposit a minimum dollar amount per contract as specified by the exchange. This amount is called *initial margin* and is required as deposit for the contract. The initial margin may be in the form of an interest-bearing security such as a Treasury bill. As the price of the futures contract fluctuates, the value of the party's equity in the position changes. At the end of each trading day, the exchange determines the day's settlement price for the futures contract. This price is used to mark to market the party's position, so that any gain or loss from the position is reflected in that party's equity account.

Maintenance margin is the minimum level (specified by the exchange) to which a party's equity position may fall as a result of an unfavorable price movement before the party is required to deposit additional margin. The additional margin deposited is called *variation margin*, and it is an amount necessary to bring the equity in the account back to its initial margin level. Unlike initial margin, variation margin must be in cash, not interest-bearing instruments. Any excess margin in the account may be withdrawn by the party. If a party to a futures contract who is required to deposit variation margin fails to do so within 24 hours, the futures position is closed out.

For investors who are considered "hedgers," there is a more favorable treatment with respect to margin requirements. Hedgers are able to put up "hedge margin." Typically, hedge margin is less than the initial margin requirement. A futures brokerage firm will provide the specific rules for obtaining hedge margin status.

Although there are initial and maintenance margin requirements for buying securities on margin, the concept of margin differs for securities and futures. When securities are acquired on margin, the difference between the price of the security and the initial margin is borrowed from the broker. The security becomes the collateral for the loan, and the investor pays interest. For futures contracts, the initial margin, in effect, serves as "good faith" money, an indication that the investor will satisfy the obligation of the contract. Normally no money is borrowed by the investor.

Since futures contracts are marked to market at the end of each trading day, each party is subject to interim cash flows as additional margin may be required in the case of adverse price movements, or as cash is withdrawn in the case of favorable price movements.

Exhibit 1: Effect of Rate Changes on Parties to a Futures Contract

	Interest rates	
Party	Decrease	Increase
Buyer (long)	Gains	Loses
Seller (short)	Loses	Gains

RISK AND RETURN CHARACTERISTICS

When a party takes a position in the market by buying a futures contract, that party is said to be in a *long position* or to be *long futures*. If, instead, a party's opening position is the sale of a futures contract, that party is said to be in a *short position* or *short futures*. The buyer of a futures contract will realize a profit if the futures price increases; the seller of a futures contract will realize a profit if the futures price decreases. This is summarized in Exhibit 1.

When a position is taken in a futures contract, the party need not put up the entire amount of the investment. Instead, only initial margin must be put up. Consequently, an investor can create a leveraged position by using futures. At first, the leverage available in the futures market may suggest that the market benefits only those who want to speculate on price movements. This is not true. As we shall see in Chapter 15, futures markets can be used to control risk. Without the leverage possible in futures transactions, the cost of reducing price risk using futures would be too high for many market participants.

TREASURY BILL FUTURES

The Treasury bill futures contract, which is traded on the International Monetary Market (IMM) of the Chicago Mercantile Exchange, is based on a 13-week (3-month) Treasury bill with a face value of $1 million. More specifically, the seller of a Treasury bill futures contract agrees to deliver to the buyer at the settlement date a Treasury bill with 13 weeks remaining to maturity and a face value of $1 million. The Treasury bill delivered can be newly issued or seasoned. The futures price is the price at which the Treasury bill will be sold by the short and purchased by the long. For example, a Treasury bill futures contract that settles in 9 months requires that 9 months from now the short deliver to the long $1 million face value of a Treasury bill with 13 weeks remaining to maturity. The Treasury bill could be a newly issued 13-week Treasury bill or a Treasury bill that was issued one year prior to the settlement date and therefore at the settlement date has only 13 weeks remaining to maturity.

Treasury bills are quoted in the cash market in terms of the annualized yield on a bank discount basis, where

$$Y_d = \frac{D}{F} \times \frac{360}{t}$$

where

Y_d = annualized yield on a bank discount basis (expressed as a decimal)

D = dollar discount, which is equal to the difference between the face value and the price of a bill maturing in t days

F = face value

t = number of days remaining to maturity.

The dollar discount (D) is found by:

$$D = Y_d \times F \times \frac{t}{360}$$

In contrast, the Treasury bill futures contract is not quoted directly in terms of yield, but instead on an index basis that is related to the yield on a bank discount basis as follows:

$$\text{Index price} = 100 - (Y_d \times 100)$$

For example, if Y_d is 8%, the index price is

$$100 - (0.08 \times 100) = 92$$

Given the price of the futures contract, the yield on a bank discount basis for the futures contract is determined as follows:

$$Y_d = \frac{100 - \text{Index price}}{100}$$

To see how this works, suppose that the index price for a Treasury bill futures contract is 92.52. The yield on a bank discount basis for this Treasury bill futures contract is:

$$Y_d = \frac{100 - 92.52}{100} = 0.0748 \text{ or } 7.48\%$$

The invoice price that the buyer of $1 million face value of 13-week Treasury bills must pay at settlement is found by first computing the dollar discount, as follows:

$$D = Y_d \times \$1,000,000 \times \frac{t}{360}$$

where t is either 90 or 91 days.

Typically, the number of days to maturity of a 13-week Treasury bill is 91 days. The invoice price is then:

$$\text{Invoice price} = \$1,000,000 - D$$

For example, for the Treasury bill futures contract with an index price of 92.52 (and a yield on a bank discount basis of 7.48%), the dollar discount for the 13-week Treasury bill to be delivered with 91 days to maturity is:

$$D = 0.0748 \times \$1,000,000 \times \frac{91}{360} = \$18,907.78$$

The invoice price is:

Invoice price $= \$1,000,000 - \$18,907.78 = \$981,092.22$

The minimum index price fluctuation or "tick" for this futures contract is 0.01. A change of 0.01 for the minimum index price translates into a change in the yield on a bank discount basis of 1 basis point (0.0001). A 1 basis point change results in a change in the invoice price as follows:

$$0.0001 \times \$1,000,000 \times \frac{t}{360}$$

For a 13-week Treasury bill with 91 days to maturity, the change in the dollar discount is:

$$0.0001 \times \$1,000,000 \times \frac{91}{360} = \$25.28$$

For a 13-week Treasury bill with 90 days to maturity, the change in the dollar discount would be $25. Despite the fact that a 13-week Treasury bill typically has 91 days to maturity, market participants commonly refer to the value of a basis point (or dollar value of an 01) for this futures contract as $25.

TREASURY BOND FUTURES

The Treasury bond futures contract is traded on the Chicago Board of Trade (CBOT). The underlying instrument for a Treasury bond futures contract is $100,000 par value of a hypothetical 20-year 8% coupon bond. However, no such Treasury bond exists. Instead, the CBOT delivery rules allow one of several Treasury bond issues to be delivered. The choice of which Treasury bond issue to deliver from among those in the pool that may be delivered is given to the seller of the futures contract.

The CBOT has established criteria that a Treasury bond issue must satisfy in order to be acceptable for delivery. Specifically, an issue must have at least 15 years to maturity from the date of delivery if not callable; in the case of callable bonds, the issue must not be callable for at least 15 years from the first day of the delivery month. Exhibit 2 shows the 30 Treasury bond issues that the seller can select from to deliver to the buyer of the June 1997 futures contract.

The futures price is quoted in terms of par value being 100. Quotes are in 32nds of 1%. Thus a quote for a Treasury bond futures contract of 108-23 means 108 and 23/32nds, or 108.71875. So, if a buyer and seller agree on a futures price of 108-23, this means that the buyer agrees to accept delivery of the hypothetical underlying Treasury bond and pay 108.71875% of par value and the seller agrees to accept 108.71875% of par value. Since the par value is $100,000, the futures price that the buyer and seller agree to pay for this hypothetical Treasury bond is $108,718.75.

Exhibit 2: Treasury Bond Issues Acceptable for Delivery to Satisfy the June 1997 Futures Contract

Issue		Conversion
Coupon (%)	Maturity	Factor
6.625	2/15/27	0.8451
6.500	11/15/26	0.8312
6.750	8/15/26	0.8598
6.000	2/15/26	0.7767
6.875	8/15/25	0.8750
7.625	2/15/25	0.9585
7.500	11/15/24	0.9447
6.250	8/15/23	0.8097
7.125	2/15/23	0.9054
7.625	11/15/22	0.9594
7.250	8/15/22	0.9194
8.000	11/15/22	0.9998
8.125	8/15/21	1.0132
8.125	5/15/21	1.0130
7.875	2/15/21	0.9868
8.750	8/15/20	1.0783
8.750	5/15/20	1.0778
8.500	2/15/20	1.0518
8.125	8/15/19	1.0128
8.875	2/15/19	1.0891
9.000	11/15/19	1.1012
9.125	5/15/18	1.1128
8.875	8/15/17	1.0866
8.750	5/15/17	1.0736
7.500	11/15/16	0.9511
7.250	5/15/16	0.9276
9.250	2/15/16	1.1196
9.875	11/15/15	1.1781
10.625	8/15/15	1.2482
11.250	2/15/15	1.3033

The minimum price fluctuation for the Treasury bond futures contract is a 32nd of 1%. The dollar value of a 32nd for a $100,000 par value (the par value for the underlying Treasury bond) is $31.25. Thus, the minimum price fluctuation is $31.25 for this contract.

Conversion Factor and Converted Price

The delivery process for the Treasury bond futures contract makes the contract interesting. At the settlement date, the seller of a futures contract (the short) is required to deliver to the buyer (the long) $100,000 par value of an 8% 20-year Treasury bond. Since no such bond exists, the seller must choose from one of the acceptable deliverable Treasury bonds that the CBOT exchange has specified. Suppose the seller is entitled to deliver $100,000 of a 6% 20-year Treasury bond to settle the futures contract. The value of this bond, of course, is less than the value of an 8% 20-year bond. If the seller delivers the 6% 20-year, this would be unfair to the buyer of the futures contract who contracted to receive $100,000 of an 8% 20-year Treasury bond. Alternatively, suppose the seller delivers $100,000 of a 10% 20-year Treasury bond. The value of a 10% 20-year Treasury bond is greater than that of an 8% 20-year bond, so this would be a disadvantage to the seller.

How can this problem be resolved? To make delivery equitable to both parties, the CBOT introduced *conversion factors* for determining the price of each acceptable deliverable Treasury issue if an issue is delivered to satisfy the Treasury bond futures contract. The conversion factor is determined by the CBOT before a contract with a specific settlement date begins trading. Exhibit 2 shows for each of the acceptable Treasury issues the corresponding conversion factor. The conversion factor is based on the price that a deliverable bond would sell for at the beginning of the delivery month if it were to yield 8%. The conversion factor is constant throughout the trading period of the futures contract.

The product of the settlement price and the conversion factor for a deliverable issue is called the *converted price*. The amount that the buyer must pay the seller when a Treasury bond is delivered is called the *invoice price*. The invoice price is the settlement futures price plus accrued interest. However, as just noted, the seller can deliver one of several acceptable Treasury issues. To make delivery fair to both parties, the invoice price must be adjusted based on the actual Treasury issue delivered. It is the conversion factor that is used to adjust the invoice price. The invoice price is:

Invoice price = Contract size × Futures contract settlement price
$$\times \text{Conversion factor} + \text{Accrued interest}$$

Suppose that the June 1997 Treasury bond futures contract settles at 108-16 and that the issue delivered is the 11.25s of 2/15/15. The futures contract settlement price of 108-16 means 108.5% of par value or 1.085 times par value As indicated in Exhibit 2, the conversion factor for this issue is 1.3033. Since the contract size is $100,000, the invoice price the buyer pays the seller is:

$100,000 × 1.085 × 1.3033 + Accrued interest
= $141,408.05 + Accrued interest

If, instead, the 6.625s of 2/15/27 which has a conversion factor of 0.8451 is delivered, the invoice price would be:

$$\$100,000 \times 1.085 \times 0.8451 + \text{Accrued interest}$$
$$= \$91,693.35 + \text{Accrued interest}$$

Cheapest-to-Deliver Issue

In selecting the issue to be delivered, the short will select from among all the deliverable issues the one that will give the largest rate of return from a *cash and carry trade*. A cash and carry trade is one in which a cash bond that is acceptable for delivery is purchased and simultaneously the Treasury bond futures contract is sold. The bond purchased can be delivered to satisfy the short futures position. Thus, by buying the Treasury bond issue that is acceptable for delivery and selling the futures, an investor has effectively sold the bond at the delivery price (i.e., converted price).

A rate of return can be calculated for this trade. The rate of return is determined by:

1. the price plus accrued interest of the Treasury bond that could be purchased
2. the converted price plus the accrued interest that will be received upon delivery of that Treasury bond issue to satisfy the short futures position
3. the coupon payments that will be received between today and the delivery date
4. the reinvestment income that will be realized on the coupon payments between the time received and the delivery date.

The first three elements are known. The last element, reinvestment income, depends on the rate that can be earned on any interim coupon payments. What is assumed is that this rate is the prevailing term repo rate where the term is the number of days between receipt of the interim coupon payment and the bond delivery. The annual rate of return on the cash and carry trade is calculated as follows:[1]

$$\text{Annual return} = \frac{\text{Dollar return}}{\text{Purchase Price} + \text{Accrued Interest Paid}} \times \frac{360}{\text{Days}_1}$$

where

Proceeds at settlement date
= Converted price + Accrued interest received + Interim coupon payment
+ Interest from reinvesting interim coupon payment

---

[1] The formula can be modified to allow for the fact that the interim coupon payment reduces the amount invested (the denominator of the first term). The modified formula is:

$$\text{Annual return} = \frac{\text{Dollar return}}{\text{Adjusted investment cost}} \times 360$$

where

Adjusted investment cost $= \text{Days}_1(\text{Purchase price} + \text{Accrued interest paid})$
$- \text{Days}_2(\text{Interim coupon payment})$

Converted price = Futures price × Conversion factor

Interest from reinvesting interim coupon payment
= Interim coupon × [1 + term repo rate × ($Days_2$/360)]

$Days_2$ = Number of days between interim coupon payment and actual delivery date

$Days_1$ = Number of days between settlement date and actual delivery

Dollar return = Proceeds at settlement date − Purchase price
− Accrued interest paid

The annual rate of return calculated for an acceptable Treasury issue is called the *implied repo rate*. Market participants will seek to maximize the implied repo rate; that is, they will use the acceptable Treasury issue that gives the largest rate of return in the cash and carry trade. The issue that satisfies this criterion is referred to as the *cheapest-to-deliver issue*. As explained in Chapter 14, it plays a key role in the pricing of this futures contract. This is depicted in Exhibit 3.

Exhibit 3: Determination of Cheapest-to-Deliver Issue Based on the Implied Repo Rate

Implied repo rate: Rate of return by buying an acceptable Treasury issue, shorting the Treasury bond futures, and delivering the issue at the settlement date.

Buy this issue:	Deliver this issue at futures price:	Calculate return (implied repo rate):
Acceptable Treasury issue #1	Deliver issue #1	Implied repo rate #1
Acceptable Treasury issue #2	Deliver issue #2	Implied repo rate #2
Acceptable Treasury issue #3	Deliver issue #3	Implied repo rate #3
. . .	. . .	. . .
Acceptable Treasury issue #N	Deliver issue #N	Implied repo rate #N

Cheapest-to-deliver issue is the issue that produces the maximum implied repo rate.

Exhibit 4: The Implied Repo Rate on March 25, 1997 for the Treasury Bond Issues Acceptable for Delivery to Satisfy the June 1997 Futures Contract[*]

Issue		Implied
Coupon (%)	Maturity	Repo Rate (%)
6.625	2/15/27	−8.48
6.500	11/15/26	−6.19
6.750	8/15/26	−4.28
6.000	2/15/26	−4.29
6.875	8/15/25	−2.76
7.625	2/15/25	−1.51
7.500	11/15/24	−1.26
6.250	8/15/23	−1.59
7.125	2/15/23	−0.17
7.625	11/15/22	0.52
7.250	8/15/22	0.54
8.000	11/15/22	1.51
8.125	8/15/21	1.81
8.125	5/15/21	1.90
7.875	2/15/21	1.81
8.750	8/15/20	2.61
8.750	5/15/20	2.67
8.500	2/15/20	2.74
8.125	8/15/19	2.76
8.875	2/15/19	3.47
9.000	11/15/19	3.47
9.125	5/15/18	3.66
8.875	8/15/17	4.09
8.750	5/15/17	4.03
7.500	11/15/16	3.36
7.250	5/15/16	3.06
9.250	2/15/16	4.63
9.875	11/15/15	4.83
10.625	8/15/15	5.10
11.250	2/15/15	5.25

[*] Calculation of the implied repo rate for these issues was provided by the Futures Basis Matic (FB)v7 of the Fixed Income Research Department of Goldman, Sachs & Co. The analysis is as of 3/25/97 based on a futures price of 108-23.

Exhibit 4 shows the implied repo rate on March 25, 1997 for each deliverable issue to satisfy the June 1997 futures contract. The highest implied repo rate is 5.25% for the 11.25% 2/15/15 issue. Therefore, it is this issue that is the cheapest-to-deliver issue.

While an issue may be the cheapest to deliver today, changes in factors may cause some other issue to be the cheapest to deliver at a future date. A sensitivity analysis can be performed to determine how a change in yield affects the cheapest to deliver. For the June 1997 futures contract, the 11.25% 2/15/15 issue would remain the cheapest to deliver if yields decreased. For a rise in yields, the cheapest-to-deliver issue would be as follows:[2]

Yield change	Cheapest-to-deliver issue	
+20 basis points	10.625%	8/15/15
+40 basis points	8.875%	8/16/17
+60 basis point	8.875%	2/15/19
+80 basis point	8.125%	8/15/21

Delivery Options

In addition to the choice of which acceptable Treasury issue to deliver — sometimes referred to as the *quality option* or *swap option* — the short position has three more options granted under CBOT delivery guidelines. The first is related to the quality option. If a Treasury bond is auctioned prior to the settlement date, then the short can select this new issue. This option is referred to as the *new auction option*. The second option grants the short the right to decide when in the delivery month delivery actually will take place. This is called the *timing option*. The third option is the right of the short to give notice of intent to deliver up to 8:00 p.m. Chicago time after the closing of the exchange (3:15 p.m. Chicago time) on the date when the futures settlement price has been fixed. This option is referred to as the *wild card option*. The quality option, the new auction option, the timing option, and the wild card option (in sum referred to as the *delivery options*), mean that the long can never be sure which Treasury bond will be delivered or when it will be delivered. The delivery options are summarized in Exhibit 5.

Exhibit 5: Delivery Options Granted to the Short (Seller) of a CBOT Treasury Bond Futures Contract

Delivery option	Description
Quality or swap option	Choice of which acceptable Treasury issue to deliver
New auction option	Choice of a newly issued Treasury bond to deliver
Timing option	Choice of when in delivery month to deliver
Wild card option	Choice to deliver after the day's settlement price for the futures contract is determined

---

[2] This information was obtained from a printout provided by the Futures Basis Matic (FB)v7 of the Fixed Income Research Department of Goldman, Sachs & Co. The analysis is as of 3/25/97 based on a futures price of 108-23.

For a short who wants to deliver, the delivery procedure involves three days. The first day is the *position day*. On this day, the short notifies the CBOT that it intends to deliver. The short has until 8:00 p.m. central standard time to do so. The second day is the *notice day*. On this day, the short specifies which particular issue will be delivered. The short has until 2:00 p.m. central standard time to make this declaration. (On the last possible notice day in the delivery month, the short has until 3:00 p.m.) The CBOT then selects the long to whom delivery will be made. This is the longest outstanding long position. The long is then notified by 4:00 p.m. that delivery will be made. The third day is the *delivery day*. By 10:00 a.m. on this day the short must have in its account the Treasury issue that it specified on the notice day and by 1:00 p.m. must deliver that bond to the long that was assigned by the CBOT to accept delivery. The long pays the short the invoice price upon receipt of the bond.

TREASURY NOTE FUTURES

There are three Treasury note futures contracts: 10-year, 5-year, and 2-year. All three contracts are modeled after the Treasury bond futures contract and are traded on the CBOT. The underlying instrument for the 10-year Treasury note futures contract is $100,000 par value of a hypothetical 10-year 8% Treasury note. There are several acceptable Treasury issues that may be delivered by the short. An issue is acceptable if the maturity is not less than 6.5 years and not greater than 10 years from the first day of the delivery month. The delivery options granted to the short position and the minimum price fluctuation are the same as for the Treasury bond futures contract.

For the 5-year Treasury note futures contract, the underlying is $100,000 par value of a U.S. Treasury note that satisfies the following conditions: (1) an original maturity of not more than five years and three months, (2) a remaining maturity no greater then five years and three months, and (3) a remaining maturity not less than four years and three months. The minimum price fluctuation for this contract is a 64th of 1%. The dollar value of a 64th for a $100,000 par value is $15.625 and is therefore the minimum price fluctuation.

The underlying for the 2-year Treasury note futures contract is $200,000 par value of a U.S. Treasury note with a remaining maturity of not more than two years and not less than one year and nine months. Moreover, the original maturity of the note delivered to satisfy the 2-year futures cannot be more than five years and two months. The minimum price fluctuation for this contract is a 128th of 1%. The dollar value of a 128th for a $200,000 par value is $15.625 and is therefore the minimum price fluctuation.

KEY POINTS

1. *A futures contract is an agreement between a buyer (seller) and an established exchange or its clearinghouse in which the buyer (seller) agrees to take (make) delivery of something at a specified price at the end of a designated period of time.*

2. *The parties to a futures contract are required to satisfy margin requirements (initial, maintenance, and variation margin).*

3. *A party who takes a long futures position realizes a gain when the futures price increases; a party who takes a short futures position realizes a gain when the futures price decreases.*

4. *For the Treasury bond futures contract the underlying instrument is $100,000 par value of a hypothetical 20-year 8% Treasury coupon bond.*

5. *Conversion factors are used to adjust the invoice price of a Treasury bond futures contract to make delivery equitable to both parties.*

6. *The cheapest-to-deliver issue is the acceptable Treasury bond issue that has the largest implied repo rate.*

7. *The short in a Treasury bond futures contract has several delivery options: quality option (or swap option), new auction option, timing option, and wild card option.*

8. *The cheapest-to-deliver issue can change over the life of the contract.*

9. *Which acceptable Treasury issue will become the cheapest to deliver if yields change can be determined.*

10. *The 2-year, 5-year, and 10-year Treasury note futures contracts are modeled after the Treasury bond futures contract.*

Chapter 13

TREASURY OPTIONS

In this chapter we look at options on Treasury securities. This financial instrument is different from a Treasury futures contract in terms of its risk and return characteristics. As a result, a Treasury option can be used to control interest rate risk in ways that are either not possible or too difficult to acheive using a Treasury futures contract. In Chapter 14, we will explain how a Treasury option can be used to control interest rate risk and how to value a Treasury option. A Treasury option may be traded either on an organized exchange or in the over-the-counter market. We will discuss both types. The most popular form of exchange-traded Treasury option is an option on a Treasury futures contract.

THE BASIC OPTION CONTRACT

An *option* is a contract in which the writer of the option grants the buyer of the option the right, but not the obligation, to purchase from or sell to the writer something at a specified price within a specified period of time (or at a specified date). The *writer*, also referred to as the *seller,* grants this right to the buyer in exchange for a certain sum of money, which is called the *option price* or *option premium*. The price at which the underlying may be bought or sold is called the *exercise* or *strike price*. The date after which an option is void is called the *expiration date*. Our focus in this chapter is on options where the "something" underlying the option is a interest rate instrument.

When an option grants the buyer the right to purchase the designated instrument from the writer (seller), it is referred to as a *call option*, or *call*. When the option buyer has the right to sell the designated instrument to the writer, the option is called a *put option*, or *put*.

An option is also categorized according to when the option buyer may exercise the option. There are options that may be exercised at any time up to and including the expiration date. Such an option is referred to as an *American option*. There are options that may be exercised only at the expiration date. An option with this feature is called a *European option*.

The maximum amount that an option buyer can lose is the option price. The maximum profit that the option writer can realize is the option price. The option buyer has substantial upside return potential, while the option writer faces substantial downside risk. We'll investigate the risk and reward profile for option positions later.

There are no margin requirements for the buyer of an option once the option price has been paid in full. Because the option price is the maximum amount that the investor can lose, no matter how adverse the price movement of the underlying instrument, there is no need for margin. Because the writer of an option has agreed to accept all of the risk (and none of the reward) of the position in the underlying instrument, the writer is generally required to put up the option price received as margin. In addition, as price changes occur that adversely affect the writer's position, the writer is required to deposit additional margin (with some exceptions) as the position is marked to market.

DIFFERENCES BETWEEN OPTIONS AND FUTURES CONTRACTS

Notice that unlike in a futures contract, one party to an option contract is not obligated to transact. Specifically, the option buyer has the right but not the obligation to transact. The option writer does have the obligation to perform. In the case of a futures contract, both buyer and seller are obligated to perform. Of course, the buyer of a futures contract does not pay the seller to accept the obligation, while an option buyer pays the seller the option price.

Consequently, the risk and reward characteristics of the two contracts are also different. In the case of a futures contract, the buyer of the contract realizes a dollar-for-dollar gain when the price of the futures contract increases and suffers a dollar-for-dollar loss when the price of the futures contract drops. The opposite occurs for the seller of a futures contract. Options do not provide this symmetric risk and reward characteristic. The most that the buyer of an option can lose is the option price. While the buyer of an option retains all the potential benefits, the gain is always reduced by the amount of the option price. The maximum profit that the writer may realize is the option price; this is offset against substantial downside risk. This difference is extremely important because managers can use futures to protect against symmetric risk and options to protect against asymmetric risk.

EXCHANGE-TRADED VERSUS OTC OPTIONS

There are exchange-traded options and over-the-counter options. Exchange-traded options have two advantages. First, the exercise price and expiration date of the contract are standardized. Second, as in the case of futures contracts, the direct link between buyer and seller is severed after the order is executed because of the interchangeability of exchange-traded options. The clearinghouse associated with the exchange where the option trades performs the same function in the options market that it does in the futures market.

OTC options are used in the many situations where an institutional investor needs to have a tailor-made option because the standardized exchange-traded option does not satisfy its investment objectives. Investment banking firms and commercial banks act as principals as well as brokers in the OTC options market.

OTC options can be customized in any manner sought by an institutional investor. There are plain vanilla options such as options on a specific Treasury issue. The more complex OTC options created are called *exotic options*. Examples of OTC options are given at the end of chapter. While an OTC option is less liquid than an exchange-traded option, this is typically not of concern since institutional investors who use OTC options as part of a hedging or asset/liability strategy intend to hold them to expiration.

In the absence of a clearinghouse the parties to any over-the-counter contract are exposed to counterparty risk. For an OTC option, once the option buyer pays the option price, it has satisfied its obligation. It is only the seller that must perform if the option is exercised. Thus, the option buyer is exposed to unilateral counterparty risk — the risk that the option seller will fail to perform.

TREASURY FUTURES OPTIONS

The underlying for a Treasury option can be a Treasury security or a Treasury futures contract. The former options are called *options on physicals*. In the United States, there are no actively exchange-traded options on physicals. Options on Treasury futures are called Treasury *futures options*. The actively traded Treasury options on exchanges are Treasury futures options.

The Basics of Treasury Futures Options

A futures option gives the buyer the right to buy from or sell to the writer a designated Treasury futures contract at the strike price at any time during the life of the option. If the Treasury futures option is a call option, the buyer has the right to purchase one designated Treasury futures contract at the strike price. That is, the buyer has the right to acquire a long Treasury futures position in the designated Treasury futures contract. If the buyer exercises the call option, the writer acquires a corresponding short position in the futures contract.

A put option on a Treasury futures contract grants the buyer the right to sell a designated Treasury futures contract to the writer at the strike price. That is, the option buyer has the right to acquire a short position in the designated Treasury futures contract. If the put option is exercised, the writer acquires a corresponding long position in the designated Treasury futures contract.

As the parties to the Treasury futures option will realize a position in a Treasury futures contract when the option is exercised, the question is: what will the futures price be? That is, at what price will the long be required to pay for the Treasury futures contract, and at what price will the short be required to sell the Treasury futures contract?

Upon exercise, the futures price for the Treasury futures contract will be set equal to the strike price. The position of the two parties is then immediately marked-to-market in terms of the then-current Treasury futures price. Thus, the Treasury futures position of the two parties will be at the prevailing Treasury futures price. At the same time, the option buyer will receive from the option seller the economic benefit from exercising. In the case of a call futures option, the option writer must pay the difference between the current futures price and the strike price to the buyer of the option. In the case of a put futures option, the option writer must pay the option buyer the difference between the strike price and the current futures price.

For example, suppose an investor buys a call option on a Treasury futures contract in which the strike price is 85. Assume also that the futures price is 95 and that the buyer exercises the call option. Upon exercise, the call buyer is given a long position in the Treasury futures contract at 85 and the call writer is assigned the corresponding short position in the Treasury futures contract at 85. The Treasury futures positions of the buyer and the writer are immediately marked-to-market by the exchange. Because the prevailing futures price is 95 and the strike price is 85, the long Treasury futures position (the position of the call buyer) realizes a gain of 10, while the short Treasury futures position (the position of the call writer) realizes a loss of 10. The call writer pays the exchange 10 and the call buyer receives from the exchange 10. The call buyer, who now has a long Treasury futures position at 95, can either liquidate the position at 95 or maintain a long futures position. If the former course of action is taken, the call buyer sells a Treasury futures contract at the prevailing futures price of 95. There is no gain or loss from liquidating the position. Overall, the call buyer realizes a gain of 10. The call buyer who elects to hold the long Treasury futures position will face the same risk and reward of holding such a position, but still realizes a gain of 10 from the exercise of the call option.

Suppose instead that the Treasury futures option is a put rather than a call, and the current futures price is 60 rather than 95. Then if the buyer of this put option exercises it, the buyer would have a short position in the Treasury futures contract at 85; the option writer would have a long position in the Treasury futures contract at 85. The exchange then marks the position to market at the then-current futures price of 60, resulting in a gain to the put buyer of 25 and a loss to the put writer of the same amount. The put buyer who now has a short Treasury futures position at 60 can either liquidate the position by buying a Treasury futures contract at the prevailing futures price of 60 or maintain the short futures position. In either case the put buyer realizes a gain of 25 from exercising the put option.

There are no margin requirements for the buyer of a Treasury futures option once the option price has been paid in full. Because the option price is the maximum amount that the buyer can lose, regardless of how adverse the price movement of the futures position, there is no need for margin.

Because the writer (seller) of an option has agreed to accept all of the risk (and none of the reward) of the position in the underlying instrument, the writer (seller) is required to deposit not only the margin required on the Treasury futures contract position, but also (with certain exceptions) the option price that is received for writing the option. In addition, as prices adversely affect the writer's position, the writer would be required to deposit variation margin as it is marked to market.

Exchange-Traded Futures Options

In Chapter 12, we discussed the various Treasury futures contracts traded on the Chicago Board of Trade (CBOT) and the International Monetary Market (IMM) of the Chicago Mercantile Exchange. Options on Treasury bond and note futures are traded on the CBOT. All futures options are of the American type. If the option buyer elects to exercise early, he or she must notify the clearing corporation which then randomly selects a clearing member that must select a short from amongst its customers.

The CBOT's Treasury bond futures contracts have delivery months of March, June, September, and December. In Chapter 12 we described the delivery process and the choices granted to the short. There are Treasury futures options that expire in the next three regular quarterly expiration months. Trading of futures options on Treasury bonds stops in the month prior to the underlying futures contract's delivery month. The day in that month in which the futures options stop trading is the first Friday preceding, by at least five days, the first notice day for the Treasury bond futures contract.

In an attempt to compete with the OTC option market, the CBOT introduced in 1994 the *flexible Treasury futures options*. These futures options allow counterparties to customize options within certain limits. Specifically, the strike price, expiration date, and type of exercise (American or European) can be customized subject to CBOT constraints. One key constraint is that the expiration date of a flexible option cannot exceed that of the longest standard option traded on the CBOT. Unlike an OTC option, where the option buyer is exposed to counterparty risk, a flexible Treasury futures option is guaranteed by the clearing house. The minimum size requirement for the launching of a flexible futures option is 100 contracts.

The price of a futures option on a Treasury bond is quoted in a 64th of 1% of par value. For example, a price of 24 means $^{24}/_{64}$th of 1% of par value. Since the par value of a Treasury bond futures contract is $100,000, an option price of 24 means:

$$[(^{24}/_{64})/100] \times \$100,000 = \$375$$

In general, the price of a futures option on a Treasury bond quoted at Q is equal to:

$$\text{Option price} = [(Q/64)/100] \times \$100,000$$

RISK AND RETURN CHARACTERISTICS OF OPTIONS

Here we illustrate the risk and return characteristics of the four basic option positions — buying a call option, selling a call option, buying a put option, and selling a put option. The illustrations assume that each option position is held to the expiration date and not exercised early. In our illustrations we will use an option on a Treasury bond since the principles apply equally to Treasury futures options. To keep the illustration simple, we ignore transaction costs.

Buying Call Options

The purchase of a call option creates a financial position referred to as a *long call position*. To illustrate this position, assume that there is a call option on a Treasury bond that expires in one month and has a strike price of $100. The option price is $3. Suppose that the current price of the Treasury bond is $100. For an investor who purchases this call option, the profit or loss at the expiration date is shown in the second column of Exhibit 1. The maximum loss is the option price and there is substantial upside potential.

Exhibit 1: Comparison of Long Call Position and Long Treasury Bond Position

Assumptions: Treasury bond price = $100
Option price = $3
Strike price = $100
Time to expiration = 1 month

Price of Treasury Bond at Expiration Date	Net Profit/Loss for	
	Long Call[*]	Long Treasury Bond[**]
$150	$47	$50
130	27	30
120	17	20
115	12	15
110	7	10
109	6	9
108	5	8
107	4	7
106	3	6
105	2	5
104	1	4
103	0	3
102	−1	2
101	−2	1
100	−3	0
99	−3	−1
98	−3	−2
97	−3	−3
91	−3	−9
90	−3	−10
70	−3	−30
60	−3	−40

[*] Price at expiration − $100 − $3, Maximum loss = $3
[**] Price at expiration − $100

It is worthwhile to compare the profit and loss profile of the call option buyer to that of a long position in the Treasury bond. The payoff from the position depends on the Treasury bond's price at the expiration date. Exhibit 1 compares the long call position and the long position in the Treasury bond. This comparison clearly demonstrates the way in which an option can change the risk/return profile. An investor who takes a long position in the Treasury bond realizes a profit of $1 for every $1 increase in the Treasury bond's price. As the Treasury bond's price falls, however, the investor loses dollar-for-dollar. If the price drops by more than $3, the long position in the Treasury bond results in a loss of more than $3. The long call position, in contrast, limits the loss to only the option price of $3 but retains the upside potential, which will be $3 less than for the long position in the Treasury bond.

Writing (Selling) Call Options

The writer of a call option is said to be in a *short call position*. To illustrate the option seller's (writer's) position, we use the same call option we used to illustrate buying a call option. The profit and loss profile of the short call position (that is, the position of the call option writer) is the mirror image of the profit and loss profile of the long call position (the position of the call option buyer). That is, the profit of the short call position for any given price for the Treasury bond at the expiration date is the same as the loss of the long call position. Consequently, the maximum profit that the short call position can produce is the option price. The maximum potential loss is the highest price realized by the Treasury bond on or before the expiration date (the price if interest rates fall to zero), less the option price.

Buying Put Options

The buying of a put option creates a financial position referred to as a *long put position*. To illustrate this position, we assume a hypothetical put option on the Treasury bond with one month to expiration and a strike price of $100. Assume the put option is selling for $2. The current price of the Treasury bond is $100. The profit or loss for this position at the expiration date depends on the market price of the Treasury bond. The profit and loss profile for the long put position is shown in the second column of Exhibit 2.

As with all long option positions, the loss is limited to the option price. The profit potential, however, is substantial: the theoretical maximum profit is generated if the Treasury bond's price falls to zero.

To see how an option alters the risk and return profile we again compare it to a position in a Treasury bond. The long put position is compared to taking a short position in the Treasury bond because this is the position that would realize a profit if the bond's price falls. Suppose an investor sells the Treasury bond short for $100. Exhibit 2 compares the profit and loss profile for the long put position and short position in the Treasury bond.

Exhibit 2: Profit/Loss Profile for a Long Put Position and Comparison with a Short Treasury Bond Position

Assumptions: Treasury bond price = $100
Option price = $2
Strike price = $100
Time to expiration = 1 month

Price of Treasury Bond at Expiration Date ($)	Net Profit/Loss for	
	Long Put ($)*	Short Treasury Bond ($)**
150	−2	−50
130	−2	−30
120	−2	−20
110	−2	−10
105	−2	−5
100	−2	0
99	−1	1
98	0	2
97	1	3
96	2	4
95	3	5
94	4	6
93	5	7
92	6	8
91	7	9
90	8	10
75	23	25
70	28	30
65	33	35
60	38	40

* $100 − Price at expiration − $2, Maximum loss = $2
** $100 − Price at expiration

While the investor who takes a short position in the Treasury bond faces all the downside risk as well as the upside potential, the long put position limits the downside risk to the option price while still maintaining upside potential (reduced only by an amount equal to the option price).

Writing (Selling) Put Options

Writing a put option creates a financial position referred to as a *short put position*. The profit and loss profile for a short put option is the mirror image of the long put option. The maximum profit from this position is the option price. The theoretical maximum loss can be substantial should the price of the Treasury bond fall.

To summarize, buying calls or selling puts allows the investor to gain if the price of a Treasury bond rises. Selling calls and buying puts allows the investor to gain if the price of a Treasury bond falls.

OTC TREASURY OPTIONS

OTC Treasury options are created by commercial banks and investment banks for their clients. Dealers can customize the expiration date, the underlying, and the type of exercise. For example, the underlying could be a specific Treasury security or a spread between yields in two maturity sectors of the Treasury market.

In addition to American- and European-type options, an OTC Treasury option can be created in which the buyer may exercise prior to the expiration date but only on designated dates. Such options are referred to as *modified American* or *Atlantic* or *Bermuda* options. With an OTC Treasury option, the buyer need not pay the option price at the time of purchase. Instead, the option price can be paid at the expiration or exercise date. For such options, the option writer is exposed to counterparty risk in addition to the option buyer.

Some institutional investors may have exposure not only to the level of rates but the spread between two sectors of the Treasury yield curve. It is difficult to hedge against yield curve risk with current exchange-traded options.[1] As a result, several dealer firms have developed proprietary products for such a purpose. These options can be structured with a payoff in one of the following ways should the option expire in the money. First, there could be a cash settlement based on the amount that the option expires in the money. Second, there could be an exchange of ownership of the two Treasury securities underlying the option. It is difficult to structure options with a settlement based on an exchange of securities, but there are institutional investors who desire this type of structure. (Goldman Sachs refers to such structures as dual exercise options (DUOPs).)

The reason for the popularity of yield curve spread options is that there are many institutional investors whose performance is affected by a change in the shape of the yield curve. We discussed yield curve risk in Chapter 7. As an example of a yield curve spread option, consider the Goldman Sachs' product called SYCURVE. This option represents the right to buy (in the case of a call option) or sell (in the case of a put option) specific segments of the Treasury yield curve. "Buying the curve" means buying the shorter maturity and selling the longer maturity; "selling the curve" means selling the shorter maturity and buying the longer maturity. The curve is defined by the spread between two specific maturities. They could be the 2-year/10-year spread, the 2-year/30-year spread, or the 10-year/30-year spread. The strike is quoted in basis points.

The yield spread is measured by the long maturity yield minus the short maturity yield. For a call option to be in the money at the expiration date, the yield spread must be positive; for a put option to be in the money at the expiration date, the yield spread must be negative. For example, a 25 basis point call option on the 2-year/10-year spread will be in the money at the expiration date if:

---

[1] While there were yield curve spread options and futures traded on the CBOT, these contracts stopped trading in the summer of 1997.

10-year yield – 2-year yield > 25 basis points

A 35 basis point put option on the 10-year/30-year spread will be in the money at the expiration date if:

30-year yield – 10-year yield < 35 basis points

Yield curve options such as the SYCURVE are cash settlement contracts. In the case of the SYCURVE, if the option expires in the money, the option buyer receives \$0.01 per \$1 of notional amount, per in-the-money basis point at exercise. That is:

amount option expires in money (in bp) × \$0.01 × notional amount

For example, suppose that \$10 million notional amount of a 2-year/10-year call is purchased with a strike of 25 basis points. Suppose at the expiration date the yield spread is 33 basis points. Then the option expires 8 basis points in the money. The cash payment to the buyer of this option is

$$8 \times \$0.01 \times \$10,000,000 = \$800,000$$

From this amount, the option premium must be deducted.

KEY POINTS

1. *An option is a contract in which the writer of the option grants the buyer the right, but not the obligation, to purchase from or sell to the writer something at a specified price within a specified period of time (or on a specified date).*

2. *The option buyer pays the option writer (seller) a fee, called the option price.*

3. *A call option allows the option buyer to purchase the underlying from the option writer at the strike price; a put option allows the option buyer to sell the underlying to the option writer at the strike price.*

4. *Treasury options include options on Treasury securities and options on Treasury futures contracts, called futures options.*

5. *There are exchange-traded Treasury options and over-the-counter Treasury options.*

6. *The only actively-traded exchange-traded Treasury options are futures options.*

7. *Treasury futures options are American-type options.*

8. *The Chicago Board of Trade has introduced customized futures options called flexible Treasury futures options.*

9. *OTC Treasury options are customized by dealers for their clients in terms of the expiration date, the underlying Treasury security, and the type of exercise.*

10. *An OTC Treasury option can be created in which the buyer may exercise prior to the expiration date but only on designated dates (so called modified American or Atlantic or Bermuda options).*

11. *An OTC Treasury option can be created whereby the buyer pays the premium at the expiration date.*

12. *Spread options can be structured with a payoff that is either cash settled or requires an exchange of ownership of the two securities underlying the option.*

13. *A common spread option is one that has a payoff based on the spread between two maturity sectors of the Treasury yield curve.*

Chapter 14

VALUATION OF TREASURY FUTURES AND OPTIONS

In Chapters 12 and 13, we explained Treasury futures and options contracts. In this chapter we turn to how to value these instruments. At the end of the chapter, we look at how to use option valuation to value callable Treasury bonds.

THEORETICAL TREASURY FUTURES PRICE

To understand how futures contracts are valued, consider the following example. Suppose that a 12% 20-year bond is selling at par. Also suppose that this bond is the deliverable for a futures contract that settles in three months. If the current 3-month interest rate at which funds can be loaned or borrowed is 8% per year, what should be the price of this futures contract?

Suppose the price of the futures contract is 107. Consider the following strategy:

Sell the futures contract at 107.
Purchase the bond for 100.
Borrow 100 for 3 months at 8% per year.

The borrowed funds are used to purchase the bond, resulting in no initial cash outlay for this strategy. Three months from now, the bond must be delivered to settle the futures contract and the loan must be repaid. These transactions will produce the following cash flows:

From settlement of the futures contract:
Flat price of bond	=	107
Accrued interest (12% for 3 months)	=	3
Total proceeds	=	110

From the loan:
Repayment of principal of loan	=	100
Interest on loan (8% for 3 months)	=	2
Total outlay	=	102

Profit = Total proceeds − Total outlay	=	8

This strategy will guarantee a profit of 8. Moreover, the profit is generated with no initial outlay because the funds used to purchase the bond are borrowed. The profit will be realized *regardless of the futures price at the settlement date*. Obviously, in a well-functioning market, arbitrageurs would buy this bond and sell the futures contract, forcing the futures price down and bidding up this bond's price so as to eliminate this profit.

In contrast, suppose that the futures price is 92 instead of 107. Consider the following strategy:

> Buy the futures contract at 92.
> Sell (short) the bond for 100.
> Invest (lend) 100 for 3 months at 8% per year.

Once again, there is no initial cash outlay. Three months from now this bond will be purchased to settle the long position in the futures contract. That bond will then be used to cover the short position (i.e. to cover the short sale in the cash market). The outcome in three months would be as follows:

> *From settlement of the futures contract:*
> | | | |
> |---|---|---|
> | Flat price of bond | = | 92 |
> | Accrued interest (12% for 3 months) | = | 3 |
> | Total outlay | = | 95 |
>
> *From the loan:*
> | | | |
> |---|---|---|
> | Principal received from maturing investment | = | 100 |
> | Interest earned (8% for 3 months) | = | 2 |
> | Total proceeds | = | 102 |
>
> | | | |
> |---|---|---|
> | Profit = Total proceeds − Total outlay | = | 7 |

The profit of 7 is a pure arbitrage profit. It requires no initial cash outlay and will be realized regardless of the futures price at the settlement date.

There is a futures price that will eliminate the arbitrage profit. There will be no arbitrage if the futures price is 99. Let's look at what would happen if the two previous strategies are followed and the futures price is 99. First, consider the following strategy:

> Sell the futures contract at 99.
> Purchase the bond for 100.
> Borrow 100 for 3 months at 8% per year.

In three months, the outcome would be as follows:

From settlement of the futures contract:

Flat price of bond	=	99
Accrued interest (12% for 3 months)	=	3
Total proceeds	=	102

From the loan:

Repayment of principal of loan	=	100
Interest on loan (8% for 3 months)	=	2
Total outlay	=	102

Profit = Total proceeds − Total outlay	=	0

There is no arbitrage profit in this case.

Next consider the following strategy:

Buy the futures contract at 99.
Sell (short) the bond for 100.
Invest (lend) 100 for 3 months at 8% per year.

The outcome in three months would be as follows:

From settlement of the futures contract:

Flat price of bond	=	99
Accrued interest (12% for 3 months)	=	3
Total outlay	=	102

From the loan:

Principal received from maturing investment	=	100
Interest earned (8% for 3 months)	=	2
Total proceeds	=	102

Total proceeds − Total outlay = Profit	=	0

Thus neither strategy results in a profit. Hence the futures price of 99 is the theoretical price, because any higher or lower futures price will permit arbitrage profits.

Theoretical Futures Price Based on Arbitrage Model

Considering the arbitrage arguments just presented, the theoretical futures price can be determined on the basis of the following information:

1. The price of the bond in the cash market.
2. The coupon rate on the bond. In our example, the coupon rate is 12% per year.
3. The interest rate for borrowing and lending until the settlement date. The borrowing and lending rate is referred to as the *financing rate*. In our example, the financing rate is 8% per year.

We will let

r = annualized financing rate (%)
c = annualized current yield, or annual coupon rate divided by the cash market price (%)
P = cash market price
F = futures price
t = time, in years, to the futures delivery date

and then consider the following strategy that is initiated on a coupon date:

Sell the futures contract at F.
Purchase the bond for P.
Borrow P until the settlement date at r.

The outcome at the settlement date is

From settlement of the futures contract:

Flat price of bond	=	F
Accrued interest	=	ctP
Total proceeds	=	$\overline{F + ctP}$

From the loan:

Repayment of principal of loan	=	P
Interest on loan	=	rtP
Total outlay	=	$\overline{P + rtP}$

The profit will equal:

Profit = Total proceeds – Total outlay

Profit = $F + ctP - (P + rtP)$

In equilibrium the theoretical futures price occurs where the profit from this strategy is zero. Thus to have equilibrium, the following must hold:

$0 = F + ctP - (P + rtP)$

Solving for the theoretical futures price, we have

$$F = P + Pt(r - c) \tag{1}$$

Alternatively, consider the following strategy:

Buy the futures contract at F.
Sell (short) the bond for P.
Invest (lend) P at r until the settlement date.

The outcome at the settlement date would be

> *From settlement of the futures contract:*
> | Flat price of bond | | = | F |
> | Accrued interest | | = | ctP |
> | Total outlay | | = | $\overline{F + ctP}$ |
>
> *From the loan:*
> | Proceeds received from maturing of investment | = | P |
> | Interest earned | = | rtP |
> | Total proceeds | = | $\overline{P + rtP}$ |

The profit will equal:

$$\text{Profit} = \text{Total proceeds} - \text{Total outlay}$$

$$\text{Profit} = P + rtP - (F + ctP)$$

Setting the profit equal to zero so that there will be no arbitrage profit and solving for the futures price, we obtain the same equation for the futures price as equation (1).

Let's apply equation (1) to our previous example in which

$$r = 0.08$$
$$c = 0.12$$
$$P = 100$$
$$t = 0.25$$

Then the theoretical futures price is

$$F = 100 + 100 \times 0.25(0.08 - 0.12) = 100 - 1 = 99$$

This is the futures price that we found earlier will produce no arbitrage profit.

The theoretical price may be at a premium to the cash market price (higher than the cash market price) or at a discount from the cash market price (lower than the cash market price), depending on $(r - c)$. The term $r - c$ is called the *net financing cost* because it adjusts the financing rate for the coupon interest earned. The net financing cost is more commonly called the *cost of carry*, or simply *carry*. *Positive carry* means that the current yield earned is greater than the financing cost; *negative carry* means that the financing cost exceeds the current yield. The relationships can be expressed as follows:

Carry	Theoretical futures price
Positive ($c>r$)	will sell at a discount to cash price ($F<P$)
Negative ($c<r$)	will sell at a premium to cash price ($F>P$)
Zero ($c=r$)	will be equal to cash price ($F=P$)

In the case of interest rate futures, carry (the relationship between the short-term financing rate and the current yield on the bond) depends on the shape of the yield curve. When the yield curve is upward sloping, the short-term financing rate will be less than the current yield on the bond, resulting in positive carry. The theoretical futures price will then sell at a discount to the cash price for the bond. The opposite will hold true when the yield curve is inverted.

Adjustments to the Theoretical Pricing Model for Treasury Futures

Several assumptions were made to derive the theoretical futures price using the arbitrage argument. Below we discuss these assumptions and explain the implications for the theoretical futures price.

Interim Cash Flows

No interim cash flows due to variation margin or coupon interest payments were assumed in the model. However, for Treasury futures contracts we know that interim cash flows can occur for both of these reasons. Consider first variation margin. If interest rates rise, the short position in a Treasury futures contract will receive margin as the futures price decreases; the margin can then be reinvested at a higher interest rate. If interest rates fall, there will be variation margin that must be financed by the short position; however, because interest rates have declined, financing will be possible at a lower cost. Incorporating interim coupon payments into the pricing model is not difficult. However, the value of the coupon payments at the settlement date will depend on the interest rate at which they can be reinvested. The shorter the maturity of the contract and the lower the coupon rate, the less important the reinvestment income is in determining the theoretical futures price.

Difference in Borrowing and Lending Rates

In deriving the theoretical futures price it is assumed that the borrowing and lending rates are equal. Typically, however, the borrowing rate is higher than the lending rate. As a result, there is not one theoretical futures price but rather there are lower and upper boundaries for the theoretical price of Treasury futures contract.

Uncertainty About Deliverable Issue

Another assumption made to derive equation (1) is that only one instrument is deliverable. But the futures contract on Treasury bonds and Treasury notes are designed to allow the short the choice of delivering one of a number of deliverable issues (the quality or swap option). Because there may be more than one deliverable, market participants track the price of each deliverable bond and determine which bond is the cheapest to deliver. The theoretical futures price will then trade in relation to the cheapest-to-deliver issue.

There is the risk that while an issue may be the cheapest to deliver at the time a position in the futures contract is taken, it may not be the cheapest to deliver after that time. In Chapter 11, we explained how the cheapest-to-deliver issue was determined. We reported that for the June 1997 Treasury bond futures contract the cheapest-to-deliver issue was the 11.25% 2/15/15 issue. Moreover, we showed how if yields increase the cheapest-to-deliver issue would change.

A change in the cheapest-to-deliver issue can dramatically alter the theoretical futures price. For this reason, many market participants use more than just the cheapest-to-deliver issue in valuing a Treasury futures contract. Market participants who do take this approach have developed proprietary models for selecting the package of issues from the deliverable pool.

Because the quality option is an option granted by the long to the short, the long will want to pay less for the futures contract than indicated by equation (1). Therefore, as a result of the quality option, the theoretical futures price as given by equation (1) must be adjusted as follows:

$$F = P + Pt(r - c) - \text{Value of quality option} \qquad (2)$$

Market participants have employed theoretical models in attempting to estimate the fair value of the quality option.

Uncertainty About Delivery Date

In deriving equation (1) a known delivery date is assumed. For Treasury bond and note futures contracts, the short has a timing option and a wild card option, so the long does not know when the security will be delivered. The effect of the timing and wild card options on the theoretical futures price is the same as with the quality option. These delivery options result in a theoretical futures price that is lower than the one suggested in equation (1), as shown below:

$$F = P + Pt(r - c) - \text{Value of quality option} - \text{Value of new auction option}$$
$$- \text{Value of timing option} - \text{Value of wild card option} \qquad (3)$$

or alternatively,

$$F = P + Pt(r - c) - \text{Delivery options} \qquad (4)$$

Market participants attempt to value the delivery options in order to apply equation (4).

VALUING TREASURY OPTIONS

Now let's look at how to value an option on a Treasury security.

Basic Components of the Option Price

The option value is a reflection of the option's *intrinsic value* and any additional amount over its intrinsic value. The premium over intrinsic value is often referred to as the *time value*. The intrinsic value of an option is its economic value if it is exercised immediately. If no positive economic value would result from exercising the option immediately, then the intrinsic value is zero.

For a call option, the intrinsic value is positive if the current price of the underlying security is greater than the strike price. The intrinsic value is then the difference between the two prices. If the strike price of a call option is greater than or equal to the current price of the security, the intrinsic value is zero. For example, if the strike price for a call option is 100 and the current price for the security is 105, the intrinsic value is 5. That is, an option buyer exercising the option and simultaneously selling the underlying security would realize 105 from the sale of the security, which would be covered by acquiring the security from the option writer for 100, thereby netting a gain of 5.

When an option has intrinsic value, it is said to be *in the money*. When the strike price of a call option exceeds the current price of the security, the call option is said to be *out of the money*; it has no intrinsic value. An option for which the strike price is equal to the current price of the security is said to be *at the money*. Both at-the-money and out-of-the-money options have an intrinsic value of zero because they are not profitable to exercise.

For a put option, the intrinsic value is equal to the amount by which the current price of the security is below the strike price. For example, if the strike price of a put option is 100 and the current price of the security is 92, the intrinsic value is 8. The buyer of the put option who exercises it and simultaneously buys the underlying security will net 8 by exercising this option since the security will be sold to the writer for 100 and purchased in the market for 92. The intrinsic value is zero if the strike price is less than or equal to the current market price.

For our put option with a strike price of 100, the option would be: (1) in the money when the security's price is less than 100, (2) out of the money when the security's price exceeds 100, and (3) at the money when the security's price is equal to 100. These relationships are summarized in Exhibit 1.

The time value of an option is the amount by which the option price exceeds its intrinsic value. The option buyer hopes that, at some time prior to expiration, changes in the market price of the underlying security will increase the value of the rights conveyed by the option. For this prospect, the option buyer is willing to pay a premium above the intrinsic value.

Exhibit 1: Relationship Between Security Price, Strike Price, and Intrinsic Value

If Security price > Strike price	Call option	Put option
Intrinsic value	Security price – Strike price	Zero
Jargon	In-the-money	Out-of-the money
If Security price < Strike price	Call option	Put option
Intrinsic value	Zero	Strike price – Security price
Jargon	Out-of-the-money	In-the-money
If Security price = Strike price	Call option	Put option
Intrinsic value	Zero	Zero
Jargon	At-the-money	At-the-money

Exhibit 2: Summary of Factors that Affect the Price of an Option on a Treasury Security

Increase in factor with all other factors held constant	Effect on call option	Effect on put option
Current price of underlying Treasury security	increase	decrease
Strike price	decrease	increase
Time to expiration (American options)	increase	increase
Expected yield volatility	increase	increase
Short-term risk-free rate	increase	decrease
Coupon interest payments	decrease	increase

For example, if the price of a call option with a strike price of 100 is 9 when the current price of the security is 105, the time value of this option is 4 (9 minus its intrinsic value of 5). Had the current price of the security been 90 instead of 105, then the time value of this option would be the entire 9 because the option has no intrinsic value.

Factors that Influence the Value of an Option on a Treasury Security

There are six factors that influence the value of an option in which the underlying is a Treasury security:

1. current price of the underlying Treasury security;
2. strike price;
3. time to expiration of the option;
4. expected yield volatility over the life of the option;
5. short-term risk-free interest rate over the life of the option; and,
6. coupon interest payment over the life of the option.

The impact of each of these factors may depend on whether (1) the option is a call or a put, and (2) the option is an American option or a European option. A summary of the effect of each factor on put and call option prices is presented in Exhibit 2.

Current Price of the Underlying Treasury Security

The option price will change as the price of the underlying Treasury security changes. For a call option, as the price of the underlying Treasury security increases (holding all other factors constant), the option price increases. The opposite holds for a put option: as the price of the underlying Treasury security increases, the price of a put option decreases.

Strike Price

All other factors equal, the lower the strike price, the higher the price of a call option. For put options, the higher the strike price, the higher the option price.

Time to Expiration

An option is a "wasting asset." That is, after the expiration date passes the option has no value. Holding all other factors equal, the longer the time to expiration of the option, the greater the option price. This is because, as the time to expiration decreases, less time remains for the underlying Treasury security's price to rise (for a call buyer) or to fall (for a put buyer) and, therefore, the probability of a favorable price movement decreases. Consequently, for American options, as the time remaining until expiration decreases, the option price approaches its intrinsic value.

Expected Yield Volatility

All other factors equal, the greater the expected yield volatility (as measured by the standard deviation or variance), the more an investor would be willing to pay for the option, and the more an option writer would demand for it. This is because the greater the yield volatility, the greater the probability that the price of the underlying Treasury security will move in favor of the option buyer at some time before expiration.

Short-Term Risk-Free Interest Rate

Buying the underlying Treasury security ties up one's money. Buying an option on the same quantity of the underlying Treasury security makes the difference between the security's price and the option's price available for investment at the risk-free rate. All other factors constant, the higher the short-term risk-free interest rate, the greater the cost of buying the underlying Treasury security and carrying it to the expiration date of the call option. Hence, the higher the short-term risk-free interest rate, the more attractive the call option will be relative to the direct purchase of the underlying Treasury security. As a result, the higher the short-term risk-free interest rate, the greater the price of a call option. The reverse is true for a put option.

Coupon Payments

Coupon interest payments on the underlying Treasury security tend to decrease the price of a call option because they make it more attractive to hold the underlying Treasury security than to hold the option. For put options, coupon interest payments on the underlying Treasury security tend to increase their price.

Factors that Influence the Value of a Treasury Futures Option

There are five factors that influence the value of an option on a Treasury futures contract:

1. current Treasury futures price;
2. strike price;
3. time to expiration of the option;
4. expected yield volatility over the life of the option; and,
5. short-term risk-free interest rate over the life of the option.

Exhibit 3: Summary of Factors that Affect the Price of a Treasury Futures Option

Increase in factor with all other factors held constant	Effect on call option	Effect on put option
Current Treasury futures price	increase	decrease
Strike price	decrease	increase
Time to expiration	increase	increase
Expected yield volatility	increase	increase
Short-term risk-free rate	decrease	decrease

These are the same factors that affect the value of an option on a Treasury security. Notice that the coupon payment is not a factor since the underlying is a Treasury futures contract.

Exhibit 3 summarizes how each factor affects the value of a Treasury futures option. The primary difference between factors that influence the price of a Treasury futures option and an option on a Treasury security is the short-term risk-free rate. For both a call and a put, the option price decreases when the short-term risk-free rate increases.

Option Pricing Models

At any time, the intrinsic value of an option can be determined. The question is, what is the time value of an option worth? To answer this question, option pricing models have been developed.

Black-Scholes Model

The most popular model for the pricing of equity options is the Black-Scholes option pricing model.[1] By imposing certain assumptions and using arbitrage arguments, the Black-Scholes model computes the fair (or theoretical) price of a European call option on a non-dividend-paying stock.

The Black-Scholes model is:

$$C = SN(d_1) - Xe^{-rt} N(d_2) \tag{5}$$

where

$$d_1 = \frac{\ln(S/X) + (r + 0.5s^2)t}{s\sqrt{t}} \tag{6}$$

$$d_2 = d_1 - s\sqrt{t} \tag{7}$$

$\ln$ = natural logarithm
C = call option price
S = stock price

---

[1] Fischer Black and Myron Scholes, "The Pricing of Corporate Liabilities," *Journal of Political Economy* (May-June 1973), pp. 637-659.

X = strike price
r = short-term risk-free interest rate
e = 2.718 (natural antilog of 1)
t = time remaining to the expiration date (measured as a fraction of a year)
s = standard deviation of the stock price
$N(.)$ = the cumulative probability density. The value for $N(.)$ is obtained from a normal distribution function

Notice that the factors that we said earlier determine the price of an option are included in the formula. However, the sixth factor, cash payments (coupon interest in the case of a bond), is not included because the model is for a non-dividend-paying stock. The standard deviation of the stock price must be estimated.

The option price derived from the Black-Scholes model is "fair" in the sense that if any other price existed, it would be possible to earn riskless arbitrage profits by taking an offsetting position in the underlying stock. That is, if the price of the call option in the market is higher than that derived from the Black-Scholes model, an investor could sell the call option and buy a certain number of shares in the underlying stock. If the reverse is true, that is, the market price of the call option is less than the "fair" price derived from the model, the investor could buy the call option and sell short a certain number of shares in the underlying stock. This process of hedging by taking a position in the underlying stock allows the investor to lock in the riskless arbitrage profit. The number of shares necessary to hedge the position changes as the factors that affect the option price change, so the hedged position must be changed constantly.

Because the basic Black-Scholes model as given by equation (1) is for a non-cash paying security, let's apply it to a Treasury strip with three years to maturity. Assume the following values:

Strike price	= $88.00
Time remaining to expiration	= 2 years
Current price	= $83.96
Expected price volatility = standard deviation	= 5%
Risk-free rate	= 6%

Note the current price is $83.96 which is the present value of the maturity value of $100 discounted at 6% (assuming a flat yield curve).

In terms of the values in the formula:

S = 83.96
X = 88.00
t = 2
s = 0.10
r = 0.06

Substituting these values into equations (6) and (7):

$$d_1 = \frac{\ln(83.96/88) + (0.06 + 0.5[0.10]^2)2}{0.10\sqrt{2}} = 0.5869$$

$$d_2 = 0.5869 - 0.10\sqrt{2} = 0.4455$$

From a normal distribution table:

$$N(0.5869) = 0.7214 \text{ and } N(0.4455) = 0.6720$$

Then, from equation (5):

$$C = 83.96\ (0.7214) - 88\ (e^{-(0.06)(2)})\ (0.6720) = \$8.116$$

There is no reason to suspect that this estimated value is unreasonable. However, let's change the problem slightly. Instead of a strike price of $88, let's make the strike price for the call option on this Treasury strip $100.25. Substituting the new strike price into equations (6) and (7):

$$d_1 = \frac{\ln(83.96/100.25) + (0.06 + 0.5[0.10]^2)2}{0.10\sqrt{2}} = -0.3346$$

$$d_2 = -0.3346 - 0.10\sqrt{2} = -0.4761$$

From a normal distribution table:

$$N(-0.3346) = 0.3689 \text{ and } N(-0.4761) = 0.3170$$

Then, from equation (5):

$$C = 83.96\ (0.3689) - 100.25\ (e^{-(0.06)(2)})\ (0.3170) = \$2.79$$

Thus, the Black-Scholes model tells us that this call option has a fair value of $2.907. Is there any reason to believe this is unreasonable? Well, consider that this is a call option on a Treasury strip that will never have a value greater than its maturity value of $100. Consequently, a call option struck at $100.25 must have a value of zero. Yet, the Black-Scholes model tells us that the value is $2.907! In fact, with a higher volatility assumption, the model would give an even greater value for the call option.

The reason for obtaining an unrealistic value for this option is the underlying assumptions of the model. There are three assumptions underlying the Black-Scholes model that limit its use in pricing options on Treasury securities. First, the probability distribution for the prices assumed by the Black-Scholes model permits some probability — no matter how small — that the price can take on any positive value. But in the case of a Treasury strip, the price cannot take on a value above $100. In the case of a Treasury coupon bond, we know that the price cannot exceed the sum of the coupon payments plus the maturity value. For example, for a 5-year 10% coupon Treasury with a maturity value of $100, the price cannot be greater than $150 (five coupon payments of $10 plus the maturity value of $100). Thus, unlike stock prices, Treasury prices have a maximum value. The only way that a Treasury's price can exceed the maximum value is if negative interest rates are permitted. This is not likely to occur, so any probability distribution for prices assumed by an option pricing model that permits Treasury prices to be higher than the maximum value could generate nonsensical option prices. The Black-Scholes model does allow Treasury prices to exceed the maximum bond value (or, equivalently, allows negative interest rates).

The second assumption of the Black-Scholes model is that the short-term interest rate is constant over the life of the option. Yet the price of a Treasury security will change as interest rates change. A change in the short-term interest rate changes the rates along the yield curve. Therefore, to assume that the short-term rate will be constant is inappropriate for Treasury options. The third assumption is that the variance of prices is constant over the life of the option. As a Treasury security moves closer to maturity its price volatility declines. Therefore, the assumption that price variance is constant over the life of a Treasury option is inappropriate.[2]

Black Model for Treasury Futures Options

The most commonly used model for futures options is the one developed by Black.[3] The model was initially developed for valuing European options on forward contracts. The value of a call and put based on the Black model is:

$$C = e^{-rt} [FN(d_1) - XN(d_2)] \tag{8}$$

$$P = e^{-rt} [XN(-d_2) - FN(-d_1)]$$

where

$$d_1 = \frac{\ln(F/X) + 0.5s^2 t}{s\sqrt{t}} \tag{9}$$

$$d_2 = d_1 - s\sqrt{t} \tag{10}$$

$\ln$ = natural logarithm
C = call option price
P = put option price

---

[2] While we have discussed the problems of using the Black-Scholes model to price Treasury options, it can also be shown that the binomial option pricing model based on the price distribution of the underlying Treasury suffers from the same problems. Later we will look at a binomial option pricing model based on a distribution for the short-term interest rate.

[3] Fischer Black, "The Pricing of Commodity Contracts," *Journal of Financial Economics* (March 1976), pp. 161-179.

F = futures price
X = strike price
r = short-term risk-free interest rate
e = 2.718 (natural antilog of 1)
t = time remaining to the expiration date (measured as a fraction of a year)
s = standard deviation of the price
$N(.)$ = the cumulative probability density. The value for $N(.)$ is obtained from a normal distribution function

There are two problems with this model. First, the Black model does not overcome the problems cited earlier for the Black-Scholes model. Failing to recognize the yield curve means that there will not be a consistency between pricing Treasury futures and options on Treasury futures. Second, the Black model was developed for pricing European options on futures contracts. Treasury futures options, however, are American options.

The second problem can be overcome. The Black model was extended by Barone-Adesi and Whaley to American options on futures contracts.[4] This is the model used by the Chicago Board of Trade to settle the flexible Treasury futures options. However, this model was also developed for equities and is subject to the first problem noted above. Despite its limitations, the Black model is the most popular option pricing model for options on Treasury futures.

Arbitrage-Free Binomial Model for Valuing Options on Treasury Securities

In developing a pricing model for valuing options on Treasury securities, it is necessary to take into consideration the Treasury yield curve. The model used to value a Treasury option should be "arbitrage free." This means that if the model is used to value an on-the-run Treasury issue, it should produce a value equal to the market price for that on-the-run issue.

The most popular model used by dealer firms to value Treasury options is the arbitrage-free binomial developed by Black, Derman, and Toy.[5] Here we will see how the arbitrage-free binomial tree is constructed and used to value a Treasury security. Then we will see how the tree can be used to value a Treasury option.

To illustrate the binomial model, we start with the on-the-run Treasury yield curve. In our illustration, we use the hypothetical on-the-run Treasury issues shown in Exhibit 4. Each bond is trading at par value (100) so the coupon rate is equal to the yield to maturity. We will simplify the illustration by assuming annual-pay bonds. Using the bootstrapping methodology explained in Chapter 5, the spot rates are those shown in the last column of Exhibit 4.

---

[4] Giovanni Barone-Adesi and Robert E. Whaley, "Efficient Analytic Approximation of American Option Values," *Journal of Finance* (June 1987), pp. 301-320.
[5] Fischer Black, Emanuel Derman, and William Toy, "A One-Factor Model of Interest Rates and Its Application to Treasury Bond Options," *Financial Analysts Journal* (January-February 1990), pp. 24-32.

Exhibit 4: On-the-Run Treasury Yield Curve and Spot Rates

Maturity (yrs)	Yield to maturity (%)	Market Price ($)	Spot Rate (%)
1	3.5	100	3.5000
2	4.2	100	4.2147
3	4.7	100	4.7345
4	5.2	100	5.2707

Binomial Interest Rate Tree Based on an assumed interest rate volatility, a binomial interest rate tree can be constructed. This tree is nothing more than a graphical depiction of the 1-period or short rates over time. How this tree is constructed is illustrated below.

Exhibit 5 shows an example of a binomial interest rate tree. In this tree, each node (bold circle) represents a time period that is equal to one year from the node to its left. Each node is labeled with an N, representing node, and a subscript that indicates the path that the 1-year rate took to get to that node. L represents the lower of the two 1-year rates and H represents the higher of the two 1-year rates. For example, node N_{HH} means to get to that node the following path for 1-year rates occurred: the 1-year rate realized is the higher of the two rates in the first year and then the higher of the 1-year rates in the second year.[6]

Look first at the point denoted by just N in Exhibit 5. This is the root of the tree and is nothing more than the current 1-year spot rate, or equivalently the current 1-year rate, which we denote by r_0. What we have assumed in creating this tree is that the 1-year rate can take on two possible values the next period and the two rates have the same probability of occurring. One rate will be higher than the other. It is assumed that the 1-year rate can evolve over time based on a random process called a lognormal random walk with a certain volatility.

We use the following notation to describe the tree in the first year. Let

σ = assumed volatility of the 1-year rate
$r_{1,L}$ = lower 1-year rate one year from now
$r_{1,H}$ = higher 1-year rate one year from now

The relationship between $r_{1,L}$ and $r_{1,H}$ is as follows:

$$r_{1,H} = r_{1,L}(e^{2\sigma})$$

where e is the base of the natural logarithm 2.71828.

For example, suppose that $r_{1,L}$ is 4.4448% and σ is 10% per year, then:

$$r_{1,H} = 4.4448\%(e^{2 \times 0.10}) = 5.4289\%$$

---

[6] Note that N_{HL} is equivalent to N_{LH} in the second year and that in the third year N_{HHL} is equivalent to N_{HLH} and N_{LHH} and that N_{HLL} is equivalent to N_{LLH}. We have simply selected one label for a node rather than clutter up the figure.

Exhibit 5: Four-Year Binomial Interest Rate Tree

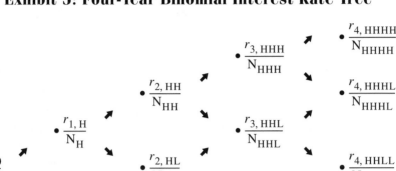

| Year 0 | Year 1 | Year 2 | Year 3 | Year 4 |

In the second year, there are three possible values for the 1-year rate, which we will denote as follows:

$r_{2,LL}$ = 1-year rate in second year assuming the lower rate in the first year and the lower rate in the second year

$r_{2,HH}$ = 1-year rate in second year assuming the higher rate in the first year and the higher rate in the second year

$r_{2,HL}$ = 1-year rate in second year assuming the higher rate in the first year and the lower rate in the second year or equivalently the lower rate in the first year and the higher rate in the second year.

The relationship between $r_{2,LL}$ and the other two 1-year rates is as follows: $r_{2,HH} = r_{2,LL}(e^{4\sigma})$ and $r_{2,HL} = r_{2,LL}(e^{2\sigma})$. So, for example, if $r_{2,LL}$ is 4.6958% and assuming once again that σ is 10%, then

$$r_{2,HH} = 4.6958\%(e^{4 \times 0.10}) = 7.0053\%$$

and

$$r_{2,HL} = 4.6958\%(e^{2 \times 0.10}) = 5.7354\%$$

In the third year there are four possible values for the 1-year rate, which are denoted as follows: $r_{3,HHH}$, $r_{3,HHL}$, $r_{3,HLL}$, and $r_{3,LLL}$, and whose first three values are related to the last as follows:

$$r_{3,HHH} = r_{3,LLL}(e^{6\sigma})$$
$$r_{3,HHL} = r_{3,LLL}(e^{4\sigma})$$
$$r_{3,HLL} = r_{3,LLL}(e^{2\sigma})$$

Exhibit 5 shows the notation for a 4-year binomial interest rate tree. We can simplify the notation by letting r_t be the 1-year rate t years from now for the lower rate since all the other short rates t years from now depend on that rate. Exhibit 6 shows the interest rate tree using this simplified notation.

It can be shown that the standard deviation of the 1-year rate is equal to $r_0\sigma$. The standard deviation is a statistical measure of volatility and we discussed this measure and its estimation in Chapter 8. It is important to understand that the process that we assumed generates the binomial interest rate tree (or equivalently the short rates), implies that volatility is measured relative to the current level of rates. For example, if σ is 10% and the 1-year rate (r_0) is 4%, then the standard deviation of the 1-year rate is 4% × 10% = 0.4% or 40 basis points. However, if the current 1-year rate is 12%, the standard deviation of the 1-year rate would be 12% × 10% or 120 basis points.

Determining the Value at a Node To find the value of a Treasury security at a node, we first calculate a security's value at the two nodes to the right of the node we are interested in. For example, in Exhibit 6, suppose we want to determine the security's value at node N_H. The security's value at nodes N_{HH} and N_{HL} must be determined. Hold aside for now how we get these two values because as we will see, the process involves starting from the last year in the tree and working backwards to get the final solution we want, so these two values will be known. (The process is called backward induction.)

Effectively what we are saying is that if we are at some node, then the value at that node will depend on the future cash flows. In turn, the future cash flows depend on (1) the security's value one year from now and (2) the coupon payment one year from now. The latter is known. The former depends on whether the 1-year rate is the higher or lower rate. The security's value depending on whether the rate is the higher or lower rate is reported at the two nodes to the right of the node that is the focus of our attention. So, the cash flow at a node will be either (1) the security's value if the short rate is the higher rate plus the coupon payment, or (2) the security's value if the short rate is the lower rate plus the coupon payment. For example, suppose that we are interested in the security's value at N_H. The cash flow will be either the security's value at N_{HH} plus the coupon payment, or the security's value at N_{HL} plus the coupon payment.

To get the security's value at a node we follow the fundamental rule for valuation: the value is the present value of the expected cash flows. The appropriate discount rate to use is the 1-year rate at the node. Now there are two present values in this case: the present value if the 1-year rate is the higher rate and one if it is the lower rate. Since it is assumed that the probability of both outcomes is equal, an average of the two present values is computed. This is illustrated in Exhibit 7 for any node assuming that the 1-year rate is r_* at the node where the valuation is sought and letting:

V_H = security's value for the higher 1-year rate
V_L = security's value for the lower 1-year rate
C = coupon payment

Using our notation, the cash flow at a node is either:

V_H + C for the higher 1-year rate
V_L + C for the lower 1-year rate

Exhibit 6: Four-Year Binomial Interest Rate Tree with 1-Year Rates*

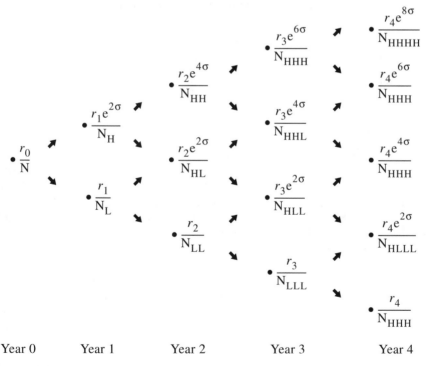

| Year 0 | Year 1 | Year 2 | Year 3 | Year 4 |

* r_t equals forward 1-year lower rate

Exhibit 7: Calculating a Value at a Node

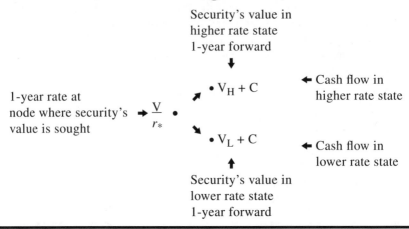

Security's value in
higher rate state
1-year forward
↓

• $V_H + C$ ← Cash flow in
higher rate state

1-year rate at
node where security's → $\dfrac{V}{r_*}$ •
value is sought

• $V_L + C$ ← Cash flow in
lower rate state

↑
Security's value in
lower rate state
1-year forward

The present value of these two cash flows using the 1-year rate at the node, r_*, is:

$$\frac{V_H + C}{(1 + r_*)} = \text{present value for the higher 1-year rate}$$

$$\frac{V_L + C}{(1 + r_*)} = \text{present value for the lower 1-year rate}$$

Then, the value of the bond at the node is found as follows:

$$\text{Value at a node} \ = \ \frac{1}{2}\left[\frac{V_H + C}{(1 + r_*)} + \frac{V_L + C}{(1 + r_*)}\right]$$

Constructing the Binomial Interest Rate Tree To see how to construct the binomial interest rate tree, let's use the assumed on-the-run Treasury yields we used earlier (see Exhibit 4). We will assume that volatility, σ, is 10% and construct a 2-year tree using the 2-year Treasury with a coupon rate of 4.2%.

Exhibit 8 shows a more detailed binomial interest rate tree with the cash flow shown at each node. We'll see how all the values reported in the exhibit are obtained. The root rate for the tree, r_0, is simply the current 1-year rate, 3.5%.

In the first year there are two possible 1-year rates, the higher rate and the lower rate. What we want to find is the two 1-year rates that will be consistent with (1) the volatility assumption, (2) the process that is assumed to generate the short rates, and (3) the observed market value of the security. There is no simple formula for this. It must be found by an iterative process (i.e., trial-and-error). The steps are described and illustrated below.

Step 1: Select a value for r_1. Recall that r_1 is the lower 1-year rate. In this first trial, we *arbitrarily* selected a value of 4.75%.

Exhibit 8: The 1-Year Rates for Year 1 Using the 2-Year 4.2% On-the-Run Treasury Issue: First Trial

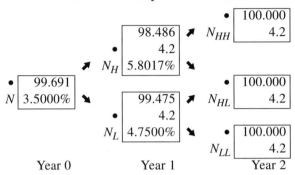

| Year 0 | Year 1 | Year 2 |

Step 2: Determine the corresponding value for the higher 1-year rate. As explained earlier, this rate is related to the lower 1-year rate as follows: $r_1 e^{2\sigma}$. Since r_1 is 4.75%, the higher 1-year rate is 5.8017% (= 4.75% $e^{2 \times 0.10}$). This value is reported in Exhibit 8 at node N_H.

Step 3: Compute the security's value one year from now. This value is determined as follows:

3a. Determine the security's value two years from now. In our example, this is simple. Since we are using a 2-year Treasury, the security's value is its maturity value ($100) plus its final coupon payment ($4.2). Thus, it is $104.2.

3b. Calculate the present value of the security's value found in 3a for the higher rate in the second year. The appropriate discount rate is the higher 1-year rate, 5.8017% in our example. The present value is $98.486 (= $104.2/1.058017). This is the value of V_H that we referred to earlier.

3c. Calculate the present value of the security's value found in 3a for the lower rate. The discount rate assumed for the lower 1-year rate is 4.75%. The present value is $99.475 (= $104.2/1.0475) and is the value of V_L.

3d. Add the coupon to both V_H and V_L to get the cash flow at N_H and N_L, respectively. In our example we have $102.686 for the higher rate and $103.675 for the lower rate.

3e. Calculate the present value of the two values using the 1-year rate r_*. At this point in the valuation, r_* is the root rate, 3.50%. Therefore,

$$\frac{V_H + C}{1 + r_*} = \frac{\$102.686}{1.035} = \$99.213$$

and

$$\frac{V_L + C}{1 + r_*} = \frac{\$103.675}{1.035} = \$100.169$$

Step 4: Calculate the average present value of the two cash flows in Step 3. This is the value we referred to earlier as:

$$\text{Value at a node} = \frac{1}{2}\left[\frac{V_H + C}{(1 + r_*)} + \frac{V_L + C}{(1 + r_*)}\right]$$

In our example, we have

$$\text{Value at a node} = \frac{1}{2}[\$99.213 + \$100.169] = \$99.691$$

Step 5: Compare the value in Step 4 to the security's market value. If the two values are the same, then the r_1 used in this trial is the one we seek. This is the 1-year rate that would then be used in the binomial interest rate tree for the lower rate and to obtain the corresponding higher rate. If, instead, the value found in step 4 is not equal to the market value of the security, this means that the value r_1 in this trial is not the 1-year rate that is consistent with (1) the volatility assumption, (2) the process assumed to generate the 1-year rate, and (3) the observed market value of the security. In this case, the five steps are repeated with a different value for r_1.

When r_1 is 4.75%, a value of $99.691 results in Step 4 which is less than the observed market price of $100. Therefore, 4.75% is too large and the five steps must be repeated trying a lower rate for r_1.

Let's jump right to the correct rate for r_1 in this example and rework steps 1 through 5. This occurs when r_1 is 4.4448%. The corresponding binomial interest rate tree is shown in Exhibit 9.

Exhibit 9: The 1-Year Rates for Year 1 Using the 2-Year 4.2% On-the-Run Treasury Issue

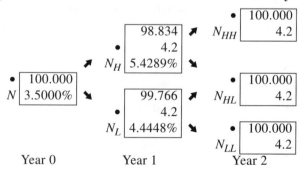

| Year 0 | Year 1 | Year 2 |

Step 1: In this trial we select a value of 4.4448% for r_1, the lower 1-year rate.

Step 2: The corresponding value for the higher 1-year rate is 5.4289% ($=4.4448\%e^{2 \times 0.10}$).

Step 3: The security's value one year from now is determined as follows:

> *3a.* The security's value two years from now is $104.2, just as in the first trial.

> *3b.* The present value of the security's value found in 3a for the higher 1-year rate, V_H, is $98.834 (= $104.2/1.054289).

> *3c.* The present value of the security's value found in 3a for the lower 1-year rate, V_L, is $99.766 (= $104.2/1.044448).

> *3d.* Adding the coupon to V_H and V_L, we get $103.034 as the cash flow for the higher rate and $103.966 as the cash flow for the lower rate.

> *3e.* The present value of the two cash flows using the 1-year rate at the node to the left, 3.5%, gives
>
> $$\frac{V_H + C}{1 + r_*} = \frac{\$103.034}{1.035} = \$99.550$$
>
> and
>
> $$\frac{V_L + C}{1 + r_*} = \frac{\$103.966}{1.035} = \$100.450$$

Step 4: The average present value is $100, which is the value at the node.

Step 5: Since the average present value is equal to the observed market price of $100, r_1 or $r_{1,L}$ is 4.4448% and $r_{1,H}$ is 5.4289%.

We can "grow" this tree for one more year by determining r_2. We would use the 3-year on-the-run issue, the 4.7% coupon bond, to get r_2. The same five steps are used in an iterative process to find the 1-year rates in the tree two years from now. Our objective is to find the value of r_2 that will produce a value of $100 (since the 3-year on-the-run issue has a market price of $100) and is consistent with (1) a volatility assumption of 10%, (2) a current 1-year rate of 3.5%, and (3) the two rates one year from now of 4.4448% (the lower rate) and 5.4289% (the higher rate). We will not describe how to complete the tree using the 3-year and 4-year on-the-run Treasury issues. Exhibit 10 shows the binomial interest rate tree for the on-the-run Treasury issues in Exhibit 4.

Exhibit 10: Binomial Interest Rate Tree for Valuing Up to a 4-Year Treasury (10% Volatility Assumed)

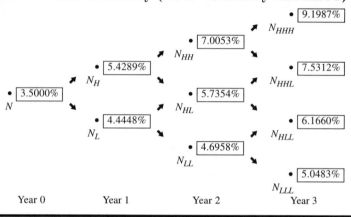

Valuing an Option-Free Bond with the Binomial Tree Now consider a Treasury issue with four years remaining to maturity and a coupon rate of 6.5%. The value of this security can be calculated by discounting the cash flows at the spot rates in Exhibit 3 as shown below:

$$\frac{\$6.5}{(1.035)^1} + \frac{\$6.5}{(1.042147)^2} + \frac{\$6.5}{(1.047345)^3} + \frac{\$100 + \$6.5}{(1.052707)^4} = \$104.643$$

If the same issue is valued using the binomial interest rate tree it should produce the same value as discounting by the spot rates.

Exhibit 10 is the binomial interest rate tree that can then be used to value any Treasury security with a maturity up to four years. To illustrate how to use the binomial interest rate tree, consider once again the 6.5% Treasury with four years remaining to maturity. Also assume that the Treasury on-the-run yield curve is the one in Exhibit 4, hence the appropriate binomial interest rate tree is the one in Exhibit 10. Exhibit 11 shows the various values in the discounting process, and produces a value of $104.643.

This value is identical to the value found when we discounted at the spot rates. This clearly demonstrates that the valuation model is consistent with the standard valuation model using spot rates.

Valuing a Treasury Call Option Now let's see how to value a Treasury call option. To illustrate how this is done, let's consider a 2-year call option on a 6.5% 4-year Treasury security with a strike price of 100.25. We will assume that the yield for the on-the-run Treasuries is the one in Exhibit 4 and that the volatility assumption is 10% per year. Exhibit 11 shows the binomial interest rate tree along with the value of the Treasury security at each node.

Exhibit 11: Valuing a Treasury Bond with Four Years to Maturity and a Coupon Rate of 6.5% (10% Volatility Assumed)

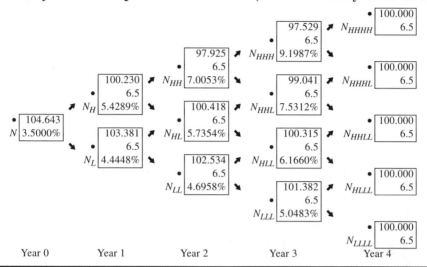

	Year 0	Year 1	Year 2	Year 3	Year 4

It is a portion of Exhibit 11 that we use to value the call option. Specifically, Exhibit 12 shows the value of our Treasury security (excluding coupon interest) at each node at the end of year 2. There are three values shown: 97.9249, 100.4184, and 102.5335. Given these three values, the value of a call option struck at 100.25 can be determined at each node. For example, if at the end of year 2 the price of this Treasury bond is 97.9249, then since the strike price is 100.25, the value of the call option would be zero. In the other two cases, since the price at the end of year 2 is greater than the strike price, the value of the call option is the difference between the price of the bond and 100.25.

Exhibit 12 shows the value of the call option at the end of year 2 (the option expiration date) for each of the three nodes. Given these values, the binomial interest rate tree is used to find the present value of the call option. The backward induction procedure is used. The discount rates are those from the binomial interest rate tree. For years 0 and 1, the discount rate is the second number shown at each node. The first number at each node for year 1 is the average present value found by discounting the call option value of the two nodes to the right using the discount rate at the node. The value of the option is the first number shown at the root, 0.6056.

Valuing a Treasury Put Option The same procedure is used to value a put option. This is illustrated in Exhibit 13 assuming that the put option has two years to expiration and that the strike price is 100.25. The value of the put option at the end of year 2 is shown at each of the three nodes.

Exhibit 12: Valuing a European Call Option on a Treasury Security Using the Arbitrage-Free Binomial Method

Expiration: 2 years; Strike price: 100.25; Current price: 104.643; Volatility assumption: 10%

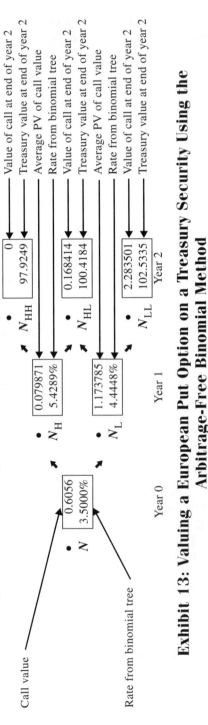

Exhibit 13: Valuing a European Put Option on a Treasury Security Using the Arbitrage-Free Binomial Method

Expiration: 2 years; Strike price: 100.25; Current price: 104.643; Volatility assumption: 10%

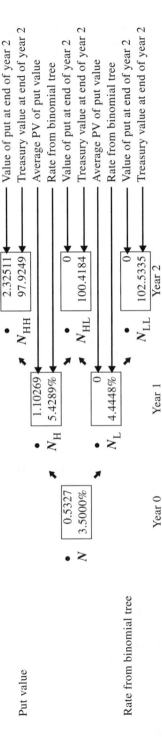

Put-Call Parity Relationship There is a relationship between the price of a call option and the price of a put option on the same underlying security, with the same strike price and the same expiration date. This relationship is commonly referred to as the *put-call parity relationship*. For European options on coupon bearing Treasury security's, the relationship is:

Put price = Call price + Present value of strike price
+ Present value of coupon payments – Price of underlying security

To demonstrate that the arbitrage-free binomial model satisfies the put-call parity relationship for European options, let's use the values from our illustration. We just found that the put price is 0.6056 and the call price is 0.5327. Earlier, we showed that the theoretical price for the 6.5% 4-year option-free bond is 104.643. Exhibit 4 shows the spot rates for each year. The spot rate for year 2 is 4.2147%. Therefore,

$$\text{Present value of strike price } = \frac{100.25}{(1.042147)^2} = 92.3053$$

The present value of the coupon payments are found by discounting the two coupon payments of 6.5 by the spot rates. As just noted, the spot rate for year 2 is 4.2147%; the spot rate for year 1 is 3.5%. Therefore,

$$\text{Present value of coupon payments } = \frac{6.5}{(1.035)^1} + \frac{6.5}{(1.042147)^2} = 12.2650$$

Substituting the values into the right-hand side of the put-parity relationship we find:

$$0.6056 + 92.3053 + 12.2650 - 104.643 = 0.5329$$

The put value that we found is 0.5327. The discrepancy is due simply to rounding error. Therefore, put-call parity holds.

Extension of Arbitrage-Free Binomial Model to Futures Options

The binomial model can be extended to value futures options. For each node at the expiration date of the futures option, a yield is given. Given the acceptable issues that can be delivered, the conversion factors, and the yield at the expiration date of the futures option, the cheapest-to-deliver Treasury issue can be determined at each node. Therefore at each node at the expiration date of the futures option, there is a cheapest-to-deliver Treasury issue and a value for that issue. From the value of the cheapest-to-deliver Treasury issue and its conversion factor, the value of the underlying Treasury bond futures can be determined.

Exhibit 14: Theoretical Call Price and Price of Underlying Treasury Security

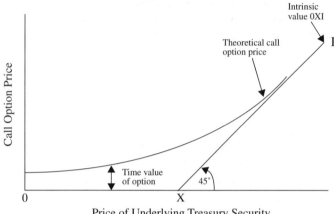

X = Strike price

Based on the strike price, the value of the option at each node at the expiration date of the futures option can be determined. The backward induction method is then used to determine the value of the futures option.

The binomial model allows the consistent valuation of Treasury bonds, Treasury bond futures, and options on Treasury bond futures.[7]

Sensitivity of Option Price to Change in Factors

To use options to control risk level, a manager would like to know how sensitive the price of an option is to a change in the factors that affect its price. Here we look at the sensitivity of a call option's price to changes in the price of the underlying Treasury security, the time to expiration, and expected yield volatility. The same concepts apply to options on Treasury futures. The magnitude of a change in the value of an option to a change in a factor is measured using an option pricing model.

The Call Option Price and the Price of the Underlying Treasury Security

Exhibit 14 shows the theoretical price of a call option based on the price of the underlying Treasury security. The horizontal axis is the price of the underlying Treasury security at any point in time. The vertical axis is the call option price. The shape of the curve representing the theoretical price of a call option, given the price of the underlying Treasury security, would be the same regardless of the actual option pricing model used. In particular, the relationship between the price

---

[7] See Soren S. Nielson and Ehud I. Ronn, "A Two-Factor Model for the Valuation of the T-Bond Futures Contract's Embedded Options," Chapter 8 in Frank J. Fabozzi (ed.), *Advances in Fixed Income Valuation Modeling and Risk Management* (New Hope, PA: Frank J. Fabozzi Associates, 1997).

of the underlying Treasury security and the theoretical call option price is convex. Thus, option prices also exhibit convexity.

The line from the origin to the strike price on the horizontal axis in Exhibit 14 is the intrinsic value of the call option when the price of the underlying Treasury security is less than the strike price, since the intrinsic value is zero. The 45-degree line extending from the horizontal axis is the intrinsic value of the call option once the price of the underlying Treasury security exceeds the strike price. The reason is that the intrinsic value of the call option will increase by the same dollar amount as the increase in the price of the underlying Treasury security.

For example, if the strike price is $100 and the price of the underlying Treasury security increases from $100 to $101, the intrinsic value will increase by $1. If the price of the security increases from $101 to $110, the intrinsic value of the option will increase from $1 to $10. Thus, the slope of the line representing the intrinsic value after the strike price is reached is 1.

Since the theoretical call option price is shown by the convex curve, the difference between the theoretical call option price and the intrinsic value at any given price for the underlying Treasury security is the time value of the option.

Exhibit 15 shows the theoretical call option price, but with a tangent line drawn at the price of p^*. The tangent line in the exhibit can be used to estimate what the new option price will be (and therefore what the change in the option price will be) if the price of the underlying Treasury security changes. Because of the convexity of the relationship between the option price and the price of the underlying Treasury security, the tangent line closely approximates the new option price for a small change in the price of the underlying Treasury security. For large changes, however, the tangent line does not provide as good an approximation of the new option price.

Exhibit 15: Estimating the Theoretical Option Price with a Tangent Line

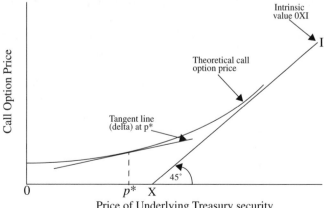

X = Strike price

Exhibit 16: Theoretical Option Price with Three Tangents

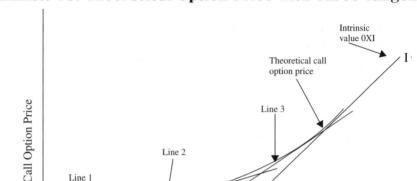

X = Strike price

The slope of the tangent line shows how the theoretical call option price will change for small changes in the price of the underlying Treasury security. The slope is popularly referred to as the *delta* of the option. Specifically,

$$\text{Delta} = \frac{\text{Change in price of call option}}{\text{Change in price of underlying Treasury security}}$$

For example, a delta of 0.4 means that a $1 change in the price of the underlying Treasury security will change the price of the call option by approximately $0.40.

Exhibit 16 shows the curve of the theoretical call option price with three tangent lines drawn. The steeper the slope of the tangent line, the greater the delta. When an option is deep out of the money (that is, the price of the underlying Treasury security is substantially below the strike price), the tangent line is nearly flat (see Line 1 in Exhibit 16). This means that delta is close to zero. To understand why, consider a call option with a strike price of $100 and two months to expiration. If the price of the underlying Treasury security is $60, its price would not increase by much, if anything, should the price of the underlying Treasury security increase by $1, from $60 to $61.

For a call option that is deep in the money, the delta will be close to one. That is, the call option price will increase almost dollar for dollar with an increase in the price of the underlying Treasury security. In terms of Exhibit 16, the slope of the tangent line approaches the slope of the intrinsic value line after the strike price. As we stated earlier, the slope of that line is 1.

Thus, the delta for a call option varies from zero (for call options deep out of the money) to one (for call options deep in the money). The delta for a call option at the money is approximately 0.5.

The curvature of the convex relationship can also be approximated. This is the rate of change of delta as the price of the underlying Treasury security changes. The measure is commonly referred to as *gamma* and is defined as follows:

$$\text{Gamma} = \frac{\text{Change in delta}}{\text{Change in price of underlying Treasury security}}$$

The Call Option Price and Time to Expiration

All other factors constant, the longer the time to expiration, the greater the option price. Since each day the option moves closer to the expiration date, the time to expiration decreases. The *theta* of an option measures the change in the option price as the time to expiration decreases, or equivalently, it is a measure of *time decay*. Theta is measured as follows:

$$\text{Theta} = \frac{\text{Change in price of option}}{\text{Decrease in time to expiration}}$$

Assuming that the price of the underlying Treasury security does not change (which means that the intrinsic value of the option does not change), theta measures how quickly the time value of the option changes as the option moves towards expiration.

Buyers of options prefer a low theta so that the option price does not decline quickly as it moves toward the expiration date. An option writer benefits from an option that has a high theta.

The Call Option Price and Expected Yield Volatility

All other factors constant, a change in the expected yield volatility will change the option price. The *kappa* of an option measures the dollar price change in the price of the option for a 1% change in expected yield volatility. That is,

$$\text{Kappa} = \frac{\text{Change in option price}}{1\% \text{ change in expected yield volatility}}$$

Duration of an Option

The duration of an option measures the price sensitivity of the option to changes in interest rates and can be shown to be equal to:

Duration for an option = Duration of underlying Treasury security

$$\times \text{Delta} \times \frac{\text{Price of underlying Treasury security}}{\text{Price of option}}$$

As expected, the duration of an option depends on the duration of the underlying Treasury security. It also depends on the price responsiveness of the option to a change in the underlying Treasury security, as measured by the option's delta. The leverage created by a position in an option comes from the last ratio in the formula. The higher the price of the underlying Treasury security relative to the price of the option, the greater the leverage (i.e., the more exposure to interest rates for a given dollar investment).

It is the interaction of all three factors that affects the duration of an option. For example, a deep out-of-the-money option offers higher leverage than a deep-in-the-money option, but the delta of the former is less than that of the former.

Since the delta of a call option is positive, the duration of an interest rate call option will be positive. Thus, when interest rates decline, the value of an interest rate call option will rise. A put option, however, has a delta that is negative. Thus, duration is negative. Consequently, when interest rates rise, the value of a put option rises.

VALUATION OF CALLABLE TREASURY BONDS

In Chapter 2, we explained how to value a noncallable Treasury bond. The valuation of a callable Treasury bond requires an understanding of the valuation of Treasury bond options. That is why we postponed a discussion of callable Treasury bond valuation until now.

The valuation model begins with the binomial interest rate tree. It is the same interest rate tree that is used to value options on Treasury bonds. The backward induction method is used to find the value of the callable Treasury bond at each node. However, the valuation procedure at a node is modified as follows. If an issue may be called at that node, then two values are determined at the node. The first is the standard value calculated by the backward induction method. The second value is par value which is the call price for a callable Treasury bond. The value that is used in subsequent calculations using the backward induction method will depend on whether or not the Department of the Treasury is expected to call the issue at that node.

To determine whether the issue will be called, the model developer must determine the criteria that the Department of the Treasury will use to decide whether or not to call the issue. We can refer to this as the "Treasury call decision rule." For example, this rule can be as simple as if the value at a node is greater than par value, then the issue will be called. One model developer, Global Advanced Technology, uses the following rule: if effective duration is less than 0.2 years, at the same point when the maturity is more than 0.2 years then the bond is deemed callable and it is called.

The theoretical value for the callable Treasury bond is then the value at the root of the tree. It will depend on the expected yield volatility assumed (since this assumption affects the binomial tree) and the Treasury call decision rule. The theoretical value of the embedded call option is then equal to the difference between the theoretical value of the issue if it is not callable and the theoretical value of the callable issue.

KEY POINTS

1. The theoretical price of a futures contract is equal to the cash price plus the cost of carry.

2. The cost of carry is equal to the cost of financing the position less the cash yield on the underlying security.

3. The shape of the yield curve affects the cost of carry.

4. The standard arbitrage model must be modified to take into consideration the nuances of the Treasury futures contract.

5. For a Treasury bond futures contract, the delivery options granted to the seller reduce the theoretical futures price below the theoretical futures price suggested by the standard arbitrage model.

6. In valuing a Treasury bond futures contract, more than one deliverable is used by some market participants rather than just the cheapest-to-deliver issue.

7. The value of an option is composed of its intrinsic value and its time value.

8. The six factors that affect the value of an option on a Treasury security are the current price of the underlying security, the strike price, the time to expiration of the option, the expected yield volatility over the life of the option, the short-term risk-free interest rate over the life of the option, and the coupon interest payment over the life of the option.

9. With the exception of the coupon interest payment, the value of a Treasury futures option is affected by the same factors that affect an option on a Treasury security.

10. With the exception of the short-term risk-free interest rate, how an option changes when one of the factors changes is the same for Treasury futures options and options on Treasury securities.

11. Several assumptions underlying the Black-Scholes model limit its use in pricing options on Treasury securities and futures options.

12. The Black model is commonly used for valuing futures options but is limited because it deals with European-type options.

13. Failure to take into account the yield curve can result in an inconsistent valuation of bonds, bond futures, and futures options.

14. Managers need to know how sensitive an option's value is to changes in the factors that affect the value of an option.

15. *An arbitrage-free binomial tree is used to value an option on a Treasury security.*

16. *A binomial tree is arbitrage free when it produces a value for an on-the-run Treasury that is equal to its market price.*

17. *The binomial method involves generating a binomial interest rate tree based on (1) on-the-run Treasury yield curve, (2) an assumed interest rate generation process, and (3) an assumed interest rate volatility.*

18. *The uncertainty of interest rates is introduced into the model by introducing the volatility of interest rates.*

19. *The put-call parity relationship is the pricing relationship between the price of a call option and the price of a put option on the same underlying instrument, with the same strike price and the same expiration date.*

20. *The put-call parity relationship is satisfied by the binomial model.*

21. *The arbitrage-free binomial model allows for the consistent pricing of Treasury bonds, Treasury bond futures, and options on Treasury bonds.*

22. *The binomial interest rate tree can be used to value a callable Treasury bond.*

23. *The delta of an option measures how sensitive the option price is to changes in the price of the underlying Treasury security and varies from zero (for call options deep out of the money) to one (for call options deep in the money).*

24. *The gamma of an option measures the rate of change of delta as the price of the underlying Treasury security changes.*

25. *The theta of an option measures the change in the option price as the time to expiration decreases.*

26. *The kappa of an option measures the dollar price change in the price of the option for a 1% change in expected yield volatility.*

27. *The duration of a Treasury option is a measure of its price sensitivity to small changes in interest rates and depends on the option's delta, the option's leverage, and the duration of the underlying Treasury security.*

28. *In valuing a callable Treasury bond it is necessary to make an assumption about the criteria that the U.S. Department of the Treasury will use to decide whether to call an issue.*

29. *The theoretical value of a callable Treasury bond will depend on the assumed expected yield volatility and the Treasury call decision rule.*

Chapter 15

CONTROLLING INTEREST RATE LEVEL RISK WITH TREASURY FUTURES AND OPTIONS

In this chapter we look at how to control interest rate risk with Treasury futures and options. As explained in Chapters 6 and 7, interest rate risk includes level risk and yield curve risk. A risk control strategy can be employed to control the interest rate risk of a portfolio without regard to the price movement of any individual bond comprising the portfolio. This type of risk control strategy is called a *macro strategy*. Alternatively, a risk control strategy can be implemented to control the risk of an individual bond or a group of bonds with similar characteristics. This type of risk control strategy is called a *micro strategy*. With a micro strategy, there may be considerably less exposure to yield curve risk.

PRELIMINARY STEPS IN ANY RISK CONTROL STRATEGY

There are four preliminary steps that a portfolio manager should take before implementing any strategy to control interest rate risk:

1. Determine which instruments are the most appropriate to employ to control risk.
2. Determine the objectives of the strategy.
3. Determine the position that should be taken in a risk control instrument.
4. Assess the potential outcome of the risk control strategy.

These steps are essential for two reasons. First, by taking these steps, the manager can assess what a risk control strategy can and cannot accomplish. Second, the steps ensure that if the risk control strategy is employed, it is set up in the proper way.

Determining which Instruments are the Most Appropriate to Employ

To control the interest rate risk of a position or portfolio, a position must be taken in another instrument or instruments. We shall focus on the use of Treasury futures and options as the risk control instruments. A primary factor in determining which instrument or instruments to use for controlling risk is the degree of correlation between the rate on the risk control instrument and the interest rate that creates the underlying risk that the manager seeks to control. For example,

255

the rate risk associated with a long-term corporate bond portfolio can be better controlled with an instrument that is affected by long-term Treasury rates rather than short-term Treasury bill rates because long-term corporate bond rates are more highly correlated with the former than with the latter.

Correlation is not the only consideration if liquidity is of concern. For a position that requires liquidity, it may not be desirable to control its risk with an illiquid instrument. When size is an important consideration, even risk control instruments that are generally viewed as highly liquid may have a liquidity problem. In such cases, it may be necessary for the manager to use several vehicles rather than one.

Determining the Objectives of the Strategy

The measures described in Chapter 6 provide information about the potential loss from a position resulting from a change in the level of interest rates. Given the potential loss and the appropriate risk control instruments to employ, the manager should then determine what is expected from the risk control strategy. For example, hedging is a special case of risk control. Suppose that a manager wants to hedge the risk associated with a current or anticipated future position of an individual bond (i.e., a micro hedging strategy). The manager should then determine what is expected from the hedge — that is, what rate will, on average, be locked in by the hedge. This is the *target rate* or *target price*. If this target rate is too high (if hedging a sale) or too low (if hedging a purchase), hedging may not be the right strategy for dealing with the unwanted risk.

Determining the Position that
Should Be Taken in a Risk Control Instrument

Given the risk control instruments and the objectives of the strategy, the position that should be taken in the risk control instruments must be determined. A position has two dimensions. The first dimension is whether the position should be a long position or a short position. For example, if a manager seeks to reduce the level risk exposure of a long position in a Treasury bond using Treasury bond futures, the appropriate position is a short position in the futures contract. The second dimension is the size of the position in the risk control instrument selected. For example, when using futures and options, it is the number of contracts. The amount of the position will depend on the dollar price volatility of the position whose risk the manager seeks to control relative to the risk control instrument used to control that risk. Later we will explain how this is done.

Assessing the Potential Outcome of the Risk Control Strategy

Given the position in the risk control instrument or instruments, the next step is to determine the potential outcome of the strategy. In many instances, this involves determining the outcome of the strategy under various scenarios that might be expected. That is, scenario analysis is performed. The scenarios analyzed will obviously involve different future interest rate levels.

In addition, because all risk control strategies make certain assumptions, it will be necessary to stress test the outcomes. For example, in the case of Treasury bond futures, a common assumption is that the cheapest-to-deliver issue will not change. In fact, the cheapest-to-deliver issue will change as interest rates change. The outcome of a risk control strategy can assess the potential impact of a change in the cheapest-to-deliver issue at different interest rate levels. As another example, it is common to make an assumption about the spread between two rates. So, a manager might make an assumption about the spread between single-A corporates and Treasuries when using Treasury bond futures to control the interest rate risk of a single-A corporate bond.

The scenarios analyzed can then be compared to the objectives established for the risk control strategy. It might be found, for example, that under a wide range of scenarios the objectives may be realized. On the other hand, it may turn out that for some scenarios that are reasonably likely to occur, the risk control strategy results in outcomes that are inferior to doing nothing at all.

CONTROLLING LEVEL RISK WITH TREASURY FUTURES

We begin with the application of Treasury bond futures to control risk. The price of a Treasury futures contract moves in the opposite direction from the change in interest rates: when rates rise, the futures price will fall; when rates fall, the futures price will rise. By buying a Treasury futures contract, a portfolio's exposure to rate changes is increased. That is, the portfolio's duration increases. By selling a Treasury futures contract, a portfolio's exposure to rate changes is decreased. Equivalently, this means that the portfolio's duration is reduced.

The same exposure can be obtained by using cash market instruments. Treasury securities can be used to alter the duration of a position. Specifically, a long bond position's duration can be reduced by shorting an appropriate amount of Treasury securities and a short bond position's duration can be reduced by buying an appropriate amount of Treasury securities.

Using Treasury futures instead of Treasuries has three advantages. First, transaction costs for trading futures are lower than trading in the cash market. Second, margin requirements are lower for Treasury futures than for Treasury securities; using futures thus permits greater leverage. Finally, it is easier to sell short in the futures market than in the Treasury market. Consequently, while a manager can alter the duration of a portfolio with Treasury securities, a quick and inexpensive means for doing so (on either a temporary or permanent basis) is to use Treasury futures contracts.

General Principle

The general principle in controlling level risk with Treasury futures is to combine the dollar value exposure of the current portfolio and that of a Treasury futures position so that it is equal to the target dollar exposure. This means that the manager must be able to accurately measure the dollar exposure of both the current portfolio and the Treasury futures contract employed to alter the exposure.

Dollar duration can be used to approximate the change in the dollar value of a bond or bond portfolio to changes in the level of interest rates. Suppose that a manager has a $250 million Treasury portfolio with a duration of 5 and wants to reduce the duration to 4. Thus, the target duration for the portfolio is 4. Given the target duration, a target dollar duration for a small number of basis point change in interest rates, say 50 basis points, can be obtained. A target duration of 4 means that for a 100 basis point change in rates (assuming a parallel shift in rates of all maturities), the target percentage price change is 4%. For a 50 basis point change, the target percentage price change is 2%. Multiplying the 2% by $250 million gives a target dollar duration of $5 million for a 50 basis point change in rates.

The manager must then determine the dollar duration of the current portfolio for a 50 basis point change in rates. Since the current duration for the portfolio is 5, the current dollar duration for a 50 basis point change in interest rates is $6.25 million. The target dollar duration is then compared to the current dollar duration. The difference between the two dollar durations is the dollar exposure that must be provided by a position in the Treasury futures contract. If the target dollar duration exceeds the current dollar duration, a Treasury futures position must increase the dollar exposure by the difference. To increase the dollar exposure, an appropriate number of Treasury futures contracts must be purchased. If the target dollar duration is less than the current dollar duration, an appropriate number of Treasury futures contracts must be sold.

Once a futures position is taken, the portfolio's dollar duration is equal to the current dollar duration without Treasury futures and the dollar duration of the Treasury futures position. That is,

> Portfolio's dollar duration = Current dollar duration without Treasury futures
> + Dollar duration of Treasury futures position

The objective is to control the portfolio's level risk by establishing a Treasury futures position such that the portfolio's dollar duration is equal to the target dollar duration. That is,

> Portfolio's dollar duration = Target dollar duration

Or, equivalently,

> Target dollar duration = Current dollar duration without Treasury futures
> + Dollar duration of Treasury futures position   (1)

Over time, the portfolio's dollar duration will move away from the target dollar duration. The manager can alter the Treasury futures position to adjust the portfolio's dollar duration to the target dollar duration.

Determining the Number of Contracts

Each Treasury futures contract calls for a specified amount of the underlying Treasury security. When the level of interest rates change, the value of the underlying Treasury security changes, and therefore the value of the Treasury futures contract changes. How much the Treasury futures dollar value will change when interest rates change must be estimated. This amount is called the *dollar duration per Treasury futures contract*. For example, suppose the futures price of a Treasury futures contract is 70 and that the underlying Treasury security has a par value of $100,000. Thus, the futures price is $70,000 (0.70 times $100,000). Suppose that a change in interest rates of 50 basis points results in the futures price of the Treasury futures contract changing by about 3 points. Then the dollar duration per Treasury futures contract is $3,000 (0.03 times $100,000). Or equivalently, it is $3,000 per $100,000 par value of the underlying.

The dollar duration of a Treasury futures position is then the number of Treasury futures contracts multiplied by the dollar duration per Treasury futures contract. That is,

Dollar duration of Treasury futures position
$\qquad$ = Number of Treasury futures contracts
$\qquad$ × Dollar duration per Treasury futures contract $\qquad$ (2)

To determine how many Treasury futures contracts are needed to obtain the target dollar duration, we can substitute equation (2) into equation (1). The result is

Number of Treasury futures contracts
$\qquad$ × Dollar duration per Treasury futures contract
$\qquad$ = Target dollar duration
$\qquad$ − Current dollar duration without Treasury futures $\qquad$ (3)

Solving for the number of Treasury futures contracts we have:

Number of Treasury futures contracts=
$$\frac{\text{Target dollar duration}}{\text{Dollar duration per Treasury futures contract}}$$
$$-\frac{\text{Current dollar duration without Treasury futures}}{\text{Dollar duration per Treasury futures contract}} \qquad (4)$$

Equation (4) gives the approximate number of Treasury futures contracts that are necessary to adjust the portfolio's dollar duration to the target dollar duration. A positive number means that Treasury futures contracts must be purchased; a negative number means that Treasury futures contracts must be sold. Notice that if the target dollar duration is greater than the current dollar duration without Treasury futures, the numerator is positive and therefore Treasury futures contracts are purchased. If the target dollar duration is less than the current dollar duration without Treasury futures, the numerator is negative and therefore Treasury futures contracts are sold.

HEDGING WITH TREASURY FUTURES

Hedging with Treasury futures calls for taking a futures position as a temporary substitute for transactions to be made in the cash market at a later date. If cash and Treasury futures prices move together, any loss realized by the hedger from one position (whether cash or futures) will be offset by a profit on the other position. Hedging is a special case of controlling level risk. In a hedge, the manager seeks a target duration or target dollar duration of zero.

Typically the bond or portfolio to be hedged is not identical to the Treasury security underlying the Treasury futures contract. This type of hedging is referred to as *cross hedging*. There may be significant risks in cross hedging.

A *short* (or *sell*) *hedge* is used to protect against a decline in the cash price of a bond. To execute a short hedge, Treasury futures contracts are sold. By establishing a short hedge, the manager has fixed the future cash price and transferred the price risk of ownership to the buyer of the Treasury futures contract. A *long* (or *buy*) *hedge* is undertaken to protect against an increase in the cash price of a bond.

Hedge Effectiveness and Residual Hedging Risk

Earlier we described the four preliminary steps that a manager should undertake prior to the employment of a risk control strategy. In the case of hedging, the manager must try to assess the hedge effectiveness and the residual hedging risk. *Hedge effectiveness* lets the manager know what percent of risk is eliminated by hedging. For example, if the hedge effectiveness is determined to be 85% effective, over the long run a hedged position will have only 15% of the risk (that is, the standard deviation) of an unhedged position.

The *residual hedging risk* is the absolute level of risk in the hedged position. This risk tells the manager how much risk remains after hedging. While it may be comforting to know, for example, that 85% of the risk is eliminated by hedging, without additional statistics the manager still does not know how much risk remains. The residual hedging risk in a hedged position is expressed as a standard deviation. For example, it might be determined that the hedged position has a standard deviation of 10 basis points. Assuming a normal distribution of hedging errors,[1] the manager will then obtain the target rate plus or minus 10 basis points 68.3% of the time. The probability of obtaining the target rate plus or minus 20 basis points is 95.5%, and the probability of obtaining the target rate plus or minus 30 basis points is greater than 99.7%.

---

[1] The properties of a normal distribution are described in Chapter 8.

The target rate, the hedge effectiveness, and the residual hedging risk determine the basic trade-off between risk and expected return. Consequently, these statistics give the manager the information needed to decide whether to employ a hedge strategy. Using these statistics, the manager can construct confidence intervals for hedged and unhedged positions.[2] Comparing these confidence intervals, the manager can determine whether hedging is the best alternative. Furthermore, if hedging is the right decision, the level of confidence in the hedge is defined in advance.

It is important for a manager to realize that the hedge effectiveness and the residual hedging risk are not necessarily constant from one hedge to the next. Hedges for dates near a futures delivery date will tend to be more effective and have less residual hedging risk than those lifted on other dates. The life of the hedge, that is, the amount of time between when the hedge is set and when it is lifted, also generally has a significant impact on hedge effectiveness and residual hedging risk. For example, a hedge held for six months might be 95% effective, whereas a hedge held for one month might be only 30% effective. This is because the security to be hedged and the hedging instrument might be highly correlated over the long run, but only weakly correlated over the short run. On the other hand, residual hedging risk usually increases as the life of the hedge increases. The residual hedging risk on a 6-month hedge may be 80 basis points while the residual hedging risk for a 1-month hedge may be only 30 basis points. It may seem surprising that hedges for longer periods have more risk if they are also more effective. However, hedge effectiveness is a measure of relative risk, and because longer time periods exhibit greater swings in interest rates, the greater percentage reduction in risk for longer hedges does not mean that there is less risk left over.

The target rate, the residual risk, and the effectiveness of a hedge are relatively simple concepts. However, because these statistics are usually estimated using historical data, the manager who plans to hedge should be sure that these figures are estimated correctly.

Risk and Expected Return in a Hedge

In a micro hedge strategy, when a manager enters into a hedge, the objective is to "lock in" a rate for the sale or purchase of a security. However, there is much disagreement about what rate a manager should expect to lock in when futures are used to hedge. One view is that the manager can, on average, lock in the current spot rate for the security. The opposing view is that the manager will, on average, lock in the rate at which the futures contracts are bought or sold. The truth usually lies somewhere in between these two positions. However, as the following cases illustrate, each view is entirely correct in certain situations.

---

[2] See Chapter 8 for an explanation of confidence intervals.

The Target for Hedges Held to Delivery

A hedge that is held until the futures delivery date provides an example of a hedge that locks in the futures rate. The complication in the case of using Treasury bond futures and Treasury note futures to hedge the value of intermediate- and long-term bonds is that because of the delivery options the manager does not know for sure when delivery will take place or which bond will be delivered.[3]

To illustrate how a Treasury bond futures held to the delivery date locks in the futures rate, assume for the sake of simplicity, that the manager knows which Treasury bond will be delivered and that delivery will take place on the last day of the delivery month. Consider the 7⅝s Treasury bonds maturing on February 15, 2007.[4] For delivery on the June 1985 contract, the conversion factor for these bonds was 0.9660, implying that the investor who delivers the 7⅝s would receive from the buyer 0.9660 times the futures settlement price, plus accrued interest. Consequently, at delivery, the (flat) spot price and the futures price times the conversion factor must converge. *Convergence* refers to the fact that at delivery there can be no discrepancy between the spot and futures price for a given security. If convergence does not take place, arbitrageurs would buy at the lower price and sell at the higher price and earn risk-free profits. Accordingly, a manager could lock in a June sale price for the 7⅝s by selling Treasury bond futures contracts equal to 0.9660 times the face value of the bonds. For example, $100 million face value of 7⅝s would be hedged by selling $96.6 million face value of Treasury bond futures (rounded to 967 contracts).

The sale price that the manager locks in would be 0.9660 times the Treasury futures price. Thus, if the futures price is 70 when the hedge is set, the manager locks in a sale price of 67.62 (70 times 0.9660) for June delivery, regardless of where rates are in June. Exhibit 1 shows the cash flows for a number of final prices for the 7⅝s and illustrates how cash flows on the Treasury futures contracts offset gains or losses relative to the target price of 67.62. In each case, the effective sale price is very close to the target price (and, in fact, would be exact if enough decimal places were carried through the calculations). However, the target price is determined by the Treasury futures price, so the target price may be higher or lower than the cash market price when the hedge is set.

When we admit the possibility that bonds other than the 7⅝s of 2007 can be delivered, and that it might be advantageous to deliver other bonds, the situation becomes somewhat more involved. In this more realistic case, the manager may decide not to deliver the 7⅝s, but if she does decide to deliver them, the manager is still assured of receiving an effective sale price of approximately 67.62. If the manager does not deliver the 7⅝s, it would be because another bond can be delivered more cheaply, and thus the manager does better than the targeted price.

---

[3] See Chapter 12 for an explanation of the delivery options.

[4] This example is taken from Chapter 9 in Mark Pitts and Frank J. Fabozzi, *Interest Rate Futures and Options* (Chicago, IL: Probus Publishing, 1989).

Exhibit 1: Treasury Bond Hedge Held to Delivery

Instrument to be hedged: 7⅝s Treasury bonds of 2/15/07
Conversion factor for June 1985 delivery = 0.9660
Price of futures contract when sold = 70
Target price = 0.9660 × 70 = 67.62

Actual sale price for 7⅝s Treasury bond ($)	Final futures price ($)[*]	Gain or loss on 967 contracts ($; $10/0.01/contract)[**]	Effective sale price ($)[***]
62	64.182	5,620,188	67,620,188
63	65.217	4,620,378	67,620,378
64	66.253	3,619,602	67,619,602
65	67.288	2,619,792	67,619,792
66	68.323	1,619,982	67,619,982
67	69.358	620,172	67,620,172
68	70.393	−379,638	67,620,632
69	71.429	−1,380,414	67,619,586
70	72.464	−2,380,224	67,619,776
71	73.499	−3,380,034	67,619,966
72	74.534	−4,379,844	67,620,156
73	75.569	−5,379,654	67,620,346
74	76.605	−6,380,430	67,619,570
75	77.640	−7,380,240	67,619,760

*By convergence, must equal bond price divided by the conversion factor.
**Bond futures trade in even increments of ¹⁄₃₂. Accordingly, the futures prices and margin flows are only approximate.
***Transaction costs and the financing of margin flows are ignored.

In summary, if a manager sets a risk minimizing futures hedge that is held until delivery, the manager can be assured of receiving an effective price dictated by the futures rate (not the spot rate) on the day the hedge is set.

The Target for Hedges with Short Holding Periods

When a manager must lift (remove) a hedge prior to the delivery date, the effective rate that is obtained is much more likely to approximate the current spot rate than the futures rate the shorter the term of the hedge. The critical difference between this hedge and the hedge held to the delivery date is that convergence will generally not take place by the termination date of the hedge. This will be the case regardless of whether the manager is hedging with Treasury bill futures or hedging longer-term instruments with Treasury note and Treasury bond contracts.

To illustrate why a manager should expect the hedge to lock in the spot rate rather than the Treasury futures rate for very short-lived hedges, let's return to the simplified example used earlier to illustrate a hedge to the delivery date. It is assumed that the 7⅝s of 2007 were the only deliverable Treasury bonds for the

Treasury bond futures contract. Suppose that the hedge is set three months before the delivery date and the manager plans to lift the hedge after one day. It is much more likely that the spot price of the bond will move parallel to the converted futures price (that is, the futures price times the conversion factor) than that the spot price and the converted futures price will converge by the time the hedge is lifted.

A 1-day hedge is, admittedly, an extreme example. However, it is not uncommon for traders and risk managers to have such a short horizon. Few money managers are interested in such a short horizon. The very short-term hedge does illustrate a very important point: when hedging, a manager should not expect to lock in the Treasury futures rate (or price) just because he is hedging with Treasury futures contracts. The futures rate is locked in only if the hedge is held until delivery, at which point convergence must take place. If the hedge is held for only one day, the manager should expect to lock in the 1-day forward rate, which will very nearly equal the spot rate. Generally hedges are held for more than one day, but not necessarily to delivery.

How the Basis Affects the Target Rate for a Hedge

The proper target for a hedge that is to be lifted prior to the delivery date depends on the basis. The *basis* is simply the difference between the spot (cash) price of a security and its futures price. That is:

Basis = Spot price – Futures price

In the Treasury market, a problem arises when trying to make practical use of the concept of the basis. The quoted futures price does not equal the price that one receives at delivery. For the Treasury bond and note futures contracts, the actual futures price equals the quoted futures price times the appropriate conversion factor. Consequently, to be useful the basis in the Treasury market should be defined using actual futures delivery prices rather than quoted futures prices. Thus, the price basis for Treasury coupon securities should be redefined as:

Price basis = Spot price – Futures delivery price

Unfortunately, problems still arise due to the fact that Treasury securities age over time. Thus, it is not exactly clear what is meant by the "spot price." Does spot price mean the current price of the actual Treasury coupon security that can be held and delivered in satisfaction of a short position, or does it mean the current price of an instrument that currently has the characteristics called for in the Treasury futures contract? For example, when the basis is defined for a 3-month Treasury bill contract maturing in three months, should spot price refer to the current price of a 6-month Treasury bill, which is the instrument that will actually be deliverable on the contract (because in three months it will be a 3-month Treasury bill), or should spot price refer to the price of the current 3-month Treasury bill? In most cases the former definition of the spot price makes the most sense.

For hedging purposes it is also frequently useful to define the basis in terms of interest rates rather than prices. The rate basis is defined as:

Rate basis = Spot rate − Futures rate

where spot rate refers to the current rate on the instrument to be hedged and the futures rate is the interest rate corresponding to the futures delivery price of the deliverable Treasury security.

The rate basis is helpful in explaining why the two types of hedges explained earlier are expected to lock in such different rates. To see this, we first define the *target rate basis*. This is defined as the expected rate basis on the day the hedge is lifted. A hedge lifted on the delivery date is expected to have, and by convergence will have, a zero rate basis when the hedge is lifted. Thus, the target rate for the hedge should be the rate on the Treasury futures contract plus the expected rate basis of zero, or in other words, just the Treasury futures rate. When a hedge is lifted prior to the delivery date, one would not expect the basis to change very much in one day, so the target rate basis equals the Treasury futures rate plus the current difference between the spot rate and futures rate, i.e., the current spot rate.

The manager can set the target rate for any hedge equal to the Treasury futures rate plus the target rate basis. That is,

Target rate for hedge = Treasury futures rate + Target rate basis

If projecting the basis in terms of price rather than rate is more manageable (as is often the case for Treasury note and bond futures contracts), it is easier to work with the target price basis instead of the target rate basis. The target price basis is just the projected price basis for the day the hedge is to be lifted. For a deliverable security, the target for the hedge then becomes

Target price for hedge = Treasury futures delivery price + Target price basis

The idea of a target price or rate basis explains why a hedge held until the delivery date locks in a price with certainty, and other hedges do not. As is often said, hedging substitutes basis risk for price risk, and the examples have shown that this is true. For the hedge held to delivery, there is no uncertainty surrounding the target basis; by convergence, the basis on the day the hedge is lifted is certain to be zero. For the short-lived hedge, at the time the hedge is lifted the basis will probably approximate the basis when the hedge was initiated, but its actual value is not known. For hedges longer than one day but ending prior to the futures delivery date, there can be considerable risk because the basis on the day the hedge is lifted can end up being anywhere within a wide range. Thus, the uncertainty surrounding the outcome of a hedge is directly related to the uncertainty surrounding the basis on the day the hedge is lifted, that is, the uncertainty surrounding the target basis.

For a given investment horizon hedging substitutes basis risk for price risk. Thus, one trades the uncertainty of the price of the hedged security for the uncertainty of the basis. Consequently, when hedges do not produce the desired results, it is customary to place the blame on "basis risk." However, basis risk is the real culprit only if the target for the hedge is properly defined. Basis risk should refer only to the unexpected or unpredictable part of the relationship between cash and futures. The fact that this relationship changes over time does not in itself imply that there is basis risk.

Basis risk, properly defined, refers only to the uncertainty associated with the target rate basis or target price basis. Accordingly, it is imperative that the target basis be properly defined if one is to correctly assess the risk and expected return in a hedge.

Cross Hedging

Earlier, we defined a cross hedge in the futures market as a hedge in which the security to be hedged is not deliverable into the futures contract used in the hedge. For example, a manager who wants to hedge the sale price of long-term corporate bonds might hedge with the Treasury bond futures contract, but since corporate bonds cannot be delivered in satisfaction of the contract, the hedge would be considered a cross hedge. Similarly, on the short end of the yield curve, a manager might want to hedge a 3-month rate that does not perfectly track the Treasury bill rate. A manager might also want to hedge a rate that is of the same quality as the rate specified in one of the contracts, but that has a different maturity. For example, it is necessary to cross hedge to hedge a Treasury bond, note, or bill with a maturity that does not qualify for delivery on any futures contract. Thus, when the security to be hedged differs from the Treasury futures contract specification in terms of either quality or maturity, one is led to the cross hedge.

Conceptually, cross hedging is somewhat more complicated than hedging deliverable securities, because it involves two relationships. First, there is the relationship between the cheapest-to-deliver (CTD) issue and the Treasury futures contract. Second, there is the relationship between the security to be hedged and the CTD. Practical considerations may at times lead a manager to shortcut this two-step relationship and focus directly on the relationship between the security to be hedged and the Treasury futures contract, thus ignoring the CTD altogether. However, in so doing, a manager runs the risk of miscalculating the target rate and the risk in the hedge. Furthermore, if the hedge does not perform as expected, the shortcut makes it difficult to tell why the hedge went awry.

The Hedge Ratio

The key to minimize risk in a cross hedge is to choose the right *hedge ratio*. The hedge ratio depends on the relative dollar duration of the bond to be hedged and the Treasury futures position. Equation (4) indicates the number of Treasury futures contracts to achieve a particular target dollar duration. The objective in hedging is make the target dollar duration equal to zero. Substituting zero for target dollar duration in equation (4), we obtain:

Number of Treasury futures contracts

$$= - \frac{\text{Current dollar duration without Treasury futures}}{\text{Dollar duration per Treasury futures contract}} \qquad (5)$$

To calculate the dollar duration of a bond, the manager must know the precise point in time that the dollar duration is to be calculated (because volatility generally declines as a bond seasons) as well as the price or yield at which to calculate dollar duration (because higher yields generally reduce dollar duration for a given yield change). The relevant point in the life of the bond for calculating volatility is the point at which the hedge will be lifted. Dollar duration at any other point is essentially irrelevant because the goal is to lock in a price or rate only on that particular day. Similarly, the relevant yield at which to calculate dollar duration initially is the target yield. Consequently, the numerator of equation (5) is the dollar duration on the date the hedge is expected to be lifted. The yield that is to be used on this date in order to determine the dollar duration is the forward rate.

An example for a single bond rather than a portfolio shows why dollar duration weighting leads to the correct hedge ratio.[5] Suppose that on April 19, 1985, a money manager owned $10 million face value of the Southern Bell 11¾s bonds of 2023 and sold June 1985 Treasury bond futures to hedge a future sale of the bonds. This is an example of a cross hedge. Suppose that (1) the Treasury 7⅝s of 2007 were the cheapest-to-deliver issue on the contract and that they were trading at 11.50%, (2) the Southern Bell bonds were at 12.40%, and (3) the Treasury bond futures were at a price of 70. To simplify, assume also that the yield spread between the two bonds remains at 0.90% (i.e., 90 basis points) and that the anticipated sale date was the last business day in June 1985.

Because the conversion factor for the deliverable 7⅝s for the June 1985 contract was 0.9660, the target price for hedging the 7⅝s would be 67.62 (70 × 0.9660), and the target yield would be 11.789% (the yield at a price of 67.62). The yield on the telephone bonds is assumed to stay at 0.90% above the yield on the 7⅝s, so the target yield for the Southern Bell bonds would be 12.689%, with a corresponding price of 92.628. At these target levels, the dollar duration for a 50 basis point change in rates for the 7⅝s and telephone bonds per $100 of par value are, respectively, $2.8166 and $3.6282. As indicated earlier, all these calculations are made using a settlement date equal to the anticipated sale date, in this case the end of June 1985. The dollar duration for $10 million par value of the Southern Bell bonds is $362,820 ($10 million/100 times $3.6282). Per $100,000 of par value for the Treasury futures contract, the dollar duration per Treasury futures contract is $2,817 ($100,000/100 times $2.8166). Therefore:

---

[5] This example is adapted from Pitts and Fabozzi, *Interest Rate Futures and Options.*

Current dollar duration without Treasury futures =
Dollar duration of the Southern Bell bonds = $362,820

and

Dollar duration of the CTD = $2,817

However, to calculate the hedge ratio, we need the dollar duration not of the CTD, but of the Treasury bond futures contract. Fortunately, knowing the dollar duration of the bond to be hedged relative to the CTD and the dollar duration of the CTD relative to the Treasury futures contract, we can easily obtain the hedge ratio:

$$
\text{Hedge ratio} = -\frac{\text{Current dollar duration without Treasury futures}}{\text{Dollar duration of the CTD}} \times \frac{\text{Dollar duration of the CTD}}{\text{Dollar duration per Treasury futures contract}} \quad (6)
$$

Assuming a fixed yield spread between the bond to be hedged and the CTD, the hedge ratio given by equation (6) can be rewritten as:

$$
\text{Hedge ratio} = -\frac{\text{Current dollar duration without Treasury futures}}{\text{Dollar duration of the CTD}} \times \text{Conversion factor for the CTD} \quad (7)
$$

Substituting the values from our example into equation (7):

$$
\text{Hedge ratio} = -\frac{\$362,820}{\$2,817} \times 0.9660 = -124 \text{ contracts}
$$

Thus, to hedge the Southern Bell position, 124 Treasury bond futures contracts must be shorted.

Scenario analysis can be used to show the potential outcome of this hedge. Exhibit 2 shows that, if the simplifying assumptions hold, a futures hedge using the recommended hedge ratio very nearly locks in the target price for $10 million face value of the telephone bonds.[6]

Another refinement in the hedging strategy is usually necessary for hedging nondeliverable securities. This refinement concerns the assumption about the relative yield spread between the CTD and the bond to be hedged. In the prior discussion, we assumed that the yield spread was constant over time. Yield spreads, however, are not constant over time. They vary with the maturity of the instruments in question and the level of rates, as well as with many unpredictable and nonsystematic factors.

---

[6] In practice, most of the remaining error could be eliminated by frequent adjustments to the hedge ratio to account for the fact that the dollar duration changes as rates move up or down.

Exhibit 2: Hedging a Nondeliverable Bond to a Delivery Date with Futures: Scenario Analysis

Instrument to be hedged: Southern Bell 11¾s of 4/19/23

Par value = $10 million

Hedge ratio = 124

Price of futures contract when sold = 70

Target price for Southern Bell bonds = 92.628

Actual sale price of telephone bonds ($)	Yield at sale (%)	Yield on Treasury 7⅝s* (%)	Price of Treasury 7⅝s	Futures price**	Gain (loss) on 124 contracts ($10/0.01/contract) ($)	Effective sale price ($)****
7,600,000	15.468	14.568	54.590	56.511	1,672,636	9,272,636
7,800,000	15.072	14.172	56.167	58.144	1,470,144	9,270,144
8,000,000	14.696	13.769	57.741	59.773	1,268,148	9,268,148
8,200,000	14.338	13.438	59.313	61.401	1,066,276	9,266,276
8,400,000	13.996	13.096	60.887	63.030	864,280	9,264,280
8,600,000	13.671	12.771	62.451	64.649	663,524	9,263,524
8,800,000	13.359	12.459	64.018	66.271	462,396	9,262,396
9,000,000	13.061	12.161	65.580	67.888	261,888	9,261,888
9,200,000	12.776	11.876	67.134	69.497	62,372	9,262,372
9,400,000	12.503	11.603	68.683	71.100	(136,400)	9,263,600
9,600,000	12.240	11.340	70.233	72.705	(335,420)	9,264,580
9,800,000	11.988	11.088	71.773	74.299	(533,076)	9,266,924
10,000,000	11.745	10.845	73.312	75.892	(730,608)	9,269,392
10,200,000	11.512	10.612	74.839	77.473	(926,652)	9,273,348
10,400,000	11.287	10.387	76.364	79.052	(1,122,448)	9,277,552
10,600,000	11.070	10.170	77.884	80.625	(1,317,500)	9,282,500
10,800,000	10.861	9.961	79.394	82.188	(1,511,312)	9,288,688
11,000,000	10.659	9.759	80.889	83.746	(1,704,504)	9,295,496
11,200,000	10.463	9.563	82.403	85.303	(1,897,572)	9,302,428

* By assumption, the yield on the 7⅝s of 2007 is 90 basis points lower than the yield on the Southern Bell bond.

** By convergence, the futures price equals the price of the 7⅝s of 2007 divided by 0.9660 (the conversion factor).

*** Transaction costs and the financing of margin flows are ignored.

Regression analysis allows the manager to capture the relationship between yield levels and yield spreads and use it to advantage. For hedging purposes, the variables are the yield on the bond to be hedged and the yield on the CTD. The regression equation takes the form:

$$\text{Yield on bond to be hedged} = \alpha + \beta \times \text{Yield on CTD} + \text{error} \qquad (8)$$

The regression procedure provides an estimate of β (the *yield beta*), which is the expected relative yield change in the two bonds. Our example that used a constant spread implicitly assumes that the yield beta, β, equals 1.0 and α equals 90 basis points (the assumed spread).

For the two issues in question, that is, the Southern Bell 11¾s and the Treasury 7⅝s, suppose that the estimated yield beta was 1.05. Thus, yields on the corporate issue are expected to move 5% more than yields on the Treasury issue. To calculate the hedge ratio correctly, this fact must be taken into account; thus, the hedge ratio derived in our earlier example is multiplied by the factor 1.05. Consequently, instead of shorting 124 Treasury bond futures contracts to hedge $10 million of telephone bonds, the investor would short 130 contracts.

The formula for the hedge ratio is revised as follows to incorporate the impact of the yield beta:

$$\text{Hedge ratio} = - \frac{\text{Current dollar duration without Treasury futures}}{\text{Dollar duration of the CTD}}$$
$$\times \text{Conversion factor for CTD} \times \text{Yield beta} \qquad (9)$$

where the yield beta is derived from the yield of the bond to be hedged regressed on the yield of the CTD [equation (8)].

The effect of a change in the CTD and the yield spread can be assessed a priori. An exhibit similar to that of Exhibit 2 can be constructed under a wide range of assumptions. For example, at different yield levels at the date the hedge is to be lifted (the second column in Exhibit 2), a different yield spread may be appropriate and a different acceptable issue will be the CTD. The manager can determine what this will do to the outcome of the hedge.

Monitoring and Evaluating the Hedge

After a target is determined and a hedge is set, there are two remaining tasks. The hedge must be monitored during its life, and evaluated after it is over. A futures hedge may require very little active monitoring during its life. In fact, overactive management may pose more of a threat to most hedges than does inactive management. The reason for this is that the manager usually will not receive enough new information during the life of the hedge to justify a change in the hedging strategy. For example, it is not advisable to readjust the hedge ratio every day in response to a new data point and a possible corresponding change in the estimated value of the yield beta.

There are, however, exceptions to this general rule. As rates change, dollar duration changes. Consequently, the hedge ratio may change slightly. In other cases, there may be sound economic reasons to believe that the yield beta has changed. While there are exceptions, the best approach is usually to let a hedge run its course using the original hedge ratio with only slight adjustments.

A hedge can normally be evaluated only after it has been lifted. Evaluation involves, first, an assessment of how closely the hedge locked in the target rate, that is, how much error there was in the hedge. To provide a meaningful interpretation of the error, the manager should calculate how far from the target the sale (or purchase) would have been, had there been no hedge at all.

One good reason for evaluating a completed hedge is to ascertain the sources of error in the hedge in the hope that a manager will gain insights that can be used to advantage in subsequent hedges. A manager will find that there are three major sources of hedging errors:

1. The projected value of the basis at the lift date can be in error.
2. The parameters estimated from the regression (α and β) can be inaccurate.
3. The error term in the regression may not equal zero.

Frequently, at least in the short run, the last two sources of error are indistinguishable. The manager will generally only know that the regression equation did not give an accurate estimate of the rate to be hedged. However, such inaccuracy could have occurred either from poor parameter estimates or from very accurate parameter estimates in conjunction with a large error term.

The first major source of errors in a hedge — an inaccurate projected value of the basis — is the more difficult problem. Unfortunately, there are no satisfactory simple models like the regression that can be applied to the basis. Simple models of the basis violate certain equilibrium relationships for bonds that should not be violated. On the other hand, theoretically rigorous models are very unintuitive and usually soluble only by complex numerical methods. Modeling the basis is undoubtedly one of the most important and difficult problems that managers seeking to hedge face.

HEDGING WITH OPTIONS

There are three popular hedge strategies employing options: (1) a protective put buying strategy, (2) a covered call writing strategy, and (3) a collar strategy. We begin with basic hedging principles for each strategy. Then we illustrate the first two strategies using Treasury futures options to hedge the Southern Bell bonds in which a Treasury bond futures hedge was used. Using Treasury futures options in our illustration of hedging the Southern Bell bonds is a worthwhile exercise because it shows how complicated hedging with Treasury futures options is and the key parameters involved in the process. We also compare the outcome of hedging with Treasury futures and hedging with Treasury futures options.[7]

Basic Hedging Strategies

Protective Puts

Consider first a manager who owns a bond and wants to hedge against rising interest rates. The most obvious options hedging strategy is to buy puts on bonds. These *protective puts* are usually out-of-the-money puts and may be either puts on cash Treasury securities or puts on Treasury futures. If interest rates rise, the puts will increase in value (holding other factors constant), offsetting some or all the loss on the bonds in the portfolio.

This strategy is a simple combination of a long put option with a long position in a cash bond. The result is a payoff pattern that resembles a long position in a call option alone. Such a position has limited downside risk, but large upside potential. However, if rates fall, the price appreciation on the securities in the portfolio will be diminished by the amount paid for the puts. Exhibit 3 compares the protective put strategy to an unhedged position.

The protective put strategy is very often compared to purchasing insurance. Like insurance, the premium paid for the protection is nonrefundable and is paid before the coverage begins. The degree to which a portfolio is protected depends upon the strike price of the options; thus, the strike price is often compared to the deductible on an insurance policy. The lower the deductible (that is, the higher the strike on the put), the greater the level of protection and the more the protection costs. Conversely, the higher the deductible (the lower the strike on the put), the more the portfolio can lose in value; but the cost of the insurance is lower. Exhibit 4 compares an unhedged position with several protective put positions, each with a different strike price, or level of protection. As the exhibit shows, no one strategy dominates any other strategy, in the sense of performing better at all possible rate levels. Consequently, it is impossible to say that one strike price is necessarily the "best" strike price, or even that buying protective puts is necessarily better than doing nothing at all.

Covered Call Writing

Another options hedging strategy used by many portfolio managers is to sell calls against a bond portfolio; that is, to do *covered call writing*. The calls that are sold are usually out-of-the-money calls, and can be either calls on cash bonds or calls on Treasury futures. Covered call writing is just an outright long bond position combined with a short call position. The strategy results in a payoff pattern that resembles a short position in a put option alone. Obviously, this strategy entails much more downside risk than buying a put to protect the value of the portfolio. In fact, many portfolio managers do not consider covered call writing a hedge.

---

[7] The illustrations in this section are taken from Chapter 10 of Pitts and Fabozzi, *Interest Rate Futures and Options*.

Exhibit 3: Protective Put: Profit/Loss Profile

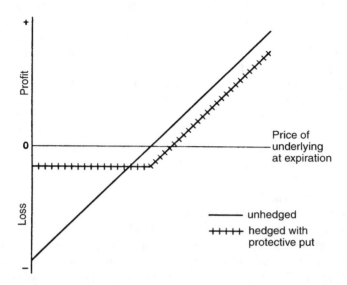

Exhibit 4: Protective Put with Different Strike Prices

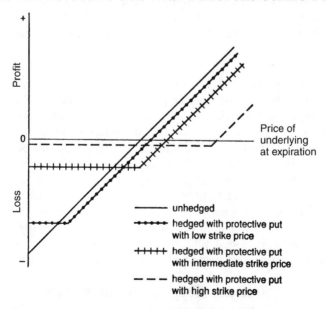

Regardless of how it is classified, it is important to recognize that while covered call writing has substantial downside risk, it has less downside risk than an unhedged long position alone. On the downside, the difference between the long bond position alone and the covered call writing strategy is the premium received for the calls that are sold. This premium acts as a cushion for downward movements in prices, reducing losses when rates rise. The cost of obtaining this cushion is that the manager gives up some of the potential on the upside. When rates decline, the call options become greater liabilities for the covered call writer. These incremental liabilities decrease the gains the portfolio manager would otherwise have realized on the portfolio in a declining rate environment. Thus, the covered call writer gives up some (or all) of the upside potential of the portfolio in return for a cushion on the downside. The more upside potential that is forfeited (that is, the lower the strike price on the calls), the more cushion there is on the downside. Like the protective put strategy, there is no "right" strike price for the covered call writer.

Comparing the two basic strategies for hedging with options, one cannot say that the protective put strategy or the covered call writing strategy is necessarily the better or more correct options hedge. The best strategy (and the best strike prices) depends upon the manager's view of the market. Purchasing a put and paying the required premium is appropriate if the manager is fundamentally bearish. If, on the other hand, the manager is neutral to mildly bearish, it is better to take in the premium on the covered call writing strategy. If the manager prefers to take no view on the market at all, and as little risk as possible, then a futures hedge is most appropriate. If the manager is fundamentally bullish, then no hedge at all is probably the best strategy.

Collars

There are other options hedging strategies frequently used by managers. For example, many managers combine the protective put strategy and the covered call writing strategy. By combining a long position in an out-of-the-money put and a short position in an out-of-the-money call, the manager creates a long position in a *collar*. The manager who uses the collar eliminates part of the portfolio's downside risk by giving up part of its upside potential.

The collar in some ways resembles the protective put, in some ways resembles covered call writing, and in some ways resembles an unhedged position. The collar is like the protective put strategy in that it limits the possible losses on the portfolio if interest rates go up. Like the covered call writing strategy, the portfolio's upside potential is limited. Like an unhedged position, within the range defined by the strike prices the value of the portfolio varies with interest rates.

Options Hedging Preliminaries

As explained earlier, there are certain preliminaries that managers should consider before undertaking a risk control strategy. The best options contract to use depends upon several factors. These include option price, liquidity, and correlation with the bond(s) to be hedged.

In price-inefficient markets, the option price is important because not all options will be priced in the same manner or with the same volatility assumption. Consequently, some options may be overpriced and some underpriced. Obviously, with other factors equal, it is better to use the underpriced options when buying and the overpriced options when selling.

Whenever there is a possibility that the option position may be closed out prior to expiration, liquidity is also an important consideration. If the particular option is illiquid, closing out a position may be prohibitively expensive, and the manager loses the flexibility of closing out positions early, or rolling into other positions that may become more attractive.

Correlation with the underlying bond(s) to be hedged is another factor in selecting the right contract. The higher the correlation, the more precisely the final profit and loss can be defined as a function of the final level of rates. Poor correlation leads to more uncertainty. While most of the uncertainty in an options hedge usually comes from the uncertainty of interest rates themselves, slippage between the bonds to be hedged and the instruments underlying the options contracts adds to that risk. Thus, the degree of correlation between the two underlying instruments is one of the determinants of the risk in the hedge.

Hedging Long-Term Bonds with Puts on Treasury Futures

As explained above, managers who want to hedge their bond positions against a possible increase in interest rates will find that buying puts on Treasury futures is one of the easiest ways to purchase protection against rising rates. To illustrate this strategy, we can use the same utility bond example that we used to demonstrate how to hedge with Treasury bond futures. In that example, a manager held Southern Bell 11¾s of 2023 and used Treasury futures to lock in a sale price for those bonds on a futures delivery date. Now we want to show how the manager could have used Treasury futures options instead of Treasury futures to protect against rising rates.

In the example, rates were already fairly high; the hedged bonds were selling at a yield of 12.40%, the Treasury 7⅝s of 2007 (the cheapest-to-deliver issue at the time) were at 11.50%. For simplicity, it was assumed that this yield spread would remain at 90 basis points.

Selecting the Strike Price

The manager must determine the minimum price that he wants to establish for the hedged bonds. In our illustration it is assumed that the minimum price is 87.668. This is equivalent to saying that the manager wants to establish a strike price for a put option on the hedged bonds of 87.668. But, the manager is not buying a put option on the utility bonds. He is buying a put option on a Treasury bond futures contract. Therefore, the manager must determine the strike price for a put option on a Treasury bond futures contract that is equivalent to a strike price of 87.668 for the utility bonds.

This can be done with the help of Exhibit 5. We begin at the top left hand box of the exhibit. Since the minimum price is 87.668 for the utility bonds, this means that the manager is attempting to establish a maximum yield of 13.41%. This is found from the relationship between price and yield: given a price of 87.668 for the utility bond, this equivalent to a yield of 13.41%. (This gets us to the lower left hand box in Exhibit 5.) From the assumption that the spread between the utility bonds and the cheapest-to-deliver issue is a constant 90 basis points, setting a maximum yield of 13.41% for the utility bond is equivalent to setting a maximum yield of 12.51% for the CTD. (Now we are at the lower box in the middle column of Exhibit 5.) Given the yield of 12.51% for the CTD, the minimum price can be determined (the top box in the middle column of the exhibit). A 12.51% yield for the Treasury 7⅝s of 2007 (the CTD at the time) gives a price of 63.756. The corresponding futures price is found by dividing the price of the CTD by the conversion factor. This gets us to the box in the right hand column of Exhibit 5. Since the conversion factor is 0.9660, the futures price is about 66 (63.7567 divided by 0.9660). This means that a strike price of 66 for a put option on a Treasury bond futures contract is roughly equivalent to a put option on the utility bonds with a strike price of 87.668.

The foregoing steps are always necessary to obtain the appropriate strike price on a futures put option. The process is not complicated. It simply involves (1) the relationship between price and yield, (2) the assumed relationship between the yield spread between the hedged bonds and the CTD, and (3) the conversion factor for the CTD. As with hedging employing futures illustrated earlier in this chapter, the success of the hedging strategy will depend on (1) whether the CTD changes and (2) the yield spread between the hedged bonds and the CTD.

Exhibit 5: Calculating Equivalent Prices and Yields For Hedging with Treasury Futures Options

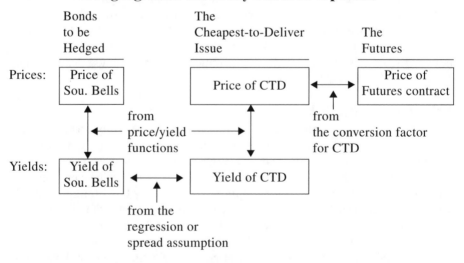

Calculating the Hedge Ratio

The hedge ratio is determined using the following equation similar to equation (7) since we will assume a constant yield spread between the security to be hedged and the CTD issue:

$$\text{Hedge ratio} = \frac{\text{Current dollar duration without Treasury futures options}}{\text{Dollar duration of the CTD}}$$
$$\times \text{Conversion factor for CTI}$$

For increased accuracy, we calculate the dollar durations at the option expiration date (assumed to be June 28, 1985 in our illustration) and at the yields corresponding to the futures strike price of 66 (12.51% for the CTD and 13.41% for the hedged bonds). The dollar durations are as follows per 50 basis point change in rates:

Current dollar duration without Treasury futures options = $326,070
Dollar duration of the CTD = $2,548

Notice that the dollar durations are different from those used in calculating the hedge ratio for the futures hedge. This is because the dollar durations are calculated at prices corresponding to the strike price of the futures option (66), rather than the futures price (70). The hedge ratio is then:

$$\text{Hedge ratio} = \frac{\$326,070}{\$2,548} \times 0.9660 = 124 \text{ put options}$$

Thus, to hedge the Southern Bell position with put options on Treasury bond futures, 124 put options must be purchased.

Outcome of the Hedge

To create a table for the protective put hedge, we can use some of the numbers from Exhibit 2. Everything will be the same except the last two columns. For the put option hedge we have to insert the value of the 124 futures put options in place of the 124 futures contracts in the next-to-last column. This is easy because the value of each option at expiration is just the strike price of the futures option (66) minus the futures price (or zero if that difference is negative), all multiplied by $1,000. The effective sale price for the hedged bonds is then just the actual market price for the hedged bonds plus the value of the options at expiration minus the cost of the options.

Suppose that the price of the futures put option with a strike price of 66 is 24. An option price of 24 means $^{24}\!/_{64}$ of 1% of par value, or $375. With a total of 124 options, the cost of the protection would have been $46,500 (124 × $375, not including financing costs and commissions). This cost, together with the final value of the options, is combined with the actual sale price of the hedged bonds to arrive at the effective sale price for the hedged bonds. These final prices are shown in the last column of Exhibit 6. This effective price is never less than

87.203. This equals the price of the hedged bonds equivalent to the futures strike price of 66 (i.e., 87.668), minus the cost of the puts (that is, $0.4650 = 1.24 \times 24/64$). This minimum effective price is something that can be calculated before the hedge is ever initiated. As prices decline, the effective sale price actually exceeds the projected effective minimum sale price of 87.203 by a small amount. This is due only to rounding and the fact that the hedge ratio is left unaltered although the relative dollar durations that go into the hedge ratio calculation change as yields change. As prices increase, however, the effective sale price of the hedged bonds increases as well; unlike the futures hedge shown in Exhibit 2, the options hedge protects the investor if rates rise, but allows the investor to profit if rates fall.

Exhibit 6: Hedging a Nondeliverable Bond to a Delivery Date With Puts on Treasury Bond Futures: Scenario Analysis

Instrument to be hedged: Southern Bell 11¾s of 4/19/23
Hedge ratio = 124 puts
Strike price for puts on futures = 66-0
Target minimum price for hedged bonds = 87.203
Option price per contract = $375

Actual sale price of hedged bonds ($)	Yield at sale (%)	Futures price[*]	Value of 124 put options ($)[**]	Cost of 124 put options ($)	Effective sale price ($)[***]
7,600,000	15.468	56.511	1,176,636	46,500	8,730,136
7,800,000	15.072	58.144	974,144	46,500	8,727,644
8,000,000	14.696	59.773	772,148	46,500	8,725,648
8,200,000	14.338	61.401	570,276	46,500	8,723,776
8,400,000	13.996	63.030	368,280	46,500	8,721,780
8,600,000	13.671	64.649	167,524	46,500	8,721,024
8,800,000	13.359	66.271	0	46,500	8,753,500
9,000,000	13.061	67.888	0	46,500	8,953,500
9,200,000	12.776	69.497	0	46,500	9,153,500
9,400,000	12.503	71.100	0	46,500	9,353,500
9,600,000	12.240	72.705	0	46,500	9,553,500
9,800,000	11.988	74.299	0	46,500	9,753,500
10,000,000	11.745	75.892	0	46,500	9,953,500
10,200,000	11.512	77.473	0	46,500	10,153,500
10,400,000	11.287	79.052	0	46,500	10,353,500
10,600,000	11.070	80.625	0	46,500	10,553,500
10,800,000	10.861	82.188	0	46,500	10,753,500
11,000,000	10.659	83.746	0	46,500	10,953,500
11,200,000	10.463	85.303	0	46,500	11,153,500

* These numbers are approximate because futures trade in even 32nds.
** From $124 \times \$1,000 \times \text{Max}\{(66 - \text{Futures Price}), 0\}$.
*** Does not include transaction costs or the financing of the options position.

Covered Call Writing with Futures Options

Unlike the protective put strategy, covered call writing is not entered into with the sole purpose of protecting a portfolio against rising rates. The covered call writer, believing that the market will not trade much higher or much lower than its present level, sells out-of-the-money calls against an existing bond portfolio. The sale of the calls brings in premium income that provides partial protection in case rates increase. The premium received does not, of course, provide the kind of protection that a long put position provides, but it does provide some additional income that can be used to offset declining prices. If, on the other hand, rates fall, portfolio appreciation is limited because the short call position constitutes a liability for the seller, and this liability increases as rates go down. Consequently, there is limited upside potential for the covered call writer. Of course, this is not so bad if prices are essentially going nowhere; the added income from the sale of call options is obtained without sacrificing any gains.

To see how covered call writing with Treasury futures options works for the bond used in the protective put example, we construct a table much as we did before. With Treasury bond futures selling around 71-24 on the hedge initiation date, a sale of a 78 call option on Treasury bond futures might be appropriate. As before, it is assumed that the hedged bond will remain at a 90 basis point spread off the CTD (the 7⅝s of 2007). We also assume for simplicity that the price of the 78 calls is 24/64. The number of options contracts sold will be the same, namely 124 contracts for $10 million face value of underlying bonds. Exhibit 7 shows the results of the covered call writing strategy given these assumptions.

To calculate the effective sale price of the bonds in the covered call writing strategy, the premium received from the sale of calls is added to the actual sale price of the bonds, while the liability associated with the short call position is subtracted from the actual sale price. The liability associated with each call is the futures price minus the strike price of 78 (or zero if this difference is negative), all multiplied by $1,000. The middle column in Exhibit 7 is just this value multiplied by 124, the number of options sold.

Just as the minimum effective sale price could be calculated beforehand for the protective put strategy, the maximum effective sale price can be calculated beforehand for the covered call writing strategy. The maximum effective sale price will be the price of the hedged security corresponding to the strike price of the option sold, plus the premium received. In this case, the strike price on the futures call option was 78. A futures price of 78 corresponds to a price of 75.348 (from 78 times the conversion factor), and a corresponding yield of 10.536% for the CTD (the 7⅝s of 2007). The equivalent yield for the hedged bond is 90 basis points higher, or 11.436%, for a corresponding price of 102.666. Adding on the premium received, 0.465 points, the final maximum effective sale price will be about 103.131. As Exhibit 7 shows, if the hedged bond does trade at 90 basis points over the CTD as assumed, the maximum effective sale price for the hedged bond is, in fact, slightly over 103. The discrepancies shown in the exhibit are due to rounding and the fact that the position is not adjusted even though the relative dollar durations change as yields change.

Comparing Alternative Strategies

We reviewed three basic strategies for hedging a bond position: (1) hedging with Treasury futures, (2) hedging with out-of-the-money puts on Treasury bond futures, and (3) covered call writing with out-of-the-money calls on Treasury bond futures. Similar, but opposite, strategies exist for those whose risks are that rates will decrease. As might be expected, there is no "best" strategy. Each strategy has its advantages and its disadvantages, and we never get something for nothing. To get anything of value, something else of value must be forfeited.

Exhibit 7: Hedging a Nondeliverable Bond to a Delivery Date With Calls on Treasury Bond Futures: Scenario Analysis

Instrument to be hedged: Southern Bell 11¾s of 4/19/23
Hedge ratio = 124 calls
Strike price for calls on futures = 78-0
Expected maximum price for hedged bonds = 103.131
Option price per contract = $375

Actual sale price of hedged bonds ($)	Yield at sale (%)	Futures price*	Liability of 124 call options ($)**	Premium from 124 call options ($)	Effective sale price ($)***
7,600,000	15.468	56.511	0	46,500	7,646,500
7,800,000	15.072	58.144	0	46,500	7,846,500
8,000,000	14.696	59.773	0	46,500	8,046,500
8,200,000	14.338	61.401	0	46,500	8,246,500
8,400,000	13.996	63.030	0	46,500	8,446,500
8,600,000	13.671	64.649	0	46,500	8,646,500
8,800,000	13.359	66.271	0	46,500	8,846,500
9,000,000	13.061	67.888	0	46,500	9,046,500
9,200,000	12.776	69.497	0	46,500	9,246,500
9,400,000	12.503	71.100	0	46,500	9,446,500
9,600,000	12.240	72.705	0	46,500	9,646,500
9,800,000	11.988	74.299	0	46,500	9,846,500
10,000,000	11.745	75.892	0	46,500	10,046,500
10,200,000	11.512	77.473	0	46,500	10,246,500
10,400,000	11.287	79.052	130,448	46,500	10,316,052
10,600,000	11.070	80.625	325,500	46,500	10,321,000
10,800,000	10.861	82.188	519,312	46,500	10,327,188
11,000,000	10.659	83.746	712,504	46,500	10,333,996
11,200,000	10.463	85.303	905,572	46,500	10,340,928

* These numbers are approximate because futures trade in even 32nds.
** From $124 \times \$1,000 \times \text{Max}\{(\text{Futures Price} - 78),0\}$.
*** Does not include transaction costs.

Exhibit 8: Alternative Hedging Strategies Compared

Actual sale price of bonds ($)	Yield at sale (%)	Effective sale price with futures hedge ($)	Effective sale price with protective puts ($)	Effective sale price with covered calls ($)
7,600,000	15.468	9,272,636	8,730,136	7,646,500
7,800,000	15.072	9,270,144	8,727,644	7,846,500
8,000,000	14.696	9,268,148	8,725,648	8,046,500
8,200,000	14.338	9,266,276	8,723,776	8,246,500
8,400,000	13.996	9,264,280	8,721,780	8,446,500
8,600,000	13.671	9,263,524	8,721,024	8,646,500
8,800,000	13.359	9,262,396	8,753,500	8,846,500
9,000,000	13.061	9,261,888	8,953,500	9,046,500
9,200,000	12.776	9,262,372	9,153,500	9,246,500
9,400,000	12.503	9,263,600	9,353,500	9,446,500
9,600,000	12.240	9,264,580	9,553,500	9,646,500
9,800,000	11.988	9,266,924	9,753,500	9,846,500
10,000,000	11.745	9,269,392	9,953,500	10,046,500
10,200,000	11.512	9,273,348	10,153,500	10,246,500
10,400,000	11.287	9,277,552	10,353,500	10,316,052
10,600,000	11.070	9,282,500	10,553,500	10,321,000
10,800,000	10.861	9,288,688	10,753,500	10,327,188
11,000,000	10.659	9,295,496	10,953,500	10,333,996
11,200,000	10.463	9,302,428	11,153,500	10,340,928

To make a choice among strategies, it helps to lay the alternatives side by side. Using the futures and futures options examples, Exhibit 8 shows the final values of the portfolio for the various hedging alternatives. It is easy to see from Exhibit 8 that if one alternative is superior to another alternative at one level of rates, it will be inferior at some other level of rates.

Consequently, we cannot conclude that one strategy is the best strategy. The manager responsible for selecting the strategy makes a choice among probability distributions, not usually among specific outcomes. Except for the perfect hedge, there is always some range of possible final values of the portfolio. Of course, exactly what that range is, and the probabilities associated with each possible outcome, is a matter of opinion.

Hedging with Options on Treasury Securities

Hedging a position with options on Treasury securities (cash Treasuries) is relatively straightforward. Most strategies, including the purchase of protective puts, covered call writing, and creating collars, are essentially the same whether futures options or options on physicals (Treasury securities) are used. As explained in Chapter 13, there are some mechanical differences in the way the two types of contracts are traded, and there may be substantial differences in the liquidity of the two types of contracts. Nonetheless, the basic economics of the strategies are virtually identical.

Using over-the-counter (OTC) options on Treasury securities frequently relieves the manager of much of the basis risk associated with a futures options hedge. For example, a manager of Treasury bonds or notes can usually buy or sell OTC options on the exact Treasury security held in the portfolio. Using options on futures, rather than options on Treasury securities, is sure to introduce additional elements of uncertainty.

Given the illustration presented above, and given that the economics of options on Treasury securities and options on futures are essentially identical, additional illustrations for options on Treasury securities are unnecessary. The only important difference is the hedge ratio calculation and the calculation of the equivalent strike. To derive the hedge ratio, we always resort to an expression of relative dollar durations. Thus, for options on Treasury securities, assuming a constant spread the hedge ratio is:

$$\text{Hedge ratio } = \frac{\text{Current dollar duration without Treasury options}}{\text{Dollar duration of underlying for Treasury option}}$$

If a relationship is estimated between the yield on the bonds to be hedged and the instrument underlying the option, the appropriate hedge ratio is:

$$\text{Hedge ratio } = \frac{\text{Current dollar duration without Treasury options}}{\text{Dollar duration of underlying for Treasury option}}$$
$$\times \text{ Yield beta}$$

Unlike Treasury futures options, there is only one deliverable, so there is no conversion factor. When cross hedging with options on Treasury securities, the procedure for finding the equivalent strike price on the bonds to be hedged is very similar. Given the strike price of the option, the strike yield is easily determined using the price/yield relationship for the instrument underlying the option. Then given the projected relationship between the yield on the Treasury security underlying the option and the yield on the bonds to be hedged, an equivalent strike yield is derived for the bonds to be hedged. Finally, using the yield-to-price formula for the bonds to be hedged, the equivalent strike price for the bonds to be hedged can be found.

KEY POINTS

1. *A macro risk control strategy is one used to control the interest rate level risk of a portfolio without regard to the price movement of any individual bond comprising the portfolio.*

2. *A micro risk control strategy can be implemented to control the risk of an individual bond or a group of bonds with similar characteristics.*

3. *There are four preliminary steps that should be taken before a risk control strategy is initiated so that a manager can assess what a hedge strategy can and cannot accomplish.*

4. *The key factor to determine which instrument or instruments to use is the degree of correlation between the rate underlying the instrument and the rate that creates the risk that the manager seeks to control.*

5. *Buying a Treasury futures contract increases a portfolio's duration; selling a Treasury futures contract decreases a portfolio's duration.*

6. *The advantages of adjusting a portfolio's duration using Treasury futures rather than Treasury securities are transaction costs are lower, margin requirements are lower, and it is easier to sell short in the Treasury futures market.*

7. *The general principle in controlling level risk with futures is to combine the dollar exposure of the current portfolio and that of a Treasury futures position so that it is equal to the target dollar duration.*

8. *The number of Treasury futures contracts needed to achieve the target dollar duration depends on the current dollar duration of the portfolio without Treasury futures and the dollar duration per Treasury futures contract.*

9. *Hedging with Treasury futures calls for taking a futures position as a temporary substitute for transactions to be made in the cash market at a later date, with the expectation that any loss realized by the manager from one position (whether cash or futures) will be offset by a profit on the other position.*

10. *Hedging is a special case of controlling level risk in which the target duration or target dollar duration is zero.*

11. *Cross hedging occurs when the bond to be hedged is not identical to the Treasury security underlying the Treasury futures contract.*

12. *A short or sell hedge is used to protect against a decline in the cash price of a bond; a long or buy hedge is employed to protect against an increase in the cash price of a bond.*

13. *The manager should determine what is expected from the hedge; this expectation is the target rate or target price.*

14. *The manager should estimate the hedge effectiveness, which indicates what percent of risk is eliminated by hedging.*

15. *The manager should estimate the residual hedging risk, which is the absolute level of risk in the hedged position and indicates how much risk remains after hedging.*

16. *The target rate, the hedge effectiveness, and the residual hedging risk determine the basic trade-off between risk and expected return and these statistics give the manager the information needed to decide whether to employ a hedge strategy.*

17. *The hedge ratio is the number of Treasury futures contracts needed for the hedge.*

18. *The basis is the difference between the spot price (or rate) and the Treasury futures price (or rate).*

19. *In general, when hedging to the delivery date of the Treasury futures contract, a manager locks in the futures rate or price.*

20. *Hedging with Treasury bond futures and Treasury note futures is complicated by the delivery options embedded in these contracts.*

21. *When a hedge is lifted prior to the delivery date, the effective rate (or price) that is obtained is much more likely to approximate the current spot rate than the futures rate the shorter the term of the hedge.*

22. *The proper target for a hedge that is to be lifted prior to the delivery date depends on the basis.*

23. *Basis risk refers only to the uncertainty associated with the target rate basis or target price basis.*

24. *Hedging substitutes basis risk for price risk.*

25. *Hedging non-Treasury securities with Treasury bond futures requires that the hedge ratio consider two relationships: (1) the cash price of the non-Treasury security and the cheapest-to-deliver issue and (2) the price of the cheapest-to-deliver issue and the futures price.*

26. *After a target is determined and a hedge is set, the hedge must be monitored during its life and evaluated after it is over and the sources of error in a hedge should be determined in order to gain insights that can be used to advantage in subsequent hedges.*

27. *Three popular hedge strategies are the protective put buying strategy, the covered call writing strategy, and the collar strategy.*

28. *A manager can use a protective put buying strategy — a combination of a long put option with a long position in a cash bond — to hedge against rising interest rates.*

29. *A covered call writing strategy involves selling call options against the bond portfolio.*

30. *A covered call writing strategy entails much more downside risk than buying a put to protect the value of the portfolio and many managers do not consider covered call writing a hedge.*

31. *It is not possible to say that the protective put strategy or the covered call writing strategy is necessarily the better or more correct options hedge since it depends upon the manager's view of the market.*

32. *A collar strategy is a combination of a protective put strategy and a covered call writing strategy which eliminates part of the portfolio's downside risk by giving up part of its upside potential.*

33. *The best options contract to use depends upon the option price, liquidity, and correlation with the bond(s) to be hedged.*

34. *For a cross hedge, the manager will want to convert the strike price on the options that are actually bought or sold into an equivalent strike price for the actual bonds being hedged.*

35. *When using Treasury bond futures options, the hedge ratio is based on the relative dollar duration of the current portfolio, the cheapest-to-deliver issue, and the futures contract at the option expiration date, as well as the conversion factor for the cheapest-to-deliver issue.*

Chapter 16

BASIS TRADING WITH FUTURES AND VOLATILITY TRADES WITH OPTIONS

In previous chapters we described Treasury futures and options, how they are valued, and how they can be used to control interest rate risk. In this chapter, we will look at two trading strategies involving these instruments. The first strategy is futures basis trading. The second strategy is volatility trades with options.

FUTURES BASIS TRADING

As explained in Chapter 15, the difference between the cash price and the futures price is called the *basis*.[1] For a Treasury futures contract, the futures price is the delivery price which depends on the particular Treasury issue delivered. The delivery price is the product of the futures price and the conversion factor for the particular Treasury issue delivered.

To illustrate the calculation of the basis, suppose that the Treasury bond futures price is 97-4/32 (97.125) and the price of the cheapest-to-deliver Treasury bond issue is 107-18/32 (107.5625). Assume that the conversion factor for the cheapest-to-deliver Treasury bond is 1.1. Then the delivery price is 97.125 multiplied by 1.1, or 106.8375. The basis is then 0.725 (= 107.5625 − 106.8375).

In Chapter 15, we explained that how the basis changes from the time a hedge is put on and the time a hedge is lifted will affect the performance of the hedge. We referred to this as the basis risk in a hedge strategy. There are trades that are put on for which the motivation is not risk control, but instead speculation on the anticipated movement in the basis. This is referred to as *basis trading*.

Buying and Selling the Basis

Basis trading involves taking a position in a Treasury futures contract and an opposite position in a Treasury issue that is deliverable into the contract in order to capitalize on the anticipated change in the basis. Specifically, the following trade is put on depending on how the basis is expected to change:

1. If the basis is expected to increase:

> sell the Treasury futures contract
> buy a deliverable Treasury issue in the cash market

---

[1] Some market practitioners refer to the basis as the difference between the futures price and cash price.

A trade done in anticipation of the basis increasing is referred to as *buying the basis* or going *long the basis*.

> *2. If the basis is expected to decrease:*
>
>> buy the Treasury futures contract
>> sell (short) a deliverable Treasury issue in the cash market

This trade is called *selling the basis* or going *short the basis*.

To understand why buying or selling the basis produces a profit if the anticipated movement in the basis materializes, we will use a simple illustration. It will be simple because it abstracts from the complexity of Treasury futures contracts. We will assume that there is only one deliverable issue and therefore we are not concerned with the cheapest-to-deliver issue. Here is the information that we will use in our illustrations:

- price of underlying (deliverable) Treasury issue is 100
- borrowing rate is 8% per annum
- cash yield on the underlying Treasury issue is 12% per annum
- futures price is 99
- there are three months to the settlement date

In Chapter 14, we showed that the fair value of this futures contract is 99. Therefore, the futures contract is fairly priced. The basis is 1 (= 100 − 99). Suppose that an investor believes that the basis will increase and takes the following position:

- buys $1 million par value of the Treasury issue
- sells 10 contracts of the Treasury futures contract

The reason for the sale of 10 futures contract is that each contract calls for $100,000 par of the underlying Treasury issue.

Now, suppose that on the next day the following occurs:

- price of underlying (deliverable) Treasury issue increases to 100.50
- borrowing rate decreases to 7%

From equation (1) of Chapter 14, the fair value of this futures contract (ignoring the one day passage of time) is:

$$100.50 + 100.50 \times 0.25 \, (0.07 - 0.12) = 99.2438$$

While the cash price and the futures price increased, the basis increased from 1 to 1.2562 (= 100.50 − 99.2438). Let's look at what happened in this trade.

Profit on the cash Treasury issue:

Value of $1 million par value of Treasury issue on next day	=	$1,005,000
Initial value of Treasury issue	=	1,000,000
Gain	= $	5,000

Loss on the Treasury futures position:

Cost of purchasing 10 contracts on next day	=	$ 992,438
Initial sale of 10 contracts	=	990,000
Loss	= $	2,438

Thus, there was a net gain equal to $2,562 (= $5,000 – $2,438). As indicated earlier, an increase in the basis will produce a profit if the basis is purchased.

Suppose that instead of the price of the Treasury issue increasing to 100.50, it declines on the next day to 99.50 but the borrowing rate does decrease to 7%. Once again, ignoring the one day passage of time, the fair value for the futures contract would be

$$99.50 + 99.50 \times 0.25 \, (0.07 - 0.12) = 98.2563$$

Hence, the cash price and futures price decreased and the basis increased from 1 to 1.2437. Buying the basis produced a net profit of $2,437, as shown below:

Loss on the cash Treasury issue:

Value of $1 million par value of Treasury issue on next day	=	$ 995,000
Initial value of Treasury issue	=	1,000,000
Loss	= $	5,000

Gain on the Treasury futures position:

Cost of purchasing 10 contracts on next day	=	$ 982,563
Initial sale of 10 contracts	=	990,000
Gain	= $	7,437

Again, an increase in the basis generated a net profit by buying the basis. Thus, regardless of whether the cash and futures prices increased or decreased, a net profit was generated because the basis increased.

It is a simple exercise to demonstrate that a decrease of the basis would generate a loss by buying the basis regardless of whether the cash and futures prices both increased or both decreased. Similarly, it can be demonstrated that selling the basis in such cases would have generated a net profit.

Basis Trading when There is More than One Deliverable

We made several simplifying assumptions in our illustration. First, we assumed that there was only one underlying for our hypothetical Treasury futures contract. This is not the case as explained in Chapter 12. There will be a cheapest-to-deliver issue. The futures price will track the cheapest-to-deliver issue. As explained later, it is in fact this complexity that the cheapest-to-deliver can change, as well as other delivery options granted to the short, that creates interest in basis trading. For now, let's look at the complexity introduced by the fact that there is more than one deliverable.

When yields change, the price of a Treasury issue will change depending on its dollar duration. The futures price will also change depending on its dollar duration. Consequently, the relative price change of both the Treasury issue and the futures contract depends on their relative dollar durations. If the dollar durations are not equal, the outcome of a basis trade is not only determined by how the basis changes but also on the relative dollar durations. That is, there is interest rate risk. In Chapter 15, we encountered the same situation in establishing the hedge ratio. That is, in equation (6) in Chapter 15, the hedge ratio required the calculation of the ratio of the dollar duration of the cheapest-to-deliver issue to the dollar duration per Treasury futures contract. A good estimate of this ratio is the conversion factor for the cheapest-to-deliver issue. By weighting the trade using the conversion factor for the cheapest-to-deliver issue, the interest rate risk in a basis trade can be neutralized.

The positions in a basis trade are determined as follows when recognition is given to the conversion factor. The par amount of the futures position taken is found by multiplying the par value of the cheapest-to-deliver issue by the conversion factor of the cheapest-to-deliver issue. For example, suppose that the conversion factor for the cheapest-to-deliver issue is 1.1 and that $1 million par value is taken in the cheapest-to-deliver issue. Then, a position of $1.1 million par value is taken in the futures contract. Since each futures contract is for $100,000 par value, this means that a position in 11 futures contract should be taken. So, if the strategy involves buying the basis, an investor would buy $1 million par value of the cheapest-to-deliver issue and short 11 futures contracts. Selling the basis would involve shorting $1 million of the cheapest-to-deliver issue and buying 11 futures contracts.

When there is more than one deliverable, a basis trade need not involve a position in the cheapest-to-deliver issue. Any deliverable issue can be used. Typically, the conversion factor of the deliverable issue is used to determine the position in the futures contract. The risk here is that the futures price may not track the cash price of the deliverable issue.

Recognition of Carry

In our simplified illustration, we assumed that the basis changed on the next day and ignored other factors that would affect the outcome of the trade. The only consequence of the trade was the net outcome after recognizing the gain and loss on the cash and futures positions. However, when pursuing a strategy of buying the basis, recognition must be given to (1) the cost of financing the cash position and (2) the coupon earned on the cash position. This is the cost of carry or, simply, carry from the trade. Similarly, when selling the basis, carry results from (1) the short-term interest that can be realized from investing the proceeds from the short sale of the Treasury issue and (2) the accrued interest payout from the short sale.

Thus, there are two components that determine the outcome of a basis trade. The first is the net gain or loss from the change in the value of the cash price and futures price. The second is the carry on the trade.

Factors that Affect the Basis

We now know what basis trading is, the positions that should be taken based on expectations of how the basis will trade, how to properly weight the trade, and the two components that determine the overall gain or loss. Next we turn to the factors that determine the basis since this is what the investor is betting on.

We know from equation (4) of Chapter 14 that

$$F = P + Pt(r - c) - \text{Value of delivery options}$$

where

P = cash market price
F = futures price
r = annualized financing rate (%)
c = annualized current yield, or annual coupon rate divided by the cash price (%)
t = time, in years, to the futures delivery date

This means that the difference between the cash and futures price is:

$$\text{Basis} = P - F = - Pt(r - c) + \text{Value of delivery options} \qquad (1)$$

From equation (1) it can be seen that the basis consists of two components. The first term is the cost of carry. The second term is the value of the delivery options. The basis will increase or decrease depending on how these two components change over time.

In a world where there is only one deliverable issue and that issue must be delivered at one specific date in the delivery month, the delivery options have a value of zero. If the financing rate and the cash yield are unchanged over time, the basis will change as the time to delivery changes. At the delivery date, t is zero and therefore the basis converges to zero. Basis trading for this simplified contract is based on predictions of how carry will change at some time in the future.

Moving on to the real world case, contract specifications of Treasury futures allow for not only more than one deliverable issue (the swap option), but also more than one delivery date. In addition, there are other delivery options that were explained in Chapter 12 (e.g., the wild card option). All delivery options are granted to the short. Betting on how the basis will change in the future then requires more than predicting changes in carry; it also requires predicting how the value of the delivery options will change.

In the case of the swap option, we explained in Chapter 12 how changes in market yields can change the cheapest-to-deliver issue. Thus, the volatility of yields becomes an important factor in assessing the likelihood that the cheapest-to-deliver will change and how, in turn, that will change the basis. Moreover, the level of yields also affects which issue will be the cheapest-to-deliver. Consequently, to the extent that changes in yield levels change the cheapest-to-deliver issue and thereby the basis, there may be a level effect in a basis trade.

In a trade in which the cash position is not the cheapest-to-deliver issue but some other deliverable issue, a basis trade is effectively a combination trade. The first is a trade that depends on the change in the basis between the cheapest-to-deliver issue and the futures contract. The second element of the trade is a bet on the price spread between the deliverable issue that a position is taken in and the cheapest-to-deliver issue.

Mechanics of a Basis Trade

In our description of a basis trade, it is assumed that both legs (i.e., cash and futures) are transacted simultaneously so that at the time of execution, the basis is known. In practice, the prices at which the two legs are executed will not be known because the two legs cannot be transacted simultaneously. This is particularly true when the cash position involves an off-the-run Treasury issue since they are typically less frequently quoted.

As a result, a simpler procedure for executing a basis trade is available so that both legs can be executed in such a way so that the basis is locked in at the time of execution. The transaction is called an *exchange for physicals* (EFP). This transaction works as follows. There are two parties to the transaction. Party A sells a futures position and simultaneously buys a cash position. The counterparty, Party B, buys the same futures position that Party A has sold and simultaneously sells the cash position that Party A buys.

An EFP is an exception to Section 4c(a) of the Commodity Exchange Act that prohibits off exchange trades and prearranged trades. As such, an EFP must satisfy certain requirements. One requirement is that (1) the seller of the futures position must be the buyer of the cash position and (2) the buyer of the futures position must be the seller of the cash position. Another requirement is that the simultaneous positions taken must be equivalent. The exception is when a position based on the conversion factor of a deliverable issue is taken. As explained earlier, this is the typical position weighting used in a basis trade. If any weighting other than that based on the conversion factor of the deliverable issue is taken, written justification must be provided to demonstrate that the cash and futures positions are equivalent.

VOLATILITY TRADES WITH TREASURY FUTURES OPTIONS

There are many types of trades in the options market. Some seek to alter a risk/return payoff while other seeks to capitalize on expectations about the direction of the market. Here we will focus on trades which seek to capitalize on anticipated market volatility. We refer to these trades as *volatility trades*. The three volatility trades that we discuss are straddles, strangles, and butterflies.

Exhibit 1: Profit/Loss Payoff at Expiration Date of a Long Straddle Strategy

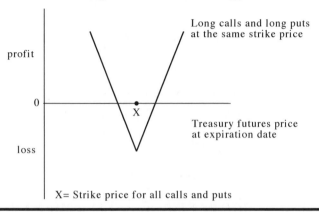

X= Strike price for all calls and puts

Straddles

A *straddle* is composed of either long calls and long puts or short calls and short puts. All of the options have the same strike price and have the same expiration date. When the position involves long calls and long puts, the strategy is called a *long straddle*. Exhibit 1 shows the profit/loss payoff of a generic long straddle at the option expiration date. The overall position is constructed to be delta neutral. That is, there is no market bias. To construct a straddle with this property, the number of long calls and long puts will not necessarily be equal.

As can be seen from Exhibit 1, if the market stays flat, the trade loses money as the options' time value disappears at the expiration date. However, if the market moves sufficiently in either direction, either the calls or the puts will end up in the money and there will be a profit on the position. Thus, the investor is betting on market volatility in a long straddle strategy.

A *short straddle* consists of short positions in puts and calls. Exhibit 2 is a generic payoff of a short straddle at the expiration date. This trade would be put on by investors who anticipate a flat market.

Strangles

A *strangle* is the more heavily leveraged cousin of the straddle. As with a straddle, the position involves either long puts and long calls or short puts and short calls, and the expiration dates for the options are the same. Unlike a straddle, however, the strike price is not the same for the calls and puts. An at-the-money strangle is composed of an out-of-the money call and an out-of- the money put. The strike price for the options are such that they are both equally out of the money and the current price of the futures is halfway between the two strike prices. Exhibits 3 and 4 show the profit/loss payoff for a generic long at-the-money strangle and a generic short at-the-money strangle.

Exhibit 2: Profit/Loss Payoff at Expiration Date of a Short Straddle Strategy

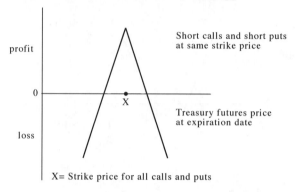

Exhibit 3: Profit/Loss Payoff at Expiration Date of a Long at-the-Money Strangle Strategy

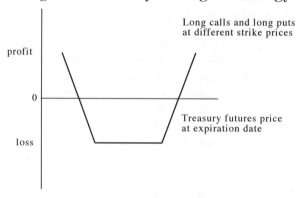

Exhibit 4: Profit/Loss Payoff at Expiration Date of a Short at-the-Money Strangle Strategy

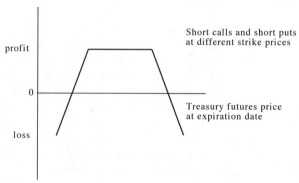

Just like a straddle, a strangle is a pure volatility play. If the market stays flat, the position loses time value; in contrast, if the market moves dramatically in either direction, the position makes money from either the puts or the calls. Because the options in this strategy are both out of the money, the market has to move significantly before either option moves into the money. However, the options are much cheaper, so it is possible to buy many more options for the same dollar amount invested in the strategy compared to a straddle strategy. This is the ideal situation for the investor who is heavily bullish on volatility and wants windfall profits in a rapidly moving market.

Writing strangles is a very risky business. Most of the time the market will not move enough to put either option much into the money, and the writer of a strangle will make the fee income. Occasionally, however, the market will plummet or spike, and the writer of the strangle will suffer catastrophic losses. This accounts for the picturesque name of this trade.

Butterflies

The straddle and strangle involve the purchase or sale of two different contract types with the same expiration date. In a straddle, the strike price of the contracts are the same; in a strangle, the strike price is out of the money for both the calls and puts. In a *butterfly trade*, the investor takes a position in three options of the same type (calls or puts) with the same expiration date. The options differ with respect to the strike price.[2] Typically the butterfly involves options with three consecutive strike prices. The options with the highest and lowest strike price are either bought or sold. The opposite position is taken in the option with the middle strike price. In a *long butterfly* the options with the highest and lowest strike price are purchased and the option with the middle strike price is sold. In a *short butterfly*, the option with the middle strike price is purchased and the options with the highest and lowest strike price are sold.

Typically, the trade is weighted so that for each option position in the wings (i.e, the options with the highest and lowest strike price), an opposite position is taken in two options with the middle strike price (i.e., the body or center of the butterfly). Exhibits 5 and 6 show the profit/loss payoff for a long butterfly and a short butterfly, respectively. Notice that in a quite market, the long butterfly is profitable; in a volatile market, the short butterfly is profitable.

A comparison of Exhibits 2 and 5 indicates that a short straddle and a long butterfly both benefit from a flat market. However, unlike a short straddle which has unlimited risk, a long butterfly has limited risk. As a result, while an investor might expect that a market will not be volatile, that investor is still exposed to unlimited risk. For this reason, an investor might prefer a long butterfly to a short straddle.

---

[2] In Chapter 11 we discussed butterfly trades in the cash market. Such trades involve a bet on changes in the shape of the yield curve.

Exhibit 5: Profit/Loss Payoff at Expiration Date of a Long Butterfly Strategy

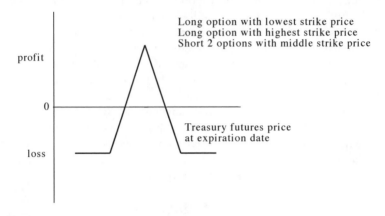

Long option with lowest strike price
Long option with highest strike price
Short 2 options with middle strike price

profit

0

loss

Treasury futures price
at expiration date

Exhibit 6: Profit/Loss Payoff at Expiration Date of a Short Butterfly Strategy

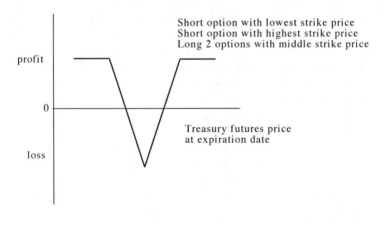

Short option with lowest strike price
Short option with highest strike price
Long 2 options with middle strike price

profit

0

loss

Treasury futures price
at expiration date

KEY POINTS

1. *Basis trading involves taking a position in a Treasury futures contract and an opposite position in a Treasury issue that is deliverable into the contract in order to capitalize on the anticipated change in the basis.*

2. *The basis is the difference between the cash price and futures price.*

3. *An investor buys the basis or goes long the basis in anticipation of an increase in the basis; an investor sells the basis or goes short the basis in anticipation of a decrease in the basis.*

4. *Buying the basis involves buying a deliverable Treasury issue in the cash market and selling the Treasury futures contract.*

5. *Selling the basis involves selling a deliverable Treasury issue in the cash market and buying the Treasury futures contract.*

6. *To neutralize a basis trade to interest rate risk, the positions are weighted by the conversion factor of the deliverable issue taken in the cash market.*

7. *The overall outcome of a basis trade consists of two components: (1) the net gain or loss from the change in the value of the cash price and futures price and (2) the carry on the trade.*

8. *When buying the basis, the trade's cost of carry is the difference between the cost of financing the cash position and the coupon earned on the cash position.*

9. *When selling the basis, the trade's cost of carry is the difference the short-term interest that can be realized from investing the proceeds from the short sale of the Treasury issue and the accrued interest payout from the short sale.*

10. *The basis of a futures contract consists of two components: (1) the cost of carry and (2) the value of the delivery options.*

12. *The basis will increase or decrease depending on how the cost of carry and the value of the delivery options change over time.*

13. *A basis trade in which the cash position is not the cheapest-to-deliver issue but some other deliverable issue is effectively a combination trade consisting of two bets: (1) how the basis between the cheapest-to-deliver issue and the futures contract changes and (2) how the price spread between the deliverable issue that a position is taken in and the cheapest-to-deliver issue changes.*

14. *Because of the difficulty of simultaneously transacting in the cash and futures markets to execute a basis trade, an exchange for physicals (EFP) transaction can be used.*

15. In the options market, volatility trades are executed to capitalize on anticipated market volatility.

16. A straddle is a volatility trade in which a position is taken in either long calls and long puts or short calls and short puts with all of the options having the same strike price and the same expiration date.

17. A long straddle benefits if the market moves sufficiently in either direction so that either the calls or the puts will end up in the money; a short straddle benefits if the market is flat.

18. A strangle involves either long put and call positions or short put and call positions with the same expiration dates but the strike price is not the same for the calls and puts.

19. An at-the-money strangle is composed of an out-of-the money call and an out-of-the money put with the strike price for the options such that they are both equally out of the money and the current price of the futures is halfway between the two strikes.

20. A strangle is basically a leveraged straddle requiring that the market moves dramatically in either direction in order for the investor to benefit from a long strangle strategy.

21. Writing strangles is extremely risky because in situations where the market plummets or spikes, the writer of the strangle will suffer catastrophic losses.

22. A butterfly trade in the options market is a volatility play in which a position is taken in three options (all of the same type) and with the same expiration date.

23. Typically a butterfly trade involves options with three consecutive strike prices.

24. In a long butterfly the options with the highest and lowest strike price are bought and the option with the middle strike price is sold; in a short butterfly the options with the highest and lowest strike price are sold and the option with the middle strike price is purchased.

25. Typically, a butterfly trade is weighted so that for each option position in the wings, two options are purchased of the option with the middle strike price.

26. In a quite market, the long butterfly is profitable; in a volatile market, the short butterfly is profitable.

27. While both a short straddle and a long butterfly benefit from a flat market, a long butterfly does not have the unlimited risk of a short straddle.

INDEX

To stay on top, you need to know a lot about key players in the fixed-income market. *Don't sweat the details, use the Capital Access Desk Reference Series.*

If you want to stay on top of the fixed-income universe, you need comprehensive, reliable information from an industry leader. Capital Access International introduces its *Desk Reference Series*— essential guides to the buyers and sellers of fixed-income securities.

The Desk Reference Series provides you with an inside look at the world of fixed-income. It gives you detailed firm profiles that include critical contact and asset information, as well as structure preferences for an array of fixed-income investment instruments.

These guides can help you assess your best prospects—and peers—in each segment of the market. They also take you a step further, by providing essential information to help you identify and reach key players.

To find out more or to order copies of the Desk Reference Series, contact us at 800-866-5987 or info@capital-access.com

Capital Access
I N T E R N A T I O N A L

430 Mountain Avenue
Murray Hill, New Jersey 07974

**Tel. (908) 771-0800
Fax. (908) 771-0330
Toll Free: (800) 866-5987**

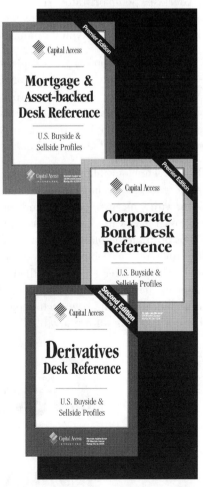

Get on the Leader Board.

Why use a putter in a sand trap? With BARRA Decision,™ even the longest shots get legs. Callable corporates? Birdie. Floating rate notes? Eagle. Swaptions? Hole in one. Analyzing re-REMICs is a chip shot. Because of our extensive database of everything from treasuries to asset-backed securities, you don't need extra strokes to analyze your entire portfolio.

With Decision, you'll drive farther off the tee than you ever thought possible. Analyze portfolio risk using OAS duration and convexity. Perform scenario analysis with your viewpoint on rates, spreads and volatilities. Structure portfolios using immunization, enhanced index strategies, cash flow analysis. Windows-based analytics make it easy, so you'll produce down the stretch like a seasoned pro.

Don't risk slicing or hooking with inferior models. BARRA's research is rigorous, consistent and accurate. We have an ongoing effort to examine, refine and enhance our work. Whether it's interest rate lattice generation, term structure modeling, path sampling, prepayment modeling, advanced risk measures like Key Rate Durations, or perform-ance attribution, you'll always be pin high.

BARRA's technology allows you to shape your shots to the circumstances. Integrate Decision with your own database and run it on your own hardware; it's ODBC-compliant and runs on multiple platforms. The flexible architecture of our object-oriented design ensures that you'll keep pace with the financial markets as new innovations appear. With our commitment to leading edge technology, you'll never find yourself facing an unplayable lie.

Decision
OAS-Based Portfolio Analytics System

⑤ BARRA

Decision, formerly a GAT product, is now available from BARRA.
GAT is a wholly-owned subsidiary of BARRA.
For more information call Winnie Chan 212•785•9630.

At Piper Jaffray we offer consultative services, expertise and strategies to government portfolio managers.

While the industry views the Treasury market as a commoditized market focused on product and price, we can consistently add value for our clients through the development of investment strategies, advisory services and highly competetive market execution.

We believe the integration of expertise, market data and management of the investment process enables us to help create customized solutions.

Managing the investment process includes:
- Establishing investment policies
- Developing customized benchmarks
- Risk management analysis
- Performance analysis

We have the tools you need and the service you deserve to help create solutions for your government portfolio.

Work with a firm that has the right solutions...Piper Jaffray.

Fixed Income Capital Markets
222 South Ninth Street
Minneapolis, MN 55402
1 800 333-6000
http://www.piperjaffray.com/

7/97-2922